Living with Handicap

Living with handicap

The report of a working party
on children with special needs

Edited by

Eileen Younghusband
Dorothy Birchall

Ronald Davie
M. L. Kellmer Pringle

Contributors

Dorothy Birchall
Ronald Davie
Dorothy F. Egan
Lucy Faithfull
Ronald Gulliford
H. C. Gunzburg
S. O. Myers
Margaret Peter

A. F. Philp
M. L. Kellmer Pringle
Ian M. Richardson
Stanley S. Segal
Robert Wigglesworth
Mary D. Wilson
Enid Wistrich
Eileen Younghusband

Published by

National Children's Bureau

(*formerly* The National Bureau for Co-operation in Child Care)

Publishers note

Reference is made throughout this work to the National
Bureau for Co-operation in Child Care. It is the former
name of the present National Children's Bureau. This new
name was adopted in November 1970 because the old title
was cumbersome and did not adequately indicate the
activities of the Bureau as an inter-disciplinary organisation
concerned with children's needs in the family, school and
society.

I.S.B.N.   0 902817 00 0

First edition 1970
Reprinted 1971

Published by
National Children's Bureau
(*formerly* The National Bureau for Co-operation in Child Care)
Adam House, 1 Fitzroy Square, London W1P 5AH
© 1970

Printed in Great Britain by
Leicester Printers Ltd
Church Gate Press Leicester and London

Contents

CONTENTS

xi

Membership of the Working Party

Chairman

The Baroness Serota, JP
(resigned on appointment as Baroness in Waiting, May 1968)

Dame Eileen Younghusband, DBE, JP
Vice-President of the National Bureau for Co-operation in Child Care

Members

Ronald Davie
Deputy Director of the National Bureau for Co-operation in Child Care

Dr Dorothy F. Egan
Medical Liaison Officer and Research Fellow, Newcomen Clinic, Guy's Hospital, London

M. Fitzgerald, MBE
Child Care Consultant to a number of Inner London Boroughs'
Children's Departments (resigned May, 1968)

Miss Lucy Faithfull
Children's Officer, City of Oxford

Ronald Gulliford
Senior Lecturer in Education; Tutor, Diploma in Special Education Course,
School of Education, University of Birmingham

Dr H. C. Gunzburg
Consultant Psychologist; Director of Psychological Services,
Hospitals for the Sub-Normal, Birmingham Area

J. Loring
Director, Spastics Society (resigned February, 1968)

S. O. Myers
Principal, Condover Hall School for blind children with additional handicaps,
near Shrewsbury, Salop

*Professor R. Parker
Professor of Social Administration, Bristol University

A. F. Philp
Supervisor and Case Work Training Officer, London Borough of Bexley

Dr M. L. Kellmer Pringle
Director of the National Bureau for Co-operation in Child Care

Dr Ian M. Richardson, JP
Director of the General Practice Teaching and Research Unit, University of Aberdeen; formerly Chairman of Aberdeen City Juvenile Court

Stanley S. Segal, JP
Principal, Ravenswood Centre of Special Education, Crowthorne; Hon. Principal, College of Special Education

Dr Robert Wigglesworth
Consultant Paediatrician, Oxford Regional Hospital Board

Dr Mary D. Wilson
Staff Inspector for Special Education, Inner London Education Authority

Mrs Enid Wistrich
Councillor, London Borough of Camden

*T. W. Cynog-Jones
Observer appointed by the Carnegie United Kingdom Trust

Observers

Department of Education and Science
Department of Health and Social Security
Home Office

Secretary to the working party

Miss Dorothy Birchall
National Bureau for Co-operation in Child Care

Mrs M. Peter analysed and collated the parents' letters which appear as Chapter 1 and she also provided suitable quotations from these for the text of the report.

* *Both were full members, and received all the papers, but other commitments prevented them from attending the meetings of the Working Party.*

Preface

The Working Party began its task in October 1967 under the chairmanship of Baroness Serota. On being appointed a Baroness-in-Waiting, she felt she had to resign – a matter of much regret. The Bureau sincerely appreciates the invaluable help she had so generously given to the Working Party in its initial stages. Fortunately, Dame Eileen Younghusband, one of the Bureau's Vice-Presidents, agreed to accept the chairmanship.

How the report was written

After laying the groundwork, for example, determining in detail the scope of the enquiry, how and from which sources evidence should be obtained, three sub-groups were formed to concern themselves respectively with medical, educational and social aspects. The task of writing chapters was shared out among all the members of the Working Party with the convenor of each sub-section being responsible for the co-ordination and sub-editing. Each chapter and the findings and conclusions were then considered by the whole Working Party. The task of editing the final report was undertaken by Dame Eileen Younghusband, Miss Dorothy Birchall, Mr R. Davie and Dr M. L. Kellmer Pringle and this editorial board accepts full responsibility for the shape and wording of this published version, though the contents are the work of members expert in different fields.

References have been added to material which only became available after the Working Party ceased to meet, for example, the Chronically Sick and Disabled Persons Act, the Green Paper on the *National Health Service*, the White Paper on *Reform of Local Government in England* and the Local Authority Social Services Act.

The report is a composite document for which the whole group has collective responsibility. This does not mean that there was complete unanimity on every issue, on the contrary on a few points there was considerable divergence; in those instances the majority view was adopted, often modified in the light of the minority opinion.

Because the brief was wide, it did not prove possible to pursue as many questions in depth as the Working Party should have wished to do or to give a detailed account of all existing services for handicapped children. Inevitably, too, more questions were raised than answered. On some issues no clear-cut solutions presented themselves, as for example in relation to categories of handicap, especially autism. But I hope that the work will stimulate further thought and action at a time when considerable changes are proposed in the structure of local government, the National Health Service, and the operation of the social services.

Acknowledgments

The Bureau is extremely grateful to all those who made it possible for this work to be undertaken; the professional and voluntary organisations who asked for a working party to be set up; the Carnegie United Kingdom Trust who made this financially possible by a generous grant; all the organisations who provided evidence; the selected local authorities who gave a great deal of information to enable case studies to be made of prevalent practice and of co-ordination between different departments; to Miss Anne Allen for her article in a national Sunday newspaper asking parents of handicapped children to write to the Working Party telling of their experiences; to the editors of many other newspapers who printed a letter with a similar request; and of course to those parents who responded to this request and took the trouble to write to us about their personal experiences, knowing in advance that this could not directly or immediately benefit their own children.

Critical comments on the main findings and conclusions were invited from Dr J. D. Kershaw, Miss C. Pratt and Miss Margery Taylor; their helpful and constructive observations were much appreciated. Mr W. L. Hooper gave valuable help with the editing of the manuscript.

The Bureau is deeply indebted to the members of the Working Party who gave so generously of their knowledge, experience and time; to our first chairman, Baroness Serota, who set us on the way; and to Dame Eileen Younghusband, whose agreement to take over the chair, enabled the work to proceed and to come to a fruitful conclusion, under her wise, able and close guidance. Very special thanks are due also to Miss Dorothy Birchall, who made it seem almost a pleasure to draft and re-draft specially difficult parts and to the secretaries who behind the scenes typed revised versions of the report. Finally, this is the first book produced by the Bureau as sole publisher. A great deal of work has been involved, and the piloting through of this venture to a successful conclusion has largely been the responsibility of the Bureau's Secretary, Mr L. E. Hancock.

COHEN OF BIRKENHEAD
President

Introduction

How it began

At the request of some member organisations, the National Bureau for Co-operation in Child Care called together a meeting of voluntary and professional bodies interested in the education, care and well-being of handicapped children. This meeting recommended that a working party be set up to review their needs, to consider how existing resources might be more effectively used and what improved or new facilities appear to be required. The Bureau's Council and Executive Committee unanimously accepted this proposal. Thanks to a two-year grant from the Carnegie United Kingdom Trust it proved possible to undertake this project.

Terms of reference

These were as follows:

  a. to recommend what could be done to use present resources more effectively and what more could be done, if additional resources were made available. An order of priority should be indicated;
  b. to suggest ways of promoting an increasingly inter-disciplinary approach in the education, care and treatment of handicapped children;
  c. to outline what arrangements should be made for monitoring new conditions arising from social, educational and medical changes;
  d. to make recommendations regarding the most suitable method for setting up a central pool of information, both regarding literature and services.

Consideration was to be given "across the board", with regard to professional disciplines, age range of children (between 0 and 18 years) and the nature of the handicap. However, it was found necessary

1

to impose restriction regarding the last mentioned topic since it soon became apparent that the canvas envisaged was too wide to encompass adequately during the comparatively short life of the Working Party. With considerable reluctance it was decided to exclude the socially disadvantaged, including young delinquents and drug addicted youngsters. The needs of children handicapped in these ways are such as to require separate and detailed consideration. From time to time, however, some reference is made to these handicaps in our report. Nor were we able to consider as fully as we would have wished the young chronic sick, whether in hospital or housebound at home; or the employment circumstances of handicapped young people.

We also do not refer to the differences in organisation, both local and central, of the education, health and personal social services in Scotland and Northern Ireland as compared with England and Wales.

The composition of the Working Party

The multi-disciplinary nature and wide scope of our terms of reference are reflected in the Working Party's composition. A number of members wore more than "one hat"; for example, two members, a father and a mother, each had a handicapped child and thus could contribute not only from their professional but also from their personal experience of what is involved both for the child and his family. Additionally, the Department of Education and Science, the Department of Health and Social Security and the Home Office were consulted through their observers; the Supplementary Benefits Commission, the Department of Employment and Productivity, and the Central Youth Employment Executive were also consulted about the relevant chapters. All this help from central government departments has been most valuable.

Sources of evidence

Evidence was obtained from four main sources. First, the experience and knowledge of all the members of the Working Party have been used in wide-ranging, inter-disciplinary discussions as well as in preparing the report itself.

Secondly, 58 professional and voluntary organisations, and some individuals, submitted written evidence. Many organisations set up special committees to prepare this evidence within the framework suggested by the Working Party. A summary appears in appendix B.

Thirdly, ten county and county borough councils in different parts of the country were invited to supply information about present provision for handicapped children in their areas. The medical officer of health, the chief education officer, the children's officer and the clerk of each authority were asked about practice and policy in relation to an early detection of handicap, assessment procedures, provision for pre-school children, special educational treatment, school leaving and employment, supportive services to families, the role of voluntary organisations, the training of staff and the co-ordination of services. From the replies, which are summarised in appendix C, it was possible to obtain some concrete illustrations of the diversity of provision in various parts of the country.

Fourthly, some indications of "consumer reactions" were obtained. In response to articles in the national press, letters were received from a large number of parents, giving valuable information about the problems they were encountering in relation to their handicapped child. These are the parents' voices in the first chapter which open the whole discussion.

Priorities and costs

Our terms of reference required us to consider what improvements could be made in services for handicapped children; what were the priorities; and which improvements could be made without additional cost. So far as priorities are concerned, we stress the need for much more comprehensive prevention, detection and treatment through health, education and social services, particularly for children under 5: an increase in day school provision for handicapped children from an early age; comprehensive and continuous assessment; and much more attention to the human and employment needs of handicapped adolescents. The emphasis in all our findings is upon the handicapped child remaining in his family and the local community wherever this is possible: to achieve this a comprehensive range of counselling and supportive services must be available to the family.

The foregoing are all interlocking parts of a total pattern. To determine priorities it is necessary to look at each element in the pattern to see where there are weaknesses or gaps and where improvement at any one point would reinforce others. For example, there is a shortage of all professional workers but better deployment and more adequate clerical and other support could result in more effective use of these and other scarce resources. There are wide differences in different parts of the country and between different services in the range, quality and amount of provision. Fragmented services and some permissive legislation can result in no provision at all, or help over a limited period for limited groups of people. Moreover, the effectiveness of any one service may depend upon what other related services may or may not provide. For example, whether or not a handicapped child goes to a day or residential school may not primarily depend upon the education authority but on whether the health department has a sufficient home help service, the welfare department is willing to make necessary adaptations in the home, or the housing department to provide suitable housing. In short, the health, education, social service and housing needs of the handicapped are so closely interlocked that only comprehensive planning can effectively determine priorities.

This leads on to the question of cost. It is idle to think that the well-being of handicapped children can be purchased on the cheap. Indeed far more resources are needed, particularly since the number and life span of multi-handicapped children are increasing. Nonetheless there are points at which alternative use of resources might yield better returns. For example, more provision for handicapped children in day schools, coupled with supportive services for the family, could result in fewer children in expensive residential schools or long-stay hospitals. To combine different types of assessment units into comprehensive assessment centres would add little to cost and much to effectiveness. The pungent arguments in the Seebohm Report for combining the fragmented and piecemeal personal social services and thus creating a more effective organisational structure and making better use of manpower and other resources are accepted in the Local Authority Social Services Act. The case for many more nursery schools for all children is even stronger for actually or potentially handicapped children. In the health service, too, babies and small children are a high priority, whether for prevention, detection or treatment.

Both priorities and costs obviously indicate a yardstick against which they are measured. The ultimate aim is the development of each handicapped child to the fullness of his potential as an integrated and independent human being. Obviously the public and voluntary services can only contribute towards but not guarantee the achievement of so personal and elusive a goal. But they can provide means without which the task would be impossible. Ability to work and to be self-supporting is crucial to adult independence. Thus one of the aims of the social services should be to make this possible – to the extent that it is realistic – for many more handicapped young people than at present. This calls for a diversity of resources, including mechanical aids to mobility and electronic and other equipment to give the handicapped control over their environment. This is a point at which personal and social benefits meet. More financial and other resources invested in handicapped children could mitigate the pervasive effect of the condition and enable them to contribute more adequately to society when they grow up.

Last but not least in the list of priorities, we must stress the supreme importance of research into the causative factors in physical, intellectual, emotional and environmental handicapping conditions. Short of prevention at the source all later remedial action is to some degree palliative.

Some assumptions in the report

The Working Party faced a hard task in trying to look at the wide range of handicapping conditions from mild to severe, and at the health, educational, family and social needs of handicapped children. And in so doing to avoid "the long-standing tendency to think in terms of specific pathological entities rather than of living people in their social setting who happen to have acquired diseases and disabilities" (World Health Organisation Report, 1967). We have tried to set the child and his family firmly in the centre of the picture, to emphasise that their needs are just the same as those of any other family but that to meet them is far harder because man has to strive to do what nature accomplishes effortlessly for those who develop normally. There is irreversible tragedy too for many handicapped children and their families.

Inevitably this report covers some familiar ground; inevitably, too, not every aspect is given equal weight. Where there is repetition this too has seemed inevitable in order to keep the focus on the child and his family rather than on specific services. To some extent the report breaks fresh ground in giving equal importance with health and education to the social care needs of handicapped children and their families. All such children are at risk of emotional and social handicap and of distorted family relationships. Hitherto, this has been insufficiently taken into account. In our report we try to bring this personal developmental aspect and family and social relations fully into the limelight.

A result is to show the poverty of supporting services for families and the failure to take sufficient account of their human needs. In this report we try to analyse the nature of these needs, which call for more extensive psychiatric, psychological and social work services than exist at present. We became well aware of the current gaps in social care, fragmented between health, education welfare, child care, welfare, and the youth employment service. For the sake of brevity we have referred to the social services department when making certain future proposals but to the existing separate services in discussing the current situation. This also applies to the local authority health services because although the government has announced its decision to unify the National Health Service under area health authorities, this decision has not been implemented at the time of going to press. The Chronically Sick and Disabled Persons Act – a private members bill given government support – and the white paper, *Reform of Local Government in England*, will also both have significant consequences for many of our findings and conclusions.

The Social Work (Scotland) Act, 1968 has already created north of the border unified social work departments unfettered by separate age or need categories. These, and those to be started in England and Wales, should in time pioneer the comprehensive, flexible and imaginative personal social services which are an essential complement to good health and education services for children with special needs.

This report starts with letters from parents of handicapped children in order that their individual stories should echo through the later chapters. Analysis, generalisation and proposals for improvement in services may otherwise seem remote from "people in their social setting". Since the Working Party was set up by the National Bureau for Co-operation in Child Care it was confined to children but we are conscious that handicapped adults share many of the same constrictions and special needs.

Reference

WORLD HEALTH ORGANISATION (1967) *Report of a Working Group on the Early Detection and Treatment of Handicapping Defects in Young Children.* Regional Office for Europe. World Health Organisation, Copenhagen.

Main findings and conclusions

The assumptions on which the report is based

1. In our view *the focus should be on the child and his family* in their community and on his developmental needs as a child rather than primarily on a handicapping condition. The physical, emotional, educational and social aspects of the child with special needs must be kept in constant balance with each other. The majority of such children grow up, and will continue to live, in a local community amongst ordinary people. They should be saved as far as possible from isolation and helped towards independence. The wide range of handicapping conditions, physical, mental, emotional and social – some slight, some severe, some temporary, some permanent – means that it is more appropriate to plan in the light of a child's all-round needs and functional capacities in every day life rather than with a too exclusive emphasis on the nature of the defect. But due attention must be given to the important direct and indirect effects on the child of the handicapping condition and the need for treatment and remedial action.

2. In this inter-disciplinary, comprehensive approach the personal, family and social needs of handicapped children should be given equal weight with those of health and education. In our view all three must play an equal part, though with different roles at different times, in assessing and meeting the needs of handicapped children. We agree with the Seebohm Report that family and social needs can only be effectively met through a unified social services department, and thus we welcome the legislation now introduced to set up such departments. We also think that a unified National Health Service working in the closest partnership with the local authorities should be better able to give the comprehensive continuing and specialist health care which handicapped children need.

9

3. The role of voluntary organisations is and will continue to be of extreme importance. We hope for closer co-operation between them and for a still wider range of imaginative experimentation.

4. Local communities also should be actively helped to become more aware of the needs of the handicapped and be involved in the care, support and acceptance of handicapped children and their families.

5. The age range covered is from 0 – 18 years, though we recognize that handicapped adults may have many needs that are similar to those of handicapped children.

6. Socially handicapped children not specifically considered. Our survey did not include socially handicapped children, except in so far as they are maladjusted or educationally subnormal. We refer from time to time to children at risk of social handicap and many of our recommendations for prevention, detection, assessment, and comprehensive provision apply to them also.

Prevention

7. A great deal is known about the prevention of handicap but some of this information is not effectively translated into preventive practice. Preventive services and action should include genetic counselling and family planning, improved ante-natal and perinatal care, especially for women in vulnerable groups, and attempts to reduce all forms of accident in childhood. Increased support for families is essential to lessen those emotional, social and learning handicaps which result from an unfavourable environment. Early identification of handicaps, together with extension of facilities for both pre-school children and adolescents is essential. This would also contribute materially to secondary prevention (*chapter 4*).

8. The sheer size of the problem of providing adequate assessment, treatment, training and supportive services for handicapped children and their families points to the crucial importance of all forms of prevention. This includes better deployment of resources, primary and secondary prevention, and research into causative factors (*chapter 4*).

Initial detection, including screening

9. It is essential that the developmental screening of the whole child population from birth onwards should be as comprehensive and

frequent as possible. Unfortunately, this is difficult in the pre-school years when some families most at risk are least likely to go voluntarily to infant welfare and toddler clinics. Hence the work of health visitors (including screening tests for auditory or visual defects) is crucial. Initial detection through medical, emotional, social and educational screening would come from general practitioners, medical officers, staffs of hospital maternity departments, as well as of premature and special care units, midwives, health visitors, day nursery, play group and nursery school staffs, social workers and of course parents themselves (*chapter 5*).

10. Once children are in school, comprehensive screening becomes relatively easy. The existing work of school health and school psychological services could be further strengthened by a more co-ordinated system of educational guidance, drawing more systematically on observation by teachers, in order to ensure that children with special educational and social needs are noted as early as possible with a view to organising special help in the form of social work support, psycho-educational assessment, education in special schools or classes, or remedial teaching, as appropriate. Research is needed to identify what characteristics of children are most predictive of subsequent educational and social difficulty. However, much more could be done now to improve methods of early identification and to give prompt help to children with special needs (*chapter 5*).

Comprehensive assessment teams

11. There should be in every appropriate local area comprehensive assessment teams competent to make the relevant physical, intellectual, emotional and social assessment of any child where initial screening or continued observation suggest he may suffer from a handicapping condition. The 'core' team should consist of a doctor interested in child health, an educationist and a social worker. It should have speech therapists, physiotherapists, and visiting medical, psychiatric and other specialists available to it; and should draw on the knowledge of the family doctor, teacher and other professionals who know the particular child or family. The team should have an assessment centre as its base, with various facilities for parents and children (including short-term residential observation). But sometimes (particularly in scattered rural areas) it should hold sessions in schools, child health centres or elsewhere. It is also important that some sessions should be held in places acceptable to adolescents (*chapter 6*).

12. Inter-disciplinary assessment, which should always be as comprehensive and as continuous as possible, must be concerned with the child's total development and functional abilities and the most effective way of meeting his needs. For some children further specialist assessment, tests or other procedures will be necessary in hospitals, psychiatric clinics or reception centres for long-term observation (*chapter 6*).

Local authority duty to compile and maintain a comprehensive register

13.* Local authorities and health authorities should have a duty to co-operate in compiling and maintaining a comprehensive register which should contain two major sections:

a. An observation section:
This would consist of children whose family background, medical history, or other circumstances, indicated a need for observation until the possibility of a handicapping condition being present or developing has been ruled out, or else confirmed, when the record would be transferred to the next section.

b. A handicapped children section:
This would contain details of children known to be handicapped or assessed by the team as having a significant defect or condition which is potentially handicapping. We recognise the difficulties of clearly identifying some children in this last group. The observation section would perhaps be the more appropriate place for certain children with defects which might develop into handicaps (*chapter 6*).

14.* Comprehensive and continuous assessment related to detection (including screening) would reveal many gaps and inadequacies in existing services. It is, however, essential that detection and assessment should steadily uncover true incidence rather than simply being related to available provision in any given locality. We recognise the size of the problem and the amount of unmet need that this procedure would reveal (*chapter 6*).

---

* The asterisks at paragraphs 13, 14, 15, 16, 55, 58, 59, 60, 61, refer to the note of dissent on page 26.

15.* Copies of the register should be kept at the assessment centre as well as by the education, health and social services authorities. Care should be taken to safeguard confidentiality in its use. It should be the duty of the social services department to ensure that every child's case is reviewed annually (or more frequently if necessary or if requested by the parents) and for this purpose to see that all necessary reports are available to the team, as well as for seeing that agreed follow-up action is taken by the services primarily concerned (*chapter 6*).

The social services department's co-ordinating function to ensure continuity of care

16.* The local authority social services department should ensure continuity of care from detection, whether at birth or later, onwards. Where necessary, it should provide casework, counselling and other services for handicapped children and their families, in close co-operation with the health, education, and employment services (*chapter 6*).

The priority needs of children under 5 years

17. There is an urgent need for more pre-school age facilities for handicapped children; in particular, day nurseries and nursery schools or classes which are able and prepared to take a proportion of handicapped children are in extremely short supply. Until many more nursery schools or classes are available pre-school playgroups have, potentially, an important role to play, provided there is professional guidance. They should be given more encouragement and support, locally and nationally. What is now known about the importance of early learning applies with even greater force to the young handicapped child. Thus it is of vital importance to make available pre-school facilities, be it nursery schools, playgroups or home teaching, in some cases even before the age of 2 years. How best to compensate for disabilities and to promote optimal learning needs further study and experimentation. Therefore, it is desirable that research and evaluation should be built into pre-school programmes (*chapters 2 and 9*).

18. The rapid all round development of small children and the losses that they may suffer from parental inadequacies or adverse circumstances indicate that society would reap rich benefits by meeting their and their parents' needs more fully at this early stage. In particular, knowledge about the risks of handicap suffered by small children in socially vulnerable families suggests that a wide range of resources, skilled help and supporting services should be concentrated on such families (*chapters 2 and 5*).

Supporting services to families with handicapped children

19. Information, advice and counselling services should be available to parents, and should be as full and comprehensive as possible. However, there will inevitably be differences between parents in their emotional and intellectual ability to grasp all the details and to accept all the implications of diagnosis, prognosis and treatment, either at the time or later (*chapter 7*).

20. Parents should be recognised as participants in the 'team' which is assessing, treating and caring for the child with special needs. The exact form which this participation might take and the extent to which it will be possible will vary from parent to parent. Their full participation in the assessment and subsequent treatment of the child and in decisions about his future would not only make it more likely that the best decision was taken but would also enable the parents to realise the reasons which lie behind decisions.

There is also a need for:
a. Adequate counselling on both practical and emotional problems.
b. Psychiatric help where necessary for all members of the family or for those working with them (*chapter 7*).

21. Parents should have the right to request a further assessment or review, in addition to their right to a second opinion. They should also have a right to a full and impartial hearing when they disagree with a diagnosis; assessment; medical, educational or child care treatment or provision. They should have similar rights if they are dissatisfied with the quality of a service (*chapter 7*).

22. A range of supporting services is necessary to enable families to care for their handicapped children at home. These should often be used in conjunction with each other to lessen the strain on parents, siblings and the handicapped child himself. They include:
a. A '*sitting-in*' *service* to allow the rest of the family to go out together. A group of part-time and voluntary workers with nursing, teaching or other experience should be available as 'sitters'.

b. *Home helps*, especially for families with a severely handicapped child at home.

c. *Laundry services* for incontinent children.

d. *Suitable housing* and, if necessary, adaptation of premises to the needs of the physically handicapped.

e. *Provision of 'aids to living'* related to the nature of the handicap.

f. A range of *day care facilities*.

g. *Holiday places* in residential centres for handicapped children, with or without their parents.

h. *Places in holiday camps* or elsewhere for the siblings of handicapped children who may otherwise miss an active holiday.

i. *Hostels* where handicapped children can stay periodically for a few days to give themselves and the family a break; or during a crisis; or during the week in term time to be near a special school; or after leaving school.

j. *An information service* about equipment, publications on the care of children with different handicaps, and information on services and available provision.

k. *Assistance – particularly to those who are housebound –* to help children and their families to develop their potentialities for creative and leisure activities (*chapter 7*).

The design and adaptation of buildings

23. There is at present no obligation on local housing authorities to provide for physically handicapped people in their housing programmes. Welfare departments (in future social services departments) have powers to make arrangements for necessary adaptations to premises, for example, widening doorways for a wheel chair to go through, installing or adapting bathroom and lavatory facilities, but the extent to which these powers are used varies. Unsuitable housing should not be a reason for a handicapped child having to live away from home. We welcome the more stringent responsibilities imposed by the Chronically Sick and Disabled Persons Act. We also look forward to more comprehensive planning by the new social services departments (*chapter 3*).

24. Unsuitably designed school buildings can also make it impossible to educate children with some handicaps in ordinary schools. In the design of many colleges, indeed of some of the new university buildings,

flights of outside steps and distance between buildings create additional hazards for some handicapped young people (*chapter 3*).

25. The employment openings for crippled or chairbound school leavers are obviously further circumscribed by the design and equipment of the building where they might be offered work, as well as by problems of transport (*chapter 10*).

26. Therefore in all new buildings proper provision should be made for access to and use of essential facilities by the handicapped (*chapter 3*).

The need for hostels as an alternative to handicapped children being mainly at home or mainly away from home

27. At present there is almost no alternative to a handicapped child either being at home – often with inadequate supporting services for the family – or else away in a residential school, hospital or children's home. The widespread provision of hostels for handicapped children by the social services and education departments seems to us an essential means to relieve the strain on families, to enable many more children to go to day special schools and remain close to their homes, and to relieve the pressure on special schools and hospitals. Hostels should be used flexibly for children to stay for weekends, holidays, a few days or for longer periods. The planning of such hostel provision – both long stay and short stay – should largely be the responsibility of the children's regional planning committees (*chapters 8 and 9*).

Special educational treatment

28. The Department of Education and Science's categories of handicapped children require revision in the light of changed incidence and knowledge since 1945.

The existing categories are:
  a. blind
  b. partially sighted
  c. deaf
  d. partially hearing
  e. educationally subnormal
  f. epileptic
  g. maladjusted
  h. physically handicapped
  i. speech defect
  j. delicate

Instead we suggest the following broad groupings which are not, of course, mutually exclusive. They are intended chiefly for educational assessment and as a guide to the use of a variety of educational facilities to suit individual children's needs rather than as separate categories for special educational treatment.

  a. visual handicap
  b. hearing impairment
  c. physical handicap
  d. speech and language disorder
  e. specific learning disorder
  f. intellectual handicap
  g. emotional handicap
  h. severe personality disorder
  i. severe environmental handicap
  j. severe multi-handicap (*chapter 9*).

29. We welcome the move towards educating handicapped children in ordinary schools, though the question whether a child should be educated in an ordinary school rather than a special school is complex. The solution depends not only on the degree of disability but on the child's personality, intelligence and additional disabilities as well as on the characteristics of the ordinary school. We also recognise other problems, such as teachers having too little expert advice and consultation available to them. This also applies to many peripatetic and home teachers (*chapter 9*).

30. Any given school for handicapped children should cater for as wide a range of handicaps and ages as possible, provided that the educational and other special needs of each handicap can be adequately met (*chapter 9*).

The education of severely subnormal children

31. We welcome the decision to transfer responsibility for the education of severely subnormal children, both in training centres and in mental subnormality hospitals, to the local education authority and thus to bring it within the main stream of special educational provision. This will entail planning to give such children the most suitable type of education and training: integrate the present staff in the education service; and bring into the main stream of teacher training the future

training of teachers of such children and of those with learning
difficulties (*chapter 9*).

Boarding schools

32. Boarding special schools should only be used where this is (at a
given time) in the best all-round interests of the physical, emotional,
intellectual and social development of the child. It is always desirable
for the child and his parents to visit the school before he becomes a
boarder. Home visits at weekends as well as for school holidays are
important. Parents should be encouraged to visit their children and
given financial or other help where necessary. The importance of the
child care function in residential schools needs greater emphasis. The
quality of the residential child care staff is in our view of paramount
importance (*chapters 8 and 9*).

33. School and home social workers of the social services department
should be jointly responsible for securing the closest possible relations
between the child, his parents and his home neighbourhood, and
between the parents and school. Primary responsibility should rest with
the social worker in the home area, though it is essential that links
should be regularly maintained with the social services department in
the school area (*chapter 8*).

Long stay hospitals

34. It is not desirable that the present number of severely subnormal
children should be in large hospital wards and cared for primarily by
nursing staff or by untrained auxiliaries. Many such children are
capable of living in a community home, or else in special units of
appropriate size with both nursing, teaching and care staff. The team
should be large enough for members to support one another and to
provide continuity of care. The children should have opportunities for
training, physical activity, stimulus and occupation, sometimes leading
to life in the open community. We recognise that this is unlikely to be
possible for some severely multi-handicapped children with very
limited mental development (*chapter 8*).

35. There are also many physically handicapped children in long-stay
hospitals whose all-round needs suggest the same careful and comprehensive planning (*chapter 8*).

Handicapped children without a parent or guardian

36. Some children who are in hospitals or independent special boarding schools or other institutions because of physical or mental handicaps, may have no one to act as an individual friend and to be responsible for taking part in planning for their future. Local authorities already have a general duty under section 1 of the Children Act, 1948, to receive into care a child living away from or without a parent or guardian. In our view this power should be used by the local authority of the area in which the hospital, independent school or other institution is situated in relation to all such children (unless there is strong reason to the contrary in a certain individual case). For those who need to remain in the physical care of the hospital, independent school or other institution, the social services department should act *in loco parentis* (*chapter 8*).

37. In situations where the parent or guardian or other relatives of children in the foregoing circumstances are unable or unwilling to visit, it should be the duty of the local authority social services department of the area in which the hospital, independent school or other institution is situated to appoint a social worker or a responsible volunteer to exercise this "outside friend and guardian" function. Every effort should be made to facilitate visits by this person, including payment of fares and other expenses if necessary (*chapter 8*).

Children in the care of the local authority

38. If a handicapped child has to be received into care because he cannot be in his own home, every effort should be made to compensate for this by such means as a foster home placement or, if he is in a boarding school, to ensure that he goes to the same foster home or children's home each holiday (*chapter 8*).

39. Our enquiries revealed a considerable number of handicapped children – especially educationally subnormal and maladjusted – in the care of local authority children's departments, often because places are not available in residential schools or hospitals. This situation should be explicitly recognised, both in the annual returns of children in care, in the schemes for community homes prepared by the children's regional planning committees and in provision for the education and care of such children. We hope that the wider powers of the new social services departments will make it possible to plan comprehensively to meet such children's needs (*chapter 8*).

School leaving and preparation for employment

40. There should be early and careful preparation by the school, the youth employment service and the social services department for school leaving and subsequent placement. This should include a realistic appraisal of the possibilities of employment for each handicapped child within broad categories based on work potential for: *a.* normal, or *b.* sheltered employment, or *c.* occupation – if employment is not possible. Transfer from one category to another may be necessary in the light of experience (*chapter 10*).

41. The school curriculum, especially in the last years, should give due consideration to the need for preparation for life after school, particularly personal independence, social relations and pre-work experience. The educational progress of many handicapped children is retarded by their handicap and they mature late. It is, therefore, desirable for many, especially severely handicapped, children to stay on at school well after the statutory school leaving age. Further education centres for them should include vocational training and continued education for independence and for social relations with their non-handicapped contemporaries (*chapters 9 and 10*).

42. There are wide variations from excellent to poor in the co-operation between schools (especially residential schools), the youth employment service, the school health service and the present welfare departments. Better co-operation should result when our proposals about continuous assessment, the register, and responsibility for continuity of care by the social services department are in operation (*chapter 10*).

43. Well before the statutory school leaving age every handicapped pupil, who will be on the comprehensive register which we propose, should be specifically considered by a careers officer with special training or experience in the placing of handicapped school leavers. For all handicapped children likely to have employment difficulties there should be a case conference, including the child, his parents, the social worker of the social services department who knows the family, the head teacher and the specialist careers officer. When necessary, specialist careers officers from particular voluntary societies and a disablement resettlement officer should be available (*chapter 10*).

44. We envisage that continuing comprehensive assessment would not cease after young people leave school. The social services department, acting in co-operation with the youth employment service and the disablement resettlement officer, would have continued responsibility for handicapped school leavers. It should ensure that continuing care is provided, whether social, medical or occupational. Close co-ordination would be necessary between the local authority services, the proposed area health authorities, the Department of Employment and Productivity, Remploy factories and the various voluntary organisations concerned. It is highly desirable that regular medical examinations should continue for all handicapped young people who need them (*chapter 10*).

Insufficient understanding of or knowledge about the aspirations and needs of adolescents who are handicapped

45. There is a surprising failure to recognise the acute problems of isolation from their peers that confront many of the more seriously handicapped adolescents, who face, often without the chance to satisfy them, the normal urges of young people for companionship, relations with the opposite sex, sport, enjoyment of leisure pursuits, travel, spending money, achievement, and the prospect of their own future home and family. We think it urgent that the needs of adolescents who are handicapped should receive more systematic study and that greater efforts should be made to meet them so far as possible (*chapters 2 and 7*).

The shortage of professionally qualified staff with suitable training

46. There is a severe shortage of professionally qualified staff with training or experience related to children with special needs, in particular:
    a. medical practitioners skilled in developmental screening;
    b. child psychiatrists;
    c. educational psychologists;
    d. specially trained teachers of the handicapped;
    e. residential child care staff in boarding schools or children's homes or hostels;
    f. social workers, especially in the personal social services, child and family guidance, and education welfare (*chapter 11*).

47. We think it important that, wherever appropriate, refresher or

specialised courses on children with special needs should be multi-disciplinary. At the initial training stage each profession should learn to understand not only the emotional, intellectual, physical and social needs of children, especially those who are handicapped, but also the role of the other related professions (*chapter 11*).

48. Students in colleges of education should devote more time to a study of the special educational needs of handicapped children, particularly the educationally subnormal (in a wide context) and the maladjusted, in view of the increased awareness of minor disabilities affecting learning and adjustment, and increased concern for environmentally handicapped children. In virtually every classroom of whatever ability level, there will be children suffering from minimal defects and handicaps, some of which will be affecting the learning process and which because of their covert nature may be distressing to the child if the learning difficulty is attributed to wilfulness, laziness, lack of concentration, failure to try, etc (*chapters 9 and 11*).

49. Accordingly we urge the need for colleges of education to consider in what ways they may prepare students better to play their part in preventive work, in early detection and to meet the special educational and other needs of children. Furthermore we suggest that each area training organisation should review its policy in relation to the teaching of children with handicaps whether in ordinary or special schools; this should also include giving the students experience of other related professions and services.

Finally, there should be comprehensive provision for experienced teachers to become knowledgeable and skilled in the teaching of handicapped children. In addition to the present advanced courses, this should include reorientation courses for teachers wishing to transfer from ordinary to special schools; a basic three-year training for teachers of the subnormal (by enlarging the present diploma courses for teachers of the subnormal); and an advanced course (after practical experience) leading to the B.Ed. in special education (*chapter 11*).

Indications for medical, educational and social data collection, research and evaluation

50. A greatly expanded programme of research and evaluation is required. In part this must rest upon adequate data collection which

would give a more accurate picture of the true incidence of handicapping conditions, be they physical, emotional or social. More action
projects and longitudinal studies of the medical, social, emotional and
educational aspects of disabilities in childhood could provide a firmer
basis for prevention, detection, assessment, treatment, care and
education services for children with special needs. This should also
result in more effective deployment of resources. There is a similar
need for technological research and the production of improved
appliances for handicapped people (*chapter 12*).

The fragmented services for handicapped children and lack of co-ordinated planning locally and nationally

51. Overall national planning of services and provision for handicapped
children – and adults – is at the present time conspicuous by its
absence. In particular, there are four government departments directly
and closely concerned; the Department of Education and Science, the
Department of Employment and Productivity, the Department of
Health and Social Security and the Home Office, with no specific
provision for integrated planning between them. There is an urgent
need for effective machinery for co-ordinated appraisal, clarification of
priorities and policy determination in relation to the total well-being
of handicapped children (*chapter 12*).

52. The weaknesses in national planning are mirrored in local planning.
At present there are four departments concerned, which often results
in no coherent and comprehensive planning either for handicapped
children in general, or for any particular child. The setting up of social
services departments will reduce the number. This, together with the
proposed unification of the National Health Service, will mean that
there will in future be comprehensive authorities for education, for
health and for the personal social services. Nevertheless problems of
'across the board' planning and co-operation will remain. We welcome
the new children's regional planning committees for a wide range of
community homes and hope that in due course these will be extended
to include residential special schools (*chapter 12*).

53. At present some barriers to an adequate range of local provision
spring from the small size of many local authorities especially in
relation to handicaps such as deafness and blindness, which are
comparatively rare. These difficulties will be lessened when the

proposals for the greatly enlarged unitary and metropolitan authorities in the Government White Paper *Reform of Local Government in England* are implemented: and also if unified area health authorities are set up with the same boundaries (*chapter 12*).

The case for a national advisory council on handicapped children

54. The evidence to us from many voluntary organisations and from parents' letters stressed the confusion, gaps, overlapping and lack of co-ordination whether in public or voluntary services for handicapped children. They emphasised the need for better information services in local authorities and for a comprehensive national council or other advisory body, covering all forms of handicap and all relevant disciplines and services. The suggested purposes included: policy formulation; fact finding and research; acting as both a forum and pressure group, making known the common needs of all handicapped children and their families; making proposals about new or improved services; and acting as a source of information about specific resources, appliances, voluntary or statutory services, research and enquiries available in relation to children with various handicaps. (*chapter 12*).

The case for two councils, one voluntary, the other inter-departmental

55* We came to the conclusion that this range of functions was too wide to be encompassed within one council and, moreover, that a council advisory to central government is necessarily different from an independent body free to arouse public opinion, and to give advice and information to parents of handicapped children. We think there is a strong case for setting up two councils, the one an independent voluntary body and the other within the several ministries directly concerned. Our more detailed proposals for each council are set out below (*chapter 12*).

An independent voluntary council

56. We propose the setting up of an independent voluntary council, largely on the lines suggested in evidence to us. Its aim would be to bring together the separate voluntary and other organisations with an interest in handicapped children:

    a. to provide a meeting ground for discussion of necessary action;

  b. to undertake publicity on behalf of such children and their
      families;
  c. to undertake studies and enquiries;
  d. to act as a comprehensive source of information for parents and
      others about facilities which already exist (*chapter 12*).

57. We considered whether the proposed council should be a separate
new body, but we came to the conclusion that this would overlap with
some of the functions of existing bodies. Much of the evidence had
suggested that the National Bureau for Co-operation in Child Care
would be the appropriate body to undertake the tasks outlined above.
We agree that there is no other sufficiently comprehensive organisation
in the children's field. Accordingly we support the adoption of this
proposal and commend it to the Executive Committee and Council of
the National Bureau. We recognise that this might run counter to some
of the Bureau's policies. We are also aware that considerable funds
would be required to implement the proposal for a co-ordinating,
disseminating and bridge-building service, in particular to provide a
central information service for individual enquiries (*chapter 12*).

An inter-departmental advisory council

58.* In central government the problem is primarily that several
vertically organised departments have responsibility for different
aspects of handicap – though the health, education, social and employment needs of the handicapped themselves are essentially horizontal
and closely interrelated. We see no way to meet this problem except by
some kind of interdepartmental machinery for a developmental,
consultative role and to achieve common policies (*chapter 12*).

59.* The possibilities are: either an advisory council set up by the
initiative of the ministers concerned, probably within one ministry but
with representatives of others and of outside interests; or an advisory
council set up by legislation. In either event, the council should have a
constitution and its chairman should have access to the ministers
concerned (*chapter 12*).

60.* No matter how the council was set up, in order to fulfil a difficult
but crucial developmental and consultative role, it should bring together the particular interests in handicapped children of the Department of Education and Science, the Department of Employment and

Productivity, the Department of Health and Social Security, the Home Office and other relevant government departments. It should also include other interests, notably the local authority associations, the health authorities, voluntary organisations, professional associations, universities and independent research institutes. It should have access to any available information it needed; it should also have the necessary staff and other resources at its disposal to undertake independent enquiries and to commission research. It would clearly need to set up various sub-committees. It should present a regular report to Parliament, which should be published. It should comment in this report, amongst other matters, on the annual returns from local authorities about comprehensive assessment, the numbers and types of children on the registers, the services provided for them, variations in different parts of the country, and the changing pattern of incidence and provision (*chapter 12*).

61.* We envisage that the council would be based in one of the four departments primarily concerned. It should be the responsibility of the designated department to ensure that other departments concerned have adequate representation. But what primarily matters is the will to ensure that it should become an effective body, constantly consulted and able to make its voice heard on the different but closely inter-related needs of the handicapped (*chapter 12*).

Note of dissent

Note of dissent by Dr D. Egan, supported by Dr R. Wigglesworth, except for the sentence within the asterisks.

Paragraphs 13, 14, 15 and 16

The need for universal periodic screening of the whole child population from birth onwards deserves far greater emphasis than has been given in the main findings of the report. The "at risk" concept has been important in arousing interest for the early identification of handicap, but its applicability is limited. There is a small group of children, estimated at some 5–10 per cent, with criteria implying high risk, and this selected group will yield 30 per cent of children with handicaps. The remaining 70 per cent can only be identified by periodic developmental screening examinations of the whole child population. This will be done by child health doctors (local health authority medical officers and general practitioners) in child health clinics. A stimulating framework for this approach has been provided in the general recommendations of the Sheldon Committee's Report, Ministry of Health, 1967.

The proposal of my colleagues in the Working Party to give local authorities the statutory duty to compile and maintain a comprehensive register which would consist of two major sections *a.* an observation section, and *b.* a handicapped children section could thus only deal with a minority of children. Moreover the proposal immediately raises problems of definition. The delineation of handicap itself is all too often blurred. Obviously it would be well-nigh impossible to define the factors which would require the statutory registration of a child as in need of observation until the possibility of a handicapping condition being present or developing has been ruled out.

It is of course essential to ensure that all infants and pre-school children should be given periodic developmental screening examinations. This must be the task of the child health team. The health visiting service is well placed to ensure that children attend child health clinics especially with their increasing attachment to general practices.

Criteria implying high risk are not easily defined and must be a matter of experienced clinical judgement. It is one thing to agree between doctors that certain babies and young children need special observation in case they develop a handicap; to ear-mark medical records accordingly, and to carry out the follow-up through health visitors who already have a statutory duty to follow-up *all* babies and young children. It is quite another thing to place the responsibility for the review of these children's cases in a social services department. This measure would be likely to arouse much unnecessary anxiety in parents, undermine the family's confidence in the doctor, and lead to a situation in which, as a result, essential medical information might well be withheld for fear of misinterpretation. When help is required to provide casework or counselling the services of a social work department can usefully be called in. *It is of interest in this connection that in the United States of America, child health programmes which hitherto were administered by the Children's Bureau – including maternal and child health services, crippled children, maternal and infant care, and health of school and pre-school children – have been transferred to the Health Services and Mental Health Administration (HSMHA), leaving the Children's Bureau able to concentrate on welfare and social services*.

A further point is the failure of the main findings and conclusions of the report to draw sufficient distinction between the provisions for babies and pre-school children, and those for the school-age child. There is a world of difference between the analyses of the motor, visual, hearing and learning developmental delay in the infant and young child in whom the somatic, intellectual and emotional factors are so interwoven, and the analyses of these in a child of school age. All of these factors are so much influenced in the young child by transitory variations in general health that there can be no substitute for the paediatrician, the competent child health doctor and the health visiting service. The concept that effort concentrated on children under 5 years is probably more rewarding than similar effort given at a later age, applies to services for early identification, to assessment and immediate treatment, and to support of the parents.

Paragraphs 55, 58, 59, 60 and 61
It seems to me entirely wrong in principle to set up a central government advisory body for advice on handicapped and potentially handicapped children. Progressive thought in recent years has moved away from the separation between handicapped and potentially handicapped children – in so far as it is even practical to define this group – and the normal child population. Furthermore a consequence of setting up a central government advisory body could be to take away effective responsibility and drive from the appropriate central government departments.

The proposed representation would be unwieldy and their effective impact on a number of central government departments extremely doubtful. Inevitably the paper work of local authorities to make the kind of reports visualised would be considerably increased, and their returns, based on registers compiled from factors which are incapable of precise definition, would be of doubtful value as national statistics. Already the Department of Health and Social Security, the Department of Education and Science, and the Home Office have the same Chief Medical Officer, and on the medical side the link between services has recently been strengthened by the appointment of a senior doctor, whose task it is to co-ordinate the medical services for children rendered under the auspices of the three central departments. Similar arrangements might well be introduced into other sections of the central departments. Encouragement can and should be given to the development of co-operation at field level. A notable example is provided by the assessment centres now being set up. Here there is the closest co-operation between paediatricians, local authority doctors, general practitioners and social service agencies.

1. The Parents' Voices

*"So here we are — one struggling grandmother who will eventually
have a nervous breakdown if nothing can be done soon, a worried father
trying to run a business, one very puzzled three year old boy who
cannot understand why his much loved sister does not respond to his
affection and wonders why she does not live at home . . . one mother who
feels . . . terrified of what she might do to her own daughter if she
comes home again and behaves as before and, in the middle of it all, one
very pretty, much loved little girl who does not understand and cannot
cope with the world and whose only means of expressing herself is
screaming."*

Letter from a mother of a five year old mentally handicapped
daughter now living with her grandmother.

In 1968 when the National Bureau for Co-operation in Child Care
planned this present study Anne Allen wrote an article in a national
Sunday newspaper asking parents of handicapped children to write
about their experiences. Subsequently, newspapers in many parts of the
British Isles published a letter from the Bureau, signed by the Director,
making the same request. The response was encouraging – 412 parents
and others wrote in about their past experiences, their hopes and their
fears. Mostly they wrote about their needs, revealing injustices,
hardships and deficiences of which the authorities may be only
remotely aware.

Are these parents typical? Possibly not. Writers to newspapers are
unlikely to be wholly representative of the general population although
there has been very little research into what kind of people they are. It
should be said therefore that no generalisations can be drawn from the

letters described here* about the characteristics of parents of handicapped children in general. Nor was it possible to check the writers' statements.

All that can be said is that such families *do* exist and that their letters offer an insight into their lives, their relations with society and, most of all, what they consider to be their greatest needs. Even if their circumstances are exceptional their presence in the community is justification for questioning the adequacy of existing provisions and reassessing the services which they require.

The families

Who wrote? Over 300 letters came from mothers of handicapped children – six times as many as from fathers. Only a few parents wrote and signed the letters jointly (*Table 1*: page 63). But the handicapped child's impact on the community is shown by letters from outside the immediate family circle: the social worker writing of a "scandalous anomaly" in the regulations affecting the family bereaved of a mentally handicapped daughter; the teachers in special schools and units; the retired couple in their seventies directing a non-profit-making company to provide outings for handicapped children, in memory of a son who had been killed in an aircraft carrier during the second World War.

These parents and other writers concerned with handicapped children wrote from all over the British Isles, from Lisburn in Ulster to Clacton on Sea, from St. Austell to Kirriemuir in the Braes of Angus (*Table 2*). The geographical distribution of the letters, in general reflected the actual distribution of the child population, although a few areas were under-represented, due no doubt to the fact that the Bureau's letter was not published in the local press.

Incomes and Occupations

Apart from the address where they live very few parents gave much information about themselves. Only 36 letters, for instance, gave the father's occupation or income. A lorry driver, one of five from whose families letters came, and a male staff nurse in a mental subnormality hospital, were struggling to support their dependents, including

---

* To avoid possible identification of individual families, names, ages and other personal details have been changed where it seemed necessary.

handicapped children, on £15 a week. Other fathers in low income occupations included four working on the land, a dustman, school caretaker, office boy and London taxi driver. A chief steward on an ocean-going liner, earning £148 monthly, a television producer, an engineer, and RAF officers – two of five fathers in the armed services – were among the minority with higher incomes whose occupations were stated.

Predictably even fewer of the mothers mentioned jobs outside the home, although a few were working full or part-time to relieve the financial strain on the family. The wife of a railway worker with a 10 year old spina bifida daughter and four other children wrote, "I have had to go out to work and put the baby in a day nursery so that we could buy and run a car . . . this is not a luxury but the only means of getting us out as a family". Others would have liked to take jobs but could not arrange suitable child-minding while away from home and the total of 24 mothers described as having full- or part-time jobs is probably close to the total number in employment since the difficulties of arranging outside employment were only too clear from the letters. A few other mothers who were able to get out found that working in schools, hospitals, offices or factories helped to ease the nervous tension as well as the financial strain and occasionally they had been encouraged to do so by understanding doctors.

Precise incomes were rarely mentioned but those stated were often pitifully inadequate. A 70 year old widow with a mentally handicapped son of 29 had been trying, unsuccessfully, to repay her mortgage out of their combined income of £3 14s 6d a week. A deserted wife, with a daughter who had been wheelchair-bound and brain-injured after a traffic accident and with three other children to bring up, depended on social security allowances of £9 2s 0d. "It is", she wrote bitterly, "an offence to neglect children; it should be an offence also to leave them destitute". The mother of a 12 year old spastic and another child was forced to take an £8 a week clerical assistant's job to keep the family while her husband was in prison for motoring offences. The ludicrous situation of trying to feed, clothe and warm a mentally handicapped daughter of two and a four year old on an income of £6 weekly, supplemented by 11s social security and 10s family allowance was described by a 30 year old woman who was separated from her husband.

Hardship was great where wives were supporting handicapped children on their own and the strains imposed on marriage by the presence of a handicapped child were emphasised by the comments of 19 parents who were divorced or separated. The father of a mentally handicapped son wrote, "I recall how my marriage went on the rocks. We couldn't go out together . . . I would come home from work – wife prepares dinner, I take over and wife goes out to where I didn't know. I didn't have time to care, I was tied up caring for the children, tending to mainly the handicap of the child. We saw each other maybe two hours an evening". Another writer, who had later reunited with his wife, described the sheer helplessness, worry and fatigue which led to the mutual recriminations, fierce quarrels and subsequent break up. Was it significant that over one-third of the writers did not specifically mention the presence of their husband or wife in the home?

Family size
The size of the families was often a factor in financial and marital strain. It varied from those with a single child to a family with 13, whose mother wrote bitterly of her battle to keep her 11 year old mongol daughter and others who were still living at home on family allowances and social security after her husband had deserted her five years earlier. A holiday for her handicapped daughter was an un- attainable dream.

About half of the handicapped children described in the letters had at least one brother or sister but because of the brevity of some writers, their preoccupation with the handicapped member of the family, the other half may not all have been 'only' children.

The children
Though they were reticent about themselves and other members of their families, many parents wrote at length about their handicapped children. Some chronicled their experiences from pregnancy to the present day; others gave blow-by-blow accounts of their tussles with local authorities – in one case 29 letters, 16 interviews and innumerable telephone calls over an 18-month period.

Four hundred and twelve handicapped children were described in all. While most were the only handicapped children in their families, sixteen of them had another handicapped brother or sister, and in each of three other families there were three. For those with three the strains might have been expected to be intolerable – but not one showed the bitterness or self-pity which characterised the letters of some of the other parents. The mother of eight, coping with an incontinent, non-speaking ten year old, an older severely subnormal daughter and a boy at a school for the educationally subnormal – all affected by phenylketonuria – wrote: "They all live at home and are happy". The mother of three deaf children, aged ten, seventeen and twenty-six, tried to meet and comfort parents when they first found out their child was deaf.

Boys predominated. There were two hundred and forty-eight, compared with one hundred and sixty-four girls. The sex of three other children was not given. Obviously these figures cannot be taken as an indication that there are more handicapped boys than girls in the country as a whole – but they might reflect greater parental concern about having a handicapped son than a handicapped daughter.

Over half of the children described by the writers were aged five to fifteen. Fifty-five were in the pre-school age group and one hundred and twenty-three were sixteen or over (*Table 3d*). Fifty-two adults over the age of twenty-one were included in this last group and the letters from or about them – including four from handicapped adults themselves – offered stark reminiscences of pre-war childhood experiences or insights into the difficulties which handicapped children in the school-age group might meet later. Thirty-five years ago attitudes to the handicapped were far less enlightened, as the letter from a 50 year old man born without a right arm indicated. "Conditions for children today are certainly improved" he wrote. "My letter really concerns my own generation – most of us feel 9th class citizens". A spastic employee, describing the strain of working from 8 am to 5 pm five days weekly, wrote: "What a difference it would make if disabled people were allowed to work fewer hours a day for a livable wage". One mother described the persistence and initiative of her partially sighted diabetic son who was now teaching in a special school and planning to marry a colleague in three or four months' time.

About three-quarters of the handicapped children lived at home with one or both parents and of the one hundred and five who were in residence elsewhere only a quarter went home for weekends or school holidays (*Table 3d*).

The majority of pre-school children were living at home without any other placement but even in the school-age group fifty-one (over 20 per cent) were wholly at home – a figure too high for complacency. Nearly one-third of the post-school group were also living wholly at home and only seventeen were in open employment. These included a teacher, telephone order clerk, assistant cook in a home for the blind, an engineering works apprentice doing an associated further education course and a plasterer's labourer. About 20 per cent of the children were not living at home, but in a residential setting of one kind or another (*Tables 3a, b, c*).

Their handicaps
Just over half the children – two hundred and nine – were described as having more than one handicap and twenty-six of these had four or more handicaps. One five year old boy was described as having seven. His mother listed five which had been diagnosed by successive doctors, punctuating each with an ironical exclamation mark: "Congenital deformity of the hip! Deaf-mute! Mentally retarded! Brain-damaged! 'Something wrong with his eyes'! But no treatment except a tranquilliser . . . " "Hyperactivity" and "behaviour problems" were also mentioned in her letter.

The most prevalent condition was mental handicap.* Two hundred and five children were mentally handicapped and many of these had other disabilities such as physical handicaps and speech defects. Twenty-three others were described as being educationally subnormal.

To assess the numbers and types of handicaps from which the children suffered was difficult. Many writers were vague, mentioning, for instance, only "physical handicap", "brain damage", or "mental handicap". Where "mental handicap" was mentioned it was sometimes possible to tell from the children's placement – in a junior training centre or a school for the educationally subnormal, for instance – if they were severely subnormal or educationally subnormal and to classify them separately.

Seventy children were unable to walk properly and spent all or most of their time in wheelchairs. This was the most prevalent physical

* The term "mental handicap" as used in this chapter, covers not only those children who were obviously severely subnormal but also those whose degree of mental impairment was not clear from the letters.

handicap. Sixty-one had cerebral palsy and nearly a quarter of the children – 48 – were unable to speak. A similar number suffered from epilepsy or from convulsions due to other causes. Twenty-five children were partially sighted, twenty-three suffered from spina bifida and at least twenty-three were autistic. Other children were handicapped by deafness, blindness, maladjustment and emotional difficulties, heart, speech and vision defects, asthma, anaemia and congenital defects. Handicaps more rarely mentioned were diabetes, dislocated hips, multiple sclerosis, coeliac disease, scoliosis and microcephalus. But concepts of what constitutes a handicap are becoming more sophisticated. One parent wrote of the "discrepancy" between her son's "verbal and performance IQs."

The frequency with which various handicaps were mentioned could be misleading. It probably has less to do with their country-wide incidence than it has with the extent of practical and other difficulties associated with particular handicaps. The incidence of educational subnormality in the school-age population, for instance, is high – yet only twenty-three educationally subnormal children were described in the letters. However, as their parents tend to be in a similar intelligence range and the management, educational and other problems may be less acute than with other handicapping conditions, the small number who were described is not so surprising.

Positive help

Needs were foremost in the majority of letters but over two hundred and thirty writers were grateful for the help they received, help not only in fundamentals like schooling and hospital treatment but also in the opportunity to lay bare their anxieties and frustrations on paper. Their gratitude was chastening.

The father of an eight year old multi-handicapped child, who had seen the Bureau's letter in his local newspaper, wrote in reply: "I cannot express to you the moral uplift I experienced on finding someone that even displayed a sincere interest in improving services as you do", and the mother of a deaf five year old interrupted a 16-page account of her tribulations with the words, "I expect you will think from my letter that I'm a right old moaner but it's wonderful to get off my chest all my pent-up feelings that a mental welfare visitor does just not seem to have the time to hear". These and similar letters were poignant reminders of parents' sense of isolation, of their feelings that they were neglected – or rejected – by society.

What help did parents receive? Their views of what constituted positive help varied according to the sophistication of their expectations and their knowledge of existing provisions both locally and elsewhere. One writer would be touchingly grateful for help from passers-by in lifting her daughter's wheelchair over a high kerb; another would complain of inadequate headroom in the school bus which collected and returned her daughter daily. While some parents wrote appreciatively of good schools and hospital clinics, other parents and children appeared to be enjoying provisions of a similar standard but referred to them without comment.

Benefits of education
Education was most frequently mentioned. Parents with children in ordinary and special schools, in junior training centres and special care units, wrote of assiduous teaching and the devotion of the staff. "Both the schools were marvellous and without them and the staff that taught them I don't know how I would have coped", wrote the mother of three handicapped children. Another writer, whose son had attended a Rudolph Steiner school, wrote typically, "No words I can use could express my admiration and gratitude to the whole staff there."

Nearly half of the two hundred and thirty-four school-age children were explicitly described as having benefitted from their education. The number probably reflects to some extent the predominance of letters about school-age children and the relative abundance of services for children in this age group.

Personal and social help
Many parents were profoundly grateful, too, for help from relations, friends and the community in meeting personal and social needs. Over 80 of the children were seen as having been helped in this way and almost as many had been assisted by voluntary organisations.

The feeling that "someone cared" was one of the most important personal and social satisfactions mentioned by writers. For the wife of a colliery worker with a two year old suffering from epilepsy there was comfort in the knowledge that the congregations of two village churches prayed for her son every Sunday. For the parents whose twenty-two year old son had severe attacks of depression there was the consolation of sympathetic friends though they added, not uncharacteristically, that these were friends whose own lives had brought them into contact with the emotionally disturbed.

Relations, particularly grandparents, had rallied round some of the families. Grandparents helped to buy the much needed wheelchair which the local authority would not provide and the parents could not afford. Grandparents gave a home to an autistic grandson so that his mother, on her doctor's advice, could take up nursing again. In the letter from the grandfather of a five year old with spina bifida there was a sketch of the old table which he had shaped into a safe play area for toy cars. Other relations – though, sadly, few – were willing to baby-sit while parents had an evening out.

Youth clubs, swimming clubs for the disabled, groups where mothers could confide their problems to each other – all these were social contacts which writers appreciated for themselves and their children. A mentally handicapped man of twenty-six had just returned from a week's holiday in North Wales and his mother wrote of her gratitude to the youth club for the holiday she would have been unable to afford. "It just makes that difference to a mother when she knows he isn't always sitting in the corner of the kitchen doing nothing". A few special schools had parent-teacher associations where parents could talk to others in the same predicament and the chairman of a group for the parents of mentally handicapped children described the social club run by non-handicapped youth which enabled the parents to have a night out once a week. A mother of a mentally handicapped child wrote about the "Mums' Club" run by their local parents' association every Friday evening where they could laugh, chat and talk about their troubles and which organised an occasional outing while their husbands did the baby-sitting.

Aid from voluntary organisations

Many of these social contacts came through voluntary organisations. Again and again parents mentioned societies like the Association for Spina Bifida and Hydrocephalus, the Invalid Children's Aid Association, the National Society for Autistic Children, the National Society for Mentally Handicapped Children and the Spastics Society; the honorary secretaries of local branches of these and other organisations wrote to describe their activities. It was not only the day nurseries, play groups, physiotherapy sessions and youth clubs which helped but the advice on home management and the moral support they gave to parents that were of immeasurable value. Such support might mean the difference between continuing the struggle and total breakdown. "I honestly think I would not have been able to cope in the first two years of Jeremy's life without the help and moral support I received from the people running the Spastic Centre", wrote the mother of a four year old boy who was cerebral palsied and mentally handicapped, and had no speech and could not walk.

Other organisations and individuals not exclusively concerned with handicapped children also helped the families. Parents referred to the annual holidays run by the Red Cross, to transport provided by members of the Round Table and to church organisations. A play-group for mentally and physically handicapped children run by a former health visitor was an example of an individual venture and one through which the mother of a mentally handicapped epileptic boy "found out more what was going on, in one day, for handicapped children than I found all the time from hospital."

Medical and related services
Medical treatment and related services like therapy and psychological assessment were taken for granted by many writers but the help and sympathetic attitudes of general practitioners, hospital and other medical staff, especially when they went beyond their formal obliga-tions, were appreciated in relation to fifty-nine of the children. More than one parent felt that the family doctor had helped them to keep their equilibrium and the mother of an epileptic child wrote that their general practitioner had been the best friend any family could have. "He taught me how not to let Sammy see my fear for him, how to really love him without spoiling him, keeping him a normal part of a big family. I often thank God for Sammy being in the care of Dr ——— at the time he went ill and for my own sanity."

In busy hospitals, too, specialists had sometimes done more than expected, helping to find sheltered employment for a handicapped school leaver or asking the local housing authorities to rehouse council tenants with a handicapped son in a bungalow. One mother, whose son had received devoted care from the staff of a mental subnormality hospital, had decided after his death to work voluntarily for mentally handicapped children in gratitude for the hospital's help.

Help from local authorities
Although many writers were critical of their local authorities, some forty parents were grateful for the help of local government personnel. The parents of a six year old with muscular atrophy and mental handicap wrote of their great admiration for the services provided by their county. "Their interest in Michael never flags. Welfare officers pay frequent visits to our home, mental welfare, education welfare, county doctor, psychiatrist . . . when one knows that one has only to ring any of these welfare officers and help of any kind will be given it is most comforting to parents". Few parents were as wholehearted in their enthusiasm for their local authorities but they recalled and recorded the initiative of individual staff: the educational psychologist who brought together six families with hyperactive children to form a pressure group for education; the youth employment officer who for two years "left no stone unturned" in her efforts to find a job for a partially sighted girl.

Health visitors, despite criticism from some parents, appear to be among the most helpful of local authority staff. A mature student at a college of education, who recounted the experiences of many handicapped families in her area, described the fortnightly visits by a local health visitor to the mother of a handicapped child. "She takes her own sandwiches or something to heat up and Mrs J. makes her a pot of tea, thus putting Mrs J. in the position of the one to do the favour. Having lunch there means the nurse can legitimately stay an hour or so and Mrs J. can have a good talk about her problems. More important, the nurse is primed with the latest gossip so that the village is taken to pieces and put together again and Mrs J. does not feel so cut off from life around her."

Parents' attitudes
Parents like Mrs J., who appreciated the help they received were often those who were positive in their attitude to having a handicapped child and they tempt speculations about cause and effect. The personality of the parents as well as their knowledge of available services and how to obtain them appeared to be closely associated with the treatment meted out to the handicapped child. Some parents seemed to be caught in a

vicious circle, alienating local authority officials, relations and their neighbours by their attitudes and becoming more and more embittered and self-pitying as a result.

Others, like Michael's parents, could write: "What has happened is that Michael has brought a greater degree of family love: the five of us are welded together firmly yet not restricted in our individual lives". Similarly the mother of a wheel-chair-bound, partially sighted four year old, who attended a day nursery and had the help and sympathy of local welfare services, could view the family situation constructively and realistically: "Is life hell at times? Certainly. Do we ask why us? Certainly. Can we stick it? We must and do. Do we get any rewards? Most certainly – a happy laughing boy with a wonderful sense of humour and the times he does a small thing he previously couldn't do, which normal children take for granted, and those big hugs and kisses all day". Another writer, who had the support of her other children and her neighbours, recalled the anguish of the birth of her physically handicapped son and her subsequent recovery. "As you can imagine when he was born my one thought was, Dear God why? Well after I had got over the shock I looked around the rest of my children and seeing how well and happy they were I took this attitude, God gave me five lovely children, this little soul was sent to show that life is not all honey."

Perhaps the greatest stoicism was shown by parents who had been assailed by a series of misfortunes, callous and insensitive officials, rejecting neighbours and yet retained, against all odds, a great fortitude of spirit. The wife of a northern farmer, with an eight year old mentally handicapped, spastic son still awaiting a place in a training centre after three years, drew strength from the moorlands around her home. Despite disillusionment with promises broken by the health authorities, with days when she was left waiting with the wheelchair on a bleak, wind-swept hillside for an ambulance which did not turn up to take her son for treatment, she could still write: "The bright days of spring, the mellow colours of summer, the purple heather and golden days of autumn, the winter and the mud and the blessed creeping carpet of snow coming down from the moors to make everywhere bright and clean again. Contentment? Yes. Far better than a row of houses never changing, the roar of traffic and harsh city smells. And a name on a waiting list for a day centre? If only . . . " The mother

of a nineteen year old physically handicapped and partially sighted
son had become disgusted with people who thought they could "act
God to these children" but concluded her letter, "If you have one of
these type of children it is a challenge and should be treated as such.
When you get over one hurdle after another you should celebrate and
go to the next one more determined than ever."

It was this kind of determination which characterised the letters of
parents who had been most successful in getting help for their children.
Where strings dangled, parents pulled them – "titled gentlemen",
local vicars, friends on the council – but, for very many, they did not
exist at all. Nevertheless, unwilling to take 'no' for an answer from local
authorities, one mother got publicity for her son's plight on the BBC
programme "The World at One", another appealed to her Member of
Parliament, and a third wrote to Mrs Mary Wilson at 10 Downing
Street.

A few parents had appealed successfully against their local authorities' decisions that their children were unsuitable for education in
school. One eight year old boy, a high grade mongol, was now
attending an ordinary state school and another child was able to
transfer from a junior training centre to the partially hearing unit of a
school for the educationally subnormal after being taught reading,
writing and arithmetic by his mother. Collective action by a group of
parents living close to an industrial city had established a day care
centre for 35 mentally handicapped children and a short-stay care
home was now being planned.

In less conspicuous ways, too, writers showed their determination
and initiative: the parents of a cerebral palsied child took him to Italy
for holidays; a mother with a deaf five year old, three other children,
her husband and two relations, (aged eighty-six and a hundred) to care
for, wrote and produced amateur plays; the mother of a spastic son
and six other children decided, after seven years' washing, that she
could not face any more nappies and toilet-trained him within three
days by placing him on the pot at hourly intervals when the alarm bell
was timed to ring.

Their needs

Only half of the writers wrote appreciatively of help they were
receiving. Nearly all wrote in about their needs. In letters varying from

an eight-line scribble on exercise book paper to 24 pages in length, three hundred and ninety writers described a multitude of needs which, if met, would revolutionise social welfare policy and raise public expenditure on the handicapped to unprecedented heights. Yet although the material needs of the parents and their children were very great – for clothes and equipment, for more schools and centres to be built and for the staff to fill them – there seemed, written between the lines, a half-conscious yearning for greater awareness by society of the problems they faced. Those who complained, for instance, about the expense of maintaining their child at home and asked for a handicapped child's allowance were, perhaps, as concerned about the public recognition of their difficulties which they felt such an allowance would signify as about the money itself. "One would at least feel someone was trying to help", wrote a driver's wife with two spastic children. "Everyone gets family allowance but it isn't everyone who has two handicapped children . . . "

Personal and social needs
Much of this concern for greater public recognition revealed itself in the writers' personal and social needs. Over 660 needs of this kind were mentioned. Nearly one quarter of these were stated explicitly; the remainder could be inferred from the letters – although the difficulties of inferring needs of these and other kinds were considerable.*

Personal and social needs varied from majority demands for relief from round-the-clock care of a handicapped child and financial help to requests for guitar lessons, training in table manners and a toy car for a child with spina bifida.

Relief from full-time care
The need for relief from the care of a handicapped child at home was the most pressing of all personal and social needs. It was evident in relation to one hundred and twenty-three of the children. Few of the writers – mainly mothers – were excessive in their demands. Many would have been grateful for the minimum of help. A couple of hours a

---

* For instance, a vague complaint about a child's travelling time to a junior training centre could conceivably be construed as the need for more centres in the immediate vicinity, for more buses to be provided by the local authorities or for financial help to enable the family to run a car and drive the child to the centre. Any classification of such needs is therefore to some extent arbitrary and dependent on individual interpretation.

week to get the shopping done, a babysitter for an occasional evening out with their husbands, the availability of a home help at times of illness and other crises were all that many asked, but the availability or lack of such minimal relief might be the difference between a united family and a broken one.

The mother of an autistic five year old who now lived with his grandparents described the effects of unrelieved strain on family life. "His screaming sessions would last for many hours and even a quick trip to the shops and back would become a dreaded nightmare . . . Home relations became very strained, little outings to the beach or park became out of the question and it became noticeable that more and more 'friends' stopped visiting us and always put me off if I suggested visiting them . . . One day last September I finally snapped and walked out leaving both children."

In situations like this the unremitting strain could tempt parents to desperate action. Though she was the only parent to admit it openly, the mother who wrote of her impulse to take the life of her mentally handicapped daughter was probably not unique in her feelings. "I feel if she doesn't go, I will have to – my husband is afraid to go to work every morning for fear I will give the child sleeping tablets", she wrote. "I no longer care about what people think when they read these terrible words, for God's sake do something before it's too late". Fortunately, as a subsequent letter showed, her daughter's situation improved and the temptation ceased. Had there been no improvement, who knows what the outcome might have been?

The parents of a mentally handicapped daughter of eleven, though united in their hardships, had been worn down by exhaustion since, because of her behaviour, the local special care unit had refused to take her. "Her life is one of boredom, frustration and terrible loneliness", they wrote. "At times she throws herself around the room knocking over tables and chairs, hurling herself at the walls. It's a distressing sight to watch and at moments like these we are powerless to help her. I've lost count of the times she has broken panes of glass in windows and doors during these outbursts . . I don't know if you can imagine what it's like to cope with this kind of situation seven days a week, week after week, and the most terrible thing is to know it will never get any better". Such expressions of despair were not uncommon. An exhausted husband and wife whose emotionally disturbed daughter, her baby and the married man with whom she was associating were creating "a living hell" for them, prayed each night that "somewhere there must be an end to it but when and where we just don't know."

Other writers asked for centres where their children could go daily during the long school holidays to relieve boredom or for short-term residential care so that the rest of the family could go away on holiday. "My wife and I have not been out together to any entertainment or holiday for forty years," wrote the father of a thirty-nine year old son with cerebral palsy.

Financial hardship

The need for financial help, mentioned in relation to more than a hundred children, was almost as pressing. Wear and tear on clothes and shoes, long journeys to hospitals and clinics, costly high-protein diets, were thought to justify extra allowances or income tax relief. One parent's suggestion of tax allowances for incontinents might raise official eyebrows but the outlay she and others described – on rubber pants at 18s 6d per pair, on nappies and extra soap powders, on higher laundering costs – could overwhelm a family living at subsistence level. Similarly, expenses of £15 to erect a high safety fence round the garden, a grabrail in a bath and a special fire guard could fall heavily on a low income clerk and his family. Five-day stays in London, at 30s a night, while their three year old daughter was being treated at the Hospital for Sick Children, Great Ormond Street, were becoming "financially impossible" for a family living three hundred miles away, and one writer suggested that overnight hostels where parents could stay cheaply in London while their children were receiving treatment would be a good idea.

The strains of supporting an educationally subnormal daughter and her illegitimate baby were described by one mother. "We keep her and the baby for nothing and yet we pay 15s extra rent for her . . . But it now means a nursery while I get a job as we are getting into debt."

The exact amount that should be given as a handicapped child's allowance was not suggested by parents, perhaps because they realised how much the needs could vary from family to family, but the parents of a six year old mentally handicapped son probably summed up the feelings of many about financial aid: "The easiest way, as a first step, towards helping to relieve the burden of increased costs a handicapped child incurs would be to make an increase in his/her allowance on income tax or, in the case of parents of very limited means, a direct grant. But for dignity's sake don't make the parents be inundated with red-tape, just a simple application, quick conferment and payment."

Social isolation

Many parents who wrote about their financial straits were also keenly aware of the benefits which money could not buy: friends for their children and themselves, youth clubs and leisure activities for teen-agers and young adults, and opportunities to meet parents of similarly handicapped children. The need for more friends and opportunities to meet other people was expressed in relation to ninety children. Parents wanted their handicapped children to be able to mix with their non-handicapped peers and to be better integrated in the normal community. Often, however, they were disappointed.

The loneliness of those who had left school was particularly acute and even those with jobs could find that at 5 pm, when the office doors shut, they were alone again. The mother of a 22 year old shipping office clerk, suffering from muscular atrophy, wrote of her daughter's frustration at being unable to go out with friends of her own age because she could not keep up their pace and the mother of a lonely educationally subnormal boy of 19 described how her son had with-drawn into himself and was no longer able to "cope with life outside the home."

The mother of an 18 year old spastic wrote of her longing for someone to befriend her daughter. "What do we need most? . . . Someone with transport to take Amelia out regularly, (these arrangements seldom last). Few people realise the hardship on handicapped young people always having to be accompanied by Mother, to cinema or any entertainment, even church. Nor do people realise the thrill it gives a mother to wave good-bye to their youngest knowing that for a few hours they will be happy in the company of someone who cares."

"Someone who cares" epitomised many of the writers' feelings not only about friends and social contacts within their own immediate environment but also about the need for radical changes in community attitudes to handicapped children and their families, by neighbours, by officials, by the towns and villages where they lived and by society at large. "We live on a council estate", wrote the mother of a child with spina bifida. "Some people think his condition is catching and others say how wonderful to have a special child. I say nothing but I cry inside."

Inferiority and guilty feelings

The feelings of isolation, of being third class citizens in an affluent society, came through letters like that from the mother of a grown-up cerebral palsied son who wrote ironically: "Indeed those who hath (including a healthy son) shall jolly well have it all". The father of another cerebral palsied child went further. He had, he wrote, come to the conclusion that the biggest criminals were not in gaol but were the parents of the handicapped for the problems their children gave to other people. A farmer and his wife who considered they were "backing Britain" by helping the country to save imports felt that apathy over their son's mental handicap was a shabby return for their efforts. Others felt cut off from the community. "You feel so completely alone", wrote the parent of an epileptic seven year old. "There is, to my knowledge, no one I can go to for help."

A deep sense of inferiority was revealed by three or four parents who felt bitterly that too much was done for immigrants, too little for them. "Black people are having all the help to stop them being second class citizens but what is done for these third class citizens – nothing", wrote the mother of a mentally handicapped girl of 13. "When you read in the newspapers about the help for educating and housing immigrant children, you begin to feel very bitter, because you know that not enough money is being spent on the handicapped child in *this* country", wrote another. The conviction that charity should begin at home was also expressed by the mother of a baby with spina bifida who sympathised with the plight of children in Biafra but thought that public concern should "look at home before going elsewhere."

Guilt feelings were closely associated with some parents' sense of inferiority. Such feelings, even when acknowledged as being irrational, assailed several writers. The parents of a teenage, subnormal boy who felt alone and neglected "in the affluent society of today" blamed themselves for their son's condition and another parent with a speech-handicapped daughter wrote of her "feelings of guilt at having given birth to a handicapped child". But it was the mother of a six year old mentally handicapped girl who suffered the greatest agony of mind. She wrote: "I have always known that a mongol child could happen to anyone but even I believed at times that it was due to severe mental strain (my first husband committed suicide and I always felt I was to blame though there were several mitigating circumstances). I even felt this was my punishment. Though I rarely admit this to anyone it is deeply embedded in my mind."

Neighbourhood attitudes
Neighbourhood attitudes to handicapped children troubled some parents more than those of the community at large: neighbours who walked past a handicapped child as though he was not there, passers-by who stared, then stopped on some pretext and lagged behind "to get a better view" as one mother put it. "People are very good at sympathising with you, but when it comes to giving practical help, they don't want to know you", wrote the mother of three young children, one suffering from mental handicap and epilepsy and unable to walk. "I have been house-bound with my children ill with bronchitis, awaiting someone to knock on the door and ask me if they could get me a bit of shopping or get a prescription from the chemist for me . . . but people just don't care. They think it is your worry and just leave you to cope with the problem". Another mother had left a local park in tears when the park keeper shouted at her deaf son who was singing on the swings. His reply, when the child's handicap was explained, was brutally curt. "I don't care if he's deaf, daft or crippled. What's he making that noise for?" Had such callousness and lack of understanding been confined to casual encounters with park keepers and other members of the public many parents might have been able to shrug it off. But it could come, too, from the very people who were expected to give most help: professional workers in child care and other local authority officials. Chilling accounts of insensitivity were given by the minority of parents who had suffered most. A member of a child guidance service had interviewed the mother of a severely multi-handicapped child with the question "Is Stewart's father a cold fish?" A mental welfare officer was reported to have told a mother on the verge of a breakdown that if she couldn't look after her mentally handicapped son how could she manage to keep a dog. A child care officer, asked for foster home placement for an emotionally disturbed and retarded boy, told the mother that he had seen plenty of widows like her who thought they could ditch their children on to the local authorities and then go off to have a good time.

The father of an autistic child had experienced "more autism" among the local authorities than he had ever found in his daughter. Any services or advice he and his wife had been able to obtain had only been extracted after constant pressure and argument. "In our borough and so many other boroughs they are just a great big file lying forgotten in an office drawer until it's brought to attention by someone" was the way another writer described local officials' attitudes to handicapped children.

Lack of advice and information
The need to educate both the general public and parents about handicapped children, to obtain advice and information on their treatment, was mentioned in relation to fifty-nine children. One or two writers suggested that there should be more newspaper articles on handicap in order to inform the public. Others were more preoccupied with getting advice for themselves. "It would be so wonderful to have a motherly, understanding visitor to pop in and see mothers of handi-capped children, someone capable of noting dangerous signs of strain in the mother and to check that the mothers are kept up to date with ideas and methods of coping with and calming their children and also to teach mothers how best to help and teach the child how to manage and cope in a rather cruel world", wrote the mother of a five year old mentally handicapped girl.

Some parents regretted the lack of any central advisory and informa-tion centre where they could obtain much needed knowledge about education, medical treatment, vocational training and employment which local authorities – and occasionally even voluntary organisations – did not give them. "The tragedy in this situation seems to us to be that there is no one central body of information to help parents of handicapped children – the onus of finding help rests solely with the parents, and it is incredibly difficult to find time from work and family commitments to help the handicapped child", wrote the parent of a child with coeliac disease. Another was more emotional: "How cruel to tell a mother there's something wrong with her baby with not a word of advice or help in dealing with a child who spends his day screaming. What do I do when he knocks the baby down each time I turn round?"

Transport, housing and equipment
A minority of writers were anxious for better transport, housing and

equipment for their children. Parents complained about the long circuitous routes taken by buses for children attending junior training centres and at least one child spent four hours a day on buses in order to spend 3½ hours at the centre. The mother of a partially sighted child wrote that she had been "worried sick" when the school bus had taken over three hours on the homeward journey and he had not returned until after 7 pm.

The indifference of some local authorities to this problem was underlined by a writer describing experiences of a mother whose daughter was attending a day special school. The education authorities insisted it was impossible to pick her up from home and that she must be taken to the town centre to be collected. To do so the mother had to leave a baby and a two year old in the house alone. She was unhappy in this situation and when the baby began walking it became intolerable. She told the education authorities that she considered her younger children to be in real danger but "nothing can be done and if you cannot cope then Sandra must go to a residential school". Fortunately for the mother and children, and others in similar difficulties, their case was taken up by a medical officer and a minibus was bought to take them from door to door.

Others complained about the difficulties of taking their children on public transport, particularly on 250-mile journeys to London hospitals for treatment, or the sheer impossibility of getting their children to a youth club or cinema because they could not afford a car and there was no-one to drive them from the remote areas where they lived.

Several parents wrote about the need for more suitable housing, particularly bungalows. The restrictions on the outdoor play of an educationally subnormal epileptic child living in a top-floor London flat and the fears of another writer that her physically handicapped daughter might fall down the concrete stairway from their apartment block emphasised the hazard of stairs to the physically handicapped and the importance of a garden. Equipment such as wheelchairs and invalid carriages would have helped some writers and their children and others stressed the need for improvements in the design of public lavatories and swimming baths so that they could be more easily used by the handicapped.

While most writers dwelt on the social, financial and physical needs of their handicapped children a few parents were also aware of the importance of their children's emotional wellbeing. "I think that their greatest need is secure love and for them to be shown that they are each a very special person in their own right, with a place just for them", wrote the mother of a baby with congenital deformities. Another added, "The one thing they want is plenty of love and understanding and not to be looked upon as something that should be shut up in an institution".

Education

After personal and social needs, education came next in writers' priorities. Criticisms of provisions and suggestions for improvements were mentioned in relation to 178 children. The educational needs of some 50 children were explicitly stated and the remainder could be inferred from the letters.

Changes which were most frequently demanded reflected in part the preponderance of letters from parents of mentally handicapped children. Improved standards of education in junior training centres, with qualified teaching staff, were mentioned time and again. The mother of a child who had previously been at a school for the educationally subnormal but had now been transferred to a training centre compared it to "something from Dickens". Another, with a 10 year old autistic daughter, commented: "The teachers at this school, the majority of whom have had no special training in teaching mentally handicapped children and certainly none in teaching autistic children, seem to be very much at a loss as to how best to deal with Susan and are merely 'keeping her occupied'." Parents who had appealed unsuccessfully to the Department of Education and Science against the local authority's decision that their daughter was "ineducable" had sent her to a private school in preference to a training centre. Several other writers pressed for the transfer of responsibility for the education of severely subnormal children from the health to the education authorities – their letters had been written two or three months before the government's decision in principle to do so was announced in November 1968.

Other parents were less fortunate. Their children were unable to attend any centre and they wrote of the urgent need for more training centres and special care units. A dairy farmer and his wife, whose nine year old son was receiving no education or training, were particularly bitter. They wrote: "We had about a dozen education people to see him over a space of three years with various excuses such as no room for any more at the junior training centre. One day a lady came and said, 'I shall be coming to you twice a week to teach your little boy . . .' We never saw that woman again, no explanation of any kind. Then in desperation we visited a titled gentleman and personal friend living nearby. He wrote a letter for us and Alan was at the training centre in three weeks". Eighteen months later, however, they were told he could no longer attend and he was now at home again. A parent who was finally successful described how she had "put on a dejected, distraught and hysterical act" in a desperate last attempt to obtain a place in a junior training centre for her child. It worked; but the necessity to resort to such an expedient was, she felt, degrading.

Pre-school and provision in day schools
Parents of children within the "educable" range tended to be concerned about pre-school provisions and about minority groups: hyperactive or autistic children, children with dual or multi-handicaps like the mentally handicapped psychotic child born without a thyroid gland whose parents were currently satisfied with her education in New York but were anxious about her school placement when they returned to England.

Among writers who wanted education for their autistic children was one whose 11 year old child had received no schooling and who had refused to pay his rates to the local authority until some action was taken.

Another parent had also felt driven to desperate measures. During her efforts to get the local authority to provide what she considered adequate schooling for her brain damaged child she had twice tried to commit suicide and had smashed the windows of the education offices with a hammer. Her window-breaking, according to her letter, had been followed by placement in a "mental hospital" where she remained until her mother wrote to the hospital management committee to question her daughter's admission and to demand her discharge. After an interview with a doctor to whom she explained the schooling problem he contacted the education authority and she was allowed to leave the hospital.

The future education of the increasing number of spina bifida children being saved by early surgery worried several parents who wanted their children to be educated in ordinary schools. "Our child's life was saved by extremely clever surgery – but what of her life in the future?" wrote the mother of a two year old with spina bifida. One father wrote hesitantly from prison with the words: "I am most reluctant to write you from the above address, not being at all proud of my present position, but I do so realising you will not condemn me out of hand because of my fall from grace". The education authority had tried to persuade him to send his four year old son to a special school but, with backing from the specialists, he and his wife hoped he would be able to attend the local village school.

A number of parents, reluctant to send their children to residential schools in order to obtain suitable education, asked for more day special schools and one or two suggested that more handicapped children should be educated in special units within ordinary schools. One writer criticised inflexible attitudes towards the transfer of children from special to ordinary schools.

While most writers seemed satisfied with teaching standards in special schools one or two felt that the teachers did not tell them enough about what was going on. One mother whose child had been at school for three years wrote: "We don't know any more than the day Michael started school. If you ask the teachers they seem to think we have no right to know and they just say he is alright."

Such outdated attitudes could be found among parents and education authorities, too, according to a teacher in training. "So far as the education of the handicapped child is concerned, the law of chance operates", she wrote. "Parents of handicapped children are regularly told: 'Isn't it grand that there are such schools. Aren't you lucky to get him in. Fancy not having to pay' and this sometimes from parents whose normal children have been very expensively educated by the state for 15 years or more. Nor is it the uninformed public who take this attitude, so do many education welfare officers. Certainly some local authorities appear to make no effort to keep abreast with current thought or do not apply it. After all the work that has been done by Bowlby and at the Tavistock Child Development Research Unit on the harmful effects of mother-child separation, many authorities can still see nothing untoward in sending a three year old deaf child with no means of communication whatsoever, with no way of understanding an explanation, to a residential school."

Not surprisingly it was writers professionally concerned with education whose comments were the most detailed. The head of a remedial department in a London girls' school criticised the lack of small teaching groups for children who were depressed, accident prone, truants or attention seekers and for adolescent immigrant girls who arrived in England with little or no school experience.

Medical and associated services

While several writers had professional experience of the education services few if any had the specialised knowledge to enable them to diagnose in detail the deficiences of the medical and associated services for handicapped children. Nevertheless dissatisfaction with medical, psychological and welfare services, therapy, diagnosis and assessment of children's handicaps was rife and writers quoted experiences which seemed serious indictments of the practitioners concerned. Dissatisfaction was explicit or could be inferred in letters about 130 of the children.

The need was not only for improved services. Writers wanted improvements in attitudes too and one or two quoted startling experiences of callousness, indifference and ignorance. The father of a mentally handicapped, 11 year old son recalled a doctor who had asked "Wouldn't it be better if the child died?" and the parents of another mentally handicapped child had been told by a school medical officer, "Your son is not important". Pre-war experiences were remembered by a father whose mentally and physically handicapped son had been taken from hospital to hospital in an attempt to get a diagnosis – "What do you want us to do, cut a lump off his head?" had been a typical reply. A common irritation, according to another writer, was that doctors always addressed them as "mother" even though their surnames were clearly marked on the files.

Doctors' ignorance or unwillingness to inform parents – it was sometimes difficult to tell which – was resented by parents. "My doctor has been no help to us at all", wrote the mother of a three year old with spina bifida. "There are so many questions I would like to ask regarding Michael but he evades everything I try to ask him, saying things like 'poor kid' and 'oh dear' ''. One or two writers thought general practitioners should learn more about handicaps and about the services of local authorities and voluntary organisations which are available to handicapped families. The chief complaint of other mothers was that general practitioners disregarded their fears and initial requests for help when handicaps were first suspected, although they did their best to make amends when the mothers were proved right.

Parents felt that medical services could be improved if family doctors and hospital specialists could take more time to assess and treat their children, more time to give advice and discuss their children's difficulties – and less time in keeping patients waiting for appointments. "We wait in hospital waiting rooms for hours then when we get to the consultant we are well aware that he can only spare a few minutes", wrote a mother whose brain damaged child was treated as an "amiable imbecile" by the medical staff. "We tell him our story, he says a few words to our child, then tells us he will study the case over and have some tests done (they never get done) and see us in six months' time. We go again, it's another man who sees us this time, we go through the same routine – with the same result. The next time it's another man again, and so it goes on". The mother of an infant with cerebral palsy complained that specialists were not frank enough with parents. "You have to pay to see a specialist privately to get to know anything. The old saying that money talks must be true". Several others had also opted to pay for private medical treatment – and one parent was paying £2 weekly to an osteopath – because they felt that the national health service was inadequate.

Other writers wanted more physiotherapy and speech therapy for their children and local treatment centres to avoid long journeys to London hospitals.

Early detection of handicaps
Closely related to the needs for better medical and associated services were those for early detection of handicaps – mentioned explicitly or implied in letters about 30 children – and for prevention.

Writers were not only concerned with delay in the detection of handicaps which could occur but also with the way in which doctors and other staff broke the news to them, as the mother of a child with spina bifida graphically described. "When David was born I was told he was 'a fine boy' and 'you've had a rough time, love, but everything is alright now', for which I will never forgive him, as he knew that nothing would ever be alright again . . . He left the midwife to tell *me* the real truth, that David was paralysed from the waist down and had spina bifida. Do you know, she only wiped David's mouth and nose when he was born, and then she wrapped him in newspaper and put him in the cot. When I asked her why my baby was wrapped in newspaper she said, 'It is to keep him warm, Margaret, don't worry' . . . The midwife and a student nurse were still with me three hours after David's birth. I know they were expecting him to die."

With spina bifida, detection by the doctors was instant; recognition of other handicaps could be delayed for years. One parent wrote that her daughter's deafness had not been detected until she was in her teens, and another child was finally diagnosed as partially deaf when she was 11, after repeated parental requests for help and a final admission by the chief medical officer that his staff had been at fault. A more typical situation was described by the mother of a physically and mentally handicapped girl whose condition was detected by their family doctor after he had maintained for two years that "Nothing was wrong."

Prevention

Interestingly, very few writers referred – and usually by implication – to the need for prevention. One mentioned inadequate medical care at birth as the cause of her daughter's mental handicap. Another who had given birth to a rubella baby wrote, "I cannot help thinking that abortion when asked for would have certainly saved us a lifetime's heartbreak – rather than trying to ease the situation afterwards. I, unlike the mothers of thalidomide babies, was fully aware of the possibility of a handicapped child, as a result of rubella, and was foolish enough to take the advice of my doctor, who took a gamble on my child's future development". The parents of a high grade mongol were more knowledgeable about preventative action than most. Dissatisfied with what appeared to be the specialist's rather casual assurance that mongolism was unlikely to recur, they insisted on having a chromosomal analysis before deciding to have another child. "We regarded the advice given to us, regarding the advisability of having a further child, as irresponsible in the circumstances", wrote the father. "Techniques are available to ascertain the chromosomes of the parents, and it is common enough knowledge that only after a chromosome examination has been made can it be said that adequate care has been taken in assessing the situation". It is very likely that prevention was mentioned so rarely because few writers were aware of preventive measures that could have been taken or because they were so preoccupied with the here-and-now of their situation.

After school and employment

What would happen to their children after they left school, and employment, and residential care for those who have already done so, preoccupied the minds of many parents. The need for more vocational training, further education and jobs in open or sheltered employment was stressed in relation to 69 of the children and more than 50 of these writers mentioned it explicitly. Perhaps the most agonising experiences of any described in the 412 letters were those of an epileptic boy who, after a rapid succession of jobs, was awaiting trial for robbery with violence. The five nightmare years since he had begun to have fits and had been treated with drugs were described by his father.

Sacked from his first job after a fight with a workmate who had taunted him about his epilepsy and from his second for "unsuitability" (after he had been seen by the factory doctor), he was made redundant by his third employer when the selective employment tax was introduced. After several months unemployment he was given a break by a sympathetic garage manager. Two weeks later, however, the manager was taken ill and when the owner came to take over and discovered the boy's handicap he was dismissed again. From then onwards his luck went from bad to worse. Accepted for training at a rehabilitation centre he failed to complete the course successfully and on his return five prospective employers turned him down when they discovered he was epileptic. He began to mix with boys who had been in trouble with the police and was given a conditional discharge after being found guilty of assault. Another job began and ended and, unemployed once more, he took and drove away a car. Shortly afterwards he and another boy robbed a man in a city street and he was charged with aiding and abetting robbery with violence. At the time of writing, he was awaiting trial at the Old Bailey.

Somewhere along the line someone had failed, wrote his bewildered father. Was it his teachers when he first began to have fits at school, the officers of the youth employment service, the rehabilitation centre, the probation service or his parents? "Now what will happen to him? A prison cell or a detention centre will only serve to turn him into an embittered man with nothing in his heart except hate and resentment . . When he appears in court, the chairman of the bench will see a hardened young juvenile delinquent. All that I see, as his father, is a scared, bewildered youngster with no one to turn to but his parents."

The less dramatic but nevertheless demoralising effects on a partially sighted school-leaver of being unable to find a job were described by her mother. For two years the youth employment officer had tried to find employment. "Slowly over those two years Mavis began to change. The cheery, sunny-natured girl became sullen, unwanted in the outside world, and a difficult person to cope with". For this girl there was final success with a job as an assistant cook in a college and a day-release course in advanced cookery but for others the longed-for job had not yet come. The mother of an educationally sub-normal teenager voiced a common plea: "Please train my child within his capabilities to take his place as a useful member of the community."

Much less than a job – hobbies or other diversions – would have been welcomed for some of the more severely handicapped school leavers and young adults. The father of a housebound mentally and physically handicapped son, now in his forties, described his attempts to find a hobbies teacher 20 years earlier. Although he had been willing to pay for the teacher the local authority had refused to help; his disgust with officialdom soared when, shortly afterwards, army conscription papers arrived in error with a request that his son should undergo a medical examination for military service. Fears of sexual complications motivated one or two other parents to find an occupation for their children. The mother of a mentally handicapped girl in her late teens was one of several who expressed their concern. "There is nothing for her to do, only to get into trouble . . . Our biggest worry is in case she would get into trouble and end up being pregnant."

Residential care

Many of the parents of teenagers and handicapped adults were haunted by fears of what would happen to their children after their own death. Only 10 referred explicitly to the need for suitable residential care but a further 58 clearly had the same problem in mind with their allusions to the future.

To describe parents as being haunted by fear is, indeed, an understatement. The sheer terror and desperation which thoughts of their children's future inspired were revealed in a series of letters. Mental subnormality hospitals were the particular dread of many writers – "hideaways of the failures of the welfare state" said one of them. A 13 year old boy was described by his parents as living with 39 others in what was known by the hospital staff as the "shit ward". Several parents, appalled by the conditions, had removed their children from residential care, including one whose son had been in a subnormality hospital where, she claimed, a male patient had been killed.

The mother of a deaf and mentally handicapped daughter in her late twenties, who had previously been in a mental subnormality hospital, wrote, "I feel so guilty that I brought her into the world to suffer and who is going to look after her when I am gone. I suppose she will have to go back and oh! how I shudder when I think about it, but I ask God to take her before me". The parents of a 29 year old subnormal son still living at home felt death would be preferable to "the possibility of cruelty and lack of care and attention" in an institution; and a widow faced with the prospect of residential care for her emotionally and mentally handicapped son wrote "I feel like – yes – giving him an overdose, then I will know he's in good hands". Yet another wrote "Mary's life lasts only as long as mine does. When I know I go I shall have to take her with me. I couldn't leave her alone."

Half-way houses where older children and young adults could stay during the week, coming home to their families at weekends, seemed to be the solution for parents who, while unable to maintain full-time responsibility, did not want to relinquish complete care of their handicapped children. "If there were only smaller, localised units that young children could attend daily, and then in later years transfer with the people with whom they have grown older to stay there weekdays and go home weekends it would save we parents endless worry for the future of our children" suggested the mother of a mentally handicapped man in his late twenties.

Residential care, in principle, was not opposed by many of the writers; it was only the grim reality of overcrowded wards and inadequate care that deterred them. More than one writer felt that most parents would have their children put into care if satisfactory accommodation were available.

New services

Many of those who wrote about personal and social needs, about education, employment and residential care, about medical and related treatment, were, by implication, suggesting extension or co-ordination of existing services. A few, however, proposed completely new services.

Most of their suggestions centred on the need for a nationally based agency to offer information, advice and services. These reflected the writers' awareness of the unevenness of provisions in various parts of the British Isles and the lack of co-ordination between local authorities or – as stressed in one letter – between voluntary organisations working for the handicapped.

"It has become painfully apparent that there is a desperate need for the care of these handicapped children to be transferred to a central department which can cover the health, education and social welfare aspects throughout the country", wrote an electrical engineer from the South Coast. "The present arrangements result in local government servants of mediocre ability attempting to administer inadequate facilities with insufficient funds. This leads to lack of co-ordination, 'buck-passing' and intolerable delays."

A mature student at a college of education also emphasised the lack of co-ordination between departments and felt the most pressing need was for some central agency to which parents could go for information. The parents of a cerebral palsied pre-school child suggested that a national body should hold a register of all handicapped children because of the variations between different counties in their interest and willingness to spend money on handicapped children. Another writer suggested a standard directory of local and national provisions for the handicapped child, to be made available in surgeries, welfare clinics or libraries.

Others saw the unevenness of local services and lack of co-ordination as justification for initiating new services at a local rather than a national level. A male staff nurse at a mental subnormality hospital recommended the appointment of a local government official who could help to co-ordinate services for the handicapped provided by different local authority departments and would be able to advise families on such problems as schooling, clothing, wheelchairs and short-stay residential care. Similarly, peripatetic family advisers were suggested by the father of a mentally handicapped boy with cerebral palsy. Groups of trained staff could be formed to visit the parents of backward children and to help them to learn up to date methods for training their children.

The mother of a five-year-old mentally and physically handicapped child expressed a similar need: "Surely what is needed is some sort of counselling clinic, similar to the child guidance clinic but dealing only with handicapped children. It would be wonderful to share one's problems with specially trained people who really know and *understand* how parents themselves feel."

Conclusions

Inevitably, the meeting of many of the needs stated by the writers – special financial grants and better residential care, for instance – involves major policy decisions and nation-wide expenditure. The establishment of a central information, advisory and co-ordinating body which could help parents both at a local and a national level might be less costly than many other improvements suggested by parents and could, perhaps, help to counteract what seemed from some of the letters to be suspiciously like a conspiracy of silence by some local authorities in order not to tax existing services.

What also emerges from the letters, however, is how much could be done to raise the morale of handicapped children and their families without the necessity for vast expenditure. Two words recurred in the letters "people stare" – words that summed up community attitudes to the handicapped which caused families so much distress. But to put the blame on the community alone is too facile. Other people's attitudes to the handicapped and their families develop through subtle interactions between the two groups. If parents of the handicapped feel "third class citizens" and show it, if through embitterment or embarrassment they get caught in vicious circles, alienating those who can help, society is more likely to take them and their children at their own estimation and withhold sympathy and practical aid. Much is written about helping the handicapped to acquire self-respect; less, perhaps, about the necessity for their families to regain theirs.

Parents who opt to keep their handicapped children at home make a very real contribution to the community, not only in saving taxpayers the costlier alternative of institutional care but, more important in setting a standard of self-sacrifice and compassion which can enrich society. Of this they can, and should be, justifiably proud.

But self-respect also depends in part on the ability to lead a normal life. So long as parents are tied to the home, physically and emotionally, by the demands of the handicapped child, self-respect is likely to be incomplete. What is needed is relief from full-time care – baby-sitting services, more home helps and holiday homes, for instance – which, ultimately, the local authorities should probably provide. In the meantime there is a case for organised voluntary help on a country-wide scale: an organisation like Task Force, perhaps, with young volunteers helping handicapped families as Task Force helps the elderly. More sympathy, more practical help – whether in taking a wheelchair-bound child for a walk or baby-sitting while parents have an evening out – could make all the difference between hope and despair, between a "handicapped family" and one in accord with the community.

Table 1. The letter writers

Mother	301
Father	51
Both	19
Mother or father (unclear which)	11
Other relation	12
Others	18
Total	412*

* Some writers or families sent a series of letters but to avoid confusion each series was counted as one letter only.

D

Table 2. Areas from which letters came

Greater London	71
Yorkshire	45
Midlands (Herefordshire, Salop, Staffordshire, Warwickshire, Worcestershire)	42
East (Bedfordshire, Cambridgeshire, Essex, Hertfordshire, Norfolk, Suffolk)	40
South East (Kent, Surrey, Sussex)	37
North West (Cheshire, Lancashire)	37
South (Berkshire, Buckinghamshire, Dorset, Hampshire, Oxfordshire, Isle of Wight)	36
South West (Cornwall, Devon, Gloucestershire, Somerset, Wiltshire)	36
North (Durham)	23
North Midlands (Derbyshire, Leicestershire, Lincolnshire, Northamptonshire, Nottinghamshire)	21
Wales	18
Scotland	5
Northern Ireland	1
	412

Table 3. Patterns of Care and Education

a. Living at home

	Total N	Age in years		
		0 – 4 N	*5 – 15* N	*16 and over* N
Entirely at home	129	38	51	40
Day nursery	9	6	3	—
Play group	5	5	—	—
Ordinary day school	21	—	18	3
Day special school	27	1	26	—
Day school (type not given)	15	—	15	—
Junior training centre	58	—	56	2
Adult training centre	12	—	—	12
Day centre	4	—	—	4
Home tuition (including one part-time at day school)	4	—	4	—
Special care unit	4	—	4	—
Further education	2	—	—	2
Open employment	17	—	—	17
Total	307	50	177	80

b. Boarding placement, home at holidays or week-ends

	Total N	Age in years 0 – 4 N	5 – 15 N
Residential special school	20	—	20
Residential school (type not given)	2	—	2
Mental subnormality hospital school	4	1	3
Total	26	1	25

c. Not living at home

	Total N	Age in years 0 – 4 N	5 – 15 N	16 and over N
Residential school	3	—	—	3
Mental subnormality hospital	22	—	9	13
Psychiatric hospital	3	—	3	—
Residential home or hostel	9	—	—	9
Further education	1	—	—	1
Sheltered employment	5	—	—	5
Miscellaneous*	36	4	20	12
Total	79	4	32	43

* This item includes 4 cases which did not make it clear where the child was being cared for; 2 living with grandparents; 1 at a private school; 1 in a residential junior training centre; and 1 in prison.

d. Overall pattern of care and education

	Total N	Age in years 0 – 4 N	5 – 15 N	16 and over N
Living at home	307	50	177	80
Boarding placement, home at holidays or week-ends	26	1	25	—
Not living at home	79	4	32	43
Total	412	55	234	123

2. Handicapped children and their families

"After the initial shock of finding that we had a handicapped child the first hurdle to overcome was the accepting of the position (some parents never do). Perhaps the greatest help we ever had at this stage was to talk about it to the parents of other handicapped children; the parents of normal children either feel sorry or close their minds entirely.

The next step is one which gives parents a problem which many never solve. This is the almost complete lack of information about the child's future. Hospital doctors seldom commit themselves, general practitioners refer you to the hospital and local authorities are singularly lacking in the dissemination of information.

Having acquired all the knowledge possible we then faced stage three – what could we do to help the child? We learned that from 0–5 years he appeared to be no-one's concern but our own. He was given physiotherapy for one hour a week at the local hospital and there was a nursery on two mornings a week, run by a local association formed by parents of handicapped children. No other facilities were available.

Just before his fifth birthday he was given an IQ test. With only about half a dozen words to his vocabulary he failed miserably and we were told he was ineducable. We refused a place for him in a residential centre 35 miles away, feeling it would be cruel to shut him up in a home. Later he was admitted to hospital for an operation on his legs and the treatment dragged on for six months and he spent his seventh birthday and Christmas in hospital. After his return home he continued with his physiotherapy and the hospital authorities offered to have him in their small school for one morning a week.

Less than a year later, however, the teacher in charge said he could go there no more – there were a lot more children to be helped and besides he

66

*could go to a residential centre. He will be nine years old next month.
He is sitting in the armchair in the corner of the kitchen with a large
waggon on his knees, pushing small cars into the back with clumsy
movements, saying 'I'm bloody fed up'. Wouldn't you be? I know I
would! He's been waiting for a place in a day training centre for four
years and yet he's still at home. If his half days at school were added up
I don't think they would total a full month's education.*

*His future, when we are not here to look after him, haunts me. The
need to train these children when they reach school leaving age at 16, is a
dire necessity in order that they may, within their limits, be able to earn
their living eventually. Our plea is that our child should, if possible,
be trained to take his place as a useful member of the community."*

Letter from the mother of a 14 year old cerebrally
palsied mentally subnormal boy
which vividly presents the struggle of parents
who have a multi-handicapped child

Learning and emotion

The assumption that emotion and learning are separate and distinct
from each other is still widespread. In fact, intellect and feelings are
so closely interwoven as to be almost indivisible. Furthermore, the basic
emotional and educational needs are shared by all children but the
presence of a disability poses some special problems. For most practical
purposes a fourfold classification is sufficient, namely the need for love
and security, for new experiences, for recognition and achievement, and
for responsibility.

The first need is perhaps the most important during the long and
difficult business of growing up. It is unconditional acceptance which
gives the child this sense of security, of "belonging", the sense of being
cherished whatever he may be like and whatever he may do. This is the
basic and all pervasive feature of parental love and of a secure environment – valuing the child for his own sake. What are the special
problems faced by the handicapped in relation to this need? To give a
sense of security, one needs to feel secure oneself. But this is just what
many parents of a handicapped child do not feel. Some are over-

whelmed by their lack of knowledge and afraid that they may not be able to meet his special needs; others feel guilty or ashamed. Some may be completely at a loss to understand the child's difficulties especially parents of slow-learning children, even if they are themselves of good intelligence while parents of limited ability are likely to be too bewildered by all the other demands of modern life to give adequate emotional support to their handicapped child.

In the great majority of cases not enough is done to help the parents of a handicapped child to face and come to terms with their own unconscious attitudes and fears (Tizard and Grad, 1961). At school, too, special difficulties are likely to arise unless the child is among the lucky few for whom an early and correct diagnosis is made, a place is available in a suitable school, whether ordinary or special, and long-term educational guidance, in the fullest sense of the term, as well as social and home support are provided throughout his school life.

It is entirely natural that parents feel concerned and often anxious. Indeed, these feelings could be harnessed to provide the motivation for giving that extra care, time and thought to the handicapped child which are so essential in helping him to overcome as far as possible the adverse effects of a disability. Instead, this natural concern often turns into over-anxiety or resentment: left without a full understanding of the nature of the handicap or of its short, as well as long-term, implications, parental uncertainty may show itself in insecure and inconsistent handling. Emotional handicap of an aggressive type additionally calls out punitive attitudes because the child seems to challenge adult authority and to be impervious to the usual rewards and punishments. The more severe, complex or multiple the handicap, the more urgent the need for comprehensive diagnosis and continuous guidance.

The second basic emotional need is for new experiences. For the small baby everything that goes on around him falls into this category: so is every one of his earliest achievements, be it the ability to walk or to examine the texture, taste and appearance of materials and objects; while learning to understand speech and to talk himself, makes possible a vast range of new experiences. New experiences can, in fact, be regarded as a prerequisite for development. A child's ability to learn, to respond to "socialisation" and education in the widest sense of the term, depends not only on inborn capacity or intelligence, but also on the stimulation and opportunity for new experiences provided by his environment.

How does the handicapped child fare regarding the satisfaction of this need? Inevitably the nature of the handicap will delay or in some cases even make impossible the acquisition of at least some new experiences. Little is known as yet about how each handicap distorts learning; for example, the physically handicapped may fail to acquire experience of space and movement which may distort concepts of distance, dimension and later of number; and the deaf, because they remain unstimulated by speech and language until much later, and even then to a more limited extent than normal children, may fail to acquire an adequate basis for abstract thought.

Not only is it inevitable that the early learning of the handicapped child will be affected, but this is a cumulative and progressive process. The precise ways in which it influences the quality of learning awaits detailed exploration. Meanwhile the ingenuity of parents and teachers will be taxed to the full if they try to provide and adapt new experiences to the child's limitations without curtailing the range of those experiences more than is absolutely necessary.

Modifications may be needed in the order and manner in which new experiences are presented; more careful grading and control may have to be used and the aid of specially devised tools, gadgets and apparatus may have to be called on to minimise difficulties and failure. Otherwise there is a danger that new experiences may become a source of anxiety and defeat instead of an exciting challenge. This danger is the more acute the more severe the disability, be it physical or mental.

One effective way of learning, open to all handicapped children except the deaf, is through speech. For some, such as the physically severely disabled, it can be a compensatory way of broadening their experience and understanding. Language and speech play a crucial part in the learning of all children; but talking to the handicapped child and encouraging him to speak from the earliest age is particularly important.

The third need, for recognition and achievement, is closely linked with the previous one. Just because learning may be a slower and more arduous process than for the normal child, a strong incentive is needed. This lies in the pleasure shown at success and in the praise given to achievement by the adults whom the child loves or admires, and wants to please. Encouragement and a reasonable level of expectation act as a spur; too little expectation leads the child to accept too low a standard of effort; too high expectations make him feel that he cannot live up to what is required of him, which leads to discouragement and diminished effort. An optimum level is geared to each child's capability at a given point in time and at a given stage of growth: a level where success is possible but not without real effort. "Children cannot become socially competent and mentally well, if they do not have feelings of success" (Tansley and Gulliford, 1960). To give such feelings to the severely sub-normal child is particularly difficult because his extremely slow pace of learning tends to engender a sense of discouragement, if not failure, in his parents.

In relation to the handicapped child there are twin difficulties here, based on assumptions which are rarely made explicit and of which we are barely conscious. The first is that we habitually praise for achievement rather than for effort. This is unjust at best and positively harmful at worst. For example, a physically handicapped child may have written only a few lines of composition but it will have cost him a great deal more in terms of concentration and effort than the bright child needed to produce twice as much; yet the latter is much more likely to be commended for his work. Linked to this is the general tendency to judge the success of the handicapped by the extent to which their achievements equal those of the normal majority. In consequence, the more severe the handicap, the less likely that the child will be rewarded genuinely and unreservedly by recognition and a sense of real achievement.

Thus if this need is to be met, the handicapped must be granted the fulfilment of another need, aptly described by Mallinson (1956) as "the need to be different and the need to be the same". To do so it must not only be recognised that the basic needs are shared by all children but also to make all necessary allowances for the differences imposed upon the handicapped child by the nature of his disability. From this it follows that each child should be encouraged to compete only with himself, since if each is individual, the handicapped child is even more unique. This means that even the slightest improvement over his previous performance is worthy of praise and recognition: the physically handicapped child who manages to walk a few steps unaided; the deaf child who repeats, though imperfectly, a word previously quite beyond him; in each case the effort deserves recognition. The effort involved in making these small steps forward is colossal compared with the progress made by the normal child with relative ease.

The fourth need, for responsibility, is met by allowing the child to gain personal independence; first through learning to look after himself in feeding, dressing and washing himself; later in permitting him increasing freedom of movement without supervision about the home, street and neighbourhood as well as increasing responsibility for his own possessions; and finally by encouraging him to become entirely self-supporting until eventually he may assume responsibility for others, at work or within his own family.

Inevitably the nature of a child's handicap may set a limit to the ultimate degree of responsibility he will become capable of exercising. But there is a tendency to set too low a limit from a sense of pity or over-protection, or else through underestimating what he might become able to do. Also there is a need to guard against a whole household revolving around the handicapped child; rather he should be given the opportunity both at home and in school to shoulder some responsibilities, however limited in scope, so that he learns to give as well as to receive. In this way, self-respect and self-acceptance are fostered. How a child feels about himself and his handicap is a much more potent factor in determining his personal and social adjustment than the nature or even the degree of his disability (Carlson, 1952; Mallinson, 1956; Pringle, 1964 a and b).

Supporting the family

Every parent wants to have a normal child and many mothers fear they may give birth to a deformed one. When this fear becomes a reality, a sense of guilt, feelings of rejection and a determination to make up, almost to atone, to the child for what has happened to him, are all present in various degrees. In most cases, rejection is modified but it may then turn into over-protectiveness and over-possessiveness which eventually can become as damaging as the disability itself. In addition, there is likely to be some conflict between meeting the needs of the handicapped child on the one hand and those of all the other members of the family on the other hand. And where continuous care is required because of the severity of the handicap, frustration and resentment are inevitable concomitants of coping with such heavy demands.

There is no easy way of helping parents to face and manage their problems, no golden rule and no short cut. However, there is no doubt that the sooner the child's handicap and all its implications are considered as openly but also as supportively as possible, the better for all concerned. As Kershaw (1961) succinctly puts it: "The temptation to procrastinate may be considerable . . . it is not always necessary to tell the whole truth at once with uncurbed frankness. A spade is a spade; there is no need to call it a 'bloody shovel' but it is dishonest and useless to pretend that it is a silver spoon."

Early, comprehensive, multi-professional and continuous assessment and guidance are essential for every child; and counselling services, both on an individual and a group basis, should be readily available to parents.

Schooling for the handicapped child

Because trained intelligence can make up or at least compensate for physical and sensory disabilities, it is essential to consider the child's educational potential early and to plan well ahead for his special needs. Every handicapped child should be looked at periodically as a growing individual whose special problems deserve special attention "in the round". This means a physical, psychological and social investigation so that all the factors, which have a bearing on deciding the most suitable educational placement, can be taken into consideration. We discuss this more fully in chapter 6.

The starting point for current thinking can be summed up by saying that the ideal is for a handicapped child to live at home with his own family and to attend an ordinary day school. This sounds obvious today but this has not always been so. For example, blind babies were thought to require special training from the earliest moment and so were taken from their own homes into residential Sunshine Homes during the pre-school years. The present climate of opinion favours parental and community care. From this it follows that removing a child from his home is considered advisable only if remaining with his family is likely to hinder or even harm his physical, emotional or intellectual development; and that attendance at a special school is advisable only when the ordinary school cannot provide the special methods or equipment which are needed to ensure the child's progress.

Practice is, of course, far less straightforward, clearcut and tidy. Home and community care can only work if the community cares in the sense of providing the necessary supportive and ancillary services. These range from adaptations of houses and classrooms, to home helps, counselling, part-time specialist teachers and special day schools within manageable travelling distance.

Some ideas, such as a comprehensive school for the various types of handicaps, have hardly been tried out in this country except for the severely multi-handicapped child; also practices such as weekly boarding, and fostering with families in the neighbourhood for children who have to attend residential schools far from their homes, could be adopted on a much wider scale than hitherto. By such means the need for "parentectomy" would be eliminated, or at least substantially reduced.

Recognition of the importance of early learning has clear educational implications for handicapped children. Pre-school provision is as vital. The ideal is nursery schools and classes willing and able to accept a few handicapped children; play groups also have a contribution to make, provided guidance from trained, experienced advisers is available.

Acceptance of the 1944 Education Act dictum that education should take account of a child's "age, ability and aptitude" has as its corollary the need for variety, flexibility and continuity of provision. This is even more essential for the handicapped than for ordinary pupils. Continuity is perhaps most important of all: partly because early learning is likely to have been delayed and partly because subsequent progress may be at a slower than normal pace on account of the handicapping condition. As a result many children will not be ready – scholastically or emotionally – to leave the world of school and further training at 16 or even 17 years. If the opportunity for remaining in either a full-time or part-time educational setting were to be continued as late as 25 years of age, many more might well become able to earn their living, or at least to make a substantial contribution to it. This applies particularly to educationally subnormal youngsters. For many handicapped adolescents a half-way house of work experience combined with continued schooling would not only cushion the transition from school to work but might well turn out to be a financial investment in terms of reduced unemployment among the handicapped.

The education of some handicapped children gets interrupted by the need for surgical interventions or other treatments, either continuously or at intervals stretching over a number of years. Both in the initial assessment and in the long-term planning, the role of the physician and surgeon is often crucial. Though no specialist can make long-range forecasts, it helps parents, social workers and teachers to know both the most favourable and least favourable prospects, depending on how successful treatment will turn out to be. This forecast should be in functional terms; for example, whether eventually the child will be able to stand and walk, with or without the aid of crutches, calipers or an artificial limb; or whether he will remain dependent on a wheel-chair.

If treatment is needed, or a series of operations, it helps to know in advance their likely timing and how long hospitalisation will have to last on each occasion. For obvious reasons only rough indications can be given, but forward planning should take into account the child's educational needs; for example, prolonged interruption of schooling is more critical at certain times than at others, or conversely, given advance notice, some adjustments can be made in educational procedures. If, on the other hand, the child's disability is likely to be permanent and will not require any major surgery or treatment, it is also helpful for everyone concerned to be aware of this.

Education in how to live with a handicap

To be handicapped is to belong to a minority group. This always poses some problems of relationships: being unable to do and to live like the majority creates a sense of isolation; consciousness of being different makes the handicapped person awkward or shy which calls out similar reactions in the normal. Moreover, few of the non-handicapped majority are completely at ease in the company of the handicapped. In addition to general unease, different handicaps arouse different emotional responses. Blindness evokes the most favourable and the most universally compassionate attitudes; pity and admiration are readily extended to child and adult alike, as is a helping hand.

Towards the deaf there is an almost diametrically opposed attitude: intolerance, irritation, and even ridicule are widespread. At best the deaf are tactfully avoided, partly because trying to communicate with them is slow and cumbersome, and partly because the non-handicapped feel embarrassed having to repeat things and to shout when doing so; even then misunderstandings occur readily and are difficult to sort out. Moreover, this irritation and embarrassment communicates itself to the deaf so that they in turn become embarrassed, anxious or aggressive, according to temperament. The fact that it is an "invisible" handicap, which the sufferer may try to conceal, just because of the response it evokes, only makes the situation worse. Knowing that he is a figure of fun – on stage, screen and television – does not help matters either.

Attitudes towards physical disabilities vary widely, covering the whole range of emotions from sympathy to ridicule; the limbless are pitied while the stammerer or clubfoot are mimicked. Visibility (*ie* how obvious) and appearance (*ie* how ugly or malformed) also determine the degree of acceptance or tolerance.

Towards children these general attitudes are usually modified by a protective pity. While this shields them during their most vulnerable years, at the same time it must make their entry into the adult world a baffling and painful, if not traumatic, experience. A sympathetic, compassionate and almost over-protective world inexplicably turns into one of embarrassed, evasive and irritated people. This may lead some handicapped young people to self-pity as well as to seeking to evoke pity; others may withdraw into the world of the disabled or the protection of their family or into their own inner world; still others may grow to resent and fight their disability in an attempt to lead an even more "normal" life than the non-handicapped.

Education in how to live with a handicap must have its roots in a deliberate and realistic appraisal of the possible. In the first place this has to be made for the young child jointly by all those concerned for his care, management and education. It begins in the home and for many years to come parents will provide this education. Meeting the child's basic emotional needs in appropriate ways is one part of this education; gradually teaching the child a clear-sighted acceptance of possibilities (and inevitable limitations) is another; helping him through periods of resentment, bitterness, apathy and despair is perhaps the most difficult and painful part when parental hopes and ambitions have also been sadly disappointed. A consoling, healing and encouraging experience for parent and child can be to meet similarly handicapped children and adults, both those struggling like themselves and those who have successfully faced, or better still triumphed over, equal or worse obstacles. Knowing what can be achieved helps to maintain high but realistic standards as well as high morale.

The pre-school period is, at least in one respect, easier than later years for the disabled child. He is not as yet fully aware of being different nor of the continuing nature of this difference. Once he starts school and is in close, daily contact with his contemporaries, he inevitably comes up against the limitations imposed by his particular handicap which mark him off from others. And as he grows into adolescence, the peer group becomes increasingly important. Then being able to compete on equal terms, be it in games, physical activities or physical attractiveness, may present difficulties and for some youngsters seemingly insuperable barriers leading to feelings of isolation and rejection. Turning to and finding security in the "handicapped world" is regarded by some as an undesirable with-drawal, and by others as a realistic desire to avoid painful comparisons. Clearly there can be no simple or "right" solution. The non-handi-capped bear as much responsibility for how this dilemma is resolved in each individual case as does the handicapped youngster.

It is not only the disabled child who has to learn how to live with his handicap. Each member of his family must find a way of doing so. As one mother put it in her letter (see chapter 1) "truly a handicapped child is a handicapped family". That the father's support is quite crucial has been clearly shown in previous studies and is implicit in our letters from parents. Where he is able and willing to share the respon-sibilities and anxieties of caring for the handicapped child, there is a much greater chance of the marriage and family life itself remaining unimpaired or even being enhanced through sharing a labour of love. Brothers and sisters too are inevitably affected, to a greater or lesser degree, depending on the age gap between them and the handicapped child, on the nature and extent of his disabilities, and on the amount of attention he has to be given.

Thus it becomes apparent that education in how to live with a handicap must be much wider than merely help for the child concerned. It must include attention to the likely effects on parents, siblings and neighbours: indeed, it is the community which needs to be helped towards greater understanding so that it wills the means necessary to improve the quality of life and of the opportunities open to the handicapped child and his family.

In the end, there are two criteria by which successful adaptation to handicap are judged in adult life: the ability to earn a living; and the ability to live an independent life. Both of these are big aims and in pursuing them it is easy to overlook that the little things of life may have a disproportionate effect, just because they happen all the time. For example, an invalid car or wheel-chair may be essential for getting about and neither needs to curtail independence seriously; but requiring constant help with feeding or toilet needs not only makes for much greater dependence but it is also much more embarrassing. Thus, developing self-help in matters of cleanliness, personal hygiene and neatness deserve the greatest perseverance. Time and energy devoted to their achievement by home and school will pay good dividends later. The fullest use should be made too of any effective aids, gadgets and new devices which come on the market; also there are many little tricks or hints which assist in learning and managing everyday activities. Many children will pick these up incidentally by watching others or discovering them for themselves. But all who have had experience in caring for and educating the handicapped have a fund of such techniques; if they are passed on to children (and their parents) to learn during the formative years it can avoid a lot of useless or wrong learning.

Another important aspect of living with a handicap is the ability to accept help gracefully as well as to invite it when required. Where possible this should be taught alongside the need for independence. Normal people are unnecessarily made to feel rebuffed when a well-meant offer of help is brusquely rejected. How to reject and how to invite help is an art worth mastering as is the understanding of when to accept it for the sake of the would-be helper, even when assistance is not in fact needed. Indeed, the handicapped themselves can play an important role in educating those with whom they come into contact to understand and accept the disabled in a sympathetic but realistic way.

Education for recreation comes a close second to education for employment. Hobbies, the various arts, games such as chess or cards, and also certain physical sports may well be within the child's capacity;

indeed, some, like swimming and riding, can be of therapeutic value. Not only do recreational pursuits provide bridges to the world of the non-handicapped; they also provide opportunities to make relations with the opposite sex during adolescence, when most young people are looking for romance and eventually marriage. This is a particularly neglected aspect of education in living with a handicap, probably because it is so fraught with hurt, damaged self-esteem and, most important of all, because there are no easy or ready answers. All this, every handicapped young person must face sooner or later; if he can do so with the help of a compassionate, understanding and honest adult, then his (and even more so her) learning will be that much less difficult. Getting to know handicapped people who have made successful marriages may give hope. For some, marriage will be an unlikely goal. The knowledge that some people are successfully and happily wedded to their work or hobby, and through these make firm friendships, may be a consolation if not an aim.

References

CARLSON, Earl R. (1952) *Born that Way*. Arthur James, The Drift. Evesham, England.

KERSHAW, J. D. (1961) *Handicapped Children*. Heinemann, London.

MALLINSON, Vernon (1956) *None can be Called Deformed*. Heinemann, London.

PRINGLE, M. L. Kellmer (1964a reprinted 1967) *The Emotional and Social Adjustment of Blind Children*. Occ. Public. No. 10 National Foundation for Educational Research, Slough, Bucks.

PRINGLE, M. L. Kellmer (1964b reprinted 1969) *The Emotional and Social Adjustment of Physically Handicapped Children*. Occ. Public. No. 11 National Foundation for Educational Research, Slough, Bucks.

TANSLEY, A. E. AND GULLIFORD, R. (1960) *The Education of Slow Learning Children*. Routledge and Kegan Paul, London.

TIZARD, J. AND GRAD, J. C. (1961) *The Mentally Handicapped and their Families* Oxford University Press, London.

3. Handicapped children and present-day services

"Somewhere along the line someone has failed."

Letter from the father of an epileptic boy
charged with criminal offences

What is a handicap?

The word "handicap" is in common usage but it is often loosely used and, in particular, is confused with "defect" and "disability". These terms may indicate differences in degree but, more important, should imply differences in kind.

A *defect* is some imperfection, impairment or disorder of the body, intellect or personality. It can, when viewed from an objective standpoint, be minor, even trivial, or it may be gross. But in itself, the word carries no necessary implication of malfunctioning or of an adverse effect upon the individual. A *disability* is a defect which does result in some malfunctioning but which does not necessarily affect the individual's normal life. A *handicap* is a disability which for a substantial period or permanently retards, distorts or otherwise adversely affects normal growth, development or adjustment to life.

Thus a congenital malformation of the external ear is a defect which is not necessarily disabling or handicapping. A severe visual defect in one eye, an auditory impairment in one ear, having one leg rather shorter than the other would all constitute disabilities but would not normally be handicapping conditions. Virtually any defect or disability can become a handicap if, for example, its presence becomes a source of major concern to the individual. Educationally subnormal or maladjusted children are by definition handicapped. The terms

79

themselves imply in the former case that the child is intellectually retarded and in the latter that his adjustment to life is affected.

The functions of medical, educational and social services are where possible, first, to prevent defects from occurring; secondly, to provide appropriate treatment either to remove a defect or to minimise any malfunctioning which may arise; thirdly, to prevent a defect or disability from becoming a handicap or to minimise its handicapping effect.

The impact of medical advances

It is now known that of all conceptions, one in five, or 20 per cent fail to develop normally and miscarry. Recent research has indicated that one fifth of these miscarriages have an abnormal chromosome constitution which proves lethal in utero. Of the embryos which grow to a viable stage, some 3 per cent are stillborn or die in the first few weeks of life and of these about a quarter will have some, usually severe, malformation. Finally, a little under one per cent of the surviving children are likely to die between one month and seven years. Over one third of these childhood deaths will also be due to severe malformations.

These facts can be summarised as follows: one in four of all conceptions either fail to survive, or survive but with serious physical defects. However, of all defective conceptions, 85 per cent succumb before they reach childhood and indeed the vast majority do not survive the perinatal period.

Nature has thus arranged the selection of the fittest. But advancing medical knowledge can and is disturbing this balance. Improved ante-natal care, directed particularly at those mothers who are known to be at risk of a miscarriage, must result in a relatively high proportion of handicapped babies born to such mothers. Improved obstetric care and techniques, again directed to those most in need, also results in a higher proportion of surviving handicapped children. Finally, this trend is accentuated by more advanced paediatric care and surgical techniques.

On the other hand, increased awareness of, and new skills for the detection of, defects which can be transmitted genetically has opened the way for improved genetic counselling so that parents can be advised of the risk of having a defective child. Furthermore, tests in early pregnancy can now detect defective chromosomes, so that therapeutic abortion may be considered.

Advancing skills and resources for the management of pregnancy and the care of the infant, discussed in chapter 4, are reducing the risk of damage to the baby in utero, during labour, in the first few days of life and later.

Advances in medical knowledge, treatment and care are thus changing nature's balance sheet. However, this is not a simple equation in which some handicapped children survive who would previously have died and others escape handicap who would previously not have done so. There is a relative increase in the number of children with congenital defects, genetically determined, and a relative decrease in the number of children whose handicap is occasioned by "external", non-genetic circumstances. Although the existence of the trend is confirmed by clinicians, there is a surprising paucity of well-documented evidence. However, the dramatic increase in the number of children with spina bifida is an example of the heightened chances of survival of a group of children with a congenital malformation; and the decreased prevalence of poliomyelitis shows how the control of infection through vaccination can reduce a particular problem to a small fraction of its former size.

Prevalence

The prevalence of different handic ʼnping conditions thus changes with time but it also changes for some c ditions with the age of the children. The prevalence rates quoted below are from two different sources: from the Seebohm Report (HMSO 1968) and from the National Child Development Study (1958 Cohort).

The prevalence rates from the Seebohm Report were obtained from a number of sources and in the main cover school children aged 5–15 years. The National Child Development Study data were obtained from the first follow-up of a large, national sample of children at the age of seven. The sample consists of every child in England, Scotland and Wales – some 16,000 in all – born in the week 3rd to 9th March, 1958. At this first follow-up, information was gathered on 92 per cent of the group, so that the results are representative of children of this age in Britain.

Table 1. Prevalence of handicapping conditions per 1,000 related population

	Appendix Q: Seebohm Report	National Child Development Study (1958 Cohort)
	5–15 years	7 year olds
Handicap		
Blind and partially sighted	1·2	1·9
Deaf and partially hearing	1·2	1·1
Epileptic	7·2	6·2
Speech defects	27·0*	23·3
Cerebral palsy	3·0	2·2
Heart disease	2·4	3·6
Orthopaedic condition	3·4	4·6
Asthma	23·2	27·4
Eczema	10·4	24·7
Diabetes	1·2	0·2
Other physical handicaps	6·7	6·7
Severely subnormal	3·5	2·7

* 5 year olds.

It will be seen that although there is overall a large measure of agreement there are some differences. The small differences will be due to sampling errors. Other differences – notably in the prevalence of eczema – are doubtless due to different criteria having been adopted. Finally, there are some discernible age effects. For example, the prevalence of diabetes increases with age and the number of children with a speech defect will tend to decrease with age. The figure for speech defects quoted in the Seebohm Report was for 5 year old children.

Aids to living: the design of buildings

To-day, the range of skills available to help handicapped children is substantial and increasing, both in quality and quantity. Developments in electronic equipment are perhaps the most dramatic. New power and clarity in the amplification of sound allied to the reduced size of components is ameliorating the effects of hearing impairment for many with a substantial disability. Blind and limbless children may shortly be enabled to sense and manipulate their environment in ways unthought of but a few years ago. But the manufacture, fitting, mastery, servicing and exploitation of these electronic aids will raise new problems in co-ordination between a variety of professions, agencies and interests, problems that must be defined and solved if demand and supply are to meet.

Similar difficulties have to be overcome if our environment is to be tailored with some regard to the needs of the handicapped. For example, unsuitably designed school buildings can make it impossible to educate children with some handicaps in ordinary schools. This is noticeable, too, in the design of many colleges, indeed of some of the new university buildings, where flights of outside steps and distance between buildings create additional hazards and limitations for some handicapped young people.

The employment openings for crippled or chairbound school leavers are obviously further circumscribed by the physical lay-out and the equipment of the building where they might be offered work, as well as by problems of transport.

At present there is no obligation on local housing authorities to provide for physically handicapped people in their housing programmes. A recent report by the Ministry of Housing and Local Government (HMSO 1969) makes reference to a paper (Dixon, 1968) which points out that special facilities for the handicapped in a percentage of local authority ground floor flats or bungalows would only fractionally increase the initial building costs but cost "quite staggering sums of money if they have to be provided at a later date". Welfare departments have powers to make necessary adaptations to premises, for example, widening doorways for a wheelchair to go through, installing or adapting bathroom and lavatory facilities, but they vary widely in the extent to which these powers are used. Unsuitable housing can be a reason for a handicapped child having to live away from home. When the Chronically Sick and Disabled Persons Act, which was a private member's bill given government backing, comes into operation it will be the duty of local authorities to make special provision in their housing plans for chronically sick and disabled people; and also to carry out necessary adaptations in their own homes.

The statutory services

The local authority health department
At present the health department of a local authority may – and at the direction of the Secretary of State must – make arrangements for the care and/or the after-care of anyone suffering from illness and/or mental disorder. For anyone falling into these categories, the local authority is empowered to provide, equip and maintain residential accommodation, to provide centres or other facilities, and to provide any ancillary or supplementary services for their benefit. These powers are transferred to the new social services department under the Local Authority Social Services Act. Mental welfare officers already provide a social work service for severely sub-normal or mentally disordered children and their families. The Government has announced its intention of transferring responsibility for severely sub-normal children's education to the local education authority.

In addition to these duties, the health authorities must provide a health visiting service, make arrangements for home nursing where this is necessary and provide, equip and maintain health centres. They may also provide domestic help in appropriate circumstances: this responsibility is to be transferred to the social services department. The Government has announced (February 1970) its decision to take the National Health Service out of local government and to institute area health authorities.

The local authority welfare department
In general terms, the existing local welfare authorities have powers to make arrangements for "promoting the welfare" of handicapped persons; and at the direction of the Secretary of State shall be under a duty to exercise these powers. The powers include the provision of instruction for handicapped persons in their homes or elsewhere in methods of overcoming their disabilities; the provision of workshops for handicapped people over the school leaving age; and hostels to accommodate them; the provision of suitable work for handicapped people over school leaving age in their homes or elsewhere and help in the disposal of their work; the provision of recreational facilities at

home or elsewhere; the adaptation of premises or the provision of additional facilities designed to secure the greater comfort or convenience of handicapped people of any age; providing the handicapped with information about the services available to them; assisting a voluntary organisation in the provision of such services; and compiling and maintaining a classified register of handicapped persons. The Annual Report of the Department of Health and Social Security (1968) shows 1,253 physically handicapped residents under 30 years of age provided for by welfare departments, mostly in accommodation provided by voluntary organisations. It is unfortunate that these figures do not distinguish between children and adults. This also applies to the registers of disabled persons.

There is a great deal of variation between authorities in the extent to which these powers are implemented. Schemes submitted by authorities under sections 29 and 30 of the National Assistance Act, 1948, usually only specify the compilation of "a register of handicapped persons *who apply for assistance*". As a result the size of these registers varies from 1·3 per cent of the population in some authorities to 7·9 per cent in others. Under the Chronically Sick and Disabled Persons Act it will be the duty of local authorities to inform themselves about the number of handicapped people in the area who need services under Section 29, and also to make information available both generally and to individual handicapped people about the services provided. It will be compulsory on local authorities to make arrangements for providing assistance in the home; wireless, library, lectures, games, outings or other recreational or educational facilities; means of travelling for these purposes; adaptations or additional facilities to secure greater comfort or convenience at home; provision of meals; help with holidays; and the provision of a specially equipped telephone where necessary. The registration of blind persons, has a much longer history, going back to the Blind Persons Act, 1920. Such registers are not related to applications for assistance and in consequence cover virtually the whole population of blind persons.

In a debate in the House of Commons on the second reading of this Bill (5th December, 1969) it was said that a London borough, described as a "very good authority", discovered for itself that "the disablement figure was likely to be about 1·3 per cent of the population". But an independent investigation "showed that it was more likely to be

4·4 per cent". These variations in the sizes of registers are in many cases paralleled by variations in the services provided. In the debate an example was also given of an authority which was spending twice the national average per 1,000 of its population on welfare services for the handicapped. The Act is not in general concerned specifically with children but a number of the clauses are relevant particularly to the severely handicapped child.

Welfare services for handicapped children or their families may be needed at any age but in any case the welfare department should be actively concerned towards the end of a handicapped child's school life so that support can be given, where necessary, when the child leaves the ambit of the education department. Close liaison is needed here not only with the education department but also with the youth employment service. Social welfare officers are usually in touch with handicapped young people and their families as school leaving approaches. The existing welfare departments are to be merged in comprehensive social services departments under the Local Authority Social Services Act.

The local authority children's department
A handicapped child is not received into the care of a children's department solely because he is handicapped. However, where a handicapped child is rejected by his parents, or has no parents, or if there are other reasons why the parents cannot discharge their responsibilities, the children's department may receive the child into care. This is referred to in more detail in chapter 8. The child will then either be accommodated in a children's home or foster home, in a hospital or in a residential special school. In this latter situation the children's department will make arrangements for him during school holidays and after he leaves school. The children's departments are to be merged in the new social services departments.

There is one apparent exception to this position. If a local health department is making arrangements for the care or after-care of a child who is "mentally disordered", the child may be accommodated in homes or other accommodation provided or supervised by the children's department.

The local education authority
The overall framework for the education authority's responsibility for

handicapped children is in essence not different from its duties towards non-handicapped children, namely that it is required to provide appropriate education according to the individual child's age, ability and aptitude. However, if a child, because of some disability, requires special educational treatment, either wholly or partly in substitution for the education which he would receive in a normal school, he is designated a "handicapped pupil" for educational purposes. Thus a child may be substantially or permanently handicapped but not be designated a "handicapped pupil" if the nature or extent of his disability is not such that special educational treatment is required.

The education authority's responsibilities for handicapped children commence when they attain the age of two years and finish at present – unless further education is indicated – one year after the statutory school leaving age, ie at 16 years. The first duty of the education authority is to discover which children within its area require special educational treatment. In order to fulfil this duty the authority may require the parents of any child of two years or over to present him for an examination in order to determine his educational needs. This examination may be carried out according to a formal procedure which includes a statutory letter to the parents and the completion by a medical officer of the local authority of a statutory form on which is recorded the results of the examination and the recommendation(s) of the examining officer. However, this formal procedure is not strictly necessary and many authorities do not now adopt it unless the parents refuse to bring the child for examination. Parents have the right to be present at any examination of their children for this purpose but the authority's decision that a child requires special educational treatment is final, subject only to the parents' right of appeal to the Secretary of State (under Section 68 of the Education Act, 1944). However, parents may take the initiative in requesting such an examination and if they do so the authority must carry out an examination "unless in their opinion the request is unreasonable."

There are at present ten recognised categories of handicapped pupil and another one will be added when the education authorities assume responsibility for severely subnormal children. The ten categories of handicapped pupils are as follows: blind, partially sighted, deaf, partially hearing, educationally subnormal, epileptic, maladjusted, physically handicapped, pupils with speech defect and delicate pupils.

In our view these categories require revision and we make proposals about this in chapter 9.

Special educational treatment may be provided in a special school, at home, in a special unit or class within an ordinary school, or otherwise by the provision of some special help within an ordinary school. When a decision has been reached on an appropriate form of special educational treatment for an individual child, the local education authority "so far as is practicable" must make the necessary provision.

The need for special educational treatment is not static. Most obviously, the facilities must match the changing prevalence of different handicapping conditions. Additionally, however, advances in medical treatment may change the functional nature of a disability thus rendering any special educational treatment unnecessary. Finally, changes in psychological or educational thought or in educational provision may materially affect the situation. The need for any special educational facilities for a handicapped child depends in the last analysis upon the extent to which existing facilities meet his needs. This may be influenced, for example, by the size of classes in normal school, the attitudes of the teachers and to some extent by the attitudes of other pupils.

In most areas the youth employment service is administered by the local education authority. Its future is under consideration by the Government. In a few others placement in employment is the responsibility of the Department of Employment and Productivity. In any event, it has responsibility for the employment of handicapped young people, covering their vocational guidance, work placement and review of progress.

The educational categories of handicapped pupils

The ten existing categories of handicapped pupils already mentioned are defined as follows in the Handicapped Pupil and Special School Regulations, 1959 and the Amending Regulations, 1962.

Teachers of the blind and of the deaf and partially hearing must have special teaching qualifications. Such additional qualification is not at present required for any other category of handicap.

Blind pupils

These are defined as "pupils who have no sight or whose sight is or is likely to become so defective that they require education by methods not involving the use of sight."

The number of pupils in classes for the blind should not under the above regulations exceed fifteen.

The central feature of welfare services for the blind, irrespective of age, is registration, which has been in existence since the Blind Persons Act, 1920. Local authorities are responsible for this registration and the three Regional Associations for the Blind (Northern, Southern and Western), together with the Wales and Monmouthshire Regional Council, collate the registration statistics for the local authorities in their areas.

Partially sighted pupils

These are defined as "pupils who by reason of defective vision cannot follow the normal regime of ordinary schools without detriment to their sight or to their educational development, but can be educated by special methods involving the use of sight."

The number of pupils in classes for the partially sighted should not exceed fifteen.

Deaf pupils

These are defined as "pupils with impaired hearing who require education by methods suitable for pupils with little or no naturally acquired speech or language."

The number of pupils in classes for the deaf should not exceed ten.

It should be noted that this definition is essentially linked to the child's ability naturally to acquire speech and language rather than to hearing loss as such.

Partially hearing pupils

These are defined as "pupils with impaired hearing whose development of speech and language, even if retarded, is following a normal pattern, and who require for their education special arrangements or facilities though not necessarily all the educational methods used for deaf pupils."

The number of pupils in classes for the partially hearing should not exceed ten.

Again, it will be noted that the definition is linked to the acquisition of speech and language. Thus, a child who is deafened by illness or injury but has and retains his naturally acquired speech and language, will be educated as a partially hearing pupil.

Educationally subnormal pupils
These are defined as "pupils who, by reason of limited ability or other conditions, resulting in educational retardation, require some specialised form of education wholly or partly in substitution for the education normally given in ordinary schools."

Classes for educationally subnormal pupils should not exceed twenty in number.

This definition is a little anomalous in that it does not specifically exclude other categories of handicapped pupils, some of whom strictly speaking would also come within this category as defined. Thus, it is well known that a substantial proportion of handicapped pupils (other than the educationally subnormal) are educationally retarded.

Educationally subnormal pupils are numerically the largest single group of handicapped pupils. It has been estimated that approximately one per cent of the school population require education in special schools for the educationally subnormal. However, the proportion of children who require some form of special educational treatment within normal schools because of educational retardation is unlikely to be much below 10 per cent and may well be higher. Special educational treatment for such children in normal schools is usually given in remedial or special classes or groups.

Epileptic pupils
These are defined as "pupils who by reason of epilepsy cannot be educated under the normal regime of ordinary schools without detriment to themselves or other pupils."

Classes for epileptic children should not exceed twenty in number.

This is the only category of handicap where specific reference is made in the definition to the "detriment" of "other pupils". In practice, this criterion is also considered for other handicaps. This is most obviously the case where a maladjusted child is disturbing the pattern of work in a class.

Maladjusted pupils

These are defined as "pupils who show evidence of emotional instability or psychological disturbance and require special educational treatment in order to effect their personal, social or educational readjustment."

Classes for maladjusted pupils should not exceed fifteen in number.

This definition of handicapped pupils is the only one which specifically mentions other than narrowly educational considerations. Thus, a child whose educational performance and overt behaviour in an ordinary school is not creating difficulties may nevertheless require the therapeutic skills available in a special school in order to effect his personal or social readjustment. The problems may be centred on the home situation and residential schooling may be indicated.

Physically handicapped pupils

These are defined as "pupils not suffering solely from a defect of sight or hearing who by reason of disease or crippling defect cannot without detriment to their health or educational development, be satisfactorily educated under the normal regime of ordinary schools."

Classes for physically handicapped pupils should not exceed twenty in number.

Pupils suffering from speech defect

These are defined as "pupils who on account of defect or lack of speech not due to deafness require special educational treatment."

The number of special schools for children with speech defect is very small indeed. There are two independent boarding schools (primary and secondary) and one other independent primary school which takes non-communicating children including those who are autistic and aphasic. For the vast majority of children with speech defect, therefore, the "special educational treatment" consists of individual speech therapy either in school or in a clinic.

Delicate pupils

These are defined as "pupils not falling under any other category in this regulation, who by reason of impaired physical condition need a change of environment or cannot, without risk to their health or educational development, be educated under the normal regime of ordinary schools."

Classes for delicate children should not exceed thirty in number.

This category of handicap, as the definition indicates, is used as a "safety net" for children who do not fit into other categories. At the present time, children with chest complaints, including asthma, comprise the largest single group in schools for the delicate. However, a substantial minority of the children have problems of emotional disturbance and/or social deprivation. For this latter group, the children's physical condition is a minor problem – if a problem at all.

The range and variety of services

The services which are provided for a handicapped child will vary with his age and depend upon the nature and severity of the handicap. They should always be geared to meet his present and likely future needs.

There is a very considerable variation between authorities in the steps taken to detect handicapped children in the pre-school years. For example, one of the authorities studied by the Working Party reported that there was no routine follow-up of babies noted to be "at risk" of handicap. Another authority said that every baby in this category received a full developmental examination at 9 months, 1 year, 18 months, and at yearly intervals until 5.

It is now increasingly recognised that the years from 0 to 5 are crucial for the later development of handicapped – as well as normal – children. The handicapping effects of a disability may be subtle and reach far beyond the obvious limitations which are imposed. For example, as we have said in chapter 2, the locomotor limitations of a physical handicap will affect a child's exploration of his environment and may inhibit intellectual growth and the development of social skills. Steps should be taken to enable the child to make these necessary explorations, for example, by the provision of equipment to minimise the problems of mobility and by encouraging the parents to bring the "environment" to the child. Thus, ordinary household articles can be placed within his grasp and he can be moved from place to place and room to room in order that he can begin to build a conceptual framework of the world around him.

More obviously, perhaps, the child with a hearing loss needs auditory training so that he can learn to listen and make the best use of his residual hearing. A teacher of the deaf will be needed to advise the mother and help the child in this. Lip reading will need to be encouraged and spontaneous vocalisation reinforced with a smile from the mother or other members of the family.

A problem which is common to all handicapped children is that of providing adequate contacts with other children. Socialisation like other aspects of development needs to be learned. And learning cannot take place without practice. The provision of a nursery school place is one way of meeting this need. Unfortunately, present provision fails lamentably to meet it, particularly since nursery school headteachers, understandably, are reluctant to accept too many handicapped children lest this disturb the overall balance of the group.

Full-time or part-time special education may be provided from the age of two and the nursery class of a special school may be the best way of ensuring that some handicapped children have the skilled attention which is necessary. A dilemma often arises when day school provision is not available. Shall the child at the age of two or three leave the security of his mother, his family and his home for the skilled attention he needs in a residential school? How will this affect his emotional development? How does one balance a child's emotional needs against his need for highly specialised education? A peripatetic teacher is one solution adopted in some authorities.

By the age of five most handicapped children will be ready for some schooling and the many possibilities here are outlined in chapter 9. Unfortunately, the full range of provision is rarely available in a given area and it is necessary to choose the best of a limited range. Sometimes there is virtually no choice.

The extent of educational provision for handicapped children varies widely from one authority to another. For example, amongst the authorities studied by the Working Party, one large county had nearly 100 children per 10,000 of the school population receiving or awaiting special education, whilst for another county of similar size the number was only a little over 50 per 10,000. For one small county borough in the survey the comparable number was over 200 per 10,000.

The school leaving age in special schools at the present time is sixteen, although some schools encourage pupils to stay longer either to attain some specific academic goal or else to continue their general education and enhance employment prospects. We discuss this further in chapters 9 and 10.

Services for handicapped children after school leaving should depend upon the needs of the individual and his family. The consideration of suitable employment should, of course, begin well before this time and for the small minority who can be readily accommodated little more than the usual care may be required. However, for the majority of handicapped children a great deal of time as well as skill is needed both in initial placement and also in follow-up. A small number who continue to need residential provision can be placed in hostels for school leavers provided by local authorities or by voluntary agencies, but such provision is quite inadequate to meet existing needs.

Further education and/or vocational training is also available from some statutory and voluntary agencies, but, again, existing needs are not being met.

A significant minority of handicapped children need some form of sheltered employment throughout their lives and others will continue to be wholly dependent upon their families and upon the community. The range of provision here is very limited. Adult training centres and subnormality hospitals partially meet the needs of some of the severely subnormal. Some welfare departments and voluntary bodies provide sheltered workshops or home occupation but for most severely handicapped young people, who are not also mentally retarded, the future too frequently holds nothing.

The problems of providing adequately for the needs of handicapped children are particularly acute in rural areas. The children are widely scattered and centralised provision of services is sometimes quite impracticable because of the distances involved in travel. A similar problem is encountered in small authorities where the number of children requiring particular forms of provision may be counted in twos and threes.

On the other hand, the relative stability of rural communities and, often, of field staff in these areas sometimes makes the early detection of handicap more likely. Further, local rural communities can often give the kind of support to the family and later to the young handicapped person which is unlikely in a shifting urban population.

The range and variety of services needed for handicapped children have been indicated above and are also dealt with at more length in various chapters of this report. However, there is another aspect of this question which should not go unmentioned. This is the range from the services provided by the best authorities to those provided by the not so good. The gap at the present time is much too wide and it is obvious that some authorities are not yet meeting their statutory responsibilities for handicapped children, not to mention the moral obligation which everyone must feel towards an underprivileged minority in our community. The proposed reorganisation of local government with a considerable decrease in the number of local authorities should improve the situation.

The role of the voluntary organisations

Voluntary organisations have made, and continue to make, an outstanding contribution to the health, education and welfare of handicapped children. Most services for the handicapped were first established by voluntary societies and the existing pattern of services throughout the country is still dependent upon their contribution. Their role in the future may change but is unlikely to diminish.

This is clearly recognised in the following extract from the Green Paper on the *National Health Service* (1970):

"Voluntary organisations have always made an important contribution to the working of the National Health Service. The unification of the health service will enable their work to be extended. Those organisations which have aimed to help particular types of patient have found the administrative barriers within the present service as an obstacle to the full achievement of these aims. Voluntary service which supports patients both in hospital and in the community will strengthen the sense of continuity throughout the health service and constitute a further force helping to knit its elements together. . . . Voluntary activity by organisations and by groups, and volunteer projects of many kinds, will receive encouragement and support from the new area health authorities, but the main working links will be with the district committees. Paid organisers of voluntary effort will be employed, for example, to co-ordinate support for a particular hospital; some might be jointly employed by an area health authority and a local authority to co-ordinate voluntary help for the elderly or mentally ill or handicapped both in hospital and in the community. Grants and subsidies paid by the area health authority . . . will be available to support

E

96 LIVING WITH HANDICAP

voluntary bodies which provide and promote services within the general
scope of the authority's responsibilities. A special and continuing effort needs
to be made to foster voluntary work with long stay patients. Many elderly,
mentally ill, mentally handicapped and younger chronic sick patients risk
losing touch with their local community. Some have lost contact with friends
and relatives. There is a special need for volunteers to visit and befriend such
patients. Voluntary effort may also be needed to enable relatives and friends
to visit when distance or disability makes this impossible without special help.
The greater the participation of the local community in its local health
services, the greater the response of the service to the community's needs and
of the community to the service's needs."

The following are examples of the range of services that voluntary
organisations provide:

Schools, hostels, clubs, assessment centres, research centres and holiday homes
The Invalid Children's Aid Association, for example, has a school for
children with speech and language disorders, one of only three in the
country. The National Association for Mental Health has hostels for
adolescents who have been at schools for educationally subnormal or
maladjusted children and who cannot live at home. The National Fund
for Research into Crippling Diseases has recently given grants to the
National Association of Youth Clubs to develop further its PHAB
(physically handicapped able-bodied) clubs and holiday centres. The
National Society for the Prevention of Cruelty to Children is undertaking research on the "battered baby syndrome" (*see also chapter 5*).
The Spastics Society's provision includes a residential centre where
spastic children's abilities can be comprehensively assessed and they
and their parents can be given advice about education and employment.

Dr Barnardo's Homes have always provided for mildly handicapped
children in their ordinary children's homes and in their boarding
special schools for children with various and often multi-handicaps.
Dr Barnardo's now see that good standards of medical and educational
care are insufficient, because as they said in evidence to the Working
Party "although the children's handicaps and educational needs have
been met, much remains to be done to meet their social and emotional
deprivation". Thus "it has been planned to develop a skilled casework
service to support families so that they may be enabled to take as much
responsibility as possible for their handicapped children. This service
might include the provision of day care and education to relieve

families under stress and to reduce the risk of total rejection of a handicapped child. Where it is impossible for the child to remain at home we shall consider what part we ought to take (in selected areas), in conjunction with the statutory services, to see that local and flexible residential care or residential education may be provided."

Advisory and counselling services
Examples of this include a parent counselling service for the parents of all blind children run by the Royal National Institute for the Blind which also has a parents' unit where parents can stay or go daily to receive guidance in understanding and caring for their blind child. The Invalid Children's Aid Association has a staff of social workers who help families with ill or handicapped children in the London area and also organise groups for the children as well as for adolescents and for parents.

Courses and seminars for professional and voluntary workers
The National Association for Mental Health, for example, has for many years held courses for those concerned with helping handicapped children and their families, notably training courses for teachers of the severely subnormal and a short course on the care of those with multi-handicaps.

Grants for research and study
The National Fund for Research into Crippling Diseases has made a grant to the Central Council for the Disabled to undertake a pilot research study in a selected area to ascertain the availability of homes, camps, guest houses, hostels, etc, suitable for the disabled and to consider the feasibility of maintaining a register of such places. The National Children's Home is financially supporting a national study of socially disadvantaged children being carried out by the National Bureau for Co-operation in Child Care.

Bringing together parents
Much of the post-war development in voluntary service for the handicapped has been initiated by parents with personal experience of handicapped children's needs and the lack of services. Examples are the Spastics Society, the National Society for Autistic Children, the

Deaf/Blind Rubella Children's Association and the National Society for Mentally Handicapped Children.

Many large towns now have organisations which group together parents with deaf, mentally handicapped or spastic children. Such associations give valuable support to parents with a handicapped child. They provide opportunities to share experiences and to learn from others in similar situations. One of the strengths of parents' associations is that they involve fathers as well as mothers, and fathers are too easily left on one side by ordinary professional services because they are usually at work during working hours. Parents' associations often require fathers' help with transport and fund raising. The father of a handicapped child is able to do something and at the same time meet other parents with similar problems. Both he and his wife see other handicapped children and can talk informally about their own child. These groups provide opportunities for social relationships which reinforce the father's role in caring for the handicapped child.

Stimulating public awareness
This is a vital role for voluntary organisations, especially since it is one which statutory services cannot easily undertake. Improvements in provisions for the handicapped will only come about as the general public becomes more understanding of handicapped people and what can be done to help them.

This is, however, an aspect of voluntary societies' activities which may disturb those in statutory services who are professionally concerned with handicapped children. They sometimes feel that voluntary societies encourage parents to make demands which cannot be met and somewhat irresponsibly increase their expectations of services which should be available to them. This raises complex issues of "rationing" in the social services and how priorities should be determined.

It is important for voluntary and statutory services to work very closely together, complementing what they can each do separately for the handicapped child and his family. But voluntary societies must never be passive partners in this collaboration. They should always be imaginative innovators and challengers of existing practices if they are to retain their vitality and make their best contribution to the statutory services. They are still needed to provide some facilities nationally, to increase public understanding of the handicapped, to press for better facilities, to stimulate self-help groups of parents and to take the initiative in developing new services.

There are, however, very many voluntary organisations concerned in various degrees with handicapped children and much of the evidence submitted to the Working Party made a case for some measure of unification or greater collaboration between them. It is confusing to the public to be asked to support by voluntary contributions a number of different societies concerned with handicapped children. It may also be wasteful of resources to have different societies competing for funds and for personnel. There is moreover a tendency for separate societies to emphasize different disabilities and so remain somewhat restricted and insular, when the needs of handicapped children as children are very similar however their handicap may have arisen. While recognising the good work which has been done by concentrating public attention on particular disabilities, we believe there is need for some machinery for collaboration both nationally and locally and perhaps also for some measure of amalgamation between different voluntary organisations with very similar objectives. We discuss this from another angle in chapter 12.

The co-ordination of services

The co-ordination of relevant services is not in general covered by any existing legislation. However, some guidance was given to local authorities on this question in a joint circular issued by the Department of Education and Science and the Ministry of Health in 1966. The circular was occasioned by the reports of two working parties which had indicated that services for handicapped children and young people are often not adequately co-ordinated. (British Council for Rehabilitation of the Disabled 1964; Carnegie (UK) Trust 1964). The circular invited local authorities to join with hospital authorities and executive councils in a "review of aspects of common concern", which was to be directed specifically to:

   i. "The earliest detection and complete diagnosis of handicap whether physical or mental, taking account of all evident or suspected disabilities of the child's general health, and assessment of practicable measures to deal with the handicap.

   ii. Regular review of medical, educational and social factors to enable an optimum service to be given in the interest both of the child and of the family; and, in due course, consideration of employment prospects and the need for welfare services in adult life.

iii. Consistent advice and continuing support to the family and, as appropriate, to the child or young person."

It was hoped that arrangements could be made to facilitate the exchange of information between departments and services about individual children and their families. Reference was also made to the special importance of co-ordination for multi-handicapped children and for all children when a change of responsibility occurs, for example, when a family moves from one area to another or when a child starts school and leaves school. The pooling of staffing resources and inter-departmental case conferences were suggested as specific ways of increasing flexibility whilst maintaining a clear understanding by field workers, and others, of the roles they are to play. The circular is reproduced in full in appendix 4.

Evidence to the Working Party from a wide variety of sources indicated a need for more co-ordination. The principal barrier to successful co-ordination is the multi-dimensional nature of the problems of handicapped children. Many professional disciplines are concerned and these are often not aware that their various roles are essentially complementary. Within the field of statutory authorities a number of government departments are involved and this is paralleled at local or regional level by local authority departments and regional hospital boards. If the three arms of the National Health Service – general practice, hospital service and local health authority – are to be unified under "area health authorities" as envisaged in a recent Government Green Paper (HMSO 1970), some problems of co-ordination may be easier but others more difficult. The voluntary and statutory agencies are not always at one and the exchange of information is often minimal. Finally, as was said earlier, within the voluntary field there is a large number of societies with overlapping functions, which is not only wasteful but sometimes confusing to the public and counterproductive.

A multi-dimensional problem needs a multi-dimensional solution and there is at present no one agency which has any responsibility for co-ordination. If appropriate educational provision is not available the local education authority is accountable. If welfare facilities are not adequate, at present the local health or welfare departments carry a measure of responsibility. But if co-ordination is lacking, no one is accountable. Without such specific responsibility, progress is bound to be slow. This question is discussed in detail in chapter 12.

References

BRITISH COUNCIL FOR REHABILITATION OF THE DISABLED (1964) *The Handicapped School Leaver*. Report of a Working Party. London.

CARNEGIE UK TRUST (1964) *Handicapped Children and their Families*. Dunfermline, Scotland.

DAVIE, R., BUTLER, N. R. AND GOLDSTEIN, H. *From Birth to Seven* (in the press).

DEPARTMENT OF EDUCATION AND SCIENCE AND MINISTRY OF HEALTH (1966). 9/66 and 7/66. *Co-ordination of Education, Health and Welfare Services for Handicapped children and young people*. HMSO London.

DEPARTMENT OF HEALTH AND SOCIAL SECURITY (1968) *Annual Report of Chief Medical Officer*. HMSO London.

DEPARTMENT OF HEALTH AND SOCIAL SECURITY (1970) *National Health Service* HMSO London.

DIXON, P. J. (1968) "The Tenant". Paper read before the Health Congress of the Royal Society of Health.

MINISTRY OF HOUSING AND LOCAL GOVERNMENT (1969) *Council Housing Purposes, Procedures and Priorities*. HMSO London.

PACKMAN, J. AND POWER, M. (1968) "Children in need and the help they receive". Appendix Q in the *Report of the Committee on Local Authorities and Allied Personal Social Services*. HMSO London.

Acts and Regulations

Blind Persons Act (1920).
Education Act (1944).
Handicapped Pupils and Special Schools Regulations (1945).
National Assistance Act (1948).
Local Authority Social Services Act (1970).
Chronically Sick and Disabled Persons Act (1970).

4. Prevention

"I cannot help feeling that abortion when asked for would have certainly saved us a lifetime's heartbreak – rather than trying to ease the situation afterwards. I, unlike the mothers of thalidomide babies, was fully aware of the possibility of a handicapped child, as a result of rubella, and was foolish enough to take the advice of my doctor, who took a gamble on my child's future development."

Letter from the mother of a rubella child

Prevention of handicap by the control of causes must be an ultimate aim of every progressive society. Though some striking advances can be recorded, for example, the reduction in the number of children suffering from poliomyelitis and hence of physical handicaps arising from this cause; or those blinded by eye infection at or soon after birth,* it must be pointed out that other handicaps may be increasing in number, spina bifida and mongolism for instance, due to improved survival consequent upon advances in medical care of infants who but a short time ago died. Information on this changing pattern of handicap is not as complete as it should be. The comprehensive and continuous assessment which we propose should result in an improved local and national record system which would allow more research to be undertaken into the distribution and determinants of all handicapping conditions at birth and beyond.

It is, however, also true that not all the preventive knowledge currently available is being applied; many of the recommendations

* The number of cases of paralytic poliomyelitis notified in 1958 was 1,419 and in 1967, 16. The number of cases of opthalmia neonatorum in 1937 was 5,050 and in 1967, 606.

102

reached by the Butler and Bonham Survey of Perinatal Mortality in Britain (1963) have not yet become universal practice. For example, in 1967, of the mothers with four or more previous children, having legitimate births at home, "one third of them were 35 years of age or more thus clearly belonging to high risk categories for whom delivery in a consultant maternity department with full facilities is constantly urged" (Annual Report of the Chief Medical Officer of the Department of Health and Social Security for the year 1968). It may, therefore, be inferred that the chance of women bearing children who are either handicapped or at risk of becoming so continues to be higher in some areas than it should be. Research should be a high priority, both into the underlying mechanisms of physical, intellectual, emotional and social handicap; into the reasons behind failure to apply knowledge now available; and into the social and educational implications of handicap for developing children.

Primary prevention

A small, but perhaps growing, proportion of handicaps is known to be due primarily to genetic transmission of biological faults both physical and mental. Some of these conditions can now be recognised by enzyme tests and thus also identified in an unaffected parent or sibling. Clearly there is in such families a need for expert genetic counselling services which can offer up-to-date information on the risk of bearing a handicapped child and which can help parents towards wise decisions.

Genetic counselling should take account of the emotional and personal problems arising for couples who may face difficult and disturbing decisions. Casework help should be made available to them if they so desire. Professional advisers most likely to come into first contact with families who need contraceptive help – usually the general practitioner and the health visitor – should be able to advise, or to refer on to special clinics, those parents who are in need of such counselling.

Management of pregnancy and the newborn infant
Though the overall provision of obstetric services in Britain is good, survey findings suggest that considerable improvement could be achieved in certain areas. In the second report of the British Perinatal Mortality Survey (Butler and Alberman, 1969), it was found that

"death rates from causes which are amenable to obstetric care are higher in rural than in urban areas."

We acknowledge and commend the continuing effort being made at all levels of the National Health Service to bring about improvement within the limited resources available, by, for example, better buildings and recruitment of more medical and nursing staff. But too much emphasis can hardly be placed upon the urgent need for better antenatal care of women in vulnerable groups; for example, there is undoubtedly a correlation between the quantity and quality of antenatal care and conditions such as prematurity, lack of oxygen at birth, and other conditions likely to produce handicap in babies. The importance of measures for improved antenatal care, medical, nutritional and social, and the likely effect of these on perinatal mortality rates has been extensively gone into in the Butler and Bonham survey already cited. Since that survey, some further preventive developments have been reported, for example, an immunoglobulin injection to prevent the development of rhesus sensitisation and the identification of affected babies in the uterus, while an effective vaccine against rubella now seems a real possibility, and there is heightened awareness of the risks to the child of exposure to radiations, drugs, and toxic substances during pregnancy. The thalidomide tragedy is still fresh enough to remind us that embryonic tissues may be damaged by new and inadequately tested chemical substances.

Special attention needs to be paid to socially vulnerable families, where medical risk to mother and child may be associated with social or mental health problems. Families at risk in this sense of the term include unmarried mothers, mentally ill and mentally subnormal women, mothers of large families living in poverty or in poor housing conditions. Such families need social work support alongside good medical antenatal care. The medical social worker as part of the hospital team is in a good position to help, in co-operation with health visitors. Local authority social workers may be in continuous touch with the family and know the mother before she becomes pregnant. In future both are likely to be on the staff of the social services department.

Comprehensive antenatal care must include a growing element of health education covering not only specific medical prevention but also wider matters such as attitude to parenthood. It is important that the husband should be involved at this stage as far as possible, not only that he may understand the physical and emotional changes in his wife, but also that he may participate in preparing for parenthood and the changes in role which this will bring. Additional factors in family dynamics and sibling rivalry arise where there is already a child in the family. The modern well-trained health visitor is competent to advise the pregnant woman not only on such traditional, but nevertheless important, topics as her own and her infant's nutrition, but also on the emotional adjustments that childbirth requires of a family. She is able to offer general advice to the family and should act in co-operation with a skilled caseworker where this seems appropriate. This kind of "preventive preparation" can be enhanced by closer co-operation, clearer co-ordination, and better communication, between health visitors, general practitioners and social workers, and between both them and the hospital. There are several encouraging signs that this working together is becoming more prevalent and we believe this recognition that adverse biological and social conditions reinforce each other will, together with the other preventive measures referred to, substantially contribute to better care of the mother-to-be and thus assist in the control of handicap in children.

Whilst recognising the great improvement that has taken place in the last decade or two in paediatric care of the newborn infant, we consider that prevention of perinatal and neonatal brain damage is so vital that every opportunity must be taken to bring up to the best standard those areas of the country where advance has lagged. The possibility of a medical crisis at birth makes it imperative that all vulnerable pregnancies should be confined in well equipped hospitals with not only specialist obstetric but also adequate paediatric staff, including nurses, junior and senior medical staff, and technicians for whatever laboratory and radiological investigations are required. Brain damage from the following causes is a particular risk at the newborn stage: trauma, vascular damage by asphyxia due to lack of oxygen during the change-over at birth from supply via the placenta and umbilical cord to supply via the lungs; jaundice due to rhesus blood group incompatibility; too little sugar in the blood and the brain cells from asphyxia or from placentally determined malnutrition; post-natal delay in feeding for one reason or another; chilling of the baby from climate; neglect to maintain warmth, or the necessity of a long journey into a special care baby unit; and finally, lung changes due to extreme prematurity and asphyxia preventing the uptake of oxygen and the escape of carbon dioxide in the lungs. While some of these conditions are preventable, the fact must be faced that present knowledge of their causes is still imperfect and their further elucidation and preventability are dependant upon the promotion of complex research. Where medical complications do arise, the mother's own needs, and her role in the situation must be borne in mind. Difficult decisions may have to be taken as to how much to tell her about the problems and the action being taken. Her husband must of course be involved in this. There may be acute anxiety for her, as well as natural disappointment at not having the child with her and sharing in his care right from the beginning.

Paediatric and other care of the infant and pre-school child
As the baby grows out of the neonatal period, there is no less need for better and earlier diagnosis of conditions which can cause brain damage or other handicaps. Diseases such as meningitis, encephalitis, dehydration and gastro-enteritis, status epilepticus, and their complications, must be promptly diagnosed and efficiently treated; and the same is true of conditions of more insidious onset, like inborn errors of body function which, though relatively rare, are being increasingly identified by research and discovered by screening methods applied to the whole population of newborn infants – for example, the testing of urine or blood for abnormalities which if untreated may hinder the child's development.

Similarly, modern developments in neonatal and paediatric surgery may reduce handicap. Thus the prompt neurosurgical treatment of hydrocephalus, and of babies with spina bifida and meningomyelocoele is likely to prevent progressive brain damage from rising intracranial pressure. These measures and others in various conditions now prolong the life of severely handicapped children who until recently would have died. Some people argue that this only causes prolonged suffering for both the child and his family. However, until these procedures have been given a chance to work, it is difficult to forecast which children will benefit.

Closely related to good paediatric care is the need for social care and support to families where a young infant is deemed to be at risk, so that parents may be helped to cope with the acute anxiety of the early period involving observation, testing and possibly hospitalisation. Then, if a diagnosis of handicap is made, the family will need skilled help to come to terms with the situation, and to be involved right from the start, in co-operation with the medical profession, in whatever treatment is appropriate. It is essential that treatment should be interpreted in the widest possible sense, as dealing not just medically with the child, but comprehensively with the total family situation. This will involve awareness by the services concerned of the parents and other children in the family and their emotional needs and responses, as well as of practical issues and material needs. A close partnership between doctors, nurses, health visitors and social workers is thus indicated.

Environmental hazards

Some environmental hazards to children are well-known sources of handicap. For example during 1967 some 989 children died in home accidents, the majority being under 5 years of age and in 1968 more children died in fires alone than people were murdered; serious injuries were sustained by about 50,000 children (the exact number is not known and estimates can only be made from hospital records of in-patients under the age of 15 years admitted as a result of a home accident). 63,962 children in Great Britain were involved in road accidents in 1968 (of these 890 under 15 years of age were killed, 15,697 were seriously injured and 47,375 were slightly injured), and in the same year some 400 children were seriously injured by fireworks. It is most encouraging to note that in a comparison of deaths and injuries in road accidents in the first nine months of 1969 with the first nine months of 1968, there is a marked downward trend; deaths are down by 4·4%, serious injuries by 2·1% and slight injuries by 3·0%. (Royal Society for the Prevention of Accidents, 1968).

Accidental poisoning of children by pills and household liquids, and accidental injury in the home and on the roads, have both received a good deal of attention; yet, despite mounting efforts by the health professions and by public propaganda, far too many children are severely and permanently handicapped by accidents that should be prevented. Other hazards are less well known by parents and those who can influence their understanding of safety measures; for example, it is important to avoid the exposure of children to lead (and other toxic agents) by banning the sale of imported toys decorated with lead-containing paint, the sucking of which may produce irreversible brain damage. Both central and local authorities should be encouraged and enabled to do far more accident prevention.

Here again, where environmental hazards are concerned, certain families may be particularly at risk and social factors contribute to faulty parenting. This may arise from family stresses of all kinds, from ill health, from poor marital relationships, from low mentality. It may arise where one of both parents are absent, *eg* with single-parent families; where a mother is in and out of mental hospital; where children are left alone inappropriately, not necessarily through intentional neglect but often because of cultural variations in child rearing (*eg* among immigrant families). In addition to general measures of accident prevention, positive preventive social work is needed in these cases. Low earnings, large families, bad housing conditions, inappropriate infant feeding and poor health of the mother all contribute.

Prevention of handicap must be thought of in medical, educational and social terms. The balance between these factors in the cause of handicap will vary from one condition to another, from one family to another, and from one cultural context to another, and thus the preventive role of health, education, and social service will vary too, but we wish to stress again the need for the relevance of *all* services to be constantly considered. The biology, psychology and sociology of handicap in children cannot be fragmented.

Educational aspects of prevention and care
These aspects suggest that preventive measures should have a beginning in secondary education in the preparation of adolescent girls (and boys) for family living and parenthood, a task which many schools are already tackling with imagination though few educators would feel certain of the most profitable ways of doing so. While average young people probably become most sensitive to information and ideas about bringing up children when the task is already upon them, there can be no doubt that previous experiences, (*eg* helping in the care of young children) provide a basis which can be built upon later. There is also the more urgent problem of the children who, because of limited intelligence or emotional disturbance arising perhaps from their own disadvantages, are the most likely to put their children at risk. Help for them includes a wide range of curriculum content; a broadly conceived

sex education, including discussion of the need to avoid illegitimate children, family and household management in all its practical aspects as well as the health and welfare of young children. But the causes lie much deeper in some potential parents, as studies of parents who batter their children have shown.

When children reach nursery or infant school age, a great deal of preventive work is done. Traditionally it has always been an important part of nursery education to work with mothers. The same is true of many infant schools though the larger number of children and the variety of demands on the infant teachers' time and thought make it less easy. As we suggest in chapter 5, the opportunity provided in the infant school of close observation of children and more easy contact with mothers, should be fully utilised to ensure that children with emotional, social or learning difficulties are recognised, observed and, where necessary, referred for whatever special examinations are appropriate. This is surely a function of the infant school which merits the highest priority and in the performance of which infant teachers should have the closest support from health, psychological and social services.

Later in school life, the teacher's knowledge of his pupils makes possible the early detection of change in their physical and mental health or in their circumstances. Early remedial action can minimise harmful consequences.

It is well known that 10 % to 15 % of pupils are sufficiently backward educationally to need some form of special educational help and that in some areas the schools will contain a higher proportion of such pupils. Various surveys have pointed to a similarly high prevalence of emotional disturbance; for example, the National Child Development Study found 13 % of seven year olds obtained scores on the Bristol Social Adjustment Guides indicative of a fairly serious degree of emotional difficulty and the Isle of Wight Study judged about 6 % to be in need of psychiatric advice or treatment. Existing specialist services are insufficient to cope with such numbers and obviously the schools must continue to be a main agency for preventing and treating all but the most serious of these problems. Many teachers already have considerable experience of these problems and many innovations in organisation, curriculum and methods contribute indirectly to preventive work. While much more could be done by initial and in-service training of teachers and by a greater emphasis on preventive work, it should also be recognised that schools with a large number of problems need more than pious aspirations. They need additional resources and especially those of trained man-power – trained non-teaching helps, remedial teachers, teacher-social workers or counsellors – who have the time for small group teaching, for liaison with homes and social agencies and all the other time-consuming efforts entailed in preventive work.

Secondary prevention

Though the aim of prevention must be to control the basic cause of physical handicap, an important consideration is the prevention of handicaps which are primarily due to or accentuated by adverse family and environmental circumstances. These are:

Physical   – for example, contracture in a child with cerebral palsy;

Emotional   – for example, separation from parents, particularly of young children; parental, sibling or community rejection or unwise handling including over-protection of a handicapped child; or failure to meet the emotional needs of children in residential institutions;

Intellectual – inadequate or incorrect language stimulation of a child with speech delay, deafness or visual handicap, too little opportunity to mix with other children, lack of play material, lack of advice to parents on developmental training, or lack of appropriate special education, together with the damaging effects of an impoverished or deprived environment on intellectual growth;

Social   – handicapped children whose parents cannot provide the security and stability of a normal home, or who receive insufficient supportive services to enable them to do so; and handicapped children for whom an adequate substitute home is not provided. These conditions can themselves cause emotional deprivation in children not otherwise handicapped.

The prevention of these family and social, causative or aggravating influences can only be attained by a more comprehensive approach to the problems of handicapped children, starting from the moment of birth (in some cases, before birth) or diagnosis, involving consultant paediatricians, obstetricians, family doctors and local authority medical officers, along with all the ancillary staff who make up the health care team, and including psychological, educational and social work skills as appropriate. This should be a continuous process designed to help the family of the handicapped child to help him to grow into his adult roles of citizen, marriage partner, parent, and worker and to fulfil these roles to his maximum social and personal usefulness. In some instances the medical team may have this primary role; in others, it may be the psycho/social and educational team, especially where defective family relationships, inadequate maternal care and poor environmental conditions place a child at risk at birth or later.

The complexity of these issues is well illustrated by the follow up of the 314 children out of some 15,000 in the National Child Development Study (1958 Cohort) who had been in the care of a children's department (sometimes quite briefly) during their first seven years. An analysis of their whole circumstances showed that: "Already then, as they lay in their cots, the group of children who later were received into care could be distinguished from the other children born during the same week. More of them were illegitimate, their mothers tended to be younger and of smaller stature, they themselves tended to have had a shorter period of gestation and to be of lower birth weight. These characteristics are not of course independent of each other but taken together they seem to indicate a group of children who were in these first few days of their life already at a disadvantage compared with other children of the same age and social class" (Mapstone, 1969). Later this poor start revealed a complex mixture of nature and nurture. By then this was a group of seven year olds "whose homes were overcrowded and lacking in comfort; who were unsuccessful in reading and number work; poorly adjusted at school; lacking in imagination, general knowledge and the ability to express themselves; and as a final blow, undersized and unattractive in appearance by comparison with their classmates" (Mapstone 1969). There are many important implications here both for prevention and for the deployment of services.

Some implications of prevention and treatment for the organ-isation of the health, social and education services
We have emphasised that prompt skilled treatment of the actually or potentially handicapped child can prevent further disability and in

this sense prevention and treatment go together. Moreover, whether the handicap be present at birth or appears after birth, or is acquired later in life, the same principles of accurate, comprehensive diagnosis and treatment apply, with the need to focus not just on the specific handicap itself but on the handicapped child as a whole person and on his total family, social and other needs.

The prevention of handicap and its management take place within the framework of services now provided by statutory and voluntary agencies. We indicate in this chapter and the next how the National Health Service, in particular, needs to be changed to improve on its already substantial contribution to the problem of handicapped children. Some of these improvements relate to the hospital service, others are concerned with expansion and re-organisation of health services based in the community. We wish to emphasise that hospital and community health services should not be separate and discrete but closely linked parts of a whole. We are glad to learn that the government has decided to unite the three separate parts of the health service.

There are many encouraging signs of awareness of the need to forge stronger bonds between professional skills inside and outside the hospital; the growth of group practice and health centre based general practitioners, the attachment of local authority health visitors, nurses and social workers to family doctors, the emergence of team concepts, the specialisation of local health authority doctors in developmental assessment, the increasing use of specialised health visitors in after-care, and the move towards co-operation with the education, and social work professions, are all evidence of a new determination to make the multi-disciplinary approach to old and new problems a reality. The new comprehensive social services departments will also be a significant move in this direction.

In this and other chapters we draw attention to many points at which family and social circumstances may be responsible for either causing or aggravating some handicapping condition. The provision of an effective range of personal social services for handicapped children and their families has been severely neglected in comparison with the health and education services, which themselves require much improvement. But since the whole emphasis in our report is upon a proper balance between the medical, social, emotional and educational needs of handicapped children, we do not think it possible to undertake comprehensive preventive measures in the absence of well-organised social services departments staffed by professionally qualified social workers.

References

BUTLER, N. R. AND BONHAM, D. G. (1963) *Perinatal Mortality*. E. & S. Livingstone Ltd, Edinburgh.

BUTLER, N. R. AND ALBERMAN, E. D. (ed) (1969) *Perinatal Problems*. E. & S. Livingstone Ltd, Edinburgh.

DEPARTMENT OF HEALTH AND SOCIAL SECURITY (1968) *Annual Report of the Chief Medical Officer*. HMSO London.

GRAHAM, P. AND RUTTER, M. (1968) "Organic Brain Dysfunction and Child Psychiatric Disorder. *British Medical Journal*. Vol 3, No 8620, pp 689–700.

MAPSTONE, E. (1969) "Children in Care". *Concern*, No 3, Nov 69.

PRINGLE, M. L. KELLMER, BUTLER, N. R. AND DAVIE, R. (1966) *11,000 Seven Year Olds*. Longmans in association with the National Bureau for Co-operation in Child Care, London.

ROYAL SOCIETY FOR THE PREVENTION OF ACCIDENTS. Personal communication.

5. Detection and Screening

"My third child was born with a cleft palate and during the first five years had several operations. I insisted on frequent visiting which led to difficulties with the nursing staff, especially Sister. My little boy had always been very sensitive and I am sure he was affected by my tense attitude when visiting, and by Sister's resentment. The surgeon was excellent but no-one explained to me what to expect or how to help John over the effects of all these operations. Once he went to school he was given some speech therapy but he disliked school and they told me he was very dull and unresponsive. When he was ten years old he had his first break: a teacher who took a great interest in him, insisted he was quite intelligent and eventually persuaded the head to refer him to the educational psychologist. He said John was a bright boy but his hearing needed investigating. This showed he was partially deaf and so was given a hearing aid. From then on he has gone from strength to strength, but it is difficult to make up years of lost hearing and backwardness. Why could he not have been given all these tests earlier, even before he went to school? So much unhappiness for him and us could have been prevented."

Quotation from a parent's letter

The present situation

Reasons for early detection

There is general agreement that the early detection of defects and disabilities is essential for three reasons. First, some of the most basic learning takes place during the pre-school years, and on its success later progress depends; for example learning to talk and listen facilitates later social relationships and educational progress; hence an undetected handicap may not only delay present but also later achievement.

Secondly, development and learning are most rapid in the early years; for example, about 50% of a child's intelligence develops between conception and the 4th year, and about 30% between the ages of 4 to 8 years (Bloom, 1964); and there is evidence that adverse social and cultural conditions have measurable effects on the emotional adjustment and educational achievement of children as early as the first few years of schooling (Bloom, 1964; Douglas, 1964; Pringle, Butler and Davie, 1966).

Thirdly, environmental conditions have the greatest effect during the most rapid period of growth and thus interventions – be they medical, social or educational in nature – are likely to have maximal benefit the earlier they can be made. Furthermore, they may prevent secondary handicaps; for example, abnormal postures and movement patterns may arise from contractures of muscles; and lack of appropriate experience and stimulation may retard intellectual development. Moreover, social and emotional problems or malfunctioning within the child's family, whether or not related to the child's handicap, may well contribute to secondary handicaps. "Emotional disturbance arises most commonly from the quality of the child's experience rather than from any direct causal link with the type and nature of his handicap." (Williams, 1968)

Early identification of developmental delay

Physical handicaps The chronic disorders of childhood such as congenital heart disease, or asthma, are normally detected in the course of customary examinations or from presenting signs and symptoms. Neuro-developmental handicaps – motor, visual and auditory – intellectual and emotional handicaps in babies and young children may, on the other hand, often be missed unless deliberately sought for by developmental screening examinations which require new paediatric procedures and skills.

Little more than a decade has passed since the then Ministry of Health first referred to the desirability of local health authorities maintaining special care registers of babies at high risk of handicapping conditions (Ministry of Health, 1957). Initially the purpose of such "at risk" registers was to ensure the follow-up by the child health services, of babies selected at or about the time of their birth because of adverse conditions during pregnancy, labour or the puerperium, or

116	LIVING WITH HANDICAP

because of a history of major handicap in the family; for example, the aim was to detect deafness by the use of standardised tests for hearing applied periodically during the first years of life. This concept was soon extended to include developmental screening procedures to detect developmental delay in all fields of development, gross motor, visual, auditory and social skills and behaviour. It was expected that among the 20% of babies thus selected some 80% of handicaps would be found. However, this hope did not materialise.

Our evidence has shown that almost all local health authorities now maintain a risk register although these vary very much in scope, and there is not at present a standardised national list of risk factors. In some areas a senior medical officer responsible for handicapped children has also been given the duty to review all cases included on it. A survey carried out by the World Health Organisation in 1966 in three sample areas showed that only 30%–60% of known handicaps occurred in children on the risk register. The failure of hospital consultants in some maternity departments to concern themselves with the identification of such babies may have contributed to this low yield in some areas. The pressing need for the appointment of a consultant paediatrician to every hospital maternity unit has been stressed in the previous chapter. On the other hand, lists of criteria for inclusion in the at risk register have been sufficiently comprehensive to take in some 60% of all handicapped children. These facts should encourage more research into the etiology of chronic handicaps to determine not only the factors which are significant, but also the level of risk involved.

Early detection of social, emotional and environmental handicaps One major difficulty is that during the most vital period – namely the pre-school years – the child does not necessarily come under the surveillance of any professionally qualified person. Furthermore, "there are few objective criteria for the measurement and recording of disabilities, especially where young children are concerned . . . no country has yet evolved a wholly satisfactory case-finding system" (World Health Organisation, 1967). During the first year or two the health visitor is in touch with the majority of babies and their families, getting to know them and their homes by periodic visits. Also most mothers take their infant at least once to child health centres but "mothers with poor standards of care and those with large families or with illegitimate children were less likely to attend. The number of children attending, at least once, fell from 76% during the first year to 20% during the fifth year". (Ministry of Health, 1967).

It is particularly during the vital years from 2 to 5 that handicapping conditions are likely to remain undetected. If a substantial proportion of children were able to benefit from nursery school provision, then the chance of detection during this period would be greatly increased. However, "not more than one child in nine in the 3 to 5 age group goes to nursery school . . . and it is rather less well known how unevenly the available places are distributed" (Blackstone, 1969). Worse still, there appears to be no relationship between social indices of need, such as overcrowding, and the availability of nursery education. Though there has been a great expansion of pre-school play groups, these too are more likely to function in socially advantaged areas where schemes of parental self-help are more readily organised.

Families where environmental conditions are very unfavourable are, of course, in most instances known to various departments of the local authority, especially children's departments, as well as to the voluntary organisations in the area. This means that social workers may be able to assist in the detection of handicapping conditions. But it is only a minority of families who will have such contact with the social services.

The battered baby syndrome has only recently received active attention in this country. The National Society for the Prevention of Cruelty to Children has mounted a research project on battered babies in which they propose to explore the factors which are critically associated with the battering of young children by their parents and to develop methods of casework intervention in the family processes which have resulted in such abuse. The subjects will be 45–50 families in which an infant under the age of 4 years has received injuries at the hands of parents or guardians. Referrals will come from two London hospitals. The team will work with the parents from the time they first bring the child to the hospital, and clinical interviews, continuing medical and psycho-social assessment and evaluation of the treatment process will be studied. Obstetric and medical records will be examined, and the physical and emotional growth of surviving infants will be assessed. It is hoped the research will contribute to the psycho-social diagnosis of a problem which has hitherto been a medical/legal matter. The project will last until 1971 initially, but may be extended for a further two years. The battered baby syndrome only began to be identified in the 1950's (initially by Silverman) in the United States. No figures are available but estimates in this country suggest that several hundred babies are injured each year. A retrospective study of 78 battered children (1969) showed that if the first child was battered there was a 13 to 1 chance that a subsequent child would be injured.

The Department of Health and Social Security and the Home Office have recently asked medical officers of health and children's officers to arrange discussions with all those who would be concerned with the problem of the battered child. It is hoped that in each area they would review the local situation and decide what further protection and assistance could be made available to the child, the parents and others at risk in the family.

The role of parents in early detection "The folly, negligence, ignorance or selfishness of a parent can do more harm to a handicapped child than the carelessness or incompetence of any of the professional workers. By contrast, the intelligent, informed and devoted parent can confer on him benefits which no professional discipline can offer. In a variety of ways the parents may be the child's protectors, teachers and therapists" (World Health Organisation, 1967). To this list might be added that potentially the parents are also the best "detectors" of handicap. More attention should be paid to that rather maligned sixth sense "maternal instinct", because it is often the mother who has the first suspicion that all is not well with her child. To be told either "not to worry" or that he will "grow out of it" is doing a disservice, if for no other reason than that this is unlikely to allay her anxiety which itself may have an adverse effect on the child's emotional development.

In contrast, some parents though suspecting a child's disability, may pretend – even to themselves – that all is well; rather than seeking help, they may then deliberately attempt to conceal the true situation from the authorities and even from their own doctor. If they believe that existing educational and treatment facilities are inadequate or not available, they are even less likely to seek a diagnosis. This is probably one reason why when suitable facilities do become available, many hitherto unknown children come to notice. Hence the apparent paradox that the prevalence of a handicap seems to increase with increasing provision for the care, education and treatment of the particular condition.

Later detection of disabilities

As soon as children come together in groups there is the opportunity for teachers to observe and bring to notice any serious deviations from normal development – indeed it should be regarded as one essential part of their work. It would be fair to say that the majority of teachers do regard it in this way but the opportunities are not always used as well as they might be. There are several reasons for this. A teacher may be troubled by a child's behaviour or difficulty but feel that she lacks sufficient experience to judge its seriousness. She may hesitate to make a fuss though she is likely to mention the matter to the doctor or the school psychologist when they next visit. It may be that a teacher through lack of knowledge or experience fails to recognise the symptoms of difficulty – a child with a hearing impairment may be thought to be naughty; a visual defect can easily go unobserved; with infants especially, it is often difficult for the inexperienced teacher to distinguish maladjusted children from mentally slow children since both may show the same failure to make progress in pre-academic and academic tasks. The remedy can only be partly sought in greater attention to these matters in initial teacher training since so much depends on experience and maturity of judgement. Here the help and advice of head teacher is essential.

Disablement due to infection or accident may arise at any time in a child's life. At present, it is only very exceptionally that steps are taken to try to alleviate its emotional effects and then to detect as early as possible following physical recovery, whether there are consequent or residual disabilities which impede the child's emotional, social, intellectual or educational progress. For example, serious scalds and burns in early childhood are likely to have emotional concomitants both for mother and child, particularly if unsightly scars remain; the question of social casework and psychotherapy for the child and his family should at least be considered as a matter of course in all such cases.

In their evidence to the Working Party, the Association of Health Visitors commented that, "While such children receive good medical care in hospital serious inadequacies arise when they return home. Often parents are given insufficient explanation, instruction and help, and sometimes unsuitable or inadequate equipment. In addition, necessary information is not always passed on to general practitioners or local health authorities by hospitals on the discharge of all children as a regular, standard procedure and not, as at present, dependent on variable relationships between the hospitals and the local health authorities."

Consequences of the present situation

"There is evidence that many children are starting school life with defects hitherto unrecognised or not reported" (Ministry of Health, 1967). Similarly, the incidence of emotional maladjustment in a national study of seven year olds was found to be 13%, a third of which were quite serious problems (Pringle, Butler and Davie, 1966). The same study revealed that even at this early stage in their school career, some 13% of children were considered by their teachers to be in need of special educational help, in addition to any which the class teacher was providing and only some 5% were in fact receiving such help. The lower the socio-economic group the higher the incidence of both educational and emotional difficulties.

Until now the routine testing of vision in the pre-school child has been largely neglected, although accurate tests using Snellen type letters can be readily and effectively carried out at least from the age of three years, using the Sheridan matching letter techniques. Other tests of vision in the every-day situation which can be used from the age of six months have also been published by Sheridan. Children should no longer arrive at school with undiagnosed errors of refraction.

In short, though recent years have seen an increased interest in and attention to early detection and screening, there is still a long way to go. To a lesser extent this is also true regarding children of school age. What then can be done to bring about earlier detection, conceived in rather broader terms than at present?

Suggestions for making detection and screening more effective

At present, local health, education and hospital authorities do not cover the same area. If all the authorities concerned were to have responsibility for the same catchment area, co-operation and co-ordination would more easily be achieved. "Of course, re-drawing some departmental boundaries will not itself solve problems, but it would be one comparatively cheap way in which better use could be made of existing resources of field-work staff, as well as offering a more humane service to individuals in need", (Hancock et al, 1969). This situation will be changed when the government decisions about the reform of local government and the realignment of the National Health Service are implemented. The boundaries of area health authorities and unitary local authorities will then be identical.

"Effective case-finding is the first step towards success. While neither risk registers nor screening procedures are infallible, it is clear that some combination of the two offers a good prospect of dividing the labour between the specialists and their colleagues . . . If a substantial part of it can be placed in the hands of child health doctors, general practitioners, nurses and others who work in the field, the benefits of early detection will be far more widely distributed" (World Health Organisation, 1967).

There are three possible types of screening procedure: using a specific test; giving a brief but systematic examination; and by observation of behaviour. Though the last mentioned is perhaps the most subjective and depends most on the perceptiveness of the observer, it has nevertheless several advantages; among them is the fact that optimally it is done while the child is in his customary surroundings and that it can be as prolonged as need be rather than having to fit into a pre-arranged time span. Hence its potential value as a screening device is considerable, despite its limitations, especially if the observations can be guided, and if necessary, evaluated by the relevant specialist.

Early identification and developmental screening of physical, sensory and neurological defects
A risk register serves to pinpoint children who must be followed up through the pre-school years. The etiology of about a quarter of handicapping conditions is, however, as yet unknown, so that at best we cannot rely solely on this procedure to reveal all handicaps. It is now generally recognised that the aim must be to carry out developmental screening examinations of all children at key ages during the pre-school years. The Sheldon Committee (1967) recognised this as a major function of the child health services.

The first step is the recognition of developmental delay and of signs and symptoms suggesting the existence of a disability. Some of the weaknesses of our services for handicapped children are the consequence of increased prevalence of congenital as opposed to acquired, and multiple as opposed to single handicaps. Continuing improvement in paediatric techniques for the neurological examination of the new-born will undoubtedly lead to more babies being selected at this stage for comprehensive assessment. But it would not be practicable for the consultant paediatrician to carry out an expert examination on every baby born in his hospital, and other babies will be born at home or in general practitioner maternity units. Moreover, although some handicapping conditions may be recognisable at this time, others such as deafness and visual handicaps may be missed unless deliberately sought for through the pre-school and even the school years. Minimal cerebral palsy and less severe forms of mental retardation, as well as learning and language disorders as yet often become obvious only as the child develops, even after school entry. We must look therefore largely to field doctors – medical officers and general practitioners doing preventive child health work – to undertake the task of identifying developmental delay through periodic developmental screening examinations, and to refer these children as early as possible to hospital paediatricians and other appropriate consultants. While this con-stitutes the core of the scheme for detection and screening for physical, sensory and neurological defects, a multi-disciplinary approach is essential and will require intelligent observation and understanding of the development of young children by all workers concerned in their care, welfare and education. Such workers include health visitors, day nursery and nursery school staff, teachers, social workers, nursery nurses and other residential child care staff. Their special knowledge of children and child development should be used to spot danger signals.

This aim appears to be quite practicable. In 1967 some 76% of all children born attended child health clinics in the first year of life (Ministry of Health, 1967). With increasing participation of general practitioners in preventive work, with greater awareness on the part of other professional workers dealing with children, and with a rising level of education in the country as a whole, this figure may be expected to increase. Indeed, an upward trend has been observed over the past ten years.

We have in the child health service, with its two main components – home visiting by the health visitor and clinic sessions where mothers traditionally seek help in the care and management of the young child – a unique opportunity to build up a comprehensive developmental screening programme. Whatever is done in the immediate future to re-design the pattern of this service, or to define the roles to be played by workers in various disciplines, these changes should reinforce rather than weaken this potential.

Early identification of intellectual, language and emotional disabilities

At present, there is only one specific screening test which may prevent a mental handicap from developing, provided a prescribed diet is followed, namely that for detecting phenylketonuria. Screening by examination is possible from quite an early age. However, developmental language and intelligence tests have low predictive value during the pre-school years and also must be administered by a psychologist; furthermore, they are time consuming and have to be given individually. The most practicable screening is done by observation of the child's developmental progress, general behaviour and the ways in which he uses language and responds to speech.

There is no screening test and no really satisfactory examination for the early detection of emotional disabilities. While serious mental illness is very rare in childhood, emotional disturbance and behaviour disorders are relatively common; for example, most children pass through a negativistic phase and occasional regression to behaviour appropriate to a younger age is so general that it must be considered "normal". Only when such deviant behaviour is prolonged need it cause concern.

Again the only practicable screening method is observation of the child in as many situations as possible. However, it is not always easy to make a sharp distinction between a young child's intellectual, language and emotional behaviour patterns. This is because these developmental aspects are very closely interrelated: language retardation inevitably has an adverse effect on intellectual growth; emotional handicap may show itself in behaviour appropriate to a much younger child thus masking normal or above average intelligence; and the intellectually handicapped child is usually emotionally immature which might be misinterpreted as emotional disturbance. The condition which exhibits this interaction to an extreme degree is autism, where the child is almost completely withdrawn from communication with the world: he neither speaks nor responds to speech, does not play in normal ways but becomes extremely obsessed and absorbed by unusual and sometimes bizarre objects, neither shows nor responds to affection but is given to unprovoked outbursts of aggression and destructiveness. Hence observation may lead one to consider the autistic child to be intellectually handicapped (which some but not all are) or to be severely deaf (which most are not).

It is primarily parents who are in a position to detect intellectual, language and emotional disabilities. To become more effective in doing so, wider dissemination of what is known about the various stages of normal child development among school leavers, engaged couples and expecting parents should lead to a greater awareness of what to expect and when to seek advice. Such advice then needs to be as readily available as is guidance on infants' and toddlers' physical health. In turn, general practitioners, health visitors and paediatric nurses need not only better knowledge of the psychological features of normal and deviant development but they must also be prepared to dispel the still prevalent feeling among parents that to seek advice on the emotional or social aspects of a child's growth is either being fussy or confessing to failure.

Hopefully, the government sponsored work in educational priority areas, the urban aid programme and the community development projects will lead to greatly increased nursery school provision. Then more children will come under the care of trained professional staff, which should assist in the early detection of these handicaps. Pre-school play-groups can also make a valuable contribution. The Pre-School Playgroups Association in their evidence to the Working Party gave several examples of observations made by supervisors which had subsequently been reported to the local authority doctor or health visitor and had led to the detection of a handicap. An example is the comment about one little girl: "We've had a lot of very slow children who suddenly come to life and join in; but she just goes on sitting and watching. She doesn't even hold a doll if you put it into her arms."

Communication and a multi-disciplinary approach
If field doctors are to play an effective role in the early detection of chronic handicap, better communication between medical disciplines, in particular between the hospital and local health authority services is essential. Early transmission of full information from hospital maternity and paediatric departments to the child health services as well as to the general practitioner is basic. Another step towards this end is the designation of certain child health doctors with special experience and

training to promote liaison in the areas and to plan community services to meet the individual needs of the handicapped child and his family. The attachment of health visitors to general practices doing preventive child health, and a national system of record keeping of data on developmental screening examinations, are essential to the scheme.

The complexity of speech and language disorders which may present as medical, psychological, educational or social problems serves very well to illustrate the need for a multi-disciplinary approach to the detection and comprehensive assessment of the handicapped child, and requires better communication between disciplines. For example, the prevention of maladjustment must depend on the skill of all professional workers in the early recognition of family situations tending towards emotional disturbance in children and the deployment of measures to alleviate stress. When a major handicap is suspected parents may be confused by the failure of professional workers to work together and by the present tendency to give unilateral advice based on a personal view of the problem. A team approach to a truly comprehensive assessment in which all are fully informed, probably offers a better chance of success. The designation of one particular worker to communicate with the family may be agreed, but it is a matter of common knowledge that parents themselves choose their counsellor and not always the obvious one.

Later detection and screening of disabilities
Ensuring that teachers know the range of special facilities which are available, is one way of helping earlier detection; the more so, as many teachers feel very involved in their "problem" pupils and would prefer to continue doing the best they can unless they are sure that something really suitable is available. Most teachers are well aware of their responsibilities to detect slow learners as well as other children who have disabilities of one kind or another. But to do so, they need to be given more help.

First we would like to see a greater emphasis on the study of child development in undergraduate teacher training, and better opportunities for continuing post-graduate study. In the second place a rapid introduction of standardised procedures for the recognition of reading backwardness and other learning difficulties is needed. Some authorities have screening procedures in primary schools which reveal educational retardation and early maladjustment. Some of these provide excellent models to show how these principles can be implemented. In the case of backwardness in reading, many school psychological services have organised surveys of backwardness in the first or second year of the junior school. Such surveys reveal those children who may need remedial teaching, special schooling as educationally sub-normal pupils and sometimes, maladjusted children. But there would be great advantage in attempting a first screening towards the end of the infant school period. Infant school teachers know their pupils very well both from learning situations and from more informal activities. Their observations and judgements could be utilised to indicate those children who at that stage should be considered for special schooling, those who will need special or remedial teaching in the junior schools and those whose emotional disturbance indicates the need for special help. The National Child Development Study (1958 Cohort) has demonstrated that teachers do not find it difficult to make judgements of this kind (Pringle, Butler and Davie, 1966).

Ideally such a procedure should be organised by the school psychological service though carried out in a way which involves teachers as much as possible. It should in fact, be part of the process of educational guidance and would help to give the filling in of record cards a real purpose by requiring decision points at ages seven, eight and nine. A screening procedure of this kind would be incomplete without investigation of the health and development of the child. Consultation with the school doctor and family social worker should be regarded as an integral part of this procedure.

The need for screening procedures is most widely realised in connection with educationally subnormal children, but it could be that screening procedures would serve an even more useful function in the early detection of children with severe learning difficulties, who, not being obviously retarded, are allowed to drag on without the specialist examinations and treatment they require. Ideally a screening procedure should also lead to the recognition of children with minor sensory or motor defects. Further research of a multi-disciplinary kind is needed to provide information about the signs to look for; but meanwhile nothing would be lost by attempting a more systematic use of teachers' observations of pupils. Help for the child, however, may as yet be long delayed, even though his difficulties may have been recognised by the teacher, because of the shortage of educational psychologists to assess the cause of his difficulties, of teachers to give him the special help that is needed, and of social workers to attempt to ease family stress or social impoverishment.

Disablement due to accident or infection may arise at any time in a child's life. A history of this kind should be regarded by the teacher, school nurse, health visitor or social worker as indicating the need for a developmental screening examination by the school doctor so that handicapping conditions whether minor or otherwise may be detected as early as possible.

Better still, all children who have suffered a potentially handicapping illness (such as meningitis) or accident (particularly when it involves the possibility of brain damage) should come under the close and continuous surveillance of a psychologist while still in hospital to help detect whether there is a need for an early comprehensive assessment or whether some educational, remedial or psycho-therapeutic measures are indicated. The earliest possible detection of functional impairment in the emotional, social, intellectual and educational sphere is essential, not least because much needs to be learned about the spontaneous recovery of mental functions and the possibilities of systematic re-training in cases of severe regression.

References

BLACKSTONE, T. (1969) "Where Nursery Schools Are". *New Society*. Vol 14, No 367, pages 560–561.

BLOOM, B. S. (1964) *Stability and Change in Human Characteristics*. Wiley & Sons, New York.

DOUGLAS, J. W. B. (1964). *The Home and the School*. University of London Press.

HANCOCK, L. E. *et al* (1969) "Areas of Concern". *Concern No 2*. National Bureau for Co-operation in Child Care, London.

MINISTRY OF HEALTH (1967). *Annual Report of the Chief Medical Officer*. HMSO London.

MINISTRY OF HEALTH (1967) *Child Welfare Centres*. Report of the Sub-Committee of the Central Health Services Council Standing Medical Advisory Committee (Chairman Sir Wilfrid Sheldon). HMSO London.

PRINGLE, M. L. KELLMER, BUTLER, N. R. AND DAVIE, R. (1966). *11,000 Seven Year Olds*. Longmans, London.

SKINNER, A. AND CASTLE, R. (1969) *78 Battered Children: a Retrospective Study*. The National Society for Prevention of Cruelty to Children, London.

WILLIAMS, C. E. (1968) Personal Communication.

WORLD HEALTH ORGANISATION (1967). *Report by a Working Group on the Early Detection and Treatment of Handicapping Defects in Young Children*. Regional Office for Europe, WHO Copenhagen.

6. Assessment – a comprehensive and continuous process

"The birth was normal except that it started early, if my memory is correct. He was very nearly dead due to strangulation by the cord; after some hours a larger area of flesh became pink and after some 18 hours he took his first full breath. Subsequently he was seen periodically by various members of the hospital's staff where he was born and we were told that despite his shaky start, he was perfectly alright and normal. When he was 18 months old my wife took him to see the paediatrician at the same hospital who told her quite casually as she was leaving 'of course, you know he has cerebral palsy and will probably never be able to walk'. I won't bore you with the shock of what that statement did to my wife, who had just had a miscarriage. Surely parents should be told the situation much sooner, assuming that it's detectable. And it was in our case. Also we wanted, and needed to know much more so as to do our best for him."

Letter from an army officer about his son

The present situation

Can this be said to be very different from the situation described six years ago? Then the following conclusion was reached in a report sponsored by the Carnegie United Kingdom Trust (1964): "All these services (medical, educational, welfare and voluntary) or particular sections of them may impinge upon the same child or family without there being any close links or inter-relationships between them. There are barriers, both administrative and professional, which tend to delimit, restrict and specialise the operations of any one individual or agency, so that there may be little contact between one diagnostician and another or one form of treatment and another (*eg* medical and

128

educational treatment). The impression presented by our case material was that a unified and integrated approach was rarely achieved; often there was no one person directing the series of consultations and programme of treatment recommended, and the personal contact between general practitioner and consultant, consultant and school medical officer, school medical officer and special school, tended to be superficial or non-existent. There were many fingers in the pie, but no cook."

There is little evidence that any substantial improvement has come about. Nor do the reasons for this seem to have changed: "Every service is short-staffed and this is their excuse when deficiences are brought to their notice. But there are also obviously far too many overlapping and unco-cordinated services . . . Local co-ordinating committees certainly sometimes bring together small armies of social workers to discuss the worst cases, but by then most of the harm has been done. If segmentation and waste are to be avoided there must be co-operation and exchange of information at the stage of first diagnosis" (Sampson, 1965). The verdict on the purely medical side is very similar: "The outcome of a medical assessment must be reported to the family doctor, the Child Health Service and, where appropriate, to the School Health Service. We doubt whether the importance of these communications is even today sufficiently realised by the various hospital departments that may be concerned with handicapped children" (Ministry of Health, 1967).

Parents too are brought into the picture far too little and too rarely. In their evidence to the Working Party the Association of Health Visitors commented on finding parents who were suffering from the worst kind of doubt and anxiety, knowing that something was wrong but having no real information. Other parents may have been told of the diagnosed handicap with no preparation (and possibly surrounded by medical students); and yet others may have been deliberately kept in ignorance for several months after the diagnosis and then find adjustment much more difficult.

Another anxiety of parents arises because often they are given totally inadequate or incomprehensible directions for the care of their child at home. Examples quoted are instructions in the use of the spitzholtzer valve for hydrocephalics and such directions as "Give one millilitre."

Conflicting views

While some are convinced that assessment should be hospital based, especially for pre-school children, others feel just as strongly that hospitals are not the right place. The former view is advanced in the Sheldon Report (Ministry of Health, 1967) but it made little mention of educational, psychological and social aspects. Similarly, the Ministry of Health (1968) recommended that two types of hospital assessment centres for handicapped children be set up by regional hospital boards, namely, district hospital centres and regional centres, usually in teaching hospitals, and again regrettably little mention is made of educational, psychological and social aspects. Examples of such assessment centres are the Newcomen Clinic at Guy's Hospital and the Wolfson Centre at the Institute of Child Health of London University and the Sheffield and Newcastle clinics.

The opposite view is held by Professor Ross Mitchell, Professor of Child Health at the University of Aberdeen (1969): "At present the initial medical evaluation is carried out at the hospital . . . this often necessitates frequent attendance at different clinics and there is inevitably lack of sufficient communication between the various specialists and between the hospital and the community agencies who share responsibility. This leads to fragmentation of effort, conflicts of advice, inadequate support for the parents and lack of appreciation of the complete picture of the child's total handicap. Moreover, young children are often tired when they arrive at the clinic and may have to wait so that the specialist is trying to examine them under less than optimal conditions". His plan for a pre-school assessment centre in Aberdeen is a joint concern between the regional hospital board, the children's hospital, the local health authority, the local education authority and the newly formed social work department. It will be sited in the large grounds of a day school for handicapped children and within a few minutes walk of the hospital. The Vranch House Centre in Exeter and the Balvicar Centre in Glasgow are also co-operatively run assessment centres located outside hospitals. A Family Services and Assessment Centre was established by the Spastics Society in London some two years ago.

In the evidence submitted to the Working Party by the London Boroughs Association Working Group details were given of two assessment and treatment centres staffed with multi-disciplinary teams of regional hospital consultants and local authority staff which had been set up by the London Borough of Hounslow in 1956. They were housed in purpose-built premises in the grounds of large day schools for physically and multi-handicapped children. The experience and expertise accumulated during the past 13 years had "shown the value of such multi-disciplinary teams and the possibility of considerable research in such a milieu with immediate feed-back into the educational, medical and psycho-social care of these children. For these reasons the Working Group considered that the advantages and disadvantages of the assessment units and associated special schools in Hounslow and their system of early detection should be investigated further and described fully to ascertain whether such units with their educational bias have enriched the care and feed-back of knowledge . . . A further advantage may be added. When professional staff from a range of disciplines constantly work together, they come to understand each other's distinctive approach. They soon appreciate what each one can contribute towards the total assessment and treatment, and equally important they get to know the limitations of the various skills available. If they are accustomed to working in the situation where education and treatment are taking place they are less likely to make unrealistic or impracticable recommendations, and they are more likely to apply practicable ones with understanding and imagination than if they are working in a hospital remote from the community in which the children live."

A middle position is occupied by Dr Mary Sheridan (1965) "The most exhaustive medical examination may, however, still leave the diagnosis uncertain, so that a period of observation is required either as a hospital in-patient or in some form of day care . . . In future, there must also be an extension of day hospital care for the same purpose. Nevertheless, many existing facilities such as day nurseries, clinics and special care centres, could be used for diagnostic observation to better purpose than at present, if there were improved relations and co-ordination of responsibilities between hospital and local authority services. What is needed is a convenient place where the handicapped child may remain for several hours daily, sometimes with and some times without his mother. The place and the staff whom he meets there would soon become part of his familiar existence . . . The administration and staffing of such special observation units might raise difficulties for hospital boards which have little experience in running day nurseries or special schools for young children, and such centres, even if geographically situated within the curtilage of the hospital unit, might preferably be administered as part of the local health and education services. In this way, a constant interchange of information and opinion between hospital consultants, local authority medical officers, educational experts, ward sisters, nursery matrons, health visitors, and social workers could be naturally and informally maintained. . ."

The value of local community based assessment centres was also stressed by a working group of the World Health Organisation (1967). Several reasons for this view are cited including the fact that "since part of assessment consists in observing the response of the child to general care, it may be convenient and useful to combine assessment and care services in one building. Indeed, such a combination of functions may make it financially possible to erect a centre for that purpose."

The "one man team"

Too often a diagnostic examination, carried out by one specialist, is still accepted as the basis for action as well as for providing a classificatory label for a handicapped child. Even for an apparently uncomplicated, single disability such a procedure is inadequate: the child's personal and health history and his emotional and social development must be known prior to planning his future; further sensory disability should be sought for; family relationships and material circumstances, such as level of income, or suitability of housing, must be explored; and the school environment, and, where appropriate, the child's educational level, must be taken into consideration in deciding how best to provide for his needs. Care must be taken to avoid the initial examination becoming a self-fulfilling prophecy. Moreover, development and growth may in fact change a child's needs, as may also a change in family structure or environmental circumstances.

Diagnostic facilities

The idea of comprehensive assessment is gaining ground so that for example, some ophthalmologists refer children for a paediatric examination. However, a co-ordinated approach is not as yet accepted among specialists as widely as it needs to be. "Whilst it is true that notable, isolated examples can be cited of unified arrangements locally for diagnosis, assessment, treatment and education of handicapped children, in general progress towards achievement of an integrated service has been meagre. In the meantime, ominous signs have appeared of sectional interests tending to perpetuate the present state of inco-ordination" (Whitmore 1969).

At present, there are different types of diagnostic facilities for different groups of children. Referral to one or other of these is decided upon largely on the basis of the presenting symptoms or the availability of a particular service. Hence physically handicapped children are examined in assessment centres or diagnostic units which are usually in hospitals; the emotionally disturbed are referred to child guidance clinics or to psychiatric units; the socially handicapped or delinquent or those found by a court to be in need of care or control, are usually assessed in reception or classifying centres; and the educationally or mentally backward are seen by the school psychological or the school health service or in assessment/diagnostic units of the local education authority. A recent survey showed that 39 per cent of local education authorities had already established some 90 such assessment/diagnostic units and a further 20 per cent were in the process of setting up a further 94 (Brennan and Herbert, 1969).

There is a severe shortage of all these diagnostic facilities, and very considerable variation not only in quantity and quality, but also geographically. Even where they exist, they cannot always be completely staffed because of the acute shortage of the required specialist manpower. In consequence, there are often waiting lists – except for children before the juvenile courts – the longest tending to be for a first examination in a child guidance clinic where the delay is not infrequently a matter of months rather than weeks.

Consequences of the present situation
The fallacy of the simple, single handicap
It should now be recognised that the simple, single handicap is rare, if it ever existed. For one thing, unless diagnosed and treated early, even minor physical disabilities may become complicated by secondary or educational difficulties. For another, in a society which sets great store on "normality", the deviant child and his family need much support to face and cope with the fact of his being different. Thirdly, there are often consequential handicaps; for example, profound deafness inevitably affects speech and language development while

barriers of communication set up social difficulties. Fourthly, although advances in medical knowledge are having the effect of drastically reducing or even entirely eliminating certain defects, they nevertheless enable a greater number of severely damaged children with multiple defects, such as those with spina bifida, to survive.

The fallacy of labels
The labels used for children with special disabilities are in many cases rather meaningless. They depend in some measure on the agency by which these difficulties have first been diagnosed; and this in turn may depend more on chance, social class and presenting symptoms than on the child's actual needs. Recommendations made are also influenced by the availability of specialist services and provision.

To give a concrete example: a 12 year old boy with an IQ of 85, a reading age of 8 years, given to occasional bouts of hay fever, who is truanting from school and has been stealing food when hungry, might get labelled educationally sub-normal, delicate, emotionally maladjusted, in need of supervision, or requiring care or control. This may be because his problem has been taken up by his teacher, the school medical officer, the family doctor, a child care officer or the police. Hence, recommendations for treatment would be made respectively by a school medical officer, a psychologist, a psychiatrist, a social worker or a juvenile court magistrate, or a combination of these. In consequence, the boy might find himself either remaining at home, or in a residential setting of some kind or another; for his education he may go to a school for the educationally subnormal, or to one for the delicate or for the maladjusted.

Partially diagnosed needs
Research confirms that different handicapping conditions are often found together: physically handicapped children frequently show difficulties in emotional adjustment; the cerebral palsied often have sensory and intellectual defects; among juvenile delinquents, there is a high incidence of educational (and to a lesser extent physical) disabilities; many maladjusted children also have learning difficulties; among the socially and culturally deprived, educational, emotional and physical handicaps are by no means infrequent concomitants and parental rejection may also play a part. Yet often diagnosis is made of one handicap only.

To give an illustration: a recent survey in a large Children's Department* revealed that among the children in residential care who were already suffering the handicap of separation from home, some 20% suffered also from one or more other handicaps, as diagnosed by the relevant specialist. Furthermore, in over 25% of these cases it appeared that admission to care would have been unnecessary had there been adequate special educational, psychiatric and social casework provision to cater for these handicaps as well as supportive services for the family. Their lack had led to the imposition of the further handicap, removal from home or "parentectomy", and its attendant risk of institutionalisation.

Two brief case histories will show the kind of situation which is probably more common the further north one moves from the Home Counties where provision tends to be quantitatively most favourable.**
"In July 1967, 12 year old Barry was placed under the supervision of a probation officer because of his failure to attend school. The children's department first became involved in June of the following year when he was brought back before the court because of continued poor attendance. After a period in care for assessment he was allowed to return home on a promise by both mother and boy that attendance would improve.

This promise was not kept and so the child was again brought before the court in October, 1968; proceedings were adjourned for four weeks, again on the promise of improvement. There was no change however, so that in November the boy was placed in care for a further period of assessment. The results led the magistrates to send the city's education department a recommendation that Barry would benefit from attending a special school for the maladjusted. He was then examined by a psychiatrist who confirmed that the boy was unable to benefit from education in an ordinary school, but added that he also needed special educational help as he was backward, both intellectually and educationally.

Since no place could be found for him, a school medical officer recommended that he be given a trial in a residential open-air school

* Personal communication from Mr J. B. Chaplin, Children's Officer, City of Birmingham.
** Provided by 2 Children's Officers, one in the north and one in the west of the country.

in the hope that later on a more appropriate placement could be obtained. In view of the recommendation the court made a further interim order in the hope that a vacancy could be found for him. In January, 1969, the chief education officer reported that no vacancy could be found and there was little hope in the foreseeable future.

Therefore at the end of the month Barry was committed to care. He was accommodated in one of the children's department's reception centres where he remained for eight months until he was transferred to a residential special school at the age of 14 years."

The second case is a girl from a middle class home. "The mother has a most attractive home and is very conscious of appearances. They have two older children and the mother is very rejecting of Susan who is a mongol. As Susan neared five they became much more conscious of her handicap. The child went to a diagnostic unit and was diagnosed as sub-normal and not suitable for education at school. Arrangements were made for her to attend a junior training centre, but the mother on the score that she could not give her the skilled care required refuses to have her at home. Fostering was attempted and succeeded for a time, but since early 1966 she has lived in a children's home and attends the training centre daily. She has made great progress, has begun to learn to read, can write and physically look after herself, and even make her own bed.

Her family have now been persuaded to have her home for a day or two each holidays and the child care officer is working to try and make the parents more accepting and less ashamed of her. She gets on very well in the children's home and though there are worries about the future as she becomes adolescent, the arrangements made in all the circumstances appear to be in the child's best interests."

The first consequence then of a fragmentary approach or the lack of suitable provision, is not only a worsening of the potentially handicapping condition over time, but possibly also the infliction of additional handicaps.

Assessment away from home
A comprehensive approach would also serve to overcome the difficulty that, except in large urban areas, the number of children with any specific handicap is insufficient to justify diagnostic centres in every locality. Hence some children are referred for assessment to residential

units a long way from home. Yet the child is unlikely to "be himself" in strange surroundings because removal from home is unsettling at best and a traumatic experience at worst. Whether he copes and behaves better or worse than usual is immaterial in this context; the crucial point is that he will show an atypical pattern of adjustment which may lead to inappropriate recommendations. This then is a second consequence of present conditions. Of course, in some cases a period of observation away from home may shed additional light on a child's needs and thus complement the initial assessment carried out while he remained with his family.

The once-and-for-all diagnosis
While as yet too few receive a comprehensive diagnostic examination, even where this is available, there is a danger that decisions may be made in isolation and may remain ineffective because no one person is responsible for co-ordinating the various tests and specialist findings and of ensuring that they are fed back to all concerned, including teachers and parents, in such a way that they become fully aware of the practical implications. Decisions are too often made in isolation and their implementation may remain a hope deferred rather than one person's responsibility. Moreover, there is a tendency for a diagnosis to be regarded as an event complete in itself, instead of as part of a continuing long-term process. It is suggested that a comprehensive approach such as is outlined in what follows would materially diminish these problems.

Suggestions for a basic, minimal and common assessment and recording procedure

The focus
This must be on the all-round needs of the child and his family which will include the particular medical or other conditions from which he is suffering. Furthermore, as much if not more emphasis needs to be given to the child's assets, as to his defects or deficiencies. There is a tendency for the diagnostic procedure to be over concerned with descriptive labels. Instead it should focus on how to prevent a defect or deficiency from becoming a handicap or disability. The primary aim must be to develop a detailed and comprehensive programme for the care, management, education and treatment of the child – to be carried out by parents, teachers, social workers and doctors.

Categories of special needs

Some categorisation may be necessary but its limitations should be borne in mind. On the one hand, it has to be recognised that it is difficult to plan provision without knowing the approximate number of children who need to be catered for; on the other hand, there is a danger that a label becomes fixed to a child as if it described him (or the required schooling) rather than his needs.

The time has come to re-examine the definitions and categories of handicap currently employed for school children which have been in existence since the Handicapped Pupils and School Health Regulations 1945 with only minor amendments. For example, "visually handicapped" might be preferable to the present descriptions of either "blind" or "partially sighted".* Also, certain types of disability which have come to be more clearly recognised since then, such as autism, do not readily fit into these categories; nor are they entirely suitable for the pre-school child. This is further discussed in chapter 9.

If a new categorisation is to be attempted, it should be done in functional terms rather than be based on the absence or limitation of abilities. A fivefold classification of conditions might prove suitable and adequate to describe the areas or aspects whose functioning is affected. These handicapping conditions may, of course, occur in combination. They are: *1*. intellectual; *2*. physical; *3*. sensory; *4*. emotional/social; and *5*. environmental conditions. Sub-divisions may also be necessary within each of these; for example, environmental conditions encompass five not mutually exclusive groups: *i*. the socially and culturally under-privileged; *ii*. families where personal relationships are impaired to some degree or where there is some emotional neglect; *iii*. families afflicted by serious or irreversible physical or mental illness, or by a disabling handicap; *iv*. the child who has one parent only, be it because of illegitimacy, divorce, desertion or death; and *v*. families stricken by sudden and disrupting crises.

Categorisation tends at present to be rather narrowly clinical, with attention focused on pathology, though whether the abolition of all categories is too extreme a step is debatable. Terms such as primary, secondary, consequential and multi-handicap need definition. The

* No doubt the Committee of Enquiry into the Education of the Visually Handicapped set up by the Department of Education and Science will consider this issue.

advisability of distinguishing between adverse conditions – whether genetically or environmentally determined – and their functional consequences in everyday life should be explored. It might clarify the situation if defect and deficiency were used for the former, and handicap or disability for the latter.

The label "maladjustment" has acquired increasing currency and decreasing precision. A redefinition is both timely and urgent. alternatively, the term might be dropped altogether in favour of an emotionally less loaded and psychologically more accurate description, which is free of any value judgment. Perhaps "emotional handicap", or "emotional disability", might meet the case? This is discussed in greater detail in chapter 9.

There is also a need to disentangle the misunderstandings which have grown around the term "ascertainment". It has acquired a semi-legal connotation while its formal implementation (represented by completing documents such as Form 2HP) has widely fallen into disuse. And few will mourn the demise of this procedure. Again, this is more fully considered in chapter 9.

The rationale for comprehensive assessment
The various diagnostic services and the methods used by them rest broadly speaking on a common rationale. The basic team of specialists is identical (or should be): a consultant paediatrician, a social worker and an educational psychologist; but in the foreseeable future it is more likely that it would consist of a doctor, an educationist and a social worker. This team then needs to be supplemented, according to the features of a particular case, by other specialists, such as a speech therapist, a teacher of the blind, a neurologist or audiometrician, to mention just a few. The family doctor, who should know the child well, should always be involved.

The emphasis would be on the varied, developmental needs of the growing child, rather than on specific symptoms or on the reasons for which he had initially been referred. Every aspect of his development would be considered, viewed not in isolation but within the family, the community and the school setting, *ie* an assessment of the "whole child."

Special attention needs to be paid to certain critical periods in a child's life: from 0–2 years, the time of the earliest learning; and the following 3 years during which period more learning will take place than during any other comparable span of time. Then there are three vital transition periods, namely starting school, changing from the primary to the secondary stage of education and, lastly, leaving school for further training or for (if possible) employment.

The assessment procedure
Ideally, a basic, multi-disciplinary assessment should be carried out as a preventive measure as soon as it is suspected that the child may have some serious disability be this a sensory, physical, emotional or intellectual defect; in the majority of sensory and physical handicaps this is likely to be during the pre-school stage. The earlier treatment, training and education are started, the more likely it is that the child will be enabled to reach his full potential; the later compensatory and remedial measures are introduced, the more difficult it becomes to undo the effects of previous discouragement and failure. The information to be obtained on this first occasion would be confined to the essential minimum on which future action can be planned, further necessary examinations be decided upon, and later reassessments and follow-ups be carried out.

From the outset, the parents must be accepted as active partners in both the diagnostic and treatment procedures, be these medical, educational or social. This means giving practical recognition to the fact, rather than paying lip-service to it as happens too often now, that both accurate .assessment and successful treatment depend on the extent to which parents can be enabled, or are allowed and encouraged, to play a part. They will have to be taken into the specialist's confidence and be made to feel that their intimate knowledge (as well as their care of the child) is an invaluable contribution to a full assessment of the extent and future implications of his deficiencies (and assets). The less educated and articulate may need special help and guidance; but the number of "difficult" because anxious, bewildered or rejecting parents is likely to be drastically reduced by allowing them to play a constructive and positive role in assessment and continued action. However, there will be a small proportion of parents whose ability to become active partners in treatment will remain extremely limited. This in no way detracts from the need to involve them as much as is possible and to provide appropriate casework support.

At the present time, however, many defects, especially in the emotional and intellectual sphere, come to light only when the child goes to school. By that time he may have had one or more "one-man-team" examinations. In practice, therefore, it will be necessary to ensure at the time of the first, basic multi-disciplinary assessment that the data are gathered together from all previous occasions, including the medical history from the family doctor, any previous home assessment and available school reports to supplement the up-to-date ones specially obtained for this occasion. In this way a baseline will be established for future decision and action. Parents, conditioned to minimal participation, may, to begin with, need help in playing their new role.

The needs of children who become handicapped later in life, as a result of accidents, illness, gross parental mishandling or severely adverse environmental conditions, must also be kept in mind by doctors, teachers and social workers. In all such cases a comprehensive assessment is advisable.

In summary, comprehensive assessment and re-assessment should include not only the child's developmental progress in all fields but also review the family and social situation. The basic initial, multidisciplinary assessment will serve as a bridge between community services on the one hand and highly specialised, probably hospital based diagnostic units on the other, for those children for whom both are needed.

It will be comprehensive in the following five ways:

i. the focus will be on the whole child in his total environment, *ie* family, school and community;

ii. there will always be a general examination of the child's physical, educational/psychological, environmental and family conditions;

iii. all handicapping conditions will be covered, *ie* sensory, physical, intellectual, emotional;

iv. the whole age range from 0–18 years will be included;

v. recommendations will relate to care, management, education and treatment.

This then is the ideal assessment procedure which would follow on or lead to the detection of handicaps. It is, however, unrealistic to recommend that this be implemented immediately for all cases because of the extreme shortage of trained personnel. Nonetheless there is no doubt in our mind that it must be put into operation as soon as possible. It will be found to result in economies in the long run because handicaps undiagnosed or misdiagnosed in childhood and not adequately treated result in greater expenditure later in terms of human suffering and in financial and social terms too.

Implementation would, however, in all probability have to be in three stages because of the number of children likely to be involved. If such comprehensive diagnostic and assessment facilities "were confined to those children with more than one handicap, the total number in this country requiring such facilities would still amount to some half a million children" (Whitmore, 1969).

Exact figures are not at present available but the most reliable estimates so far suggest that at least 13%–15% of the child population will need special help for intellectual, physical, educational or social difficulties (Pringle, Butler and Davie, 1966; Packman and Power, 1968).

At the initial stage, we recommend two steps which could be taken now and at very little additional cost. First, as many as possible of the present different types of assessment units and centres should be combined into comprehensive assessment centres, ie reception, remand and classifying centres; school psychological services; diagnostic units of local authorities; and possibly also child guidance clinics. This would mean that practically every area would have at least one fairly accessible assessment centre. The constituent units would continue their previous work but begin to co-ordinate their procedures in co-operation with the social services department. A worker from that department should be permanently seconded to the centre to ensure that environmental and family circumstances would be taken into consideration in every case.

The second step that should be taken now is to provide a baseline for the future functions of assessment centres by building up an overall picture of local need. To this end, every child for whom any special educational, medical or social measures or treatment is provided or who has been identified as possibly having special needs, would be notified to the assessment centre to be placed into one of the two sections of a "special care register"; one section would contain children "at risk" or needing observation, the other would have the names of those diagnosed as handicapped. Minimal information only would be required at this stage. In addition to the name, address and date of birth, the reason for observation or the handicapping condition together with any recommendation made or action taken would be reported. For example, a hospital might notify a baby which is limb deficient, or one who has a hare lip and cleft palate, needing surgical interventions; the children's department a child who has been received into care for more than a week; the welfare department a child whose parents are both deaf; the general practitioner a pre-school child who is epileptic or showing severe behaviour disorders; the school a pupil who is being placed in a special class because of learning or behaviour difficulties or who is truanting; the school medical officer a child who is being recommended for speech therapy or for placement in a special school. If the assessment centre were to be informed not only of a recommendation but also when it is implemented, it would accumulate the knowledge necessary for planning local provision, in terms of staff, premises and specialised facilities of all kinds. In return, every depart—ment of the local authority which may be concerned with a family who has a handicapped child, would be notified by the assessment centre of the first and subsequent contacts.

In the second stage the following development is desirable. A follow-up enquiry should be made into the current progress and adjustment of every child listed in the two sections of the register; in the case of pre-school children and those over the age of 13 years, this would be done annually; in the case of all others every two years because the years "in between" are not quite so crucial for eventual "outcome". If the information returned indicated either that there had been little progress or that the particular condition had grown worse, then a comprehensive assessment as described earlier would be arranged in the centre. Following it, there would be the same annual or bi-annual review of progress as suggested above so that a re-assessment could be undertaken whenever necessary. There would, of course, always be feed back by the assessment centre to all concerned.

From such a review procedure several advantages would accrue. First, it would be an incentive for observing and recording a child's progress and response to treatment in the knowledge that the information would be used, and indeed demanded, for the review procedure. Secondly, parents, teachers or for that matter anyone else, not satisfied with the treatment – be it medical, social or educational – which is being given, would be reassured by the knowledge that its efficacy would regularly come under scrutiny. Thirdly, it should hasten the day when no handicapped child remains in a hospital, school, special class or in his own home making little or no progress without at least a regular reconsideration of the position. Of course, this is not to deny that there will probably always be some children so severely physically or mentally handicapped, that only minimal change can take place in their condition.

In the third stage, the goal would be an initial comprehensive assessment for every child where a handicapping condition is suspected as well as an annual review procedure for every case on the observation and handicapped register.

Record keeping and registers of children with special needs
For detection, screening and assessment to become a co-ordinated, continuous and comprehensive process, it is essential to make methods of record keeping more effective. Currently, they tend to be highly individualistic if not idiosyncratic; yet every doctor, teacher and social worker has to keep records of sorts. Busy practitioners will continue to be impatient with "all that paperwork" so long as "much that is already collected is stored undisturbed by human thought" (Peterson *et al*, 1967). Once it is seen that records are used to gain further knowledge and to improve practice, time would more readily be given to them.

The key issues are simplicity; availability; and confidentiality. Simplicity means rationalisation so that records are both easily kept and easily understood by all concerned. Availability implies that they are kept somewhere accessible to all who will need to consult them or else that duplicates are readily available; remembering, however, that the more duplicates there are, the more difficult it is to ensure that each is kept up to date. Confidentiality – where it is really essential between different professional groups – could be maintained by the professional worker concerned keeping a separate note of facts which must not be divulged. For example, a strong case can be made for not recording a child's actual IQ but only whether he is intellectually handicapped, of normal or above average intelligence, together with the name of the test and the date when it was administered. Under appropriate circumstances the details of the child's performance would be communicated.

What is suggested then is that a national record card be designed to contain all the findings of the basic, initial assessment; the child's family relationships and home circumstances; his physical condition; and his psychological (ie emotional, social, intellectual and educational) characteristics. Of course, every local authority and indeed every assessment centre would be free to record as much additional information as they judged to be necessary over and above the agreed "national minimum". The record card would be available to the family doctor, the health authority, the school, the social services department and the hospital. Its design would make it suitable for all ages, from birth to eighteen years, and it would be completed for any child found to have a handicapping condition or where, following detection and a first screening, the suspicion persists that such a condition may develop. It might be convenient to have two differently coloured cards, one indicating that further observation is required, the other that one or more handicapping conditions are present.

We concluded that – whatever the type of recording decided upon – the full record card should be kept at and by the assessment centre; it would also be responsible for entering any new information and for initiating further or follow-up examinations as recommended.

Such comprehensive records would also provide the necessary information for a register of children with special needs in a locality or region. It need only contain basic information, such as dates of interviews, where and by whom the child and family were seen, what action, if any, was taken, and what recommendations were made. Copies of this register would be kept by the health, education and social services departments, as well as in the assessment centre. If our proposal is accepted that the social services department be responsible for the continuity of care for all handicapped children and their families, then it would seem sensible to make it also responsible for seeing that other departments and the assessment centre have copies of any relevant additional information; the administrative mechanism for this might well be through the social worker seconded from the social services department to the assessment centre. A register of this kind would have three aims:

  i. to keep under review the changing needs of the individual child and his family;
 ii. to monitor the adequacy of local and regional assessment and treatment facilities in the light of changing trends;
iii. to provide comparative figures on the incidence of handicaps and provision on a national scale.

It seems preferable to us to have one register of children with special needs, incorporating the differently coloured cards, rather than keeping two separate registers, one for observation and one for the handicapped. It would provide essential information for regional planning boards and for this and other reasons the keeping of such registers should be obligatory on local authorities. Also it should be their duty to make annual returns to a central government department which in turn should publish them annually.

The case of each child on the register should be reviewed biannually and eventually once a year, the nature of this review to depend on the particular circumstances of the individual concerned. The keeping of the register would be intimately linked with continuous assessment and treatment, be this medical, educational or social.

As long as treatment facilities remain seriously inadequate, there is the risk of children not being put forward for assessment. When little is likely to happen other than perhaps a confirmation of what has been suspected, it appears to be a waste of time to go through a referral procedure, however simple, It will be necessary to counter the very natural discouragement of the teacher or general practitioner by bringing it home that putting a child forward for assessment and getting it placed on the register is bound to have a positive effect in the long run by providing definite evidence of unmet "need"; so long as this is difficult to prove, provision is bound to lag behind. Thus referral is a constructive action: even if it fails to obtain appropriate treatment for the individual child in question, it will hasten the day when such provision becomes available for other similarly affected children.

An objection to such a register is that it may stigmatise a child for life. In fact, the opposite ought to be the case: it should be the means for ensuring that appropriate care, treatment, education, training and employment are available at the earliest possible time. Just as it would be simple to move the child from the observation to the handicapped register, and vice versa, so it should be quite simple to remove his record card from the current to closed cases, once there is no further need to keep an eye on his development.

Location, staffing and premises of assessment centres

Location

Hospital or community based? The Working Party agreed that the hospital outpatient department is not the best place for an assessment centre, notwithstanding the Sheldon Report (Ministry of Health, 1967). For very young babies one might make a case for it to be sited within easy reach of a hospital, because for a minority a wide range of expertise may need to be readily available. As the child gets older, and the nature and degree of the handicap begin to be clarified, there is an increasing shift of emphasis towards educational needs, which makes a community setting more appropriate. Moreover, irrespective of age, the personal social services are important.

Indeed, most of us felt that the advantage lies with comprehensive assessment being community rather than hospital based. Three arguments in particular point in this direction. First, only a minority of all handicapped children is likely to require the highly sophisticated methods of medical examination such as can only be carried out within a hospital setting; secondly, educational, psychological or social expertise is not readily available in hospital nor can continuity of family support be realistically ensured unless it is community based; thirdly, many people react with apprehension if not fear, to hospitals because they are associated with physical pain and disease whereas many defects, particularly in the mental sphere, involve neither.

A variety of actual places was thought to be desirable because the idea of a central location is relatively new and there is thus much room for experiment. Infant welfare and child health centres, reception homes, schools and health centres are among existing premises which may prove suitable. Some sessions should be arranged in places and at times acceptable to adolescents. Wherever the location, it was urged that in addition to providing a service, assessment centres should include in their function both teaching and research.

Local, regional and national centres. Local assessment and treatment centres are needed to deal with all cases not requiring more complex procedures only available regionally; they would have firm roots in, and close continuing contact with all treatment and educational facilities available in the locality. Because many handicaps are multiple, it is essential that both regional and local centres should deal with all types of handicap.

Regional centres need to be easily accessible and should fulfil four purposes; to do so adequately, they would require residential facilities for some children and their families:

   i. To undertake the assessment of complex cases which need sophisticated equipment and skilled staff with special training and experience.

  ii. To link assessment with both short and longer term observation, experimental education and training in order to give advice both to the parent and to the education services on how to maximise the child's assets and minimise his deficiencies. The practice adopted by the Spastics Assessment Centre, and the Tavistock Institute of Human Relations, whereby local social workers accompany the family seems commendable; if medical practitioners were also to do so, at least in some cases, it would be a further improvement. This would be a practical means of keeping the regional centre in close touch with what is actually available locally, as well as enabling them to press for more treatment provision where its absence makes nonsense of available assessment procedures and resulting recommendations. It is hoped that such close liaison will ultimately develop at the Paul Sandifer Day Centre at the Hospital for Sick Children, Great Ormond Street, London, where, in conjunction with full investigation and treatment of physically handicapped children and help to their mothers, efforts are being made to build up contacts with the medical officers from the catchment areas.

 iii. To provide teaching for the various professional workers.

  iv. To carry out research.

There would seem to be very serious limitations to having national centres. Inevitably contact with facilities and procedures at regional and local level cannot be close, and often attendance at a national centre would involve the family in a long journey. "The value of assessment centres is undoubted but their usefulness to the individual child varies inversely with the distance between the child's home and the centre" (World Health Organisation, 1967). The emphasis should therefore be on regional and local centres. A national centre might be seen as a last "appeal" court or as the most high-powered assessment device for the most complex and difficult cases.

Staffing of assessment centres

The shortage of every type of trained professional staff means that even existing assessment facilities are not always working at full strength. Some pooling and integration of available resources would mark a real step forward. In addition to using scarce resources more effectively, there would be a number of additional advantages: specialists would widen their range of interests and experience; a more comprehensive and at the same time more comparable pattern of diagnosis and prognosis might be evolved; while many smaller authorities, who cannot establish every type of assessment facility, would be enabled to set up at least one comprehensive, multi-disciplinary unit.

It would be very desirable that every assessment centre should have at least one professional, full-time staff member. Otherwise it would be very difficult to ensure co-ordination, continuity, adequate feed-back and all the other "bridging activities" which assessment centres ought to undertake. There might be advantages if, in addition to being trained in one of the "helping" professions and participating in the work of one or more diagnostic teams, the full-time worker accepted the task of co-ordinator, "link-man and interpreter": he would be responsible for ensuring that records are complete; that they are passed on, suitably edited when necessary; that children are recalled according to past decisions or because of unexpected developments; and that the parents understand the findings and recommendations as well as their own part in the education and treatment of their handicapped child. It may well be that this kind of task should not be undertaken for longer than 5 to 7 years when a resumption of the earlier professional role would be advisable for at least a period of time. The social worker seconded from the social services department might be the most suitable person or the director of the assessment centre, be he a paediatrician, psychologist or social worker. Of course, the parents would be quite free to discuss their child with any member of the assessment team.

The other members of the basic professional team might well work on a sessional rather than a full-time basis and be drawn from different sources. Thus general practitioners as well as child health or hospital-based doctors, with a special interest in the handicapped, will increasingly be attracted to this work. It must be clearly understood that the efficient practice of these skills requires substantial training in developmental paediatrics which must include the development of community minded attitudes and a willingness to search out need rather than wait for demand to be expressed. The medical examination would include a paediatric investigation and assessment of neurological function, motor ability and skills; visual and auditory function; and psychiatric screening.

The psychologist might be attached to a child guidance clinic, school psychological service or also be hospital-based. He would carry out a basic developmental screening, including emotional, social and language development as well as scholastic attainments. The social worker's main affiliation would be to the social services department. Her task would be to gather information in order to assess the child's personal, family and environmental background; and either the assessment centre or the social services department (preferably the former) would be responsible for working out and acting upon a regular review procedure by gathering written reports. Ongoing casework support to the family would be the responsibility of the social services department.

Multidisciplinary case conferences under the leadership of the responsible consultant whether medical, psychological, educational or social, to which all are expected to contribute, would serve not only to define the role of each worker in a comprehensive assessment scheme, and to promote respect for each others skills, but also provide probably the best kind of in-service training. Such conferences increase the general pool of knowledge and help towards a better understanding of the child's disabilities and assets which the piece-meal approach commonly fails to achieve. It is also an essential preliminary in some cases to the setting up of remedial and treatment services to meet individual needs.

Premises
Unless purpose-built units become available, existing premises, such

as schools, school health clinics, reception centres or premises adjacent to district hospitals, might well be used. The idea of mobile "caravan units" also deserves consideration, particularly in rural areas. Once specially planned buildings are contemplated, they should be designed to meet a number of practical needs. Even the basic and minimal assessment may be impossible to achieve at one or two interviews, and require a period of skilled observation. For this purpose play and work rooms for children of different ages will need to be provided. In most cases assessment is more satisfactory if the child can remain in his familiar surroundings; for a minority residential facilities will be needed, including accommodation for the mothers where pre-school and young children are concerned. Supervised play facilities are also required for young siblings, who may have to accompany the mother; otherwise talking frankly to the various specialists may either be inhibited as well as constantly interrupted, or else things will have to be said which are not appropriate for young ears.

One interesting model is provided by the Katharine Elliot School in Shropshire. Opened in 1964, it is financed jointly by a local authority and two trusts. Here, in purpose-built premises, an assessment and observation centre functions within the premises of a day school. Initially only pre-school children were catered for but now the upper age limit has been extended to 11 years. A wide range of sensory, physical and mental defects are included for assessment, treatment and education, and there is close co-ordination and co-operation between the local authority services, the hospital, voluntary agencies and the community at large. (For a description see chapter 8 in *Caring for Children*, Pringle 1969.)

If the costs of providing assessment centres were borne jointly by the committees of local authorities chiefly responsible for children, the burden on any one would be less onerous. The proposed children's regional planning committees set up under the Children and Young Persons Act, 1969, to plan a range of community homes could well be used to undertake this task too, though unfortunately this would probably not be possible under present legislation. It must be accepted that because assessment requires highly trained staff, and good physical facilities, it can never be anything but costly. However, inappropriate treatment, resulting from inadequate assessment, is bound to be even more expensive in the long run.

Early, comprehensive and continuous assessment

When? How? By whom? How often? These are questions which can only be answered in specific terms for specific children. But in general, assessment is at present too often characterised by delay, duplication and departmentalisation; and it happens too late – the pre-school years are the most vital ones. Too many people, on separate occasions and in separate places, may see the same children and the same families, giving similar tests and asking similar questions, while other children completely slip through the net. The current introduction of developmental screening in child health settings is a move in the right direction.

Every handicapped child should if not annually at least periodically be looked at as a growing individual whose special problems deserve continuing special attention "in the round". Of course, this does not mean that every possible physical, psychological, educational and social investigation needs to be carried out in every case but all these dimensions must be taken into account during the initial assessment. An exhaustive assessment will be necessary, however, in some cases but the proportion is likely to be small.

"Co-operation, co-ordination and communication are all essential" (Wigglesworth, 1969). As long as assessment is everyone's and no-one's responsibility, early detection, appropriate treatment and renewed intervention will remain a hit-and-miss affair where those with the least ability to help themselves will suffer the most. If the same basic information were to be available about all children with special needs be these medical, educational or social, it might hasten the development of an agreed minimum recording scheme, accepted by all the local government departments, hospitals and voluntary organisations concerned with children and their families. Much would be gained by some standardisation of assessment schemes and by developing a common basic recording scheme; it would also make possible the study both of failures and of those who, despite several or severe defects, win through. Being able to predict future needs is valuable; seeing prediction beaten because the child has done better than expected is invaluable.

The adoption of comprehensive and continuous registers of children with special needs would facilitate the development of an organised system of prevention, early treatment, appropriate educational guidance and social care for all children who may have special needs at one time or another of their lives. This would replace the present, at times haphazard, system of ascertainment of those requiring special attention, whether it is medical or educational treatment or social care. Yet even at best, assessment can only be a series of approximations, not certainties.

Fundamental to any planning is the premise that handicap is not a static condition but as much a developing process as growth itself. Hence, planning too must be dynamic rather than static; assessment cannot be adequately done by a "one-man-team", however eminent the specialist, but requires a core team consisting of a doctor, an educationalist and a social worker. But the most comprehensive assessment and the most adequate long-term planning are of little avail unless they are matched by treatment and supportive services which are equally adequate in quality as well as quantity.

References

BRENNAN, W. K. AND HERBERT, D. M. (1969) "A survey of assessment/diagnostic units in Britain". *Educational Research*, 12, No 1, 13–21.

CARNEGIE UNITED KINGDOM TRUST (1964) *Handicapped Children and their Families*, Dunfermline, Scotland.

MINISTRY OF HEALTH STANDING MEDICAL ADVISORY COMMITTEE (1967) – *Child Welfare Centres* – Report of a sub-committee (Chairman, Sir Wilfrid Sheldon) HMSO London.

MINISTRY OF HEALTH (1968) Memorandum to Medical Officers of Health, June 28th, 1968. Reference F/H1/2.

MITCHELL, ROSS (1969) Personal communication.

PACKMAN, J. AND POWER, M. (1968) "Children in Need and the Help they receive". Appendix Q, pp 348–356 in the *Report of the Committee on Local Authority and Allied Personal Social Services*, HMSO London.

PETERSON, O. L. *et al* (1967) "What is value for money in medical care? Experiences in England, Wales, Sweden and the USA". *Lancet, i,* 771–776.

PRINGLE, M. L. KELLMER, BUTLER, N. R. AND DAVIE, R. (1966) *11,000 Seven Year Olds.* Longman in association with the National Bureau for Co-operation in Child Care, London.

PRINGLE, M. L. KELLMER (ed), (1969) *Caring for Children*, Longman in association with the National Bureau for Co-operation in Child Care, London.

SAMPSON, O. C. (1965) "The Wide Mesh of Welfare. *The Times Educational Supplement*, 4th June.

SHERIDAN, MARY (1965) *The Handicapped Child and his Home*. National Children's Home, Highbury, London.

WHITMORE, K. (1969) "An Assessment Service for Handicapped Children". *The Medical Officer*, Vol 22, No 3199, pp 263–267.

WIGGLESWORTH, R. (1969) Personal Communication.

WORLD HEALTH ORGANISATION (1967) *Report of a Working Group on the early Detection and Treatment of Handicapping Defects in Young Children*. Regional Office for Europe, WHO, Copenhagen.

Acts and Regulations
Children and Young Persons Act, 1969.
Handicapped Pupils and School Health Regulations, 1945.

7. Personal and social needs of parents and children

"Truly a handicapped child is a handicapped family."
Mother of a 21 year old spastic girl

The child and the family

Introduction

Like all children, those with handicaps need first and foremost to be accepted and loved by their own families. But they also urgently require the appropriate treatment, therapy and education which will mitigate their disabilities and help them towards adult maturity and independence. In a sense, this is no more than we ask for normal children and therefore we would expect it to be possible for handicapped children to have basically the same place in family life as their more fortunate brothers and sisters.

However, there are various reasons why today many handicapped children are unable to live with their families. Some can only get the specialised treatment or education they need by going to residential schools or long-stay hospitals, sometimes because the strain of looking after them has proved too much for their families. There are also those who have to be offered residential care because their homes cannot provide the stable background necessary, or because their behaviour is too disturbed or delinquent to be tolerated in their own communities. A small number of children will have been totally rejected by their parents and some have been abandoned in long-stay hospitals. Where the handicapped child has become the scapegoat for family problems or where, at the other extreme, he is over-protected to the point where he cannot develop his full potential at home, he may

155

need care away from his family at any rate for a period. We discuss various aspects of residential care more fully in chapter 8.

As a general principle, it is clearly desirable that a handicapped child should lead a normal family life; the deprivation of habitual close family relationships should not be added to the burdens he already has to bear and the problems he has to face, especially in his early years. Therefore unless there are special reasons why he is better off away from home, it is preferable for all the various facilities for treatment and schooling to be within daily reach, with assistance available to support the parents. This has important implications in planning special schools for example, because from the viewpoint of the child's personal needs, the special day school catering for a number of handicaps is in general preferable to the highly specialised one dealing with a single handicap which has to be residential because pupils are drawn from a wide area.

Stress and distortion of family life
The impact of the arrival of a handicapped child on the life of a family is tremendous, sometimes overwhelming. Dr Goldie (1966) has described the experience succinctly: "There are two questions which every mother asks after her baby is born – 'Is it a boy or a girl?', a question which is usually answered with ease; and 'Is it all right?' – meaning normal. Any representative group of mothers discussing this point will tell of their tremendous relief and pleasure when the answer to this second question is 'Yes'. In the case of the handicapped child the reply is either evasive or 'No'. Therefore from this moment on the whole family, and in particular the parents, are living with a dual problem. On the one hand they are attempting to accept, love and live with their handicapped child, while at the same time they are mourning the normal child whom they had hoped for and of whom the handicapped child is a perpetual living reminder. Inevitably also, the husband and wife have to face their personal relations and explore in this context their whole relationships and the family situation. They will have to deal with both their individual and mutual disappoint-ments and their possible secret feelings of guilt, blame, chagrin and persecution. Simultaneously, they are confronted with the reactions of their immediate family and their neighbourhood in general". The shock may be no less great when a normal child becomes handicapped

by illness or accident. The onset of maladjustment or mental illness is slower and may produce different stresses.

As the parents' letters in connection with our enquiry vividly illustrate, the handicapped child's disability affects the lives of his parents and his brothers and sisters, both by presenting them with practical problems and by affecting their feelings about themselves and their relationships with others.

It is, therefore, important to consider whether and to what extent the family of a handicapped child can accept and cope with the extra stress involved. Is the pattern of life in the family too changed and distorted by having an unusual child in its midst? Do the practical and emotional burdens impose intolerable strains on the parents or on their other children? Can a single parent manage alone without the help and comfort of a spouse? In asking a particular family to accept and cope with their handicapped child, are we asking too much? Precise answers to such questions are hard to give. Dr Mary Sheridan (1965) and others have drawn attention to the emotional problems which parents face in accepting and coming to terms realistically with their child's handicap and the distress which they have to overcome. There may be "feelings of grief and mourning which are sometimes permanent, the resentment and depression which cannot always be faced . . . and the defences used in dealing with these painful feelings". (Gould, 1968). Parents' feelings of love, acceptance and protection for their handicapped child can alternate with rejection of him and anger at their predicament. At different times and stages in the child's development, these feelings will grow or recede. Some families will find it easy to accept a physically handicapped child, others can cope more readily with the child who is "slow"; but it is not always given to each family to have the handicap they can best tolerate.

The Carnegie Trust study of handicapped children (1964) suggested that there is "a different kind of balance in the family containing a handicapped child, a restructuring of attitudes and roles which has implications for all members of the family". One of the few systematic studies made of families with handicapped children provides some interesting conclusions which do not appear to bear this out. In a survey of 180 families of children with cerebral palsy living at home in the East Midlands area Hewett (1967) concluded that "on the whole parents of spastic children are self reliant and adaptable . . . by and large they appear to have reacted to adversity in a thoroughly 'normal' way. This research", it was pointed out, "has looked rather carefully for criteria which might distinguish families with handicapped children from other families with children of similar age living in the same geographical area, and has conspicuously failed to find them". Such patterns of family activity as parental outings, the father's involvement with the children, the methods of child rearing and family discipline, the jealousy of brothers and sisters were much the same as in other families and the differences which did occur were usually related to the handicap.

Another important survey made by Tizard and Grad (1961) of 250 families with mentally subnormal children living at home and in institutions showed greater evidence of stress. It was found that a third of the mothers had physical and nearly a fifth mental health problems. There was, however, no significant difference in the ill health of all members of the family whether the child was at home or in an institution. Significantly, more mothers with children living at home had good mental health compared with those whose children were in institutions, suggesting that the ability to cope with a handicapped child at home may depend on the mother's good emotional health. The study showed that 45 % of the families with mentally handicapped children living at home had limited social contacts. There was also a general lowering of material living standards, and the strain of managing the child was often considerable. Better housing, more outside day care and services to help within the home might have helped a quarter of the families with children in institutions to keep them at home. It may be significant that 100 of the surveyed families had children of over 16 years of age.

A recent pilot study of thalidomide children (Pringle and Fiddes, 1970) showed that "the incidence of stressful circumstances was high: in a quarter of the families one or both parents showed symptoms of emotional strain or there were impaired relationships between the parents, or between them and the child. Our study can offer no evidence on the extent or the degree to which the child's disability contributed to the disturbed emotional climate of the home; that it was not the main causative factor is obvious from the facts as known. The evidence suggests that the presence of a very severely disabled child in a family produces one of two diametrically opposed and extreme situations: either the parents cope admirably, indeed heroically, and the child thrives almost as well as any normal one; or the family proves unequal to the tremendous strain, the mother breaks down, the marriage flounders and the child is either wholly rejected or causes tension and dissent which is inevitably reflected in his own maladjustment."

At present there is insufficient evidence available to indicate what factors put the greatest stress on family life. It may be that physical and sensory handicaps which are susceptible to treatment are less burdensome because families' have hope that their child's disability will be mitigated. The child's age may be significant because a greater degree of dependence may be acceptable in a young child but not in an adolescent. The community's attitude to the handicap affect the family's feelings. All these factors interact with the child's own feelings about his predicament and again on his family's attitude towards him.

The association between broken or unstable family life and children's emotionally disturbed behaviour is now well documented. As adults these children may perpetuate the unstable family life and reproduce the same circumstances for the next generation. Such general evidence serves to emphasise the especial importance of a stable family background in bringing up a handicapped child and providing the circumstances which will enable him to reach maturity in a happy environment. Anything that the community can do to support and assist the family will help in their task and reduce some of the inevitable strains.

Practical supportive services for the child and the family
The handicapped child inevitably places an extra burden on the family, a burden which increases with the degree of disability. The strains are partly financial, partly physical, as the parents – and particularly the mother – have to continue to care for the handicapped child day by day with little relief.

Nevertheless, the fact that the handicapped child is a financial burden to his family seems often to be ignored. It may be that society is so anxious that the family should care for him that it accepts the parents' sacrifices without question rather than giving a higher family allowance for a handicapped child. Yet the handicap may prevent his mother going out to work as she would otherwise expect to do as her children grew older. The family may need a car to take the handicapped

G

child out because they cannot take him, and perhaps his wheelchair, on public transport. They may have to make long journeys to visit him at a residential school or hospital. His disability may require the father's presence at home and so limit his freedom to work away, to accept promotion or to enjoy his leisure.

We welcome the provision in the new National Superannuation and Social Insurance Bill of an attendance allowance of £4 a week for those who are so severely disabled physically or mentally that they need a great deal of attention. Decisions about claims will be made by an Attendance Allowance Board. The allowances may be payable to parents of handicapped children.

At present the cost of home helps is too high for the ordinary wage earner to use the service except for short periods of acute need but if we want parents to care for their handicapped children at home, then there must be generous and flexible provision of home helps, and where necessary, home nursing. Parents of incontinent children should also have either a laundry service or, when the local authority does not have one, a service from which they can obtain incontinence pads without charge.

Parents can also be helped by measures which give them temporary relief. In some parts of the country, parents' groups or voluntary organisations arrange "sitters in" so that someone with experience can provide care while the parents go out together. Such schemes could certainly be extended if there were a greater appreciation of the need.

In some areas there are pre-school play groups where handicapped children and their mothers are welcomed. Some children are too disabled or disturbed to join such a group but many others can profit from the experience and their mothers derive benefit from being accepted, and having their children accepted, in the group.

Holidays present problems to the parents of a handicapped child although they need them more perhaps than most people. The family must decide whether to go away together or whether it would be of most benefit to have a temporary separation from the handicapped member. If they all go away together, they must know where they can take a child who may be incontinent, confined to a wheelchair, have difficulty in feeding himself or be noticeably "strange". It is not easy to obtain information about holiday places suitable for parents with handicapped children. It is to be hoped that more seaside resorts and holiday camps will pay attention to this when preparing their publicity brochures.

Many parents need a holiday free from the care of the handicapped child. They want to be sure that he will be cared for and have a holiday himself. Here again flexible and imaginative provision is called for both by local services and voluntary organisations. If the child is quite young it is probably not desirable for him to go away from home and parents but it may be possible for him to remain in his own home cared for by his grandmother or other relatives while his parents have a holiday. The success of such arrangements may depend on whether the local authority can provide home help for the relative while the family are away. Or it may be possible to give the mother temporary relief by caring for him for occasional days in a children's home or hostel or with a foster mother so that when the parents want a holiday he is left in surroundings and with people already familiar to him. Arrangements of this kind can provide the holiday needed for everyone's benefit without subjecting the child to sudden separation from those who normally care for him. We discuss holidays for children at residential schools in chapter 8.

Older children may enjoy a holiday away from their parents as those without handicaps do. It may be with other handicapped or normal children. What is needed here is a social worker whose contact with the family is close enough to be able to appreciate what long summer holidays are likely to mean to both children and parents in terms of frustration and boredom as well as lack of opportunity to do things together. With an intimate knowledge of the family, plans can be made for family or separate holidays or perhaps periods of day care. Local authorities must, however, be as ready to help children and their parents during holidays periods as they are during term time.

Caring for the physically handicapped child at home can be made very much harder by unsuitable accommodation. We must prevent situations where parents in tenement buildings without lifts care for children in wheelchairs, where incontinent children are without water closets, and where blind children may have nowhere safe to play. Local housing authorities should consider it their responsibility to provide appropriate accommodation for families with handicapped children.

Planning for the disabled demands special technical knowledge, and we hope that all who have a part in erecting or adapting buildings which are or should be used by physically handicapped people, will be guided by a Report published by the Royal Institute of British Architects in 1967. Unfortunately this work, excellent though it is, gives little attention to the needs of children.

Local authorities should make full use of their present powers to make adaptations and supply aids for the disabled. We welcome the fact that these powers are now mandatory. Simple adaptations such as stair rails, ramps, wider doorways, handrails in the lavatory and bathroom can enable a handicapped child to be more independent and to be cared for at home. Parents may not know that assistance of this kind is available and the extent to which local authorities use their powers differs widely. A simple information booklet for parents of handicapped children should be available at the comprehensive assessment centres and elsewhere. The social services department with its continuing responsibility for the handicapped child should ensure in consultation with the parents that the necessary adaptations and aids are provided.

Further attention is required to the design of aids. It is encouraging to note that studies on the design of wheelchairs are now being undertaken at Loughborough College and the Royal College of Art under the sponsorship of the National Fund for Research into Crippling Diseases. Further thought also needs to be given to the design of such aids as calipers and surgical boots which change very little in spite of new materials available, and to the design of clothing for incontinent children. In all these matters there are several aspects to be considered: the article must do the job it is designed to do as cheaply and as well as possible; at the same time it should be relatively attractive, look "modern"; and clothing in particular should not single out the child too obviously from his age group. For some handicapped children, their wheelchair, hearing aid or calipers may be so indispensable as to become part of their personality and the aid's appearance may affect their relationship with others. This is commonly accepted for spectacles for which a variety of frames is available, but insufficient attention is paid to the appearance of other aids.

Advice and Support
If families of handicapped children are to cope well with their problems,

it is generally agreed that they will need a good measure of support from social workers and indeed from all professional workers concerned with the child. In the evidence submitted to the Working Party the need for more "counselling" to the family was stressed time and again. Counselling can take many forms and it is worth examining the people involved and the type of help which comes within this very broad term.

Providing information. When a child's handicap first becomes known, the immediate need of the parents is for information on the nature of the handicap and the prognosis for the future. The responsibility for providing it falls chiefly on the doctors, psychologists and other workers who have made the diagnosis.

The moment in which they learn that their child is handicapped whether at birth or by later illness or accident must be for any parents one of the watersheds of life. There is initial shock and emotional upheaval. This is a very difficult moment, too, for whoever has to tell the parents. How it is done may affect the parents' attitude to their child and to medical and social services for a long time. The information may be given in many different ways, for example, with clinical detachment, with a sense of hopelessness for family and child, or with a compassion which conveys the continuing interest and concern of the community for the parents and child without making falsely optimistic promises to them. It is obvious which is in the child's best interests.

The following is an example of good practice when a baby is born handicapped " . . . I usually ask the father whether he would like to tell his wife about the baby or whether he would prefer me to do this with him present or alone. Infinite care and sensitivity is needed to tell the mother about the handicapped baby and the reactions in the crisis situation need to be allowed for, understood and helped, and above all the feeling of guilt and self-reproach countered; also the fears of inadequacy and not being able to cope. Reassurance of support and community concern needs to be given, and follow up, assessment and care promised" (R. Wigglesworth 1967).

The amount of care taken in this matter varies enormously. In recent years there has been a notable increase in the attention paid to parents' experience of medical services, but it still seems likely, judging for example, from the parents' letters, that parents not infrequently learn of their child's handicap from someone who does not have the time, the training or the personal security to help them over the shock, or else they are given false reassurance for a long time after they themselves are uneasily aware that there is something wrong.

Initially, parents may be unable to take in very much of what they are told because of the shock they are suffering. A series of interviews may be necessary, but the aim should be to give them full and balanced information and advice. However serious this is, it is far less alarming to parents than half the information, augmented by scraps let fall by other people, which leads them to suspect that something far worse is being hidden.

A well worded letter from the doctor or other appropriate member of the assessment team which sets out clearly the report and prognosis on the child's handicap can also give families the opportunity to absorb the information at their leisure away from the stressful conditions of the consulting room.

In spite of valuable work by voluntary organisations, it is not easy for parents to obtain information in a simple but accurate form on either handicaps or the provision of services to the handicapped (including residential provision and "aids to living"). There is need for an adequate local authority information service and a comprehensive range of leaflets on handicaps. A World Health Organisation Working Group (1967) has suggested the publication of a series of parents' guides on the care of children with particular handicaps. Better still, there might be a Parent's Guide to Handicapped Children and the help available to them, somewhat similar to the *Consumer's Guide to the British Social Services* (Willmott, 1967). Such a guide would bring the information together and at the same time avoid the arbitrary separation of children who are handicapped in different ways. What services are given must depend on the circumstances of each individual case but a publication of this kind could provide a framework for parents' expectations and their thinking about their child's welfare and and future. It would also make clear what parents have a right to demand for their children and what their rights of appeal are against administrative decisions. Evidence to the Working Party in parents' letters and from voluntary organisations strongly reinforces the case for both local and national comprehensive advice and information services.

Advice on practical care and therapy. As the implications of a child's handicap are absorbed, the immediate need is for advice on practical care and management. The doctor plays an important role in giving information and advice about physical handicaps, but more will usually be needed than can be obtained from periodic visits to a hospital or clinic. The question of who is best fitted to advise depends partly on the nature of the handicap and a great deal on the training of different workers. In general, for children under five years, the health visitor is likely to be the most suitable person since she has a ready and normal access to every home, an understanding of the care of normal children, and she can call on more specialised services within the National Health Service or the local authority. Health visitors are, however, likely to need more education and training in the care of handicapped children than they receive at present, whether initially or subsequently in refresher courses. Some local authorities employ specialist health visitors for this purpose.

Some handicaps require specialised advice to parents very early. For example, parents of deaf children must be shown how to help develop speech if vital time is not to be lost in the child's education. Autistic children present special and unusual behaviour problems which are bewildering to the uninformed and inexperienced. Highly specialised help must be given to parents to assist in the management of the child and is often best given in the privacy and quiet of the home. Home teachers, physiotherapists, speech therapists, social workers and others all have a part to play in giving practical advice to parents on how to help the child. At a later stage, teachers and psychologists also have an important role in this respect. The child's likely future in the outside world will also be uppermost in the parents' minds.

Emotional problems and support. Apart from advice on practical matters, all parents need the opportunity to come to terms with their feelings towards their handicapped child and the situation in which they find themselves. There should, therefore, be the possibility of consistent social work support for families throughout the long period of childhood and adolescence.

The caseworker's importance here is as a person to whom the family can turn for information and for support at times of difficulty. She will be concerned more directly than any other professional workers with the parents' and the child's feelings about their situation and will need to be able to listen, to understand and accept them without responding defensively to their demands or losing sight of the realities of the child's needs or the community's ability to provide for him.

There is some pressure on parents of handicapped children to be impossibly "good", forever understanding, forbearing, self-sacrificing. They are expected to be able to respond to the child's needs whatever his age, to take him for appointments without much reward and without much consideration for the other demands on them. They cannot complain about their burden without feeling – and being seen by others – as "rejecting" their child. A handicapped child has seen the situation more realistically: "Parents often feel some resentment when they are faced with the fact that they have a handicapped child. Why does it have to happen to me? What has my boy done to deserve this? Of course this is a natural reaction when faced with such a big problem. The point is not that these feelings exist, but how they are allowed to develop – whether the parents bring them out between themselves, or pretend that they do not exist at all. I think the atmosphere in my home is a lot freer because my family and I can argue quite openly about our feelings" (Younis, 1966).

This freedom is probably exceptional and it is part of the social worker's task to give opportunity for the recognition and expression of feelings in safety. Some feelings are more acceptable than others, even to those professionally concerned. There is a readiness to appreciate feelings of guilt and self-reproach but it seems less easy to accept parents' anger at being singled out, burdened and restricted, an anger which is often turned on medical and social services. Similarly, the sense of grief and loss experienced by parents of handicapped children is little recognised. They can be over pressed to be active and not "give way". It is only when there can be an ongoing relationship with time to listen and to talk about more than practical problems that the sense of loss can have expression and parents may be helped to find greater pleasure in the child they have.

The immediate, overwhelming and perhaps crucial crisis is when the handicap is first diagnosed. The way in which this crisis is resolved may to a large extent determine the family's future attitude to the child, their degree of acceptance of the child's handicap and their willingness to help him. It is also of course a crisis for the child too if he is old enough to understand his situation. "Crisis intervention" theory suggests that this is the best time to help people because at that time events are more traumatic, background personality problems and previous disturbances of the parents are thrown up and the situation can be dealt with before the protective defences are raised (Wolff, 1969). Other times of crisis when help is likely to be important are when the child is 3 or 4 years of age and there is anxiety about his schooling; at the time when he goes to school or a change of school is being considered; and when he is adolescent and there are problems of employment, status in the outside world with his peers and the opposite sex, and fear for the future after the parents' death. Continuing support is particularly important for families with mentally handicapped children.

The aim of supportive social work to the family should be to provide continuing care and service. There must be comprehension of how the handicapped child interacts with every member of the family and of the other stresses with which the family is having to cope. For this type of care centred on the home, there is no doubt that the local authority social services department should provide social workers whose concern would be the family's total needs. Unified social services departments organised on the lines foreshadowed in the Local Authority Social Services Act (1970) would certainly strengthen the concept of a comprehensive service to the family. This would include both family caseworkers and specialised social workers, residential staff for a variety of institutions and others. It would be unrealistic to think that one family caseworker could supply every need of a handicapped child or his family. There are many situations when another social worker may be in a more favourable position to provide such help. For example, when a child with spina bifida has had to undergo a series of operations, a hospital medical social worker may be best able to help. Where a child is receiving psychiatric treatment, the psychiatric social worker may co-operate with the family caseworker. When a child is at a residential school, the school's social worker or counsellor should be jointly responsible with the social services department in the home area for maintaining the links between school and home. It is always important that any other social workers should work in co-operation with the family social worker. The Green Paper *National Health Service* (1970) suggests that the social work staff of the hospital authorities

168 LIVING WITH HANDICAP

might transfer to the local authorities. This would have advantages in efficiency, flexibility, career structure and continuity of social workers.

Other professional workers such as doctors, nurses, teachers and residential child care staff provide essential emotional support. Professional workers who have an understanding of the problems and who have been able to come to terms with their own feelings on the subject can give invaluable support. Much will depend on the individual family's needs. Provided the opportunities are made available, a family is likely to discover for themselves the best source of support, which may change over the years with changing circumstances.

While various professional workers at particular times or places may play the major part in helping the child or the family, the main responsibility of providing a *continuing* service should rest with the family social worker of the social services department. His job will be to maintain contact, to recognise changing needs and interpret them to other professional staff, and to call together all relevant evidence for the periodic review which forms part of our continuous and comprehensive assessment proposals. While the individual social worker will change, the social services department will always provide a readily accessible point of contact between the handicapped child and his family and the community's services.

Finally, psychiatric help should be available if necessary to the parents of handicapped children and to their brothers and sisters who may be in difficulties. The handicapped child's own adjustment to his predicament will depend a great deal upon the attitudes to him of his parents and close relations. Therefore, for his sake as well as for his family's, their good mental health is of vital importance.

The child, the parents and professional workers

Parental participation

In the comprehensive assessment procedure we advocate, the basis should be laid for sound co-operation for the child's sake between parents and professional workers. To the parents suffering from the shock and distress of realising that their child is handicapped, the effective removal of decisions about his future to professional advisers may be a further blow to their self-confidence. If the parents can be drawn into the assessment procedure the chances are far greater that they will understand and accept their child's handicap, its implications and the best available treatment. Because of this acceptance, they will be better able to co-operate fully with the decision taken and the advice given. A working party of the National Society for Mentally Handicapped Children (1967) commented that "viewing assessment as a process involving all-round co-operation would enable the parents themselves to play a valuable part. It would elicit a more positive attitude than does the present procedure. At present parents are often the passive recipients of a diagnosis from a specialist who acts in an authoritarian role. Co-operative contact with members of the team would be stimulating and helpful to the parents' own understanding."

Whether parents are invited to participate in at least some part of case conferences where assessment and discussion of a child's progress is carried out, must be a matter for decision in individual cases. Some parents would not want to take part, or would feel overwhelmed and dismayed by the clinical, objective analysis of their child's difficulties. But assessment teams should do their best to include parents who wish this. Parents' observations on everyday behaviour and on day to day management of medical problems could, if properly handled, be as useful to an assessment team as the contribution of residential child care staff at a boarding school.

Where there are active, knowledgeable parents, they are usually able to ensure the co-ordination of services themselves by pressing for further treatment facilities or fresh reviews of progress. This can also lead them to seek out further professional advice or to obtain a second opinion to which they have a right within the National Health Service. This may be greatly resented by professional workers, even though they know of cases where a faulty diagnosis or prognosis has been made. The parent who presses for reassessment or further treatment may well be actively helping to secure them for other children as well as his own. A survey of families with cerebral palsy children in the East Midlands showed that one in four of the parents had at one time sought other advice or treatment, mostly a further medical assessment or physiotherapy, but that only one in twelve had obtained more than one further opinion. (Hewett, 1967).

It would be the task of the social services department to act as an advocate for the handicapped child. It could provide help and advice to the parents in their dealings with the authorities and, where parents are inactive, follow up individual children's cases and act as a co-ordinator of services and progress chaser. As we have said in chapter 6, a full reassessment of the child would not be necessary on the occasion of every review, but the review would give everyone concerned with the child the chance to reconsider his situation and to present their ideas for his future progress.

Parents of handicapped children should have access to the periodic review which is an essential part of the continuous assessment procedure. The responsible worker of the social services department, should have the duty of getting the parents' views on their child's progress and their wishes on possible changes in treatment and care. They may wish to bring a "friend" with them if they come to discuss their child at a review conference. It should be possible by these means to safeguard every child's future, to provide parents and professional workers with a regular opportunity to reconsider and, if necessary, challenge any aspect of the work being carried out, and to co-ordinate the many contributing services in the child's best interests.

It is equally important that parents of handicapped children should have access to independent advice and information which will enable them to seek out services and to question and challenge on their child's behalf. Some voluntary societies are excellent agencies for providing this help, but not every parent has access to one. A central information and advice agency, independent of the school, social services and hospital authorities, would be an excellent service. We discuss the case for this more fully in chapter 12.

The system of appeal against administrative decisions needs to be made clear to all parents. In practice, it would appear that parents' rights to appeal against decisions of the education authority are limited and negative. They are outlined below. The Secretary of State for Social Services has set up a Hospital Advisory Service to help to improve the management of patient care and to advise him about conditions in hospitals. At present it is concentrating its attention on long-stay hospitals. Steps are also being taken to introduce more uniform and better publicised procedures for the handling of complaints about hospitals.

The most practicable way that parents have to raise a grievance is to write to their local councillor or member of parliament. The local councillor has access to the education, health and social services departments. The MP can raise an issue with the relevant Minister and prompt a letter of enquiry from the department to the local authority concerned. If necessary, he can refer to an individual case of grievance in a parliamentary question. The power of elected members, both nationally and locally, to compel reconsideration of administrative decisions is often highly effective. In the White Paper on *Reform of Local Government in England* (1970) the Government propose the appointment of about ten Local Commissioners for Administration whose function would be to investigate complaints of maladministration in local government. These complaints by individual citizens would be routed through local councillors. The Commissioner's reports would go to the local council concerned and the public would have a right to know the contents.

Lastly, there is the question of faulty professional judgment which can lead to incorrect diagnosis or treatment or placement in an unsuitable school. The comprehensive, continuous assessment which we propose should greatly reduce the risk of perpetuating errors.

The parents' legal rights
Local education authorities have a duty under sections 8 and 33 of the Education Act 1944 to provide schools sufficient in number, character and equipment "to afford for all pupils opportunities for education and offering such variety of instruction and training as may be desirable in view of their different ages and aptitudes". They must ascertain what children in their area require special educational treatment and see that it is provided "either in special schools or otherwise" and this shall take place in special schools "so far as is practicable" where the disabilities are serious, but "where that is impracticable or the disability is not serious" the education may be given in any maintained local authority school or in one assisted by them.

Parents on their side have a duty under the Act to see that their children receive "efficient full-time education", and may select the school accordingly. The education authority may appeal to the Secretary of State for a direction determining which school the child must attend. Thus if a parent wishes his child to attend a particular school,

either an ordinary or a special one, the authority may appeal to the
Secretary of State against the parent's wishes. If a parent wishes to
withdraw his child from a special school and the authority disagrees,
he has a similar right of appeal. He may also appeal to the Minister
against a certificate issued by the medical authority stating that the
child suffers from a disability and therefore requires special education.
The categorisation of children as unsuitable for education in school will
cease when the junior training centres are taken over by the local
education authorities.

Parents have rights of appeal to prevent their children from being
ascertained as handicapped or being educated in special schools, and
some right to place their children in a particular school of their choice.
But where parents feel that the education authority is not providing the
appropriate special education for their handicapped child, their rights
to get it do not appear to be strong. Suppose for example that a child
who was both deaf and physically handicapped had to travel a long
distance daily to attend a special school for the physically handicapped
where there was moreover no provision for helping to develop his
speech. Could his parents contend that the provision was inadequate?
In theory, the parents could complain to the Secretary of State or
bring an action in the courts under section 99 of the Education Act
1944 that the authority had "failed to discharge its duty" and the
Secretary of State could direct it to do so. Apparently, no parents have
ever brought an action of this character in the law courts nor has the
Secretary of State ever made a direction in this context. If parents were
to do so, the local authority could argue that it was not practicable for
the type of special schooling sought to be provided, or that what was
provided was quite adequate. This issue would be largely one of
judgment and a claim in the courts might prove difficult to sustain.
Similarly, appeal may be made to the Secretary of State under Section
68 that the authority had acted "unreasonably" in carrying out any
of its duties and the Secretary of State could direct it to act otherwise.
Again, the issue would be one of judgment as to what was "unreasonable" and would not be easy to prove.

The child's emotional development and needs

The basic needs of children for a stable home and accepting parents
are the same whether or not they are handicapped. But handicapped

children face far greater problems than normal children, and it is far harder for them to come to terms with the outside world. The stresses to which they are subject are many and may lead to psychiatric disorder. Some of these difficulties arise from obvious deprivations due to the nature of the handicap: a deaf child has to overcome feelings of isolation; a blind child has to overcome feelings of insecurity as he moves around; a spastic child has to cope with the frustrations of his clumsy, slow movements. The child handicapped after birth by illness or accident has particular problems of adaptation to his new position. Other stresses arise from the difficult situations a handicapped child has to face. Pain, discomfort, and periods in hospital are common experiences for physically handicapped children. The ridicule and scorn of normal children and inability to join in their activities have to be met. The indifference of the outside world to his problems awaits the handicapped adolescent. Moreover, the reaction of adults, including his own family, may make it unduly difficult for him to come to terms with his dilemmas and problems. It is worth examining a few of these stresses and problems to see how they could be lessened.

The early years
The child's separation from his mother is likely to cause the greatest emotional disturbance in the early years from about 6 months up to four years. Yet many physically handicapped children will have had to spend periods in hospital for treatment at this time, and have had to suffer pain and discomfort. All become aware of their imperfect bodies and wonder why they are unlike other children. During the "animistic" stage of personality development, lasting from two to seven years, the child perceives his world in magical and authoritarian terms, in which there are no impartial, natural causes for events. "Anything that happens is likely to be seen as a punishment, and, because he lives in an egocentric world, a punishment for something he has done himself . . . If he is ill and homesick for his mother in hospital, the explanation that he must have been naughty and she was cross with him comes to him readily. His authoritarian and magical view of the world leads him to suppose that had she really wanted to, she could have saved him from his illness" (Wolff, 1969). Feelings of anxiety and guilt result and these can lead to regression and to behaviour disorders. They may be accentuated by the unresolved and continuing anxieties of the parents, who are thus unable to give their children the necessary reassurance.

Maladjustment in physically handicapped children may be caused by faulty patterns of relationship between parents and children in the earliest years (Pringle, 1969). The handicapped infant may fail to release appropriate parental reactions by his behaviour, or may stimulate inappropriate reactions. For example, a blind child does not react to his mother's approach with excitement and anticipation but remains quiet and still to hear her better. The mother may conclude that the baby is quiet and requires little attention. A hyperactive infant with minimal brain damage may cause his mother anxiety because problems of handling are more pronounced and the child's behaviour is unexpected; this can lead to a negative attitude towards him. Certainly more study and understanding of these interactions and of the difficulties which can arise is needed before parents can be helped to adjust their own attitudes to favour the development of harmonious relations and good adjustment in the child.

The school years
During this time children are concerned with their position in relation to others in a school community, as well as in their families. If a child fails to keep up with his school fellows at work or sport he feels inferior. Low self-esteem causes anxiety or apathy and if it continues over a long period, is very damaging to the healthy development of personality. Teachers know that a child who cannot keep up in the classroom is unhappy and often behaves badly. Teachers can play a key role in helping slow learners and children who show disturbed behaviour by allotting them work with which they can cope and which gives them satisfaction, and by recognising those in need of special help and seeing that they get it. As with all children, the handicapped should not feel that the pressures on them to succeed are too great, either at home or school. The extent to which teachers can tolerate and manage unusual children will determine how many with mild handicaps can be retained in ordinary schools.

A study of psychiatric disorder among school children in the Isle of Wight (Graham and Rutter, 1968) showed that physically handicapped children have a higher incidence of psychiatric disorder than the general population of school children. Of children aged 10–11 chosen at random, 6·8% showed psychiatric disorder compared with 11·5% of children with physical handicaps not involving the brain and 34·3%

of handicapped children suffering from neuro-epileptic conditions.*

The study concluded that whilst the incidence of psychiatric disorder in physically handicapped children is high, physical handicap in itself does not lead to disorder and therefore other social, intellectual and familial influences must contribute. This was emphasised by the fact that physical handicaps could not be associated with particular psychiatric disorders or specific types of behaviour.

These are important conclusions for those concerned with the care of physically handicapped children. First, they are more liable to behaviour problems and psychiatric disorder than normal children and therefore, doctors, teachers, social workers and others need to be on the alert for signs of trouble. Secondly, schools and other centres for the physically handicapped will need a higher ratio of psychiatrists and other members of the team than for the general population, both to diagnose and treat the children and to discuss problems with other professional workers. Thirdly, the parents of these children will need to show great understanding in the care of their children to try and avoid these disorders. In this they will need good support from social workers who understand the particular problems they face, and the problems that unusual or disturbed behaviour presents.

The emotional problems of severely handicapped children who are housebound or in hospitals or other long-stay institutions are likely to be even more severe. The strain on the family will also be very much greater.

Adolescence

Finally, there are the problems that the adolescent handicapped have to face. Their uncertainties about the role they can play in adult life are far greater than for normal children. Handicapped adolescents share the desire of most young people to lead as normal a life as possible and not to be conspicuous because of their handicaps. But many are aware of their growing isolation from the social life of their normal peers. Some of these factors are discussed in chapter 2. When and how should handicapped youngsters be made aware of their limitations in relation to the unsheltered world outside their special

* The highest incidence (58·3%) was shown by children suffering from lesions above the brain stem and who also suffered from fits. The conclusion drawn was that the very high rate of disorder shown in the last group was due to dysfunction of the brain.

schools? How can a young man's unrealistic career ambitions be discouraged without crushing his faith in himself and his future? Should a girl's fantasies about marriage and babies be broken by reminding her that she is unlikely ever to marry, or is it more cruel to let her leave school with hope that is bound to be shattered? What kind of sex education should be given to adolescents who ought never to marry because of their social and emotional immaturity? These difficult questions must be posed and answered if handicapped young people are to be adequately helped.

The child and the community

The adjustment of the handicapped child to the outside world depends a great deal on the attitudes of the public towards him. While he lives and works in the sheltered community of a special school and his family there is always the thought of the real world outside with which he must eventually come to terms. At the same time, the community needs to adjust to the presence of the handicapped in its midst, to recognise handicaps and make allowance for them without sentimentality, and to accept those with handicaps as people with their own personal qualities and differences.

One can imagine an ideal community in which the handicapped family finds moral support and practical help available naturally. Grandparents, the extended family, would respond with understanding and extra pairs of hands; neighbours would share some of the burdens, providing extra attention for the brothers and sisters of the handicapped child and, through small services, giving the mother relief so that she might have some life apart from the child. It is still true that some support of this kind is given, but it is spasmodic and not available to everyone. Greater mobility and less close ties within the extended family group have meant that, increasingly, families have no relatives to turn to for help. There are many neighbourhoods where there is little communication between residents and no habit of exchanging small services. In such situations, the birth of a handicapped child may increase a family's isolation rather than establish new relationships and call forth offers of help.

Moreover, a handicapped child does not necessarily awaken compassion in other people; the response may be fear or revulsion, leading to estrangement from the family. In a study of the mentally handicapped and their families it was found that: "There were few families that did not comment on the sense of humiliation they felt or had felt on occasions in the past when strangers stared at their child or made comments . . . Again, neighbours and friends, though sometimes sympathetic and considerate were often indifferent and unhelpful. There were few instances of active hostility but many women commented that they were unable to ask neighbours and relatives to look after their handicapped child as they would have done had the child been normal" (Tizard and Grad, 1961).

What type of community can best tolerate the unusual? Is the stable village, either urban or rural, better able to accept the handicapped than an urban area with a shifting population? No studies appear to have been made of this specific question but several general conclusions appear common. First, at least in initial contact, some handicaps are more easily tolerated than others. Physical handicap is generally more accepted than mental handicap, normal appearance causes less fear than physical deformity, a child who can communicate creates less anxiety or avoidance than one who cannot, and a child whose behaviour is disturbed is very hard to take. Second, there may be a limit to the number of deviants a normal group can successfully absorb. Third, and most important, acceptance cannot exist in the abstract. It depends on personal knowledge of handicapped children so that they are considered as children first, and only incidentally as handicapped.

It has been said that "The general public, and children in particular, will only behave in a kindly but unsentimental way towards the handicapped if they have the opportunity to learn to live with people who, while in some way different from themselves, are accepted without stigma in the community of which they are members. One of the strongest arguments which has been put forward in favour of an integrated community type of care for the handicapped, is that it prevents the stigma inherent in segregation" (Tizard, 1964). If we accept this view, it is important to examine how to foster and provide more contact between handicapped children and normal children. A number of clubs for normal children which accept the handicapped exist already but more are needed. The Scout and Guide and the Boys Brigade movements have also set an example here and others should be encouraged to follow suit. Mixed youth clubs are formed in some areas for both handicapped and normal youngsters. There might be more contact between ordinary schools and special schools in an area for specific activities such as music or art. Play groups can help by accepting handicapped children. Parents who encourage their handicapped children as far as possible to mix with other children and to move freely in their neighbourhood are helping to lessen their own and their children's isolation.

As far as the general public is concerned, the World Health Organisation Working Group, already cited, has described three principal objectives for public education:

1. to prepare the way for acceptance of the handicapped as equal members of society through promoting a better understanding of their problems;

2. to arouse and stimulate the interest of people who might wish to make a professional career in or give voluntary help to services for the handicapped;

3. to create a climate of public opinion which will regard the use of public resources in providing services for the handicapped as a well-justified social investment" (World Health Organisation, 1967).

By involving voluntary workers in the care of the handicapped personal links can be forged. Individual volunteers can be asked to help by baby-sitting with handicapped children, by taking them out on excursions, and by offering them holidays. Senior pupils in local schools can be drawn into projects of this nature. The local voluntary societies catering for the handicapped can also, if they are outward-looking, forge links with the community by contributing to local events such as fairs and fund-raising bazaars. Articles in newspapers and magazines, programmes on radio and television, plays and films can all contribute towards the public's general education.

The creation of an accepting climate of opinion is vital to handicapped children and their families. It is also important for the good health of the community itself. In everything that is done, careful thought should be given to making it possible for handicapped children and their parents to give – service, friendship or whatever it may be – as well as to receive. This reciprocal giving and receiving is an essential element in enhancing self worth, human dignity, and confidence in being accepted and wanted by others.

References

CARNEGIE UNITED KINGDOM TRUST (1964) *Handicapped Children and their Families.* Dunfermline, Scotland.

DEPARTMENT OF HEALTH AND SOCIAL SECURITY (1970) *National Health Service.* HMSO London.

GOLDIE, L. (1966) "Psychiatry of the Handicapped Family". *Developmental Medicine and Child Neurology.* Vol. 8, No. 4, pp 456–462.

GOLDSMITH, S. (1967 revised) *Designing for the Disabled.* Royal Institute of British Architects.

GOULD, B. (1968) "Working with Handicapped Families". *Case Conference.* Vol 15, No 5, 1968.

GRAHAM, P. AND RUTTER, M. (1968) "Organic Brain Dysfunction and Child Psychiatric Disorder". *British Medical Journal.* Vol 3, No 5620, pp 689–700.

HEWETT, S. (1967) *Handicapped Children and their Families.* University of Nottingham Press, Nottingham.

HEWETT, S. WITH NEWSOM J. AND E. (1970). *The Family and the Handicapped Child.* Allen and Unwin, London.

MINISTRY OF HOUSING AND LOCAL GOVERNMENT (1970) *Reform of Local Government in England.* HMSO London.

NATIONAL SOCIETY FOR MENTALLY HANDICAPPED CHILDREN (1967) *Stress in Families with a Mentally Handicapped Child.* NSMHC, London.

PRINGLE, M. L. KELLMER (1965 reprinted 1969). *Emotional and Social Adjustment of Physically Handicapped Children.* Occ. Public No 11. National Foundation for Educational Research, Slough, Bucks.

PRINGLE, M. L. KELLMER AND FIDDES, D. O. (1970) *The Challenge of Thalidomide.* Longman, London.

SHERIDAN, M. D. (1965) *The Handicapped Child and his Home.* National Children's Home, Highbury, London.

TIZARD, J. AND GRAD, J. C. (1961) *The Mentally Handicapped and their Families.* Oxford University Press, London.

TIZARD, J. (1964) *Community Services for the Mentally Handicapped.* Oxford University Press, London.

WIGGLESWORTH, R. (1967) "The Handicapped Child – towards helping the family in the community". Paper given to the Paediatric Group, Institute of Medical Social Workers.

WILLIAMS, C. E. (1968) "Behaviour Disorders in Handicapped Children". *Developmental Medicine and Child Neurology.* Vol 10, No 6, pp 736–740.

WILLMOTT, P. (1967) *Consumers' Guide to the British Social Services.* Penguin Press, Harmondsworth, Middx.

WOLFF, S. (1969) *Children under Stress.* Penguin Press, Harmondsworth, Middx.

WORLD HEALTH ORGANISATION (1967) *Report of a Working Group on the Early Detection and Treatment of Handicapping Defects in Young Children.* Regional Office for Europe, WHO, Copenhagen.

Younis, M. (1966) "The Way I See Things". Chapter 10 in: *Stigma, ed.* Paul Hunt. Geoffrey Chapman, London.

Acts and Bills

Education Act, 1944.

National Superannuation and Insurance Bill, 1969.

Local Authority Social Services Act, 1970.

8. Residential care for children and young people

"Never will we forget the day we took her to leave her at the school. Never will we forget the look of reproach on a young child's face. She actually thought we were dumping her . . . I am now firmly of the opinion that the setback caused by forcing these children to leave a good home where they are wanted, is such that it may never be recovered . . . She would come home on her holidays full of excitement but would gradually sink during the last five days leading to final crying and appealing not to go back."

Letter from a grandparent of a spastic child

"He is in a ward with 40 other children, two of whom are blind. For the most part he sits in a corner with his fingers in his ears because, as the nurses say, it is too noisy for him . . . for the most part he is just existing, the nurses just do not have enough time to see to anyone individually."

Letter from the mother of a blind and mentally
handicapped son of school age

Introduction

Children with a handicap, are entitled to family and community life, no less than others. Thus, so far as practicable, the assessment, treatment and training of such children should fit into the framework of the family, the home surroundings, relatives and friends. Having stated the need of all children to feel part of their family, it is not inconsistent to add that there are some children, handicapped children included, who need to go to a residential school, hospital or hostel for varying periods at given points in time in their lives. In considering whether a residential setting for part of a year may be a wise form of care the same four factors which we considered in the previous chapter must be taken into account.

181

182

First, the need to give a handicapped child specialised and appropriate treatment, training and education which cannot readily be
provided within daily reach of his home.

Secondly, the family's need to lead an active normal life, which might
not otherwise be possible when they have the demanding task of caring
for the handicapped child. Parents require both time and energy to
respond to the emotional and material needs of other children in the
family, as well as having their own adult life and interests.

Thirdly, the need of handicapped children, particularly as they grow
older, to experience independence apart from their families. Some
handicapped children are prevented by their over-conscientious and
over-protective parents from developing their own personalities and
expressing their own individuality.

Lastly, there may be parents who are themselves delicate or
handicapped or inadequate to the task of caring full time for their
handicapped child.

It cannot be stated categorically which children should remain at
home and which should go to a residential school. Professional workers
in the education, medical and personal social services should be
prepared to listen sensitively to both parents and children in order to
understand the needs of a particular child and its family, to weigh up
often conflicting priorities, and to reach the best possible decision in all
the circumstances. A partnership, with joint planning, is necessary to
mitigate the sense of rejection and temporary loss of emotional ties with
his home that the handicapped child in residential care is liable to feel.
Such help will also reduce the parents' sense of guilt associated with
relief at being released from a demanding task, and also prevent "out
of sight out of mind" attitudes on the part of brothers and sisters.
Residential care also tends to relieve the local community of its
responsibilities and can sever the handicapped child's social contacts
in his home area. It is important to avoid these dangers.

Existing planning powers and provision for residential care

So far as special education is concerned, the Department of Education
and Science has no statutory authority to require local education
authorities to build any particular type of special school. Nevertheless,
it determines the scale of new building, both day and residential,

which may be undertaken in a given period. In inviting local education authorities to submit proposals for inclusion in the building programme, the Department draws attention to the special needs of particular types of handicapped children. In deciding which projects to approve in the building programme, it also takes account of the same priorities, both in the country as a whole and in the areas of individual local authorities. Since the authorities' proposals for buildings normally exceed the financial limit of the programme, these priorities have considerable effect. In addition, the Department's inspectors in discussion with individual directors of education have opportunities of emphasising the needs in their areas of particular classes of handicapped children.

The Department of Health and Social Security is at present responsible for the medical, educational and social care of severely subnormal children in hospital. There is an inadequate number of beds for such children; while conversely it is probable that some already in hospital could certainly be cared for by other means. In 1968 there were 1,730 severely subnormal children on hospital waiting lists in England and Wales. There are no well defined procedures by which a parent can apply for their subnormal child's admission to hospital. The general well-being of the young chronic sick in hospital also requires far more all-round provision than exists at present.

Local authority residential services for handicapped children are fragmented and there is no "one door on which to knock". At present, according to the type of handicap, a child may be dealt with by the education department, the health or welfare department or, if there is the added handicap of rejection or homelessness or inability to care for the child, by the children's department. This situation will be substantially altered when the children's and welfare departments and some responsibilities of the health department are combined in social services departments. The local education authority deals with general education and treatment of handicapped children and provides for such children under Sections 9 (5), 33 and 34 of the Education Act, 1944. The Department of Education and Science publishes a list of special schools for handicapped pupils in England and Wales under the Handicapped Pupils and Special Schools Regulations (1959) (S.1 1959 No. 365). This list (List 42–1969) does not include independent schools, which are recognised as efficient under Rule 16 (List 70–1968). As has been said in other chapters, there is an inadequate number of residential schools for maladjusted children, nor is there sufficient variety; for instance, there are few schools for highly intelligent maladjusted boys, notable exceptions being Redhill and Finchden Manor. No such school exists for girls.

The local health authority has power to provide hostels in the community for the mentally handicapped under the Mental Health Act, 1959. In 1965 there were in England and Wales only 50 such hostels with places for 900 children; it was then forecast that by 1971 there would be 129 hostels for 2,219 children. In 1968 there were 1,350 children living in hostels. It was then planned to have 158 hostels for 2,706 children by 1976. In 1968 there were 196 children under 16 years awaiting hostel vacancies and 779 over 16 years. Some local authorities do not make use of these powers; indeed the Seebohm Committee found that provision ranged from 0 to 0·18 per thousand. The welfare department has permissive powers to provide hostels for the physically handicapped. It is not known how many young people under 18 years of age are living in such hostels. In time the new social services department may increase residential provision for the physically or mentally handicapped who do not need continuing medical supervision.

Local authority children's departments, soon to become part of the new social services departments, stand *in loco parentis* to handicapped children who for one reason or another must be received into care. This department often finds itself having to provide for such children because there are no vacancies in schools, hospitals or hostels. Conversely, it may be impossible to discharge a child from hospital because there is nowhere suitable for him to go. In evidence from a medical social worker we were told of an eight year old boy admitted to hospital after a road accident which left him with severe brain damage. His elderly grandparents were unable to care for him and, in spite of requests for alternative care, he remained in hospital for four years. This illustrates the lack of suitable provision for the young chronic sick.

As there is an increasing number of children with handicaps who are surviving through medical skill (*eg* cases of spina bifida) but whose parents cannot care for them, there is an increasing number of handicapped children in the care of local authority children's departments. This came out clearly in the information supplied by the ten local authorities whom we consulted (see appendix C). It has been suggested that as many as 25 % of the children in the care of some local authorities may be physically, intellectually or emotionally handicapped. Unfortunately this information is not available in the Home Office annual returns of children in care. A few children's departments make special provision for some handicapped children: others may be placed with voluntary organisations like Dr Barnardo's, the National Children's Home, a Rudolph Steiner school or a special boarding school.

The planning of residential care by children's departments is likely to improve under the Children and Young Persons Act, 1969, which sets up children's regional planning committees. These will consist of representatives from a group of local authorities with a duty to plan the most effective range of residential resources (both voluntary and statutory) in community homes of all kinds, including hostels. Residential special schools will not be part of this regional planning.

Acute problems are posed by adolescents whose behaviour is so severely disturbed that a succession of schools and children's homes have been unable to hold them. The provision for these young people is quite inadequate. A few hospitals have adolescent units, but the choice is often between an adult ward in a mental hospital or yet another holding operation in a school, a hostel, children's home, approved school or borstal. Some children's departments have created special units with a higher ratio of staff to children than in ordinary homes in an effort to provide an answer. The Home Secretary has taken powers under Section 64 of the Children and Young Persons Act, 1969 to provide education, training and psychiatric treatment under secure conditions for boys and girls between 12 and 19 who have been committed by a court on a care order and found to be too psychiatrically disturbed and disruptive for a local authority community home. The first of these four youth treatment centres is to open in 1970, with a psychiatrist as director and with provision for research and evaluation.

Better overall planning of residential resources of all kinds is essential if adequate facilities are to be provided and in particular if an improved distribution and more flexible use of residential services is to be achieved. Fewer children may then have to be sent far from their homes and the opportunity for parents to establish a real partnership with a children's home or boarding school could be offered. This situation may be improved when the much larger unitary and metro-politan local authorities come into existence and are able to plan a wider range of services than exists at present in some areas.

The present wide scatter of many services dealing with handicapped children and the lack of co-ordination between them often leads to a situation where there is no comprehensive follow-through of a given child's overall long-term progress. For instance there are children without parents and children who have been virtually abandoned by their parents in a hospital or children's home. Others may have families who take only a casual and indifferent interest in their progress. In such instances while a child is receiving treatment, custodial care or schooling from the health or education authorities, no one department is responsible for following up his progress and planning for his future unless he is in the care of the children's department. It has been known for such children to be "lost" in an institution for years with no one to visit them or to press for a review of treatment and care. They may be well-cared for by the staff of the institution but have no legal guardian. We have come to the conclusion that all such children in hospitals or independent schools and other residential institutions should, unless there is good reason to the contrary in an individual case, be received into care under section 1 of the Children Act 1948 which is already wide enough for this purpose. They might remain in or return to the hospital or other institution but the social services department of the area in which this is situated would be in loco parentis, responsible for long term planning with the hospital, or other institution, for regularly visiting and for taking a personal interest in the child. This would give him that regular contact with a parent figure outside the institution which has been found to be so important for mental health (Pringle, 1965).

Where there is a parent or guardian unable or not willing to visit, it should be the duty of the hospital or other institution to notify the social services department which should, wherever desirable, have a duty to appoint a member of staff or a volunteer as a "friend" to visit the child. Efforts should also be made to trace lost parents and help them to visit their child. Sometimes they do not visit because they cannot afford the fare, or they feel they are not wanted, or that the child is indifferent to their visits.

A practical consequence of the multiplicity of different authorities responsible for residential or home care is brought out in the Green Paper, *National Health Service* (1970):

". . . at heavy cost the hospital service cares for patients who could well be treated at home if the right local services were available on a large enough scale. Many patients are in hospital who could live outside, would prefer to live outside and would fare better outside. In many such cases care at home with the support of the community health services would be the better and cheaper solution. At the same time other patients who really need care in hospital make demands on the local authority services while they wait to be admitted.

Often the barrier to discharge from hospital is the lack of adequate services for people who would prefer to stay in their own homes. When deciding what priority to give to their health services as against the competing needs of their other services, it is clearly difficult for local authorities to take full account of the advantages which would accrue to the health service as a whole. It is not surprising that local authorities, faced as they are by many competing needs, may often not be able or ready to spend money from the rates on caring for patients who are being looked after by the hospital service but could be discharged. At present neither the hospitals' resources nor those of local health authorities are used to maximum advantage."

Residential or home care: the decision

Babies and young children

If adequate support could be given by the medical and social work professions the majority of parents would not want residential care for their baby or very young child. During the early formative years the emotional bonds between parents and child are formed and the foundation of a child's good mental health is established through the warm, loving relationship with parents. As we have said in another context in chapter 2, during these early years all supportive services and aids of the community should be provided to enable babies and young children to remain in their parents' care if possible.

Nonetheless, there are some parents who for various reasons want residential care for a baby or young child, particularly if it is spastic or mentally handicapped. As far as can be judged, the few parents who request residential care for their severely subnormal babies are in situations where the constant care of the baby would seriously curtail the parents' lives or where the child is so severely mentally handicapped that family life is disrupted, for example, by a constantly screaming child. There are also parents so shocked by their baby's handicap that they reject the child. There are other parents who cannot cope with the care for a severely handicapped baby.

The dilemma of these cases is acute for the medical and social work professions: on the one hand every baby needs his or her own parents and home care; on the other hand if parents cannot accept their baby's handicap or are too inadequate or otherwise unable to cope with it, it would seem that alternative care may have to be considered. For very young children this should wherever possible be in a foster home rather than an institution. In some localities this has been achieved for a number of handicapped babies through payment of a substantial boarding-out allowance to a foster mother. Unfortunately such children inevitably consume a disproportionate amount of a foster mother's time and energies. In heavily populated areas where foster homes are rare, placement in a residential nursery or hospital may be inevitable. But it is quite essential so to plan the regime that babies and small children have a continuous warm relationship, ideally with one but certainly not more than two or three staff members. In some hospitals, lay women (often young grandmothers) are employed to give individual unhurried attention to a child; some married women who have developed skill in mothering through their experience of bringing up their own children can be invaluable as ancillary staff and aides in hospitals.

Battered babies, who will have suffered serious physical, mental and emotional damage, often come into the care of the local authority, which must seek an appropriate home for the child. The parents, who have often themselves suffered parental ill-treatment in childhood, require highly skilled casework.

School children
Parents of school children, together with the medical, educational and social work professions, acting through the comprehensive assessment centres, must decide whether the handicapped child should go to a residential school; if so, at what age and to which school, hospital or hostel. Parents whose educational background includes "going to boarding school" will more easily accept the idea of a residential school; whereas those who regard going away from home as "being put away" are likely to feel resistant to and guilty about a residential placement. Furthermore, how the child interprets going away often depends on the social group from which he comes.

The partnership of parents and the medical, educational and personal social services

The ultimate responsibility for a child lies with the parents. Therefore it is essential that at all stages they should take part in discussions about the possible future of their child. In chapter 6 we propose that the social services department should be responsible for co-ordinating the medical, educational and social care recommendations concerning a child. The decision that, on balance and in the long term interest of both child and family, residential care is advisable should be reached through close consultation between the parents and the medical, educational and social workers involved. It is best if the final decision can be taken jointly at a case conference where the parents are also present if this is practicable.

Difficulties in determining priorities arise when a residential school meets some needs but may be detrimental in other ways. For example, a severely deaf child will emotionally need the care of parents; if however, they are unable to help the child to speak and local facilities are not available, the child's emotional deprivation may in the long run be worse if he or she never learns to communicate. Deaf children must be taught to communicate at an early age but to be sent far away from home without being able to understand the reasons or to speak may be a highly traumatic experience. In such circumstances there are immense difficulties in weighing up all the different elements in the total situation, bearing in mind not only the present but also the child's future developmental needs.

Residential school care

The choice of school

Ideally, a school should be chosen by agreement amongst all concerned to meet the needs of the individual child and his family from the point of view of what it has to offer, including reasonable proximity to home. Unfortunately, there is often no choice, it is simply a question of accepting any vacancy. Sometimes there is no vacancy at all, especially for older children who need a school for maladjusted children, or those with multi-handicaps, for whom few schools are available. One of the parents' letters gives a sad example of bad practice some years ago.

"At the age of five, the specialist registered Ellen as a partially sighted person, and down came the local authority on our heads, informing us that she

190 LIVING WITH HANDICAP

must be educated at a residential special school about 100 miles away. At no time were we asked our opinion, we were just told she must go there and we had to sign papers to say that we would not take her away from there until she was sixteen. We were not taken to see it in order that we could see what the school, its teachers and the other children were like. We were just told to sign the papers."

Geographically, schools for handicapped children have "grown up" unplanned, mainly through voluntary initiative, and are not equally dispersed over the country. Thus parents are often forced into sending their child far from home and may only be able to visit him infrequently or not at all.

The child's introduction to the school
Many residential schools have accommodation for parents, enabling them to stay a day or two seeing the school and getting to know the staff; some bring their children on the first visit; some visit again at a later date to introduce their child to the school. Accommodation for parents enables those at long distances to stay overnight. It is important that both parents and children should understand the function of the school; the child will then have a sense of coming to school away from home for a positive purpose and parents will feel that they are giving their child training and education which they themselves cannot provide otherwise and thus they are not rejecting their child but helping him.

In the majority of cases a full medical, educational and social history is submitted to the school but it is not always kept up to date. Failure to send initial and subsequent comprehensive reports is detrimental to the child. The continuous assessment procedure which we propose, with responsibility for follow-up resting with the social services department, should improve this situation.

Siting, architecture and garden play space
A number of schools stand in their own grounds in a rural setting. This creates problems of isolation for staff and children. Other schools are in a village or small town thus enabling them to be part of a community. All residential schools need gardens and good play space. The buildings should comprise both school and home; both should provide some privacy, including individual lavatories, baths and some small rooms where children can be on their own if they so wish. Children need their own possessions kept in their own lockers, chests of drawers and wardrobes.

Much of a child's life is spent in the home side of the residential school; indeed schools cannot and should not attempt to replace the child's own home, but the home side of a school needs to be so built and organised that children are cared for in small groups, receiving individual care and attention from residential child care staff.

Residential child care staff

Home care requires skilled, professionally trained and experienced people. All forms of residential care must be so organised that it is possible for each child to have a dependable relationship with one staff member in particular.

Children away from their own homes need the experience of personal relationships but the emphasis and significance of these relationships will be different for each child according to his or her needs. A child with an emotionally satisfying home background who has regular visits from family and friends will draw on the school relationships in a different way from the child whose home background is insecure and emotionally unsatisfying. Residential child care staff need to be sufficiently skilled to give to each child a personal relationship, a sense of worth, identity and self-confidence, thus helping him towards emotional maturity. This individual work must be carried out while maintaining a balance within the group. In the course of their home making duties, the staff must be aware of and respond to the child's emotional development, his physical and his recreational needs. They must provide both the peace and stimulation, sensory, physical and intellectual, needed by the children in their care. Furthermore, such relationships must be fostered in such a way that they do not supplant the parents' place in the child's affections. Residential child care and teaching staff must be able to assess the depth and significance attached by the child to school relationships. Careful planning will be necessary for the child who is due to leave school and for whom the school relationships mean more than the home relationships.

There is greater recognition nowadays of the value of this service with all that this implies in the personal care of children who have to spend their school days away from home and their need to experience life in a therapeutic community. This improvement has been accomplished in many schools through a fruitful co-operation between teachers, child care staff and the administration, leading to improvement of the physical facilities for the children within the school,

H

together with a more personal and homely attitude to their general care. The significant role of professionally trained and skilled residential child care staff is, at last, being recognised (see also chapter 11).

Opportunities for both teachers and child care staff to pursue personal interests are more likely to result in balanced healthy relationships in the care and stimulation of the children, besides helping to bring the children and the local community together.

Increasingly the work of some residential child care staff is so organised that they are able to sleep out; this requires careful thought so that the children do not suffer emotional deprivation. It is also essential to attract to residential child care work more men interested in the home care of children, some working full-time, others part-time.

One residential school for the visually handicapped, which functions mainly on a five-day week basis, has for many years employed three non-resident married housemothers with considerable success.

Reviews of children in boarding schools and the need for flexibility
The case of every handicapped child in a residential school should, as part of continuing comprehensive assessment in general, be reviewed at least every year by the parents and the team of medical, educational and social workers concerned with the child. It is important that the wishes of the child should be listened to sensitively and handled with wisdom and professional skill. There should be freedom to change; that is to say, the system of care at home or in a hostel for part of the time and care in a residential school should be flexible enough to allow a child to move from home or hostel to residential school and vice versa in order to meet his individual needs at any point of time. At present this is seldom possible as there are not sufficient vacancies in residential or day schools to allow for such flexibility.

The role of the medical, educational and personal social services
There should obviously be regular communication between the health, education and personal social services of the area in which the child lives and the residential school. What has not yet been satisfactorily resolved is the role of the social worker or school counsellor (if such posts exist in the school) and the social worker in the child's home area.

In our view, it is crucial that the social services department should be held accountable to the parents, the home local authority, the school and the child himself. Thus when comprehensive social services departments come into being they should be the accountable authority, in conjunction with voluntary agencies and social workers in hospitals or boarding schools. We agree with the Seebohm Report that social work in schools should be the responsibility of the social services department because this comprehensive service would make it possible to deal with the child in his family and neighbourhood as well as in school. We also agree that because of the wide catchment area of some boarding special schools it would not always be possible for the social services department in the child's home area to be responsible for the social work in various, perhaps distant, schools. Hence there will often have to be some degree of dual responsibility.

We do not, however, agree with the Seebohm Report that the responsibility for ensuring that suitable arrangements between the school and the child's home area are made, however they are discharged, should, as it recommends, "reside unambiguously with the social services department in whose area a particular school is located". On the contrary we think that the responsibility should rest with an equal lack of ambiguity on the social services department where the child lives. This department will have known him before he goes away to a residential school, will be responsible for holiday arrangements, for on-going work with the family, for possible changes from residential to day school, for co-operation with the youth employment service and for aftercare. The situation is different in regard to long-stay children in hospital who may have no effective home base. For them, as we have said earlier in this chapter, the social services department in the hospital area should have certain responsibilities.

Parents with handicapped children need skilled support and help without being made to feel that they themselves are always receiving and not giving. Maladjusted children may indeed be reflecting their parents' difficulties, therefore not to work with the parents is to some extent to waste the resources expended on the child; knowledge and understanding of his home is of basic value in guiding any child and particularly a child with disturbed behaviour. Considerable skill is required if parents are to have a sense of partnership with a school, children a sense of being cared for in their own right, and the child, family and school together to experience a common, equal relationship. This may well be more than any one professional worker can achieve.

Many head teachers value having a school counsellor or social worker to act as the link between home, school and child.

It is evident that the school based social worker cannot work systematically with a family; moreover when the child is at home this social worker is not available to give immediate help if needed. There must therefore be close understanding between the school social worker and the social services department in the home area.

Inevitably, social workers change but the social services department continues and parents should be aware of a "door on which to knock" in their own home area where they should receive any help required; furthermore, they should know where to go to give help. Some parents of handicapped children offer help with other children, sometimes for holiday periods and day care.

Holiday arrangements
The social worker in the home area social services department should regard it as part of his or her responsibility to make the best possible arrangements for children during the holidays. To ensure this, boarding schools might even refuse to take children until they have a firm assurance of stable and satisfactory holiday plans. This particularly applies to children in the care of a local authority. Such children suffer grievously if they have no settled holiday base. With persistence and conviction child care staff have found regular holiday foster homes for children in care who are at residential schools. This has given children a sense of belonging rather than rootlessness. If a child cannot go home and has no foster home, then he or she should return to the same children's home each holiday on a planned basis with accommodation reserved for him. If no foster home can be found and the child must return to the children's home each holiday, a carefully vetted family prepared to take an interest in the child can be helpful to him. If there are good home care arrangements in a residential school some children might do better to stay at school for part of the holidays. It is not always in the child's interest for schools to close completely every holiday.

Children in long-stay hospitals
The British Psychological Society's Report on Children in Hospitals for the Subnormal (1966) showed that in a sample of 155 children who proved testable, 24% of the sample had IQ's above 50 (14% had IQ's

over 70, and 4% had IQ's over 100). The explanation for the presence of children with mild or even no intellectual defect among children of much lower intellectual capacity, is that they have additional handicaps such as behaviour difficulties and/or physical disabilities. Pauline Morris' (1969) more recent sample showed 4·3% of children with IQ's over 50, but 44·6% not tested by the hospital; 38% of the children were multi-handicapped. We discuss other aspects of this in relation to education in chapter 9.

We think that many children in hospitals for the subnormal need only be there if they have an additional handicap besides their intellectual one. They may have behaviour disorders of various types which make it difficult to cater for them in day facilities, or physical handicaps which require expert and constant treatment. Hospitals for the sub-normal should have provision specifically for these needs. Yet few hospitals have cerebral palsy units, facilities for the blind, speech therapists, specialist audiometry and other facilities such as psychological services which give direct help to the classroom teacher, rather than simply providing psychometric assessments.

Mentally handicapped children who cannot be cared for in their own homes, in hostels or elsewhere are admitted to subnormality hospitals where there is a vacancy. These hospitals cater for anything from a hundred to 2,000 children and adults. Lately there has been much discussion about better services for severely subnormal children and adults. In the autumn of 1969 the Secretary of State for Social Services instituted a comprehensive review of long-stay hospitals. This is to be published, giving a full analysis and proposals for action.

Homes for about 25 mentally retarded children have been suggested (Tizard, 1960; Kushlick, 1967). Experimental pilot schemes are being undertaken, for instance in the area of the Wessex Regional Hospital Board which has carried out a complete survey of the mentally handicapped. Whether it is decided to set up comparatively small units or continue with the large institutionalised units, the type of care offered in hospitals is in need of re-appraisal. It has been pointed out repeatedly in recent years that the problems of mentally handicapped children are social and emotional rather than primarily medical. It is essential to concentrate on the child's educational and social development as well as on good medical care which at present dominates the others.

Children cared for in a hospital ward regime tend to become depersonalised and to miss much of a child's right to play and to develop his identity. The hospital setting invites an approach to the patients which is "ward centred" rather than "home centred", so that children lack mental and physical stimulation and continuing close relationship with an adult. Since the hierarchical medical and nursing approach seems detrimental to the needs of the developing child, it is suggested that a complete re-orientation of outlook, approach and management within the institutional framework is essential.

Subnormality hospitals may have to continue to provide some residential care, but they do not necessarily need to be hospitals, and nurses may not necessarily have duties associated with nursing physically ill or handicapped or mentally disordered patients. Another approach, modelled on child care practices and home-like handling, could be incorporated, even in large institutions, to the great benefit of the children's development. In addition to nursing staff, some subnormality hospitals have to rely on numbers of auxiliaries with no training at all. Some have valuable help from voluntary visitors who play with and take an interest in the children. The National Association for Mental Health plans to run an experimental short course for staff concerned with "ward bound" children in such hospitals, to explore the problem as it exists and ways in which these children might enjoy a richer life.

It is suggested that institutions where mentally handicapped children have to live for long periods should be broken down into small, mainly self-contained, units with house-mothers and house-fathers, a proportion of whom should be state registered or. enrolled nurses but whose first obligation would be to run a home which provides a warm supportive climate for the children, rather than to run a ward. Supervision and support by senior staff would obviously be necessary but with the emphasis on child nurture rather than on standards which are a necessity in a general hospital but quite out of place in a substitute home. In such a concept of institutional care the continued wearing of nurses' uniforms is unnecessary.

Pauline Morris (1969) comments:
"It is widely believed that shortage of staff is a vital factor preventing the implementation of many improvements now generally recognised as being necessary if mental subnormalty hospitals are to be brought into line with

current medical thought. Our data seem to suggest that staff shortage is perhaps only one factor in producing poor staff morale. Equally important are the isolation of the hospital, the debasement of the nursing role, and the failure of communication, all of which tend to stultify creative thinking. Furthermore the fact that staff turnover is so slow, particularly at senior level, means that there is little opportunity for new ideas to penetrate the service. The fact that so few patients are physically ill and requiring medical attention places the nursing staff in a position of power *vis à vis* patient care which would not be possible in a hospital where the medical staff had a more obvious and positive role to play. Under the present circumstances only those doctors in subnormality hospitals who are interested in the psychiatric treatment of patients, or in research, have any major role to play. For those who are concerned primarily with the physical care of patients, the subnormality hospital offers very little."

Current concern about children in subnormality hospitals should not distract attention from the equally pressing needs of physically handicapped children in hospital. Little published material exists about these children yet all that has been said about the childhood needs of the sub-normal applies, sometimes with even greater force, to them.

The size of the problem of residential care

Michael Power and Jean Packman undertook for the Seebohm Committee a study of children in need and the help they received. This is published as appendix Q of the Seebohm Report. They calculated that 21,000 physically handicapped children were away from home in boarding schools or hospitals in 1966, of whom 5,000 were long-stay patients in hospital. There were 24,000 mentally handicapped children away from home, including severely subnormal, educationally subnormal, maladjusted and psychiatrically disordered children, 10,000 of these in hospitals or hostels. In addition, there were 115,600 children who received help away from their own homes including 69,000 in the care of children's departments. Many of these were not in residential care and only a minority are likely to be handicapped but, as has been said earlier, the Home Office annual returns unfortunately do not give information about this and the Department of Health and Social Security figures do not differentiate between children and adults.

The total number of children in residential institutions is thus very considerable, particularly when it is remembered that more provision is required to meet the all round shortage of residential accommodation. The task is also formidable from the point of view of the standards of

of staffing, premises and other amenities which we consider essential
if a substantial number of handicapped children are to develop their
potentialities sufficiently to lead a life of their own when they grow up.

References
BRITISH PSYCHOLOGICAL SOCIETY (1966) *Children in Hospitals for the Subnormal – A
Survey of Admissions and Educational Facilities.* The British Psychological Society,
Tavistock House, London, WC1.

COMMITTEE ON LOCAL AUTHORITY AND ALLIED PERSONAL SOCIAL SERVICES
(1968) *Report of the Committee* (Seebohm Report). HMSO London.

DEPARTMENT OF HEALTH AND SOCIAL SECURITY (1970) *National Health Service.*
HMSO London.

DEPARTMENT OF EDUCATION AND SCIENCE (1968) List of Independent Schools
in England and Wales Recognised as Efficient under Rule 16 (List 70).
HMSO London.

DEPARTMENT OF EDUCATION AND SCIENCE (1969) List of Special Schools for
Handicapped Pupils in England and Wales (List 42). HMSO London.

KUSHLICK, A. (1967) "Comprehensive services for the mentally subnormal,"
Chapter 38 in: *New Aspects of Mental Health Services,* Freeman and Farndale
(ed.), Pergamon Press, London.

MORRIS, P. (1969) *Put Away.* Routledge and Kegan Paul, London.

PACKMAN, J. AND POWER, M. (1968) "Children in need and the help they
receive". Appendix Q in the *Report of the Committee on Local Authority and Allied
Personal Social Services.* HMSO London.

PRINGLE, M. L. KELLMER (1965) "Emotional adjustment among children in
care: a firm friend outside", Chapter 11 in: *Deprivation and Education.* Longmans,
Green & Co. London.

TIZARD, J. (1960) "Residential care of mentally handicapped children"
British Medical Journal. 1960. *1.* pp 1041–6.

Acts and Regulations
Children Act, 1948.
Children and Young Persons Act, 1969.
Education Act, 1944.
Handicapped Pupils and Special Schools Regulations, 1959.
Mental Health Act, 1959.

9. Special educational treatment

"So far as the education of the handicapped child is concerned, the law of chance operates."

Letter from a parent of a deaf child

Part I. The nature and aims of special education

Introduction

The measures which have been described in previous chapters to ensure early recognition and diagnostic assessment of handicapped children must be complemented by an adequate range of educational provisions. Adequacy of provision means not only that there should be a sufficient variety of special schools and classes to cater for the variety of special needs, but that they should be available in ways which facilitate the achievement of the aims of special education.

The aims in the education of handicapped children are essentially the same as those for ordinary children – to promote their fullest personal and educational development. There are, however, some differences in emphasis. Since handicaps are liable to impede emotional and social adjustment as well as educational progress, it is necessary to pay particular attention to creating the best conditions for personal and social competence both through the learning experiences provided in school and by considering other influential factors of school organisation and home-school co-operation. And since many handicaps make it more difficult for children to adjust to life and work after leaving school, it is necessary to ensure that special education includes more specific attention to the development of knowledge, attitudes and skills needed in post school life. Severely handicapped children who may not prove able to sustain complete integration into normal living nevertheless need the fullest personal and social competence they can attain.

199

These broader personal and social aspects of special education have practical implications. The effectiveness of special schooling depends upon the timing and efficiency with which various forms of other help have been and are provided – diagnosis and assessment, continuing assessment, parent guidance and continuing social work. Moreover, the need for special education cannot be assessed only in terms of academic or special instructional requirements nor in terms of the degree of disability. The child's personality and home circumstances are always an important aspect of the assessment; and the facilities and attention available in normal schools must be considered.

The present position

In the last twenty-five years, considerable change and development have occurred in the provision of special education. As the figures in Table 1 show, there has been development of provision which was inadequate or lacking in 1938, particularly for maladjusted, educationally subnormal and speech defective children.

Table I. Children in Special Schools

1. 1938		2. 1968	
Blind	4,640	Blind	1,122
		Partially sighted	1,855
Deaf	4,527	Deaf	3,213
		Partially hearing (excluding children in partially-hearing units)	1,608
Mentally defective	16,375	Educationally subnormal	48,818
Physically defective (including 16,541 delicate children)	33,323	Physically handicapped (plus 3,766 in Hospital Schools)	8,227
		Delicate	7,555
Epileptic	606	Epileptic	860
		Maladjusted (plus 2,592 in Independent Schools)	4,303
		Speech defective	251

1   Report of the Board of Education – *Education in* 1938, HMSO 1939.
2   Department of Education and Science – *Statistics of Education* 1968, Vol 1 HMSO 1969.

The numbers of handicapped children in some categories have declined (*eg* the blind, physically handicapped and delicate) and, more significant, the kind of handicaps have changed, with important consequences for education. This shows most clearly in the physically handicapped category where the emphasis has shifted from acquired conditions like tuberculosis or poliomyelitis to congenital conditions such as cerebral palsy and spina bifida which are liable to have diffuse effects on children's capacity for learning and adjustment. Improved methods of detection have actually increased the number of hearing impaired children receiving special education.

There has also been a trend to differentiate the kinds of special education provided: for example, increasing provision of selective secondary education for children with physical and sensory handicaps. The increased incidence of multi-handicaps has led to the establishment of special schools for these children. Thus, there are special schools for blind children who are subnormal or physically handicapped; for hearing-impaired children who are maladjusted; for physically handicapped children who are deaf or subnormal. A related trend has been to include in special education children who previously would have been thought too handicapped to benefit from education and this trend is about to be reinforced by the transfer of responsibility for the severely subnormal to education authorities. The way in which special education is organised has become more varied; in addition to day and residential schools there are schools which offer both; there are more special classes and units in ordinary schools; home teaching is available in most areas, etc.

An underlying influence has been changing concepts about the growth and development of children. In general, these have emphasized the importance of the family and the community, the need to promote integration where possible and to ensure as normal an experience as possible. Developments in the psychological study and assessment of children, and the application of technologies to treatment and teaching are but two examples of the increasing sophistication of methods in the field of special education. However, these have resulted in new problems emerging as well as in new opportunities for tackling old ones.

These changes have been briefly outlined in order to emphasise that the problem of defining and providing for special educational needs is not static. It is not a question of there being a set pattern and incidence of handicaps and of working towards sufficient provision. Needs change as a result of social and economic factors; medical advances prevent some handicaps and reveal others; psychological and sociological concepts influence both the recognition of handicaps and thinking about the organisation of provision. The problem therefore is how to provide as well as possible for needs which are clearly recognised in the present and to be alert as well to changing trends which have implications for the future.

The adequacy of present provision

It is extremely difficult to establish how far the provision of special education matches the need for it. One reason for this is that while surveys of the incidence of particular disabilities are undoubtedly of great value this is not the same thing as identifying the need for special education. Whether a child with a handicap requires special schooling depends upon a variety of factors such as the degree of disability and the capacity of ordinary schools to provide suitable education. This is most obvious with educational subnormality and maladjustment in which it is difficult to make clear-cut definitions of the need for special education. Ordinary schools vary in their capacity to cater satisfactorily for backward and disturbed children; a child may be a misfit in a particular area yet be readily provided for in others. Whether children are ascertained as educationally subnormal or maladjusted is also influenced by the availability of special school places. In the post-war years waiting lists for educationally subnormal schools remained long in spite of annual increases in the number of places provided, because as children on the waiting lists entered schools others replaced them who would previously not have been ascertained because of the shortage of places. This situation appears to be stabilizing, though in 1967 there were still nearly 4,000 children who had been waiting for a place for more than a year. It is probable that even if the number of educationally subnormal school places continued to increase there would still be a waiting list; the task now is to focus attention and resources on provision for educationally subnormal children in ordinary schools.

Some measure of the adequacy of special school provision can be gleaned from ascertainment rates of handicapped children in different parts of the country. Relevant information is given in *The Health of the School Child*, 1964/5, which shows considerable variations in ascertainment between regions.* In general, the rate of ascertainment for all handicaps is high in the South East and the Metropolitan areas but varies elsewhere. The differences are most marked in relation to educationally subnormal and maladjusted children. Thus 92 per 10,000 were ascertained educationally subnormal in the South East compared with 68·6 in the North Midlands. In the maladjusted category, 28·3 were ascertained in the Metropolitan area, 20·3 in the South East but only 6·7 in the Midlands and 3·4 in the Northern region. These figures are no doubt related to the distribution of child guidance staff for ascertainment work, as well as to the availability of special schooling for the maladjusted. Such marked differences would not be expected in the ascertainment of physical and sensory handicaps but a similar trend is clear when the South East is compared with other regions. Thus, the Metropolitan region ascertained 5·0 per 10,000 children as partially sighted whereas the Southern, Welsh and Northern regions ascertained about 2·0 per 10,000. Combining deaf and partially hearing pupils both the Metropolitan and the South East ascertained 10·8 per 10,000 whereas the figures for the Southern region are 6·7 and North Midlands and the South West 7·9. For the physically handicapped there is a marked difference between the North Midlands with 12·6 per 10,000 contrasted with over 20 per 10,000 in the Northern, Metropolitan and South East regions.

There are obviously many reasons for these differences. Some are no doubt due to differences in the density and characteristics of the population but perhaps the most important factors are the availability of staff for detecting and assessing handicapped children and of school places for the particular handicap. It is a common experience that establishing any kind of special school facility results in the discovery of more children needing it than was estimated originally. Needs can in fact easily be concealed either by failure to ascertain because there is no suitable provision, or because some placement, though not altogether suitable is made. The school for delicate children for example is a convenient though not necessarily an ideal placement for children with a variety of problems.

While provision in general for a particular handicap may be satisfactory, there can be difficulties locally in placing children

* Recent figures are given in *The Health of the School Child* 1966/68 for the number of handicapped children receiving and awaiting special education.

because of geographical factors, and with particular age groups or with multi-handicapped children. Our evidence indicates difficulty in placing seriously disturbed adolescents. The pressure to find more places in schools for the maladjusted suggests that the number of such children in need of special schooling is larger than the official figures show. Children with speech and language disorders who are of low intelligence or emotionally disturbed are difficult to place in a school for speech defective children.

Clearly, we have a long way to go before there is an adequate spread of special educational opportunities over the country as a whole to cater for the variety of handicaps. There is even further to go in organising this provision so that the opportunity for special education is available in ways which are least disruptive to the child and to his family. We need more information on the prevalence of handicaps and evaluation of these in terms of the kind of provision needed – provision in ordinary schools, day or boarding special schools, specialised provision for multi-handicapped children, etc.

Educational categories of handicap

In the evidence submitted to the Working Party, there was little reference to the present categorisation of handicapped children. Nevertheless, suggestions are made from time to time that the present categories are due for revision. On the one hand, there are those who fear that categories are too rigid or are sometimes too narrowly interpreted – some even suggest that categories are unnecessary. On the other hand, there are those who consider that some of the present categories are too broad (*eg* the educationally subnormal) or in need of better definition (*eg* the maladjusted). Other reasons for some re-formulation might include: the impending assimilation of the severely subnormal into the education service, the increased incidence and recognition of multi-handicapped children, the sharpened awareness of serious social handicaps and of severe learning difficulties. The emergence of conditions such as autism, for which there is little specific provision, suggests the possibility of additional categories, while the decline in the number of truly delicate children raises a question mark over what in practice has been a useful all-purpose category.

What are the purpose and value of categories of handicap? In the legislative context, categories were originally needed to specify disabilities which local authorities had the responsibility of ascertaining in children and then for providing special educational treatment. Thus the 1921 Education Act specified five types of defective children: the blind, the deaf, the physically defective, the mentally defective and the epileptic. Section 33 of the Education Act of 1944 empowered the Minister to make regulations defining "the several categories of pupils requiring special educational treatment and making provision as to the special methods appropriate for the education of pupils of each category". Eleven categories, subsequently reduced to the following ten, were defined: blind, partially sighted, deaf, partially hearing, physically handicapped, delicate, maladjusted, educationally subnormal, epileptic, speech defect (see also chapter 3 for more details). The categorisation provided in the Handicapped Pupils and School Health Service Regulations, 1945 certainly had a beneficial effect. Notably, the educationally subnormal category gave a fresh start to arrangements for the most educationally backward children; the separate categorisation of partial from severe sensory defects promoted development and change that was needed at the time; and the two new categories of maladjustment and speech defect promoted special education for these groups.

It could be argued that knowledge of handicapping conditions is now so widespread and special education so widely available that categorisation is unnecessary; that it would be sufficient to give local authorities the responsibility of identifying handicapped children and of providing suitable special education. This point of view is further supported by the possibility that new disabilities may well be distinguished as a result of experience and medical/psychological research. Moreover, the increasing occurrence of multi-handicapped children and the increased awareness that any major handicap is liable to be associated with emotional, social and intellectual limitations, makes it important to avoid rigid classifications. Recognition that there are many characteristics and educational needs which are common to all categories of handicap in children implies the need for workers in particular fields of special education to be open to ideas and experience in other branches. For example, there is a great deal of research and experience with mentally retarded children which is highly relevant to teachers of some physically handicapped children. Equally, the insights into the nature and treatment of emotional disturbance obtained by child guidance teams, teachers of maladjusted children and social workers need to be assimilated into the theory and practice of work with other handicapped groups. There are signs of increasing communication and co-operation between teachers specializing in different handicaps, but the question has far reaching implications, for example, for the training of teachers for special education. A further consideration is the possibility that it may become more usual to group children with different handicaps in the same school, especially to provide adequately for some of the rarer disabilities in less populated areas, and to avoid the need for residential schooling. In brief, many factors indicate the need to avoid rigid categorisation and to recognise that categories are not mutually exclusive.

In our view there is a place for some form of categorisation chiefly perhaps because those concerned with planning and providing special education require some indication of the variety of needs to be met but also because delineating a category helps to focus attention upon it and promotes the provision of the necessary resources. Reformulating categories from time to time in the light of experience and research is more than changing labels; it involves a re-thinking of the nature of special educational needs. Experience of the categories "defined" in the 1945 Handicapped Pupils and School Health Service Regulations amply confirms this. Whereas earlier legislation specified children who required special schooling on account of defects (deafness, blindness, physical defect, intellectual defects and epilepsy), the 1945 regulations introduced the concept of need for special educational treatment. This shift from a criterion of defect to one of educational need was particularly clear in the broad definitions of educational subnormality and maladjustment. We consider that this trend should be taken further and categorisation be viewed not so much as a categorisation of handicaps nor categorisation of children but as a categorisation of special needs and moreover the concept of special needs should include personal and social needs as well as more strictly educational ones. It follows that categories do not need to be rigidly defined nor rigidly applied in practice; they do not need to differentiate all the varieties of disability nor specify all the varieties of special education. They do not need to carry the implication that children placed in a particular category should necessarily go to a particular kind of school nor that one kind of school necessarily caters for only one kind of special need.

In our view the following groupings – a more detailed breakdown of those proposed in chapter 6 – of children with special needs more nearly reflect current knowledge:

a. visual handicap
b. hearing impairment
c. physical handicap
d. speech and language disorder
e. specific learning disorder
f. intellectual handicap
g. emotional handicap
h. severe personality disorder
i. severe environmental handicap
j. severe multi-handicap

Each of these groups will now be briefly considered:

Visual handicap

These children have needs for special methods of education and care. We know that there is a considerable body of informed opinion which advocates the combining of blindness and partial sight into the one category of visual handicap. For a variety of reasons – the small number of children involved, the uncertainty of the border-line between educational blindness and partial sight, the varying effectiveness of a certain degree of visual acuity in the same person for educational, social and practical purposes – we agree that this new category is a reasonable and practicable suggestion. Nevertheless, the very varied needs of the partially sighted and the totally blind should always be borne in mind, particularly the real fear that close association of totally blind pupils with partially sighted pupils can have the mutual disadvantage of reducing the independence of the blind and unnecessarily restricting the activities of the partially sighted.

The concept of the visually handicapped group will be of particular benefit to a large number of children with defective vision (possibly as many as 25% of the total) who lie in the "no-man's land" between educational blindness and partial sight. There should also be a general benefit for all visually handicapped pupils if there is a realistic effort to carry out the policy of a general shift towards integration.

At present there are separate residential schools for blind and for partially sighted children and there are already two residential schools for the visually handicapped. For partially sighted pupils there are day schools and special classes in normal schools, but there is no such provision for blind pupils. Blind children of appropriate ability and temperament may well profit by joining day schools and special classes which would now be designated for visually handicapped children. Partially sighted children with good prognosis from the point of view of vision, ie no likelihood of deterioration, are some of the most obvious candidates for complete integration into normal education, some blind children may also be able to achieve this goal. Resource centres for visually handicapped pupils in normal schools seem an obvious method of increasing the opportunities for integration. It is, however, appropriate to sound a note of warning: careful selection of visually handicapped candidates for integration is necessary. Too often, in the past, pupils with poor sight have been allowed to proceed rather ineffectively through schools for the partially sighted and even in normal schools. At school leaving, they have found work placement difficult and have had to receive assessment and training in the two vocational assessment centres for blind adolescents.

We can envisage visually handicapped pupils profiting from the varieties of educational provision according to individual needs and geographical position. The many issues in this field are at present being considered by a committee of enquiry set up by the Department of Education and Science under the Chairmanship of Professor M. D. Vernon.

Hearing impairment
The 1945 Handicapped Pupils and School Health Service Regulations categorised the deaf and the partially deaf separately in order to distinguish their different educational needs. Separate classes were organised for partially deaf children in deaf schools and from 1947 units for the partially hearing began to be organised in ordinary schools. The term partially hearing was adopted in 1962. This differentation of provision is now well established so that there is probably no need for separate categorisation.

The need for educational provision for hearing impaired children has increased largely because of improved methods of ascertainment. In 1938 there were 3,585 deaf children in general schools for the deaf;

in 1966 there were 2,923 deaf children and 3,479 partially hearing pupils, a total of 6,402 pupils. In addition, improved methods of screening for hearing impairment in schools have identified other children in ordinary schools who have some special needs. It is interesting to note, for example, that the number of children in ordinary schools who have been supplied with hearing aids rose from 714 in 1957 to 6,006 in 1967.

A major development has been that of partially hearing units. Education Survey No 1 (Department of Education and Science, 1967) gave a useful account of the aims and methods of this kind of organisation as well as some of the difficulties and weaknesses which need to be guarded against. Education Survey No 6 (Department of Education and Science, 1969) examines the services provided by peripatetic teachers of the deaf.

The main need in the education of the deaf is to organise the application of methods of educational treatment which we know to be necessary and about which a great deal of knowledge and experience exists. In particular, we know that early detection of impairment is necessary and that early auditory training and advice to parents are essential if the hearing impaired child is to have the best chances of acquiring good language and communication. We agree with one of the organisations submitting evidence which proposed that educational provision for young hearing impaired children should be an obligatory responsibility on local education authorities and not, as at present, a permissive one. Particular attention needs to be given to family counselling and to the provision of nursery education. In a number of places, a small group of partially hearing children attends a particular nursery school and is able to have the benefit of normal nursery experience as well as teaching from a teacher of the deaf. Without this skilled teaching deaf children may benefit little from nursery school provision.

Successful progress in hearing impaired children requires a degree of expertise, continuity and efficiency of education which is one of the most demanding in special education – both for teachers and pupils. There is not only a shortage of teachers of the deaf to meet the requirements of units for the partially hearing and peripatetic services but there is also a need for a close look at the length and content of training and the need for further training. The teacher of the deaf not only requires to know about methods specific to teaching the deaf, and about recent developments in audiology and linguistics, but also, in view of their widening functions, needs knowledge of other branches of special education, developments in ordinary education and methods of working with parents.

Physical handicap

The present category includes a wide variety of disabilities, a common factor being the need for some degree of medical surveillance, treatment and therapy. In so far as epileptic children and delicate children share this need, it would be appropriate to place them in this group, which would not preclude the provision of special schools and classes for them, just as at present there are some schools for physically handicapped children catering for specific disabilities.

As we have noted, the population of schools for these children has changed markedly during the last twenty years. Congenital disorders requiring early treatment and, ideally, early special education, form the highest proportion. There is a great need for pre-school education and improved parent guidance and counselling. If a positive approach to this is started early in the child's life, a very considerable difference can be made to the family and to the child's subsequent response to schooling. Since many of the physical handicaps are associated with specific psychological disabilities affecting learning, it is to be hoped that more psychological diagnosis and educational advisory work and more special training for teachers of physically handicapped children and social workers will be made available.

One of the problems in this branch of special education is the wide range of capacities and needs. At one extreme are pupils who need secondary, further and even higher education. At the other extreme are pupils additionally handicapped by subnormality or sensory defects, who need consideration as multi-handicapped. In between are children who can gradually be integrated into normal schools. The discussion later in this chapter about criteria for placement in ordinary schools is important in relation to this group.

Speech and language disorder

The speech defective category was introduced in the Handicapped Pupils' and School Health Service Regulations, 1945. We suggest the term speech and language disorder as a more correct description of the handicap, which is largely a failure in the acquisition of and communication by language. In 1967 there were 227 pupils being educated as speech defective children and 65,000 children were treated by speech therapists. In the main, special schooling entails residential schooling although some special classes have been established. More such classes are needed in order to avoid residential placement, to facilitate early special education and to cater for those children (usually less intelligent or additionally handicapped) who cannot be placed in one of the special schools.

Children with language disorders often present a difficult diagnostic problem and it is essential that any special educational provision should be supported by adequate diagnostic services. There are, of course, children placed in other kinds of special schools who have the additional handicap of a speech and language disorder which makes it a matter or urgency that the shortage of speech therapists should be remedied and also that teachers training for special education should be better prepared to recognise and help with these problems.

Specific learning disorder
A grouping, specific learning disorder, is proposed with a view to drawing attention to the needs of a variety of children who do not easily fit into any of the existing categories. A child of average or good intelligence but virtually no reading attainment could in theory be considered educationally subnormal and in need of special educational treatment in a special school. A school for educationally subnormal children would in general be an unsuitable placement. Sometimes such a child is placed in a school for delicate children. More frequently part-time remedial teaching at a child guidance centre or within the child's own school is provided and sometimes this is successful. There are cases, however, where the disability is severe and continuing. The child commonly languishes in a backward class, lacking the intellectual stimulation from which he could benefit, or alternatively he struggles along in a class of his peers, unable to participate fully in academic work which involves much reading and writing. This kind of problem is sufficiently common to merit separate consideration from the present educationally subnormal group.

Attention has been drawn in research to other learning difficulties in which perceptual, perceptual-motor disabilities or specific weaknesses in cognitive processes provide a significant impediment to learning. Where such difficulties occur, together with a generally low level of functioning, it may be appropriate that special help be given in a school for the educationally subnormal, but otherwise some other means of special educational treatment is required. One school for cerebrally palsied children includes a class for such children, although they are not motor-handicapped. A school for delicate children is sometimes a suitable placement or a special or remedial class may provide adequately. The actual placement is less important than ensuring a thorough diagnostic assessment with special teaching designed to meet the specific perceptual cognitive or other difficulty.

The special needs of autistic children present some difficulty in categorisation. In concluding a survey of research and theory on autism, Rutter (1968) suggested that "contrary to earlier views infantile autism is *not* anything to do with schizophrenia and that it is *not* primarily a disorder of social relationships. The presence of mental subnormality is not sufficient to account for autism and it seems unlikely that psychogenic and faulty conditioning mechanisms are *primary* factors in aetiology, although they may be important in the development of secondary handicaps . . . of all the hypotheses concerning the nature of autism that which places the primary defect in terms of a language or coding problem appears most promising". Clearly the nature of the disorder is still uncertain and the nature of the special need cannot be defined. If the assumption of a perceptual or cognitive defect affecting communication and learning is correct, the special needs of autistic children are comparable to those of multi-handicapped children.

Intellectual handicap

The category of educationally subnormal which replaced the pre-war category of mentally defective is an example of a successful re-direction of thought and practice about a handicap. The definition of the category was a broad one: "pupils who by reason of limited ability or other conditions resulting in educational retardation require some specialised form of education wholly or partly in substitution for the education normally given in ordinary schools". This defined a group of pupils in terms of educational retardation and the need for special teaching, and helped to remove the stigma which had become associated with certification as mentally defective. It indicated a large group of children – perhaps 10% of the school population – for whom skilled help was needed in special schools or in ordinary schools, though it was not proposed that more than about 1% would need special schooling.

There has been a considerable expansion of special school places (there were 48,000 children in schools for the educationally subnormal in 1968) and a vigorous development of ideas and practices in teaching educationally subnormal children in special schools. The development of provision in ordinary schools has been much less satisfactory and one of the urgent needs for the future is discussion and experiment about methods of organization in ordinary primary and secondary schools. This is a question which impinges on many educational issues: the work of remedial teaching services, the trend away from streaming in primary schools, towards mixed ability groupings in secondary schools, and the shortage of teachers experienced and trained for work with backward pupils in ordinary schools.

One consequence of the inadequate arrangements in ordinary schools is that special schools for educationally subnormal children have increasingly included children who are not markedly limited in intelligence. Thus a survey in South Wales (Chazan, 1965) showed that 38% of children in such schools had IQ's above 70. In some areas nearly 50% of the children in these schools have similar IQ's. These are usually children who have additional problems, particularly emotional ones, and social disadvantages. The special educational needs of these children are not in doubt. What must be questioned and discussed is whether many of these children could not be provided for in special classes in ordinary schools and also whether some special schools might provide a remedial and compensatory form of education with the aim of returning these pupils to ordinary schools after a temporary period of rehabilitation. These would be some of the children included in the environmentally handicapped group which we have proposed.

If we can posit a "typical educationally subnormal child" it is one whose intellectual limitations and slower development seem to indicate as far as one can predict, the need for a continuous period of special schooling, with emphasis on preparation for meeting the basic demands of working and social life after leaving school. An important feature of the teacher's skill is knowing in what sequence and how to facilitate learning for children whose ability to learn and to think is limited. With this in mind, we suggest that the term intellectual handicap should be used to include all children in educationally subnormal schools and training centres whose primary difficulty is intellectual retardation. This would distinguish those training centre children who would be more correctly placed in a multi-handicapped group and those children in educationally subnormal schools who would be more correctly placed either in a category of environmental handicap or of specific learning difficulties. The intellectually handicapped would form a group of children on whose behalf we need to utilize current knowledge of intellectual development including the contribution of genetic, organic and social factors in mental retardation and the psychology of learning, to develop methods of teaching which would promote their mental functioning and improve their learning capacity.

In junior training centres, apart from the special needs arising from severe multi-handicap which we have already distinguished, the main need arises from intellectual handicap and its implications for the content and methods of learning and teaching. Likewise in schools for the educationally subnormal, we can distinguish pupils whose main need arises from intellectual handicap (genetically or organically determined) from those others who are handicapped environmentally or socially rather than intellectually. Although in practice it may be necessary to distinguish between mild and severe degrees of intellectual handicap, any sharp division is impossible (as it is between degrees of visual handicap and hearing impairment). Nor is it possible in practice to make a sharp distinction between special educational needs arising from severe environmental or mild intellectual handicaps. This does not mean, however, that the distinction should not be attempted conceptually; indeed it must be made if justice is to be done to both groups.

It may be suggested that this would be in the nature of a return to the pre-war category of mental defect. Certainly it would be a return to a comparable group of children but with a very different set of concepts about the nature of their disabilities, and the aims and methods of their education. We envisage also that ascertainment would be informal – part of a process of educational guidance – with considerable emphasis on initial and continuous diagnostic assessment as a basis for special teaching.

It would be an essential feature of the proposal that arrangements for educationally backward children in ordinary schools should be more carefully organized, advised and supervised. Shortages of space and suitable staff will no doubt continue to limit what can be done by means of special classes within primary schools, and special classes in selected schools drawing from a wider area than that normally covered. But some further development in this direction would avoid some placements in special schools on the one hand, and on the other hand, would enable remedial teaching services to concentrate their efforts on advisory work, on tutoring children who need temporary remedial teaching, and on more thorough remedial work with children who have special difficulties.

At the secondary level, the present situation is fluid. Some schools have developed well-organized remedial departments or classes for the backward. Some have done little more than cater for backward children in a backward stream which suffers from the low morale of staff and pupils, and from low esteem in the school. The trend towards mixed ability grouping has stimulated experiments in providing remedial resource rooms and other ways of offering remedial help. What is needed is a careful study of the different kinds of special educational needs at the secondary level and an appraisal of the various ways of providing it. This should have a two-way relation to the work of the comprehensive assessment teams.

Emotional handicap
An important step forward in educational history was taken when emotional instability or psychological disturbance were recognised as grounds for special educational treatment. Furthermore, the aims of this form of special education were clearly stated as being to effect the personal, social or educational readjustment of the child. This means that local education authorities can give special consideration to the emotional needs of children who are not necessarily failing in a narrowly academic sense. We endorse this generous interpretation of the aims of education.

The term "maladjustment" is thoroughly disliked by many people, partly because of the implications of the prefix "mal" and partly because its lack of precision leads to its being bandied about rather too freely. It should, however, be remembered that it is merely an administrative term indicating that a pupil needs special education and, avoiding any assumption about the nature of the adjustment difficulties, whether these are psychological or social. Such blanket terms have their usefulness and we have found it difficult to suggest an alternative which would cover the different kinds of pupil being placed in this category. One common feature among maladjusted children is their difficulty in making satisfactory relationships with other people but even this difficulty may range from extreme withdrawal through timidity, anxiety, indifference or suspicion to hostility or violently anti-social behaviour. With such a heterogenous group of children it is not possible to say to what extent constitutional or environmental factors pre-dominate. Certainly, many maladjusted children suffer from severe emotional deprivation, family discord, instability of relationships or inconsistency of discipline but in other cases – notably some brain injured or psychotic children – this cannot be demonstrated. The inclusion of all these social/emotional/psychological difficulties in the one group of emotionally handicapped does not mean that they all receive identical treatment any more than using the term "visually handicapped" means that blind and partially sighted children will be taught by the same methods. It is also true to say that existing schools for maladjusted children vary greatly in their approach to the problem. Nevertheless, the following common principles are accepted by most who have had experience in this field:

1. The teacher's attitude to the pupil should be one of personal concern.

2. A framework of control adjusted to the child's level of develop-ment should be established on non-punitive lines.

3. Opportunities should be provided for the child to gain insight into his own behaviour, the attitudes of others and how one affects the other.

4. The child should be given skilled help in overcoming the educational retardation which is so often associated with emotional handicap.

5. Use should be made for therapeutic purposes of the expressive subjects such as art, music and drama.

There is least agreement on the nature of the control to be exercised; some schools favouring a permissive regime, with or without a degree of self-government, others depending on a benevolent authoritarianism. In our view there is room for more experiment in different treatment for different groups of children, provided that the educational aims for each child are clearly stated and the results systematically observed and recorded.

The principle of inter-disciplinary co-operation in the treatment of maladjusted children has been well established though hampered by shortage of personnel.

Severe personality disorder
Attention has been drawn above to the range of problems covered by the category of maladjusted pupils. Although practitioners in this field of special education rarely suggest a stricter classification according to type of problem there are some groups of children who may consistently fail to respond to the forms of treatment evolved for emotionally disturbed children and whose presence may arouse considerable anxiety in other pupils and their parents. These groups include those whose personality disorder appears to be rooted in constitutional abnormality, traumatic brain damage or early emotional deprivation of such lasting severity as to leave the capacity for normal relationships permanently impaired. Children described as psychotic and others called psychopathic have been contained in schools for maladjusted children without in the long run appearing to benefit from the regime. Such children may need an intensity of specialized treatment which would be better provided in a hospital setting with a suitable educational contribution. Severely brain injured children and some autistic children might also be included in this category. These children respond to an educational approach with adequate medical consultation but again require an intensity of care, generosity of staffing and very specialised methods which differ from those suitable for other emotionally disturbed children. Official recognition of severe personality disorders – though there is no suggestion that such a diverse group should be educated in the same place – might encourage the co-operation of education and hospital authorities in making more adequate provision than is at present available.

Severe environmental handicap
It seems undeniable that severe degrees of social or environmental disadvantage create special educational and personal needs which are

218 LIVING WITH HANDICAP

as real as those of children with sensory, emotional and intellectual handicaps.

Environmental disadvantages has been increasingly recognized as a problem which schools have to take into account and compensate for. Developments are beginning to take place, including the designation of educational priority areas and schools, programmes of compensatory education and efforts to improve the co-ordination between education and social work. Though these are not part of our terms of reference, we are, however, concerned with those children in whom the need for special educational treatment arises in a considerable measure from very adverse family and social factors. At present such children may be classified as educationally subnormal if they have a low level of mental functioning or language development, or maladjusted if they show marked emotional disturbance. Some become delinquent and have been committed to approved schools. Approved schools as such are abolished by the Children and Young Persons Act, 1969, though some community homes will probably continue to provide especially for certain types of delinquent and unruly children, while in the broad range of community homes for children in the care of local authorities or voluntary societies a high proportion is likely to have suffered environmental handicap. Schools for delicate children have increasingly included educationally retarded and socially disadvantaged children. Most of them will be found in remedial classes in ordinary schools.

In our view, the designation of severe environmental handicap would promote experiment and development of educational and social services for these children, would help to ensure that their needs are distinguished from those of other retarded children, and would facilitate the provision of additional resources such as remedial teaching and co-ordination of effort by schools, the social services departments and the health authorities. In some urban areas there may well be a case for some special schools and classes to provide temporary special educational treatment for such children. We prefer the term severe environmental handicap to social handicap.

Severe multi-handicap
During the last twenty years, several schools have been established for children who are multi-handicapped. Thus there are two residential schools for blind children with additional handicaps (subnormality,

physical handicap, deafness); there are several residential schools for cerebrally palsied children who are deaf or subnormal; there are several schools for deaf children with additional handicaps. The incidence of multi-handicap has grown during this period and may be expected to continue to do so.

We consider that it would be advantageous to recognise the need by a separate grouping which would include some of the children at present in junior training centres and subnormality hospitals, or else in schools for the blind, deaf or physically handicapped. A separate designation would promote the further development of educational provision and services, and its administration would stimulate thinking about the variety of forms of provision needed as well as about the nature and aims of the education and care required.

For example, there is a need for local and regional development of schools and centres for the multi-handicapped which would facilitate services to the families and also promote easier incorporation into adult life. Since 75%–80% of this group are likely to have a severe intellectual handicap, the most frequent post-school placement will be in adult training centres for mentally or physically handicapped adults, although there are also the problems of other multi-handicapped young people of normal intelligence who have severe employment problems (see also chapter 10).

Organisation of special educational provision

Educational provision for handicapped children was once thought of largely in terms of special school provision. It was never really valid to think in this way because there have always been many backward and otherwise handicapped children in ordinary schools, but it is even less valid at the present time owing to the trend towards the provision of special school classes and units in ordinary schools, and the inclusion, where appropriate, of fairly severely handicapped children in ordinary schools and classes. Indeed we have to think of a wide range of provision from very specialised care and education needed for severely handicapped and, often, multi-handicapped children, to arrangements whereby a handicapped child is educated in an ordinary school with little more than watchful care for his progress and adjustment.

In fact it is possible to distinguish the following varieties of educational facilities:

1. Full-time residential special schools.
2. Hospital schools.
3. Residential special school provision on a five-day week basis. (This is already carried out successfully by a number of local and regional schools).
4. Residential special schools which serve as a base from which pupils attend appropriate ordinary day schools in the neighbourhood, part-time or full-time.
5. Residential hostels providing tutorial help for pupils attending ordinary schools full-time.
6. Multi-purpose hostels providing the facilities suggested in paragraph 5 but for a variety of handicapped pupils, and also providing short-stay facilities for children in care, holiday facilities for handicapped children, and relief in family crises (see also chapter 7).
7. Day special schools.
8. Day special schools allowing some pupils to attend neighbouring ordinary schools.
9. Special classes in ordinary schools, and special units attached to ordinary schools.
10. Peripatetic teaching.
11. Resources centres in ordinary schools.
12. Full integration in ordinary schools.
13. Home teaching.

Within these provisions there are possibilities of variation and one school might well exercise more than one function. For example, a residential school might have some pupils who are full-time resident, others who go home for some weekends, and others who use the school as a base from which to go for some education in a neighbouring school. In the evidence presented to the Working Party there was a frequently recurring suggestion that it should be possible to provide education for several kinds of handicapped pupil within the same school, the most often stated reason being to avoid sending children to schools far from their homes. While we support the suggestion, we must point out that it would, of course, be necessary to provide for different pupils the necessary specialist teachers and specialised teaching techniques, educational apparatus, and therapeutic services.

Many organisations presenting evidence to the Working Party were adversely critical of residential school provision, especially when this meant pupils being separated from home by long distances, and often being accommodated in remote buildings in the country. We accept the validity of much of this criticism but we think that the question of residential school provision should be approached from the point of view of the positive benefit that handicapped children might receive from this type of education. There is no need for children to be sent permanently to a residential school for the whole of their school lives. Nevertheless a period, or periods, of this type of education might well be beneficial at the appropriate stage of a child's development.

The most important factor in our view is that for each individual child the educational facilities should be used flexibly, with the over-all aim of achieving the maximum appropriate integration with normal children and society, while realising that for some children full integration is neither possible nor advisable. We have already discussed different aspects of this complex issue in the two preceding chapters.

Home teaching is provided when a child by reason of temporary or permanent incapacity is unable to attend school. This service provided by local education authorities varies considerably in quantity and quality. Home teachers frequently have no special training for their work which nevertheless requires great skill and considerable experience, since the children often cover a wide age range and present diverse teaching problems. Two major shortcomings of many services are the inadequate supervision of home teachers and the lack of support, which results from their relative isolation from the general educational service.

Peripatetic teachers may carry out some home visits to young handicapped children principally to give support and guidance to parents, although peripatetic teachers of the deaf, for example, will also help young deaf children with lip reading, speech development and auditory training. The major work of most peripatetic teachers, however, is done in schools where they will teach individual children or groups and also advise class and headteachers. The two principal groups of peripatetic teachers are teachers of the deaf and remedial teachers for educationally retarded children.

Educational guidance or placement

Decisions about placement of handicapped children in the variety of ways outlined above are educational decisions. The findings of a medical or psychological examination are only one ingredient in the local education authority's decision regarding suitable placement. As we indicated earlier, assessment of degree of *disability* is not the same thing as assessing the degree of *educational handicap*. Ideally, placement should be made as a result of a team decision with the parents, in which due weight has been given to medical, psychological, social and educational information. The disciplines involved will vary according to the nature of the handicap. The head teacher of the receiving school should certainly be involved in the decision rather than being simply informed of a new entrant. Schools for maladjusted children commonly require to assess whether a particular child will fit into existing age groups and the kinds of problem currently prevalent in the school; and a similar need exists in other special schools.

Not the least important of the persons to be fully involved in the decisions are the parents. They should be clearly informed of the reasons for the recommendation, and their agreement and co-operation sought. It has been suggested that all admissions to special schools should be voluntary, the end of a process of educational guidance rather than of formal ascertainment. This has in fact been taking place in special schools for educationally subnormal children since Circular 11/61 indicated that formal ascertainment was not necessary. One likely consequence is that medical officers, psychologists, teachers, social workers and administrators will have to spend more time on discussion and explanation. This would, of course, be a good thing; many of these workers already give time for this purpose, particularly when parents are uncertain.

The real difficulty arises when parents behave unreasonably or irrationally, and for the small number of cases where this occurs, it is probably desirable to keep the existing compulsory element in use as a last resort, just as parents sometimes have to be compelled by law to send children to an ordinary school which has not been their first choice. This is a safeguard of the child's interests, just as the means by which parents can appeal to the Secretary of State is some safeguard of the parents' interests.

Special school or ordinary school

Ideally, we should provide each child with the kinds of special help he needs and do so with the minimum degree of separation from his normal fellows and the minimum disturbance of normal family life. This concept makes unnecessary such controversies as whether handicapped children should be educated in special or ordinary schools. We start from the assertion that wherever possible they should be educated in an ordinary school. But we have to consider deeply what we mean by "wherever possible". There are two broad kinds of question. First, whether the child has needs for special teaching, medical treatment or personal care which would be difficult to provide in ordinary schools. For example, it would be difficult in an ordinary school to give profoundly deaf children the specialized continuous help they need. Physically handicapped children receive physiotherapy and other treatment in the special school which might otherwise entail wasteful and tiring visits to hospital. We also have to ask whether the ordinary school has suitable organisation, design of buildings, staffing, methods, knowledge and attitudes to make a sufficient and positive provision for the handicapped child. A preliminary answer to these questions is that there are many children in special schools who could be educated in ordinary schools if resources were organised to cater for them. Some of the information we have received indicates that some local education authorities have taken steps towards this end, at least in relation to certain handicapped groups and as a supplement to special school provision.

Secondly, it is important that the child's real needs should be met. It is possible for a handicapped child to be *contained* in an ordinary school, if he presents no serious problems; he may even make progress in school attainments. But we have to ensure something more than containment. The criteria to be applied concern not only educational progress but progress towards personal and social adjustment, towards confidence and competence. It can well be that the ordinary school has the best intentions yet over-protects the handicapped child in some ways and provides insufficient support in other ways. It can be that the handicapped child feels strongly a sense of being different, of being an object of wonder and curiosity. Sometimes an ordinary school provides richer opportunities for a child's general personality development. But for others the demands can be too great.

Clearly, very many factors have to be taken into consideration in deciding whether a child is likely to be successfully placed in an ordinary school. For many handicapped children a special class with a teacher trained and experienced in special education would be needed. For others, who may not need placement in a special class, there is often a need for remedial teaching, for speech therapy and other specialist services. For yet others, who can manage in ordinary classes, the attitudes of teachers and therefore of other pupils to the handicap is important. An informed attitude is needed with the realisation that sympathy is not enough. The handicapped child needs to be helped to make a just appraisal of his assets and limitations; the school needs to balance expectations and allowances. In addition, much depends on the personality of the child and the degree of support and encouragement provided by the home. It is not always sufficiently realised that suitability for education in the ordinary school cannot only be judged on the degree of disability but depends equally on these factors in the school, the home and the child's personality and development.

To facilitate integration of handicapped children into ordinary schools a number of half-way stages are needed. In addition to special classes in ordinary schools, part-time attendance in ordinary schools is also possible. Thus a number of schools for the physically handicapped arrange for pupils to attend nearby secondary schools for certificate of secondary education or general certificate of education courses. The same thing happens in at least one school for the blind. A few schools for the educationally subnormal have arranged for one or two pupils to attend a local art school or further education college for periods during the week. Maladjusted children often attend a local secondary school when they are ready to make the transition. This kind of development is one which will surely increase, and it has implications for the siting of special schools and for the suitability of secondary school buildings, especially where physically handicapped children are concerned. Likewise, a special class in an ordinary school should not be a separate world of its own but rather a home base from the security and comfort of which children are able to venture out to benefit from the wider opportunities in the school generally. While the special class has a function in providing a continuous special experience over a period of time, it may also be viewed as a half way house helping children to make the transition to normal schooling.

The need for special classes in ordinary schools has been canvassed for many years, and for some types of handicap there has been a considerable development of provision. Units for partially hearing children, which started in London in 1947, had increased to 162 in 1966 and were intended to enable pupils to benefit from the conversation in a normal environment and to attend some classes with normal children. Special classes for partially sighted children have been a way of providing for a group of children who do not occur in some areas in sufficient numbers to warrant a school. There has been some development of classes for maladjusted children but many fewer than anticipated by the Underwood Report (1955). Recent figures show that there are now 159 special classes for the maladjusted *(Health of the School Child,* 1969).

There are also some classes for delicate children – for example, in Birmingham, for delicate children of secondary age to which they are transferred from junior schools for delicate children. There is also a need to provide classes for children with speech and language disorders. While there are several residential special schools for such children, there are insufficient places and in any event special classes would sometimes obviate the need for residential schooling. The provision of special classes for the educationally subnormal as an alternative or supplementary aid has long been advocated.

The potential advantages of special classes are many. They provide the opportunity for handicapped children to mix with ordinary children, thus benefiting from verbal and social interaction inside and outside school. It is possible for children to participate in some general activities and to use a wider range of school resources. Integration into normal society should be facilitated by integration at school age and normal pupils will grow up learning to accept and understand their less fortunate fellows. Transfer from special or ordinary class should be eased and, in particular, the transition can be watched and assisted by the special class teacher. Special classes should also enable more children to go to a school in their neighbourhood rather than having to travel some distance to a day school or, in the case of rarer handicaps, having to live away from home.

Some of the possible disadvantages may not be so obvious. There are the problems of finding not only space but suitably equipped rooms for special classes and enough trained, experienced staff to undertake a responsibility in which they will, in many cases, be rather on their own. Moreover, the single special class in particular leaves the children vulnerable to a situation where no replacement can immediately be found for a teacher who leaves. One of the advantages of a special school organisation is that it provides an in-service training of teachers. The new recruit receives guidance and help from the head teacher and his colleagues. As he meets new problems he can turn to colleagues for advice. In other words, in any increased provision of special classes there would be need for considerably more attention to and provision for teacher training, both full-time courses and in-service training. It also follows that the special class teacher, being rather on his own, needs to feel not only part of his school but also part of the special school service. He needs contact with other teachers working with handicapped children and he needs adequate support from advisory and other specialist services. The expansion of units for the partially hearing naturally drew staff from deaf schools, which suffered consequent depletion and an increased rate of staff turnover. There would not at present be sufficient trained staff for special classes for the educationally subnormal and the maladjusted.

An important problem in organising special classes is ensuring continuity of education. In a special school, catering for children from infant age through to school leaving, there can be continuity of curriculum and method, as well as continuity of knowledge and understanding of individual children. Special classes need to be organised in such a way that there is not too wide an age range and that children can move from one age group to another. It would be important, for example, that those children who need continuous special education have somewhere to go after attending junior special classes. It is not easy to organise classes in this way and to ensure that there really is continuity through the age groups and through inevitable staff changes.

Another problem is ensuring that special classes shall be used for those children who can really benefit from them. The temptation to use a local special class rather than some other specialised provision may well result in children being placed in them as a matter of convenience, and a very mixed group in terms of age, ability and severity of handicap can result.

In summary, the laudable aim of integrating handicapped children as far as possible in normal education and living should not be approached in a doctrinaire fashion. It is easy enough to express an opinion favourable or unfavourable towards the integration-segregation issue. It is harder to appreciate the complex factors on both sides, and even harder in practice to make a judgment about a child's needs in individual cases and to organise adequate arrangements in ordinary schools. The comprehensive assessment team should make an important contribution to this by periodic case conferences on individual handicapped children.

Pre-school needs

Pre-school education was strongly urged in much of the evidence submitted to us. At present, this is provided for the deaf and the blind and occasionally for other groups; for example, some schools for physically handicapped children have a nursery class and some sporadic provision is made for mentally subnormal children.

There is a strong tradition of belief in this country that nursery education makes an important contribution to the development and welfare of children. The McMillans' pioneering practice was enriched by the research and writing of Susan Isaacs and in time received considerable theoretical support from studies of both intellectual and personality development. Researches by Kirk (1958) and Tizard (1964) into the early education of handicapped children have given an impetus to the belief that nursery school experience could make a significant contribution to the development of mentally retarded children, and recently the American emphasis on pre-school experience as the key to compensation for cultural deprivation has received considerable publicity. But the present strong climate of opinion in favour of nursery education probably owes most to the experience which teachers, doctors and psychologists have had of its benefits for children who have difficulties in development. Special school head teachers with knowledge of a nursery class speak highly of the value of its social experience and activity for children whose handicap might otherwise deny them this, and also of the ready contact with parents at a period when they are most in need of guidance and most receptive of advice.

How can nursery education be provided? Clearly, a variety of means are likely to be needed according to the frequency of particular handicaps, the nature and severity of the handicap and their geographical spread. If the considerable expansion of nursery schooling as envisaged in the Plowden Report (1967) takes place and, if the work done by day nurseries is enriched by a more educational orientation, it should be possible for more handicapped children to be included in normal nursery schools and day nurseries. Some modest steps in this direction have already been taken in many places though the number of handicapped children in any one unit has to be kept small in order to maintain a balance between a normal range of children and various kinds of priority placements. Provision for partially hearing children in a nursery school can be especially valuable, so long as adequate arrangements are made for teaching by a teacher of the deaf or general supervision by a peripatetic teacher of the deaf. An obvious place for new provision is by the addition of nursery classes to special schools, particularly for physically handicapped children, the severity of whose handicap or whose need for physiotherapy or other special help precludes attendance at a normal nursery school. Likewise, severely subnormal children and their families would benefit from pre-school provision in junior training centres or, failing this, well-organised and educationally supervised play groups attached to infant welfare centres. There is a need for a variety of provisions in order to obviate lengthy travelling time due to distance.

A number of schools for the educationally subnormal already cater for very backward children in the age group 5 to 8. A nursery class continuing into such an infant class at the beginning of the educationally subnormal school would be a means of improving their potentiality for education and of making continued observation and assessment possible.

In recent years, a number of diagnostic or assessment units have been established in many parts of the country in response to the Department of Education and Science Circular 11/61. This suggested that one way of making provision for backward pupils for whom suitable arrangements cannot otherwise conveniently be made might be by the "establishment of diagnostic centres, especially for very young children who appear to be exceptionally handicapped, to help the authority determine the best form of treatment for each child". A number of such classes have been established, sometimes in special schools, sometimes in ordinary schools, sometimes elsewhere. They cover a great variety of approaches and a wide range of handicaps; some have good facilities for assessment and diagnosis but others do little more than provide a nursery or infant type class room experience for very handicapped children. While such classes provide an opportunity for assessing children's suitability for special school, normal school or training centre, one of their main values is providing nursery education for children who would not otherwise get it. In future they should be closely linked with the work of the comprehensive assessment teams.

The nature of nursery education is sometimes only superficially understood in special education. The external trappings of nursery schooling (sand, water, paints, play materials) are provided but there may be little true understanding of how the environment is used by a trained and experienced nursery school teacher to guide and stimulate activity, thought and language. We hope that the need for more trained nursery school teachers will be met particularly in special education. Likewise, there is an expanding need for nursery nurses who for a period of time will work with handicapped children (see also chapter 11).

Special teaching

It is important that discussion of such questions as assessment, organisation and provision should not lead to neglect of the teaching process itself. There was little reference to this aspect in the evidence submitted to us apart from references to teacher training.

A major problem in special teaching is knowing what can be expected of pupils, what their particular difficulties in learning are, and how to organize teaching for individual needs and characteristics. Schools have always used observation of pupils as a starting point and there is increasingly available in schools knowledge and expertise about methods of assessment. But with some pupils more is needed and we agree with the evidence of the Association of Educational Psychologists that: "An important gap as far as the school psychological service is concerned is on-going support for special schools once children attend". The shortage of psychologists is the critical factor here but we commend the practice in some services whereby certain psychologists specialise in the assessment and follow up of particular categories of handicap. We also welcome the suggestion in the Summerfield Report (1968) that psychologists experienced with particular handicaps might work on a regional basis.

Sophisticated methods of psychological assessment need to be followed by teaching based on that assessment. There is a fair amount of experimental teaching going on within the context of a sound educational approach but there are many ideas emanating from research which need to be evaluated in practice; there is also much scope for development of methods and materials. There is indeed a considerable body of knowledge from research and theory which is under-used because it is not sufficiently widely disseminated. One of the suggestions we received was that there should be instructional materials centres for special education. In the USA a number of these have been established in university departments of special education. In Britain, this kind of development would come better through teachers' centres, one advantage being the possibility of a two-way communication between teachers in ordinary and special schools. It is easy for teachers in special schools, immersed in the specific teaching problems of their own pupils, to have too little contact with developments in ordinary education, or even in other branches of special education which may well have value for their pupils.

There is also little precise evidence about the nature of special educational treatment and its results. In a field of education in which so much depends upon what teachers can do for their pupils, the lack of research comparable to that in the medical field is disturbing, even though the quality of concern and expertise in many special schools is very considerable.

At the primary stage, the need in general is to promote the development of handicapped children in all aspects and to develop curricula and methods which aim to remedy psychological disabilities. Retardation in perception, thinking, language, as well as in the early stages of basic educational skills, require not only a congenial and stimulating school experience but also in many cases a more systematic attack on weaknesses and difficulties. The need for a thorough consideration of the content of special education is very apparent in relation to severely subnormal children and to children with multi-handicaps.

One of the main problems at the secondary stage is organising suitable provision for the widening range of educational capacities. At one extreme are children who may go into higher education; at the other, there are those for whom education must be conceived in ways very different from the academic. With all children, in varying degrees, it is necessary to begin to consider their future prospects after leaving school and the implications that these may have for their education (see also chapter 10).

There has been an increasing concern about the provision of secondary education for more able children in various categories of handicap. As noted earlier, there are selective schools for children with physical and sensory handicaps, some long established like those for the blind, some more recent like those for the physically handicapped and the deaf. In view of the small numbers involved, it is inevitable that selective secondary education for particular handicaps should necessitate boarding away from home though some experience has been gained of handicapped children attending local secondary schools either full-time or part-time. There remains the problem of children who do not measure up to the requirements of the selective schools, though they certainly need and can benefit from secondary courses, including work towards external examinations such as the certificate of secondary education or the general certificate of education. In small all-age schools, the staff and resources may well be insufficient to provide these courses adequately. Part or full-time attendance at a local secondary school is one solution and another is the grouping of pupils from several kinds of special school.

With a middle range of pupils, a number of needs compete for time and attention. With many pupils there is the need to continue improving basic educational and communication skills, the need to ensure social competence and to promote emotional maturity, both needs being basic to successful post-school adjustment. There is also the need for a broad educational experience providing knowledge, ideas and aesthetic experiences without which education would be simply utilitarian. At the same time, the curriculum should include the development of knowledge, skills, and attitudes relevant to living, at work, in the family and the community. These varied requirements are not always achieved by non-handicapped, backward or socially disadvantaged youngsters. They are much more difficult for those with marked handicaps, with limited experiences and personal immaturities. For many pupils, the time is all too short; the requirements of living loom up before they have mastered the requirements of learning, which prompts the suggestion in some of our evidence that they should have a later statutory leaving age. We prefer greater flexibility about the age of leaving school or of transferring to vocational training and assessment (where provided) with more opportunities and encouragement to facilitate staying on longer at school for those children who really need it (see also chapter 10).

Evidence submitted to us stressed the need to develop realistic and purposeful curricula for these children. There is certainly a need for experiment and discussion about this. Some of the reports by the Schools Council are relevant; but there would be value in a separate programme of enquiry, discussion and development closely related to the needs of handicapped adolescents. A working party set up by the Schools Council is currently considering curricula for slow-learning children of all ages.

The increasing number of handicapped children with very limited abilities and with multi-handicaps, together with the belief that few children are incapable of benefiting from education, broadly inter- preted, is posing many questions about the aims, content and methods of special education for children with the lowest educational potential. What they need, and are capable of responding to, is very different from the conventional education provided in ordinary schools and even from much of special education. With children in the pre-school and primary age groups, it is sufficient that the opportunities and experiences for learning provided should aim at promoting their maximum develop- ment in all aspects of physical and psychological functioning. We are unfortunately a long way from knowing fully how to translate these aims into teaching sequences; progress has been made in social rather then cognitive aspects of development. We also lack methods and materials, so that compared with ordinary primary education we are groping and experimenting. The general aim with younger children, however, is clear enough.

It is as these very handicapped children grow older that uncer- tainties arise. While not precluding the possibility that education may alter the prediction for some children, it may be realistic to modify the child's education to take account of likely future prospects. The implications of this idea have scarcely been worked out for the intelligent but unemployable physically handicapped child or for the retarded multi-handicapped child, though a number of schools and units have experience of the problems. It is a question we shall have to face increasingly in the future; consideration of it may at least release us from too close an adherence to notions inherent in the words "school" and "education". A somewhat different concept of education is developing, not limited to the acquisition of attainments and skills nor to the work of the teacher and the classroom.

Part II. Severely subnormal children
Introduction

At the time of writing, the severely subnormal are still provided for outside the educational system, but responsibility for them is to be transferred from the health to the education service. Although the necessary administrative changes can no doubt be executed in a comparatively short time, it will take considerably longer before a new direction can be adopted in a field which has for so long been neglected by educationists. While the act of extending the educational umbrella to the excluded children will bring satisfaction to their parents, it must also be seized as an opportunity to re-think the educational aims, not only for severely subnormal children but also for other severely and multi-handicapped children, for whom Kershaw's concept of "planned dependence" or limited independence may be a more realistic goal than fully independent adulthood (Gardner, 1969).

Throughout this century, society has made increasing provision to help physically handicapped, blind, deaf and educationally subnormal children to overcome their disabilities, but the severely subnormal have usually been considered too handicapped to justify much remedial action. Society's obligation was thought of mainly as providing for the child's physical needs, protecting him from difficult or dangerous situations, and training him in elementary skills of self help which could be provided outside the educational system.

Special education for this group of children did in fact originate outside the education system. The first known educators of mentally defective children were physicians who turned to educational methods when medicine failed to cure the deficiency. Itard and his student Seguin developed a physiological method based on the sensationalist philosophy of the time which profoundly influenced the work done in idiot asylums throughout the 19th century. When state education became compulsory in 1870, the attention of teachers was drawn to children who failed to learn adequately and by 1892 special day provision was already being made for them in London. Unfortunately for the severely subnormal, a serious controversy arose at about this time between the more optimistic followers of Itard, Seguin and Montessori, and the genetists who argued that innate mental defect was incapable of amelioration. The outcome of the prolonged controversy in Britain was the Mental Deficiency Act of 1913, which permitted the special educational treatment of feeble minded children and initiated the segregation of lower grade defectives, who became the responsibility of mental deficiency committees. This separation of higher and lower grade subnormal children has persisted in some form ever since. Nevertheless, recent evidence has demonstrated that some severely subnormal children are capable of greater social competence than their limited intelligence and educational achievement would lead one to expect.

Looking at the situation from a strictly economic point of view, it appears sound reasoning to attempt to reduce the large expenditure which would be required for permanent custodial care by investing in these children's future, through giving them a form of education and training which in their adulthood would make them less of a constant liability to society.

Ascertainment and provision

At present severely subnormal children may be placed either in day training centres or hostels provided by local health authorities or in subnormality hospitals. The size of the problem is a matter of discussion and enquiry. The official figures for the number of severely subnormal children in pre-school age groups are generally considered to be an under-estimate, partly because of the difficulty of diagnosing subnormality at an early age, partly because children may not have been notified to health authorities, and partly because some children who will later be deemed "unsuitable for education" continue in all kinds of special schools, and sometimes even in ordinary schools. Accepting the fact that estimates of what is needed are too low, there are at present inadequate provisions even for the known needs. Published figures indicate that there is an overall shortage of places for the mentally handicapped child, even if only the "disposal problem" is considered without paying attention to the quality of education and training provided, or the difficulties caused in travelling to training centres and hospital schools some distance away. At the same time, it should be said that of 22,285 places provided in junior training centres in 1968, only 19,955 were taken up.

It has been estimated that in a population of 100,000 there will be 30 severely subnormal children in the age group 0–4. In addition we can expect 66 such children in the age group 5–15 (Kushlick, 1967). As a result of his survey in Wessex, Kushlick points out that a comprehensive service for severely subnormal children would require facilities in the community which exceed considerably the present provisions. Furthermore, if children were to live in the community rather than in hospitals or institutions, not only special residential care would have to be provided but the junior training centres would have to be expanded. In 1968 there were approximately 20,000 under 16 in junior training centres (including all-age centres) 6,620 were in subnormality hospitals and 1,730 children were awaiting places.

A study of the provisions of training centres, hostels, etc. by various local authorities, shows great differences. Sometimes this is due to a considerably higher proportion of severely subnormal children in one local authority than in others. However, the main reasons for the wide variation in the figures of ascertained prevalence rates seemed to depend on factors such as *a*. the quality of service provided, *b*. whether severely subnormal children under 5 are registered, *c*. whether there are diagnostic and community care services for very young children, *d*. the keenness of local authorities to ascertain new cases, *e*. different attitudes of local education and health authorities towards children on the borderline between mental subnormality and educational subnormality, f. the provision of schools by the local education authorities for educationally subnormal children.

Moreover, the provision of new facilities does not automatically reduce appreciably the demand for them; in fact, very often it seems to create a new demand which has not been foreseen. This is illustrated by the fact that local authorities provided in four years (ending 1966)

6,670 new places for the severely subnormal but the waiting list fell off by only about 190 in that time. The transfer of children from schools for the educationally subnormal and even private schools may partly account for this.

A consistent national ascertainment policy is essential for the planning of provisions to give the children the type of education and training most suitable for their particular handicap. This would be made more possible by the comprehensive assessment centres which we propose.

The education of severely subnormal children

The first occupation centres for mentally handicapped children were opened by voluntary organisations at the end of the first World War. Until the 1950's there was only a relatively slow growth of provision and most of it was housed in church halls and community centres which presented obvious difficulties for organising a good educational environment. The Mental Health Act, 1959, gave a much needed impetus to developments. Occupation centres were renamed training centres, and new purpose-built accommodation began to be provided so that at the beginning of 1969 there were 316 junior training centres and 109 centres shared with adults.

In addition to inadequate facilities, most staff were untrained except by experience and they have not been supported by educational advice and services. In spite of these limitations, they performed a difficult task well. Though they are the first to regret the earlier lack of training opportunities they have nevertheless acquired an understanding of severely subnormal children and their families which should not be under-rated. Future developments depend not only on recently trained personnel but on the fusion of their new ideas with the wisdom of experienced workers (see also chapter 11).

The main task will be to examine and work out in practice how best to educate severely subnormal children. A number of small investigations have indicated some of the problems. Marshall (1967) in a survey of attainments of 165 children aged 14 and 15 has shown the low educational, intellectual and social attainments of the subnormal. A number of studies have examined time-tables and procedures in junior training centres. Norris (1961) found that a disproportionate amount of time was spent on routine matters and too little on teaching but in a later study (1968) he found some improvement. Researches such as those by Kirk (1958) and Tizard (1964) demonstrate the improvements in language, personality and social development which result from a stimulating educational experience. Practical experience in several settings shows that similar gains result from providing children with home-like conditions for growing up. Indeed it is to be expected that to give children activity and experience which meets their childhood needs would have beneficial effects on their personal and social development.

A more fundamental question is whether there are more specific teaching methods, experiences and procedures which could be directed at the deficits of subnormal children. Gunzburg (1963) has developed charts for assessing the acquisition of social competence, communication, self-help, socialisation and occupation, which are widely known in centres and are useful for focusing on areas of deficit. For example, communication is frequently poor. But a more basic psychological assessment is required for the development of teaching methods designed to stimulate weak intellectual and language functions. There is a considerable body of research which has a bearing on this question. O'Connor and Hermelin (1963) have explored the linguistic and conceptual processes in the subnormal. Clarke (1966) has studied the learning of the subnormal and concludes that there is considerable scope for specific training, which, he has shown, has marked transfer effects. Woodward (1963) has utilized Piaget's account of the stages and processes of intellectual development for studying the subnormal child, first of all in the six stages of sensory-motor intelligence and more recently in the pre-operational stage. Work on the latter should be of immense significance for the education of the subnormal since the majority in training centres remain in this phase of thinking throughout their life. Normal children progress spontaneously and fairly rapidly through this early intellectual development, ie by 6 or 7 years of age. It is possible that a close look at these findings will provide the basis for educational programmes which would have something in common with nursery and infant education but also, no doubt, show differences resulting from individual and group differences in learning and thinking.

Age limits
Though there is provision for children past the age of 16 years to stay in

junior training centres and hospital schools, the prevailing practice is to move them at that age to an adult training centre or hospital maintenance departments; however, in practice there is often a bottleneck at 16 while youngsters wait for places in adult centres. This is an unhappy arrangement, because many slow maturing children are becoming responsive to more formal education at about that age and would be able to profit from further education. There is now much evidence that mental ability continues to develop after the age of 16, but it certainly requires the stimulation of an educational environment.

The present practice is partly due to the increasing pressure exercised on the junior training centres and hospital schools to accept more young children, which means making room at the senior level, and partly to inadequate provision in the junior training centres and hospital schools for stimulating the abilities of their older pupils.

It is desirable that education should be continued after the junior training centre and hospital school stage, and adequate provision should be made in the adult training centre to give further education and to consolidate by practice and experience what has been learned in the preceding stage.

Adolescents who leave the junior training centres and hospital schools are very often not given opportunities to apply and practise their social skills and learning achievements, because industrial assembly work predominates in the adult centres. We accept that it is often very difficult to make room for educational activities in workshops and on the timetable because it may interfere with the efficient running of an industrial set-up. It might be better to plan for the older age group in an extension of the junior training centre and hospital school by arranging a "transition stage". This would not be wholly educational nor wholly industrial but would allow a realistic tapering off of the junior stage and give a matter of fact introduction to the problems of life and work. This particular aspect of practical social education is so important that it should not merely be attached to the adult stage activities when in fact it demands its own programme and approach. This transition stage should provide the connecting link between the school phase and the workshop life at a time when many severely subnormal people are maturing and able to benefit from a realistic and directed social training. It would also help to establish a liaison between the junior and adult stage which at present is very often completely missing. It would call for co-operation between the local education and the health authorities as well as the social services department (to which the adult centres are to be transferred).

The role of educational advisory services

Advisory services for the staff of training centres have been limited. The Department of Health and Social Security has had a staff of only six inspectors; similarly few local authorities have employed advisers or organisers for training centres. One of the benefits of transfer should be an increase in advice and help from national and local inspectors. Though few have any intimate knowledge of training centre work, there are many who have experience of special schools, including those schools which cater for children with multi-handicaps and for children with low levels of intellectual and social achievement. There are even more inspectors whose special interests in nursery, infant education, and physical education as well as in practical and creative work are relevant to the nature and organisation of education for severely subnormal children.

It is to be hoped, too, that training centre staff will feel welcomed to refresher courses on general aspects of education and to meetings, particularly of organisations for teachers in remedial, special and nursery education. This process has already begun.

A survey by the British Psychological Society (1966) showed that only about one third of educational psychologists had open access to junior training centres. When access becomes completely open, there will still be the problem of finding enough psychologists to work with the subnormal. The shortage of educational psychologists is felt throughout special education (see also chapter 11). However, it is to be hoped that some psychological services will be able to give a psychologist special responsibility for work in this field, not only in assessment but in helping to develop methods of education derived from psychological assessment.

Following the transfer of responsibility, inspectors, advisers and psychologists will need courses on the needs of the severely subnormal. At least one university has already held a 3 day course for psychologists on methods of assessing subnormal children. It is important, too, that the content of advanced courses for experienced teachers and masters degree courses (which are one source of recruitment for lecturing and advisory posts) should include the education of subnormal children (see also chapter 11).

The organisation of special schools for severely subnormal children

One of the major problems will be the organisation of schools. The Department of Education and Science has already suggested in its consultation document of March 1969 that centres need not necessarily remain as separate institutions. There are already two examples of a training centre and school for the educationally subnormal being combined under one headmaster. Longford School, Gloucester, was the first to pioneer such a merger, when a new centre was built on the same campus as the new school. In Abingdon, the school and junior training centre are also in charge of the same headmaster though separated by two miles.

A complete combination of the severely and educationally subnormal in the same unstreamed school might be difficult in view of the wide IQ range in many schools for the educationally subnormal. It would certainly arouse serious doubts among some of their staff, at least at first. If our proposals for distinguishing the intellectually handicapped, the severely multi-handicapped, the environmentally handicapped and children with severe learning difficulties were accepted as realistic, and resulted in separate provisions being made, some experiments might be feasible in organising different kinds of provision for educationally handicapped children. Then severely subnormal children might be assimilated rather than transferred or simply attached to education. In other words, some subnormal but not multi-handicapped children and some intellectually retarded but not environmentally handicapped children might be provided for in one school since they have comparable needs for assessment and education. Likewise, it is possible that units for multi-handicapped children might provide for children at present in centres and in various kinds of special school. There is, of course, some danger in a search for homogeneity of grouping because handi-capped children need the stimulus of a range of abilities. Certain benefits of heterogeneity have to be balanced against the benefits of homogeneity, for example, the concentration of expertise and services for one kind of problem.

Different patterns of organisation will evolve from experience and experiment. Experience of different forms of organisation in the educational system (for example, combined versus separate infant-junior departments) suggests that organisation is not crucial; it is what teachers do within a given organisation that counts most. The main task is to develop a coherent and constructive approach to the educational needs of severely subnormal children.

Multi-handicapped children

It has been a convenient administrative procedure to regard children with an IQ below 50 to 55 as severely subnormal and not suitable for ordinary educational provision, because intelligence test scores provide a convenient classification method. It has nowadays become recommended practice to repeat assessments frequently because children's scores may change. Low IQ's are often the result of emotional disturbances or additional handicaps, and children who are mis-diagnosed on the basis of a low IQ score may well not receive the type of educational treatment which would help them to function nearer their real potential.

Williams (1968) mentions that in 1965 24% of blind children aged 2–4 and 32% of the age group 5–15 were considered unsuitable for education; 336 of these children were in hospitals and 239 were at home. 44% of the blind children unsuitable for school had additional defects besides intellectual subnormality. The same author and others (Pringle, 1964) estimate that at least 30% of blind children are so disturbed as to be ineducable. It follows that a hospital for the subnormal should also treat the psychiatric problems of the severely subnormal child who might well be under-functioning. We know of little systematic work in that direction in subnormality hospitals.

There is unfortunately very little evidence available which would provide the basis for an estimate of the extent of multi-handicap in the severely subnormal population. Bland's survey (1968) of 31 hospital schools gave an indication of the known number of children with additional handicaps. 9·4% of the children had defects of hearing and/or vision, 16·5% had physical handicaps and 48·3% displayed speech defects.

The fact that personality difficulties interfere with efficiency generally was pointed out in an investigation by Marshall (1967). She showed that in a sample of 165 severely subnormal children aged 14–16 the maladjustment syndrome of unforthcomingness and withdrawal were significantly correlated with inadequate social competence. It may well be that far too little attention is paid to emotional disturbance in the severely subnormal child because efforts are directed towards overcoming the effect of the intellectual handicap.

Neither hospital schools nor training centres are able at present to give the necessary attention to the child with multiple handicaps. Children with higher intellectual ability, who have to live and work in an institutional environment designed for children with low mental capacity, face the danger of deterioration. They are deprived of appropriate educational stimulation and having to mix with children who are severely handicapped or severely disturbed may be seriously damaging.

Bland's survey (1968) of 31 hospital schools also indicated how little specialist treatment is available for the well known handicaps; there was one teacher for 57 deaf or blind children, one teacher for 42 children with physical handicaps, and one speech therapist for 118 children with speech defects.

Hospitals and education

Special problems will be presented when local education authorities become responsible for children in subnormality hospitals. The lesser problem is that of hospital schools since special services departments of local education authorities have much experience of running schools in all kinds of hospitals for children. Existing schools in subnormality hospitals range from good to very inadequate and little information is at present available about them. Pauline Morris (1969) found in her survey that 30 hospitals out of 34 visited had some teaching facilities. However, three had no classrooms, 17 no playground and 20 no sanitary annexe; and 67·5% of the teaching staff were untrained.

One of the main problems will be staffing. Bland's survey (1968) showed that 82% of assistant teachers are unqualified compared with about 60% in junior training centres. Of head teachers, about a quarter are unqualified, 38% have a Training Council diploma and 38% are qualified teachers. The first task, therefore, will be to improve the status and general conditions of teachint in hospital schools.

The nature of educational work with children who do not go to hospital schools poses questions and practical problems for which solutions are not so easy to propose. These are children who are of very low mental development or multi-handicapped or both.

Despite their difficulties, such children require the full range of personal, social and emotional relationships which they ought to receive at home, and to a lesser extent would receive in good boarding schools. We do not wish to labour here the point that institutionalising children is, in itself, an unhappy though often necessary step, but we feel strongly that the present arrangement for the residential care of children in mental subnormality hospitals could be vastly improved by a different outlook which regards the multi-handicapped child primarily as a child rather than a patient.

Chapter 8 deals with the desirability of providing caring home-like conditions for the severely subnormal. Here we would like to stress that the environment in the school *and* in the wards (however organised) should be educationally stimulating and that the nursing staff should help to continue and consolidate much of the work done during school hours. Whilst we do not expect that nurses, who have a different kind of training, should be teachers in the traditional sense of the word, we think they should nevertheless become fully aware of the educational aims pursued with each individual child and try to follow up in the ward environment and in a different context what the child has been trying to acquire at school. Apart from measures aimed at giving nurses a greater understanding of principles and methods such as those offered in training courses in child care, it would be an advantage if more nursery nurses could be available for an organised educational programme in the wards. It is also desirable to employ residential child care staff.

We do not think that case conferences and reports by themselves are adequate to achieve this sort of integrated effort. In most hospitals it appears that teachers are scarcely ever consulted in arriving at decisions, and the educational contribution is regarded as insignificant compared to medical and nursing considerations. Pupils may, or may not turn up at school, may be kept back, may be discharged but the teaching staff are neither informed of this nor asked to comment on possible alternative decisions. This attitude results from regarding institutions for the mentally subnormal primarily as hospitals, and the children as primarily medical problems, when in fact many decisions need not be dictated by medical considerations at all. Hospitals for the multi-handicapped child should be altered to provide boarding school or residential child care accommodation with excellent medical and nursing care but they should not be dominated by this.

Such boarding arrangements would emphasize the educational processes of environmental stimulation throughout the child's development, and would try to provide the environmental setting necessary for it. This would avoid the hospitals present role as a "storage community" giving food and lodgings until something is done for the child, for example, going to school or being seen by the doctor. We would like to emphasise again that the changes we envisage do not depend on making special funds available, but on drawing the logical conclusions from regarding the severely subnormal child as a child with many handicaps which require adequate attention and on acknowledging that his emotional needs must be met first of all.

There are various ways in which the children's section of hospitals can be made to look less institutional and less like a hospital. This must obviously be done locally. We suggest, therefore, that the Department of Health and Social Security should encourage hospital administrators to delegate some of their responsibilities for the children's section to a team of professional workers. They should include the senior medical staff, the chief nursing administrator, the headmaster of the school, the psychologist and the social worker. This team should be responsible for taking a fresh look at the provisions made for the children's education, accommodation and daily routine; the aim should be to evolve a pattern of care in each individual hospital more in conformity with modern educational and child care concepts.

In the evidence given to us by the Counselling and Advisory Officer of the National Society for Mentally Handicapped Children it was suggested that a working party or committee should be set up "with the power to invite suggestions and to examine practices elsewhere, and with the power to make recommendations with particular reference to the quality of care and to the quality of educational stimulation needed if the handicapped child living in an institution is to have a chance to develop as much of his own potential as possible". It is pointed out, that "the purpose of the subnormality hospital needs to be rethought and, if it is to continue to serve as a place where some severely subnormal children must live, it is essential that it be redesigned as a place for children to grow up in and for adults to live in."

Our proposals for continuous comprehensive assessment, even of children in long-stay hospitals, no matter what their handicap, could have important consequences here; as would our proposal that all such children without a parent or guardian should be received into the care of the local authority while remaining in the hospital, and that all unvisited children should have a "friend" appointed for them by the local authority social services department (see also chapter 8).

References

BLAND, G. A. (1968) *Education in Hospital Schools for the Mentally Handicapped.* College of Special Education, London.

BRITISH PSYCHOLOGICAL SOCIETY (1966) *Children in Hospitals for the Subnormal. A Survey of Admissions and Educational Facilities.* The British Psychological Society, London.

CENTRAL ADVISORY COUNCIL FOR EDUCATION (ENGLAND) (1967) *Children and Their Primary Schools* (Plowden Report). HMSO London.

CHAZAN, M. (1965) "Factors associated with maladjustment in educationally subnormal children". *British Journal of Educational Psychology.* Vol 35, pp 277–85.

CLARKE, A. D. B. (1966) *Recent Advances in the Study of Subnormality.* National Association of Mental Health, London.

DEPARTMENT OF EDUCATION AND SCIENCE (1966) *The Health of the School Child.* HMSO London.

DEPARTMENT OF EDUCATION AND SCIENCE (1969) *The Health of the School Child.* HMSO London.

DEPARTMENT OF EDUCATION AND SCIENCE (1967) Education Survey No 1. *Units for Partially Hearing Children.* HMSO London.

DEPARTMENT OF EDUCATION AND SCIENCE (1969) Education Survey No 6. *Peripatetic Teachers of the Deaf.* HMSO London.

DEPARTMENT OF EDUCATION AND SCIENCE (1968) *Psychologists in the Education Services.* (Summerfield report). HMSO London.

GARDNER, L. (1969) "Planning for planned dependence". *Special Education,* Vol 58, No 1.

GUNZBURG, H. C. (1963) Progress assessment charts. National Association for Mental Health, London.

KERSHAW, J. D. (1961) *Handicapped Children.* Heinemann, London.

KIRK, S. A. (1958) *Early Education of the Mentally Retarded.* University of Illinois Press, Urbana, Illinois.

KUSHLICK, A. (1967) "Comprehensive services for the mentally subnormal", chapter 38 in: *New Aspects of the Mental Health Services*. ed. Freeman and Farndale. Pergamon Press, London.

MARSHALL, A. (1967) *The Abilities and Attainments of Children leaving Junior Training Centres*. National Association for Mental Health, London.

MINISTRY OF EDUCATION (1955) *Report of the Committee on Maladjusted Children*. (Underwood Report) HMSO London.

MORRIS, P. (1969) *Put Away*. Routledge and Kegan Paul, London.

NORRIS, D. (1961) "Education in the training centre". *Journal of Mental Subnormality*. 7, 62–66.

NORRIS, D. (1968) *Some Observations on the School Life of Severely Retarded Children*. Journal of Mental Subnormality. Monograph.

O'CONNOR, N. AND HERMELIN, B. (1963) *Speech and Thought in Severe Subnormality*. Pergamon Press, London.

PRINGLE, M. L. KELLMER (1964) *The Emotional and Social Adjustment of Blind Children*. Occasional Publication No 10. National Foundation for Educational Research, Slough.

RUTTER, M. (1968) "Concepts of autism" in *Aspects of autism* (ed Mittler, P. J.). The British Psychological Society, London.

TIZARD, J. (1964) *Community Services for the Mentally Retarded*. Oxford University Press, London.

WOODWARD, M. (1963) "The application of Piaget's theories to research in mental deficiency" in *Handbook of Mental Deficiency* (ed Ellis, N. R.). McGraw-Hill, New York.

WILLIAMS, C. E. (1968) "Psychiatric problems of blind children" in *Mental Health and Subnormality* (ed O'Gorman, G.). Butterworth, London.

Acts and Regulations

Children and Young Persons Act, 1969.

Department of Education and Science Circular 11/61 (1961).

Education Act, 1921.

Education Act, 1944.

Handicapped Pupils and School Health Service Regulations, 1945.

Mental Health Act, 1959.

10. School leaving, employment and continuing care

"*Our daughter, . . . had been registered as a disabled person, but no job had been found for her. The local youth employment officer came to see her, and was Sheila's friend from then on . . . For two long years she left no stone unturned in her efforts to find Sheila some kind of employment but to no avail. Nobody wanted to know. Having left school, she was outside the education authority, and there was nothing and no-one to fill the gap. Slowly over those two years she began to change. The cheery, sunny-natured girl became sullen, unwanted in the outside world, and a difficult person to cope with. She was sent on a course at a rehabilitation centre for the blind . . . three months later she was home again, still without employment. The youth employment officer was still concerned about Sheila, and said there was only one person left to whom she could appeal. He came to see Sheila and offered her a job at a Sunshine Home for the Blind . . . After she had been there for eighteen months the head noticed her interest in cooking and arranged for her to go on a day release course to a local college. At the end of two years training by sighted methods Sheila obtained a City and Guild Certificate in cookery.*

She accepted a job as assistant cook at the college and was able to continue her course for advanced cookery.

She is to begin a new job shortly at a residential school for handicapped children, for she says she cannot be truly happy until she is back cooking for her disabled children. She is now a happy, assured adult and a very strong ally of the underdog. She often takes a tumble, particularly down concrete steps with no white line on the edge of them, but she picks herself up, shrugs, and says it is her own fault!

A success story really, but please, please *do something about the gap between school and work for the many unfortunate people like Sheila.*"

Letter from the mother of a partially sighted girl

Introduction

The education of handicapped children should not finish abruptly at the end of the school period without any preparation for the life they will lead afterwards. This is true for all children, but with handicapped children there is a great need for careful preparation for school leaving and subsequent placement. Parents are concerned about the future early in the secondary stage of their children's education. A mother of a 14 year old educationally subnormal boy with chronic asthma wrote: "My main anxiety is what happens in two years time when he has to leave school". A further statement-cum-question is so often put by parents that its very frequency tends to dull its urgency to the school teachers to whom it is posed: "He will be all right while we are alive, but what will happen when we have gone?" Yet to both fathers and mothers this uncertainty is of vital importance and unfortunately too often the answer at present has to be vague.

Often parental guidance about employment is treated as something which ends after a handicapped child is safely settled at school. This is mentioned at the beginning of this chapter to give prominence to the fact that parents should be consulted and kept informed as soon as discussions begin about what their youngsters on the threshold of adulthood will do when they leave school.

The last years at school

Handicapped pupils, according to their handicaps, their abilities and the educational facilities available, will leave a variety of schools: secondary schools for ordinary children, special boarding grammar schools, boarding special schools and day special schools dealing with specific handicaps and with multi-handicaps. It will have been possible to make some choice of different types of school placement for children with some specific handicaps, particularly for the educationally subnormal, in centres of large population. But the choice of school may be limited for children with less common handicaps and may necessitate pupils going to schools a long way from home. Since placements in work and occupation are likely to be made in the leavers' home areas, this reinforces the arguments in chapters 8 and 9 for the education of handicapped children in their home area whenever possible.

Where selection of schools at the secondary stage is not possible and the pupils have to attend one specific school, the curriculum of this school will be varied according to the individual child's intellectual abilities. Handicapped pupils (like normal pupils) need as wide a general education as possible. It is even more important in our view that the curricula of secondary schools for handicapped pupils should be strongly weighted towards life after leaving school, in particular towards personal independence, social behaviour and pre-work experience in school, and, where practicable, outside school. The special educational needs of handicapped pupils make it desirable for many of them, especially the severely handicapped, to stay on at school for a considerable time beyond the normal school leaving age. Children at special schools, particularly boarding schools, need relationships with normal children and adults. These contacts should be for specific purposes, for example attending classes, joint activities and expeditions, rather than unplanned school or class visits.

It is better for handicapped children visiting organised activities for normal children and young people to go individually or in very small groups, with definite plans for absorbing them as soon as possible into the usual activities of the organisation. Groups of more than about three handicapped young people tend to remain unintegrated when they visit youth clubs, scouts, guides, etc. They should go to these normal organisations to carry out some pre-planned activity, not just "to mix".

While it is preferable for handicapped children and adults to join normal clubs and activities, it may sometimes be advisable to establish special clubs for the handicapped. These benefit from visits by normal people, especially where joint activities are possible. If it is necessary to have such specialised clubs, it would be well to encourage member-ship by non-handicapped people. The establishment of PHAB (physically handicapped and able-bodied) clubs in various parts of the country is proving a successful means of enabling handicapped young people to take part in youth club activities.

The enjoyable use of leisure presents difficulties for many handicapped children and adults. In planning a school programme, teachers should bear this in mind. For pupils in residential schools more time is available to plan for leisure time interests than for pupils in day schools. For the latter, some part of the school timetable should be devoted to the development of hobbies and interests. This is particularly important for those who will not be able to compete for open employment.

In selecting secondary education for handicapped children, either through choice of school or through choice of curriculum within a school, we suggest that consideration should be given to the child's employment potential, in addition to his intellectual ability and specific handicap. If it is thought that a boy or girl is likely to find work in open employment, there is a strong case for integration into normal education some time during school life. If a multi-handicapped child is likely to be admitted to a senior day training centre near home, there is also much to be said for choosing a school near his home. As stated, the time has come to experiment with the education of those with different types of multi-handicap in the same school instead of trying to define the principal handicap and choosing a school on this basis. There are two important arguments against placement according to principal handicap. First, it often leads to education at a school far from home. Secondly, it is hoped that training centres will accept all kinds of handicapped young people but the segregated education of children as deaf with other handicaps, blind with other handicaps, etc. often leads the staffs of training centres to think that very special techniques are required for dealing with the particular handicaps, thus hindering the rightful admission to the centres of those who could be managed there fairly easily.

The need for social education and for the development of independence has already been stressed. In addition, many who work with handicapped adolescents are convinced that they experience an acceleration in maturation after the age of sixteen, which is, at present, their statutory school leaving age. In the later years of adolescence, many severely handicapped young people make progress at an increased rate, provided these years are passed in an appropriate educational setting. There are, therefore, strong reasons for advocating the extension of education for some handicapped young people well beyond the age of sixteen. It is interesting to note that in some continental countries this continues to the age of 21 years. Nevertheless, we do not suggest that the statutory school leaving age of 16 for handicapped pupils should be raised, even when the general school leaving age is raised to 16. There are a few handicapped pupils who are ready to leave at this age, particularly the less severely handicapped, and some parents and children would resent a compulsory extra period at school.

We do, however, strongly urge that parents and local authorities should encourage handicapped young people to remain at school, or in some form of educational provision, well beyond the statutory school leaving age. Grammar schools for the handicapped have, for many years, achieved very good results in general certificate of education "O" and "A" level examinations. More recently secondary modern schools have had encouraging successes in certificate of secondary education examinations.

We are not advocating extra education only for the small proportion of handicapped children who can take examinations and for those who will succeed in independent work. We think that extra years of education for severely handicapped children are extremely important, provided that some form of practical, social and maturing opportunities are planned in order to fit the boys and girls for the life they will lead as adults.

The problem of children from residential special schools was pungently expressed in evidence to the Working Party from the National Association of School Masters:

"There are far too many children leaving the residential schools ill-equipped to deal with the demands of a modern society. Many have been isolated in what is largely an artificial environment for up to ten years, and it is ludicrous to expect them to deal adequately with the work situation without thorough preparation. In their last year or eighteen months at school every effort should be made through work experience, youth club movements, the Duke of Edinburgh Award Scheme, youth hostelling, etc, to re-establish links with their contemporaries in ordinary schools and therefore to prepare them in part for the kind of people they can expect to meet when they go out to work at the end of their school days. The education of the child takes place outside as well as inside the classroom, and it must be remembered that, for many of these handicapped children, social training and adjustment is often as important as what may be called classroom work. Children must be made to feel adequate to deal with the unexpected and the new situation, and the schools must be prepared to embark on an intensive programme of such activities for their school leavers."

Staff

The staffs of special schools need to be outward looking for two reasons:

First, teachers should keep in touch with schools for normal children to counter the tendency for special schools and their staffs to become isolated. Sustained contacts between special and ordinary schools would help to make it easier for handicapped and normal children to meet and work together.

Secondly, it is important for teachers in special schools to be aware of what will happen to their pupils when they leave school. It was suggested to the Working Party that careers teachers in special schools should have actual work experience of the types of employment undertaken by handicapped people; and that careers officers specialising in the placement of handicapped school leavers should take some part in the special schools' curriculum and daily life.

In those areas where specialist careers officers have been appointed there is considerable evidence of the great value of this. We realise that there are many interesting and effective new schemes of careers advice in action or being planned. The suggestions that careers officers should work in schools and careers teachers should have contact with employment are not alternatives but complementary to each other. It is important that teachers in special schools who know that their leavers will go to vocational training centres, sheltered work centres or adult training centres, should become familiar with such places. This could also have the beneficial corollary that school pupils could more readily make pre-transfer visits to these centres.

Administrative provision for school leaving, placement in employment and after-care

Provision for the after-care of handicapped pupils varies widely. Satisfactory schemes have been evolved in certain localities and for certain handicaps. The evidence presented to the Working Party, however, indicated many serious gaps and deficiencies in exchange of information concerning pupils and in liaison between both individuals and departments.

Some careers officers find a lack of co-operation from the staff of some special schools. Some boarding special schools do not even inform the youth employment service about the existence of prospective leavers. The information provided by many special schools about pupils' handicaps is too vague. Sometimes secondary handicaps are not fully reported. Part of the trouble here may well be due to the forms in use; although some of these have recently been revised there may still be difficulties arising from attempts to standardise these documents to make them universally applicable while there are such differences in local provision and employment opportunities. Unless careers officers have detailed knowledge of children's handicaps well before school leaving age, they cannot carry out their work effectively. The situation is complicated by the fact that, as far as schools are concerned, handicaps are defined medically and this may not be the only factor of occupational significance.

On the other hand, some schools find that they do not obtain the services of specialist careers officers or not as early as they would wish. We received complaints of lack of communication between schools and school medical officers, and between the education and welfare departments of the same local authority. There is no doubt that the school leaver situation in certain areas is confused and often there is no clearly defined plan about leaving procedures and no definite decision about who is primarily responsible. However, some local authorities have devised integrated schemes. We know of some schools for the educationally subnormal which are responsible for their own placement of school leavers and for some follow-up; there is a nation-wide scheme for dealing with blind school leavers; while one city's scheme includes the preparation of particularly difficult educationally subnormal school leavers for life in industry. (Hall *et al*, 1969). The headmaster of one boarding special school, which receives pupils from many local authorities, commented to us on the great variation in co-operation and liaison which his school experiences. Good liaison almost invariably results where local authorities have good facilities for handicapped school leavers and poor liaison from local authorities with poor facilities.

At the time of transfer from primary to secondary education, some consideration should be given to what might be loosely described as the work-potential of the pupil. This could have a bearing on the specialised form of educational treatment which might be available for a particular child. At least two years before statutory school leaving age, every handicapped pupil likely to have employment difficulties, who will be on the comprehensive register of children with special needs which we propose, should be interviewed with his parents by a careers officer who has special training or experience in the placing of handicapped school leavers. This interview should be followed by a case conference, which might profitably include the child, his parents, representatives of the school health and psychological services, the social services department, the head teacher and the specialist careers officer. When necessary, specialist careers officers from particular voluntary societies and a disablement resettlement officer should be available. The first case conference may be able to make definite suggestions about the training and employment of some prospective leavers, or may decide that further information or tests are necessary, or that it is too soon to make realistic decisions about some pupils. The social services department should have responsibility for ensuring that any further action is taken, as well as that on-going support is available to the family.

The social services department, acting in co-operation with the youth employment service or the employment exchange, should also take responsibility for handicapped pupils when they leave school. It should ensure that continuing care is provided, whether social or occupational. In short, we envisage that continuing comprehensive assessment would continue after the young people leave school. Close co-ordination is necessary between the local authority service, the Department of Employment and Productivity, Remploy factories and the various voluntary organisations concerned. The need for a good co-ordinated service with a known department taking responsibility may well become intensified when handicapped young people leave the sheltered educational environment and have to cope with employment in the ordinary world, or else with the frustrations of non-employment, limited spending money and few outlets for normal adolescent interests and desires. It is envisaged that a national study, financed by the Department of Health and Social Security, and undertaken by the National Bureau for Co-operation in Child Care into the further education, training and employment facilities for school leavers with severe or multi-handicaps will shed some light on this particularly intractable problem. In the view of the Society of Medical Officers of Health, all handicapped young people should be regularly examined by the school health service at least up to the age of 18 years. This objective of keeping handicapped adolescents under regular health care is most desirable; when comprehensive assessment centres come into existence these might be more acceptable to young people than going back to school for the purpose. The future of the youth employment service is at present being considered by the Government.

Vocational training and further education

Most handicapped young people will need vocational training or some other form of further education to provide opportunities for maturation, not simply a continuation of the normal school curriculum. In the evidence submitted to the Working Party it was suggested that this period of extra education, which could well be named further education, should take place in institutes of further education geographically separate from the secondary school and that it should cater for adolescents with different handicaps. It was also suggested that this type of education might be associated with further education for normal young people. This is an attractive idea for those handicapped adolescents on the borderline between integration into open employment and sheltered work; indeed it might help some who might not otherwise attain open employment. Special consideration should be given to maladjusted young people, many of whom cannot adapt to an abrupt transfer from school to employment or further education. Provision of hostels near their schools would help to bridge the gap. Work preparation courses, which include transition courses in special schools, remedial workshops within special schools, transition workshops in technical colleges, and other introductory schemes are being developed in various parts of the country. A central source of information about the development of these various schemes would be useful to parents, teachers, social workers, careers officers and others.

We see no reason why vocational training and specialised further education directed to personal independence and social acceptability should not take place together. The Institute of Careers Officers in its evidence to the Working Party stated that, though a distinction can be made between further education and training, this is especially unfortunate for handicapped school leavers for whom social education and vocational training are necessarily interrelated. After referring to the Department of Education and Science plan to establish a further education centre at Coventry, the Institute recommends that there should be more experiments in setting up special units in technical colleges within daily travelling distance of substantial numbers of young handicapped people. Such special units should also provide residential facilities and allow students who live at a distance to spend weekends at home.

Educational provision of this type would not be suitable for many

K

severely handicapped and multi-handicapped young people. Staff of schools catering for such boys and girls think that many of them could benefit from extended educational facilities. Some experimental special schemes for the multi-handicapped seem to prove that they do indeed benefit considerably, both socially and from the point of view of work potential, from extended education provided it is planned realistically and based firmly on the handicapped young peoples' abilities and needs.

Classification according to work-potential

There are of course complicated problems for handicapped school leavers. In chapter 9 we have surveyed the intricate pattern of education for children with varied types of handicap, and the wide range of possible methods of education. At some stage before children approach school-leaving (and with some seriously handicapped children this could well be at the beginning of the secondary school stage) there ought to be a realistic appraisal of the possibilities of ultimate employment for each pupil. There are three broad groups of handicapped pupils, as far as work is concerned. Firstly, there are those pupils who should be able to find work in normal employment.

These would include:
a. some boys and girls whose handicaps are not very severe, for example the mildly intellectually handicapped, many partially sighted and partially hearing pupils, the less severely physically handicapped, and b. those who are quite severely handicapped – some totally blind, some severely deaf, some severely physically handicapped – who, if they have the right qualities of character and temperament, can be found jobs in normal employment. The methods of preparation for employment and the selection of work for these two types of school leavers, the mildly handicapped and the more seriously handicapped, will naturally vary. The former may well need little more than the usual procedures carried out for work placement for normal school leavers, except for a more careful selection of the type of work recommended. The latter, the more seriously handicapped, will need much more specialised vocational assessment and training and considerable follow-up after actual work has begun.

A second group consists of those boys and girls who cannot be expected to find work in normal open employment, yet who have some work potential. They are the school leavers for whom it is reasonable to provide some sort of sheltered work. Young people in this group have a wide variety of individual capabilities, ranging from those who can only carry out very simple work slowly and perhaps not very effectively, to those whose work can be effective and of good speed, but for whom the rigours of normal employment are not possible. Handicapped people in this group will need continuing care and frequent review since they will have fairly severe or severe handicaps and they may need adjustment of treatment, apparatus, work placement, social support, etc.

A third group would contain those very severely handicapped young people for whom sheltered work, even as envisaged for the less able people of the former group, is not possible because of the gross nature of their handicaps, or it would not be possible consistently because of temperamental and personality problems or because of mental illness. Now that children previously labelled severely subnormal are to be included in educational provision, there will be a fair number of school leavers in this group able to work in sheltered workshops. This has already been demonstrated by the staffs of junior training centres, whose leavers, in some areas, have for years worked well in senior training centres.

The first two groups are similar to those placed on the Department of Employment and Productivity register of disabled persons. Grouping according to work potential is advocated because this may help to assess the work placement of individual handicapped young people; also, as has been said, consideration of the children in this fashion may have some effect on their school placement and on the school curriculum planned for them.

Provision of employment, occupation and continuing care

There is no need for radically new legislation to provide the work possibilities implied in the above list of categories. But extended and more diverse facilities are necessary, including a continual search for suitable work, the provision of more vocational assessment and training centres, more adult training centres for mentally handicapped adults and various centres for those who are physically handicapped. The responsibility for providing these will in future rest with the social services department. A re-evaluation is also needed of the contribution which Remploy could make to the employment of handicapped school leavers. At present, children under statutory school leaving age are not able to participate in "industrial exposure" for part-time employment. While safeguards are necessary, an amendment of the law may be desirable so far as handicapped children are concerned.

The basis for a scheme for the employment, occupation and continuing care of handicapped adults is in existence though it may not have been stated as explicitly as the following:

    hospitals with associated training centres;
    provision of work and occupation at home;
    training centres for mentally handicapped adults, with associated hostels;
    sheltered work centres or sheltered workshops, with associated hostels;
    Remploy and other factories;
    employment in open industry, business and the professions.

We welcome the provisions in the Chronically Sick and Disabled Persons Act (1970) designed to give disabled people better access to buildings and to enable them to benefit from improved travel facilities. Many handicapped people face acute problems of transport and difficulties arising from the unsuitable design of many of the buildings in which they might otherwise work. We suggest a further amendment of the law through the Industrial Training Act 1944, in order that capital grants could be made available to employers who were prepared to make alterations to premises such as installation of ramps, widening of doors, etc. This would enable some sympathetic employers to consider employing young people with a wider range of handicaps than at present.

There are many gaps in the provision throughout the country, especially the lack of hostel accommodation. We hope there may be further development of such pioneer projects as residential centres with social and occupational facilities, village communities and so forth. In a properly functioning scheme it should be possible for individuals to transfer from one section to another. Review of individual cases would be one of the functions of the continuing comprehensive assessment and care service which we propose.

Various voluntary societies acting independently have raised money to provide work schemes, training, etc (see also chapter 7).

Some local authorities through the initiative of senior welfare officers, supported by enthusiastic staff appointed to run centres for the disabled, have provided good examples of the way in which handicapped people can be given a fuller, more satisfactory life. The youth employment service and the Department of Employment and Productivity through the disablement resettlement officers often show great initiative, persistence and imagination in finding jobs for those who are hard to place.

The following are examples of developments in various fields of vocational guidance, employment and occupation which, if expanded to the whole country and all types of handicap, would provide a more satisfactory system.

During the 1939/45 war there was a considerable change in the education of blind adults. Many who had previously worked in sheltered workshops for the blind on economically unsound traditional crafts, for example basket work, brushmaking and machine knitting, were found work in normal factories and elsewhere where they carried out the same work as sighted colleagues. Many blind workers stayed on in open employment at the end of the war and many more blind people now work in normal jobs instead of in sheltered workshops.

A Working Party set up by the then Ministry of Labour on Workshops for the Blind (1962) recommended that blind school leavers should no longer be trained in the traditional crafts. Nowadays the great majority of such school leavers pass into normal occupations, according to their abilities and educational standards, through universities to the professions, through special training schools to physiotherapy, piano tuning, shorthand typing and secretarial work; and, by means of two national vocational assessment centres concentrating mainly on visually handicapped school leavers of normal ability, to a variety of selected occupations in open industry. It is, however, necessary for continued, vigorous action to be taken to find new types of suitable work and to persuade firms who have never employed blind people to give them opportunities to prove their worth. One striking example of success has been the employment in simple machine tool assembly by a firm in a Midlands city of a deaf-blind young man, who communicates only through the deaf-blind manual. On leaving school he attended one of the two vocational assessment centres and was found the job by an enthusiastic and persuasive specialised disablement resettlement officer. The difficulty of communication at work has been overcome by a number of workmates who have learned the deaf-blind manual. This shows that the barrier of acceptance of the handicapped by normal people can be overcome. It is also interesting to note that this year a girl from a school for the blind has been accepted for training in mental nursing. A few others have successfully trained as social workers.

The Spastics Society is developing services throughout the country to advise cerebral palsied school leavers and offering vocational assessment and help towards their placement. The Society's Centre at Garretts Green, Birmingham, is an example of a thriving work centre profiting from specialised work based on the Society's own activities: the manufacture of wheelchairs and a substantial production of Christmas cards sold to raise funds. The use of machinery and the clever breakdown of work so that individual processes can be carried out by a variety of handicapped men and women are interesting features of the factory. Most of the workers, although not capable of work in open industry, have a reasonable output. The Spastics Society find difficulty in placing seriously handicapped people because of a lack of suitable centres. Other physically handicapped people are, unfortunately, not able to profit from the finances and services of the Society because its charter only enables it to help people suffering from cerebral palsy.

To someone unaccustomed to meeting severely subnormal people, and feeling perhaps some stirrings of repulsion combined with compassion, a visit to a well-run, busy senior training centre for mentally handicapped adults, of which there are many scattered throughout the country, is a heartening experience. They are mostly run by a staff recruited from industry and able to use their know-how and engineering skill in breaking down fairly simple processes into even simpler tasks so that very severely handicapped people can take their place in a production line packing goods for a neighbouring firm, or building up coffee tables by a series of processes varying in the skills required to carry them out. The manager of one centre said to a member of the Working Party, "After you've worked with these people for a time you largely forget their mental handicaps and remember chiefly that they are persons." This sums up the feelings of many people and reinforces current moves to integrate the severely subnormal into the main stream of education and welfare.

References

BRITISH COUNCIL FOR REHABILITATION OF THE DISABLED (1964) *The Handicapped School Leaver*. Report of a Working Party. Tavistock House, London.

HALL, T. *et al* (1969) "Preparation of immature and educationally sub-normal school leavers for a life in industry." *The Lancet*, Vol 1, No 7599, pp 830–832.

MINISTRY OF LABOUR (1962) *Report of the Working Party on Workshops for the Blind*. HMSO London.

SMITH, R. (1970). Further education, training and employment of handicapped school leavers. (Personal communication on on-going research of the National Bureau for Co-operation in Child Care.)

Acts

Chronically Sick and Disabled Persons Act 1970.
Industrial Training Act, 1944.

11. The training, supply and deployment of staff

"It would be wonderful to share one's problems with specially trained people who really know and understand *how parents themselves feel."*

Letter from a mother of a five year old mentally and
physically handicapped child

No measure to advance the well-being of children with special needs is as crucial as the staffing of the health, education, employment and social care services. It is upon the numbers, personality and training of professional and other staffs and their ability to work with each other and with the child and his family that his well-being depends. Yet in every field there are severe staff shortages, inadequacies in the provision of training – whether basic or advanced – and insufficient co-operation and communication between all the professional workers.

The evidence to the Working Party mentioned especially:
the shortage of qualified staff;
the inadequacy of counselling services, of professional advice on management and of practical help to support the families of handicapped children;
the inadequate co-ordination of services and the lack of mutual understanding between different professional workers.

The medical profession

Medical practitioners need to understand the cognitive, social and emotional development of young children if they are to notice signs of deviation in good time. They must also know enough about other services to ensure that handicapped children can receive adequate treatment and education, and their families good counselling.

Much evidence suggested that the basic training of doctors paid too little attention to general aspects of child development. In the opinion of the Society of Medical Officers of Health in evidence to us, all doctors should have instruction in the physical, emotional and social problems of handicapped children. The Green Paper, *National Health Service (1970)* points out that " . . . post-graduate medical education will need to be extensively developed in the future."

General practitioners
Family doctors are given financial encouragement to undertake post-graduate training but may have difficulty in leaving their practices. The development of group practices should make this more possible; in addition participation by general practitioners in preventive child health work should extend their knowledge and improve co-ordination with other branches of the profession, (Sheldon Report, Ministry of Health, 1967).

Doctors in public and school health services
It is desirable that all doctors in the public health service, whether they are general practitioners or medical officers of the health authority, should have post-graduate training in child health. There are courses leading to the diploma in public health on the one hand, and the diploma of child health on the other and, in addition, six week courses are organised by the Society of Medical Officers of Health for experienced public health doctors.

Hospital doctors
When a child is born in hospital, the doctor delivering the child is likely to identify severe cases of handicap which can be diagnosed from birth. Our witnesses felt that he should also be responsible for putting the parents in contact with the local authority social services department for continuing support to the family. In our opinion either he or the medical social worker should tell the parents as fully as possible about the nature of the handicap and help them to come to terms with it.

Paediatricians
These, though relatively few in number, are fairly well distributed throughout the country and develop extensive knowledge of

handicapping conditions. Post-graduate courses in developmental paediatrics are available for experienced doctors. In evidence to us the British Paediatric Association said that the average consultant paediatrician has little time to talk to parents and others. This was often illustrated in the parents' letters. The need for genetic advice also has implications for both staffing and training.

Training in developmental paediatrics

There should be more training in developmental paediatrics for all doctors concerned in the detection, diagnosis, care and management of the handicapped child. There is a shortage of paediatricians with special interest and experience in this field, which may delay the setting up of assessment centres. There are courses of varying length: long courses extending over an academic year for local authority doctors with special responsibilities for handicapped children; medium courses dealing in depth with special disabilities; introductory courses and short refresher courses. The considerable experience of the Society of Medical Officers of Health in the organisation of such courses was specifically mentioned in the Sheldon Report. It must be recognised that general practitioners cannot undertake the identification of all forms of developmental delay without some formal training. It is desirable that the foundations of this knowledge should be laid in periods of under-graduate and post-graduate training.

Psychiatrists

These, especially those qualified to work with children, are quite insufficient in number and unevenly distributed throughout the country. They are qualified doctors with a post-graduate training leading to the diploma in psychological medicine. Some receive clinical training as registrars or senior house officers in psychiatric hospitals containing children or in child guidance clinics. At present they are usually employed by a regional hospital board but many are seconded to child guidance clinics administered by local education authorities. Here they work in a team including educationists and can often make direct contact with schools. Psychiatrists working in child guidance clinics are primarily concerned with emotional disturbance or learning difficulties in children, though others in hospitals work with severely subnormal or mentally disordered children. It is usually considered desirable for a school for maladjusted children to have a consultant psychiatrist, but such appointments are still rare in schools for educationally subnormal or physically handicapped children. An outline three year training programme prepared by a sub-committee of the child psychiatry section of the Royal Medico-Psychological Association provides for the consultant to have had adequate experience in a paediatric unit, in general practice and in child health clinics.

Psychologists

Psychologists are employed either in the hospital services or, more commonly, the education services. The work of educational psychologists is partly clinical, including the assessment and treatment of children with special problems, and partly advisory. Advisory work in a range of schools demands an understanding of the educational system and of teachers' problems. Thus, it has usually been considered necessary that educational psychologists should have had teaching experience before training as psychologists.

Children with special difficulties may also be helped by clinical psychologists, employed by local health or hospital authorities, whose assessment of children's handicaps is similar to that of educational psychologists; in some progressive hospitals where a sufficient number of psychologists are employed, their assessment of children may be more intensive and comprehensive. Unlike most educational psychologists, they may also have opportunities for research. Clinical psychologists are rarely used to advise teachers, even in their own hospital schools, where their clinical understanding of the particular children there and their familiarity with research into mental development and learning would be of value. Clinical psychologists in hospitals should obviously have an advisory role in the educational treatment of the children they have studied intensively.

The Summerfield Report (1968) commented on the shortage of psychologists in the education service. At the time of its survey there were 326 full-time equivalents in England and Wales, giving a ratio of 1 psychologist to a school population of 24,000. The Report recommended a ratio of 1 : 10,000 and put forward suggestions for speeding up the training of psychologists. These include a two-year post-graduate training in educational psychology with practical work in schools, clinics, nurseries, etc. While appreciating the reasons for this recommendation, we hope that there will be no reduction in the number of experienced teachers seeking training by the traditional methods. Unfortunately, the salary scales for educational psychologists do not take previous teaching experience into account, which may act as a deterrent to experienced teachers.

The shortage of educational psychologists means that too little time can be given to studying in depth the complicated learning difficulties and the emotional problems of all the different groups of handi-capped children. It is desirable for every special school to have the regular services of a consultant psychologist.

Another effect of the shortage of psychologists is that they do not necessarily take part in the assessment of educationally subnormal children for placement in a special school. Of the ten local authorities we consulted, only one mentioned that an educational psychologist took part in this process. The examinations of children put forward for special school placement are usually carried out by school medical officers approved for this purpose, but some children may already have been seen by an educational psychologist. We think that the examination of the child should not be repeated and that in any case, close co-operation between school medical officers and educational psychologists is essential. Educational psychologists working in the school psychological service have free entry to ordinary and special schools but do not normally visit training centres for severely subnormal children. This situation will no doubt change when the training centres are transferred to the education authorities, and indeed some training centres are already inviting the co-operation of psychologists in their areas.

Psychotherapists

Psychotherapy is a method of treating emotional problems by increasing the patient's insight into his own difficulties and his confidence in the establishment of human relationships. Methods of psychotherapy with children differ from the treatment of adults, depending less on verbal expression and more on the interpretation of play. Psychotherapy is within the province of psychiatrists, but in child guidance clinics or hospitals the psychiatrist spends an increasing proportion of his time in diagnostic work. A non-medical psychotherapist is, therefore, a valuable addition to the team.

A psychotherapist is usually a graduate in psychology who has had some experience of children, followed by a period of training in one of a number of recognised centres. The training, which includes a personal analysis, is lengthy and expensive so that the number of recruits is small. The Summerfield Report showed that of 115 local education authorities consulted, only 31 employed psychotherapists. When emotionally disturbed children are referred to child guidance clinics, only a small proportion receive individual psychotherapy. This is not entirely due to the shortage of psychotherapists but also because not all maladjusted children respond to this form of treatment. In addition to their work in hospitals and child guidance clinics, psychotherapists are sometimes employed to work in day and boarding schools for maladjusted children, though at present in insufficient numbers. In boarding schools, where the aim is to provide a therapeutic environment, it is likely that a smaller proportion of children will be thought to require individual psychotherapy; and here the role of the psychiatrist or psychotherapist is more often to act as a consultant or give support to members of the teaching and child care staff. There are differences of opinion as to whether it is better for the psychotherapist to be part of the school team or to work from an outside centre. There is no right or wrong procedure and it is important that experiments should be made and evaluated.

Health visitors, midwives and nurses

Health visitors

Health visitors are key people in the early detection of handicaps not apparent at birth. Since they are expected to visit all homes where there are newly born infants, they should be able to detect early deviations from normal development, especially those which might escape the notice of inexperienced parents. If the parents do not consult their general practitioner or attend the child health clinic, the health visitor may be the only person able to detect a handicap in the pre-school years. Health visitors are qualified to spot abnormalities in physical development but they are less skilled and less informed on deviations in emotional and cognitive development. Some evidence to us suggested that even the medical content of their training is insufficient to ensure that they will inevitably be able to detect physical handicaps.

Health visitors are state registered nurses with midwifery experience or a three-months' obstetrics course as a pre-requisite qualification. Their training is organised by the Council for the Training of Health Visitors, established under the Health Visiting and Social Work (Training) Act, 1962. This training is provided at 38 institutions, including university departments, polytechnics and colleges of further education in the United Kingdom. There are six integrated nursing/ health visitor courses. Health visitors should be competent to advise parents on the management of handicapped children and to listen constructively to the parents' worries and difficulties. This relationship between the health visitor and the parents involves considerable overlap with social workers. In the proposed reorganisation of the National Health Service health visitors will be employed by the area health authorities. Social workers will work in the local authority social services departments. This follows the Seebohm Committee in recognising that the health visitor's role in health education is distinct from social work. We agree, however, with the Royal College of Nursing that health visitors and social workers should co-operate closely. There has been a steady increase in the attachment of health visitors to general practices.

Midwives

If children are born in their own homes, domiciliary midwives will be the first people to notice abnormalities at birth. They should then make this known to the health authority for the child's inclusion on the "at risk" or handicapped registers.

Nurses

Nurses come into contact with handicapped children who have to be periodically in hospital, with the young chronic sick, with those in hospitals for subnormal children, in schools for physically handicapped and delicate children and, to some extent, in other kinds of special schools, or as school nurses. Nurses in special schools may be either state registered or state enrolled. Their skill and understanding is crucial to the well-being of children and their parents.

We agree with the Williams Report (1967) that the certificate in residential child care is more appropriate than a nursing qualification for the care of children in subnormality hospitals, since many do not need continuous medical and nursing care. For large numbers, those qualified as teachers or in residential child care have more to offer (see also chapter 8). Nevertheless, it is important for boarding schools for physically handicapped and delicate children to have a staff member with nursing qualifications. Where these are children who are particularly vulnerable, such as those with severe epilepsy or diabetes, the nursing staff should preferably be residential, but in other cases they could well be non-resident.

Therapists

Physiotherapists

Physiotherapists concentrate on the physical treatment of children and work only under the direction of medical practitioners. They work in hospitals, clinics, schools, or sometimes privately.

This form of treatment is extremely important for children who suffer from cerebral palsy and it is vital that the physiotherapy should start when the children are young in order to avoid secondary complications. Physiotherapists should, therefore, understand the general needs of young children and be able to make easy contact with them.

Physiotherapists receive a three-year training given in some 34 centres in England and Wales. Examinations are conducted by the Chartered Society of Physiotherapists, established in 1894. The content of the course is naturally biased towards physical conditions but recently some psychology has been included. There is still very little study of social problems and the social services. Where physiotherapists are employed in schools, sometimes by the local education authorities and sometimes on secondment from hospital staff, this gives them opportunity for close co-operation with teachers, especially those who are interested in physical education. The practice of employing physiotherapists in schools has the further advantage that the children do not have to miss schooling in order to visit hospital. Although there is undoubtedly a shortage of physiotherapists it has not been possible to estimate how far the supply falls short of reasonable demands.

Physiotherapy attracts some men, and has been one of the main employment avenues open to blind people, but most physiotherapists, particularly those working with children, are women. Many leave after marriage and perhaps not very many return to work later. After three years' training, the salary of a physiotherapist currently begins at £795 a year and goes up by stages to a point where the principal of a training school may receive £2,050 a year. These salaries are comparable with some other professions recruiting the same type of candidate for the same length of training but less than others and the career prospects are too limited to attract staff in sufficient numbers, particularly men. It might be possible to improve the career structure in this and other forms of therapy by creating some posts of responsibility for in-service training and co-operation with members of other professions.

Speech therapists

The shortage of speech therapists was the one most frequently stressed in our evidence. This is important in view of the large proportion of handicapped children who need this kind of help. In addition to children, who are categorized as speech defective, similar speech problems are found in some educationally subnormal or physically handicapped children.

Speech therapists are trained to deal with defects of voice and articulation and also with emotionally related difficulties such as stammering. In recent years they have become increasingly interested in general delay of language in young children. They receive a three-year training organised by the College of Speech Therapists and available at 11 schools throughout England and Wales. The syllabus is comprehensive and includes child psychology. One university offers a BSc in speech which covers approximately the same ground as the examination for the Licentiate of the College of Speech Therapists. They may proceed to higher qualifications including Membership and Fellowship of the College.

The shortage of speech therapists and physiotherapists is due to the same causes. Most speech therapists are women and the loss by marriage is therefore greater than in physiotherapy which has been able to attract some men. There is a similar but even more serious lack of career structure. Salaries currently range from £729 to £1,429. There are few posts of responsibility except for those speech therapists who become teachers in the training schools. The College of Speech Therapists in their evidence made a strong pleas for an improved career structure. A third factor making for the shortage of speech therapists seems to be the relative isolation in which they work.

Of all speech therapists 75% work for local education authorities. If they are based in schools they can develop fruitful co-operation with teachers, but more often they work either in speech clinics or hospitals where they may have very little contact with colleagues of their own or other professions. Unlike physiotherapists, they do not normally work in close co-operation with a doctor, and the College of Speech Therapists pointed out that many doctors have little knowledge of, or interest in, speech problems. The College recognises that there is danger in some speech correction work being undertaken by anyone without full training, but this does not apply to all aspects of speech therapy and many therapists see their role in the future as being consultants in speech to members of other professions. At present little use is made of speech therapists in the comprehensive assessment of the needs of handicapped children. It is important that this omission should be rectified and, where comprehensive assessment centres are set up, that a speech therapist should be available as a member of the team.

We are glad to know that a joint committee under the chairmanship of Professor Quirk has been set up by the Department of Education and Science, the Department of Health and Social Security, the Secretary of State for Scotland, and the Secretary of State for Wales to look into the various aspects of speech therapy. Its terms of reference are: "To consider the need for and the role of speech therapists in the field of education and of medicine, the assessment and treatment of those suffering from speech and language disorders and the training appropriate for those specially concerned in this work, and to make recommendations."

Occupational therapy
Occupational therapists, whose training covers the treatment of both mental and physical handicaps in adults and children, are more likely to be employed in hospitals providing for handicapped children than in educational establishments. In schools it is often difficult to distinguish their role from that of teachers on the one hand and physiotherapists on the other. In the physical treatment of children, the occupational therapist's aim is to "convert the children's physical abilities into functional skills" (Miss Lynne Frood, unpublished paper). This raises a query as to whether the occupational therapist's work places sufficient stress on function. Occupational therapists also concentrate on helping parents to solve problems related to the daily activities of their children such as dressing, eating and movement. In

the treatment of emotionally disturbed children the club activities organised by occupational therapists, and their therapeutic use of art and music, are more inclined to overlap with the work of teachers. Where occupational therapists and teachers are employed by the same authority, there is some difficulty over this point.

Unfortunately it often happens that a spastic child, for example, has to leave his classroom on successive occasions to receive speech therapy, physiotherapy or occupational therapy. Many workers in these professions recognise that there is something unsatisfactory in this situation. We have been interested to hear of some experiments being carried out in this country on the Peto method of treating cerebral palsied children, which originated in Hungary. In this method called "conductive education", physical training, social training, speech therapy and education are carried out by the same person, who naturally has to receive a long course of training. In England, where experiments with the method are being made without staff trained in conductive education, several professionals work simultaneously with the children, doing similar work and sharing their expertise. Thus each member of staff plays an important educative role in guiding members with related skills. Even without using the methods of conductive education, this development of teamwork has, we believe, much to offer to handicapped children.

Use of the arts as therapy
Art, music, drama and dancing are increasingly used therapeutically in work with handicapped children. Therapists working through the arts are concerned with the child's emotional life. Through mainly non-verbal forms of communication they seek to build a relationship which fosters feelings of self-confidence. These techniques are particularly valuable with severely retarded, non-communicating and emotionally disturbed children. They help to develop self-expression, enable the child to cope with anti- and a-social emotions and prepare the retarded child for a learning situation.

In clinics or hospitals for the subnormal or mentally ill a therapist works to best advantage in a team with psychiatric and nursing staff. In schools the problem is rather to make teachers more aware of the therapeutic as well as educational value of the expressive school subjects. An experienced teacher of the handicapped will have realised for himself that he must do more than impart a knowledge of music and art and teach skills, but that he must adapt his work to the level and developmental needs of the child. Unfortunately many colleges and schools for the arts ignore the teaching of arts to the handicapped. There is now a movement among therapists to remedy this gap. A one-year post-graduate diploma course for professional musicians on the use of music with the handicapped is run by the Guildhall School of Music and the British Society for Music Therapy. The Standing Conference for Amateur Music has a sub-committee on music for the handicapped which organises courses and discussion meetings for teachers of handicapped children. The new College of Speech and Drama is the first to appoint (in 1969) a lecturer in drama therapy, and an association of teachers of drama has recently been formed to promote the therapeutic use of drama.

Teachers

Among professional people, teachers – apart from nurses and residential child care staff – have continuous day-to-day contact with handicapped children over a long period. Their influence is, therefore, second only to that of parents. Thus it is important that they should be given every opportunity to acquire understanding of handicapping conditions and specialised teaching skills and be able to offer to the children a helpful and understanding relationship. The teacher's role in special education is very wide, since a narrow concentration on scholastic progress is quite out of place in view of the effect of handicap on all aspects of development. The emphasis on other aspects of a child's development is clear in schools for maladjusted children where the main educational aim is the child's emotional readjustment, but even before these schools started, attention was paid to physical, social and emotional well-being. Teachers also have an important role in assessment. More effort should be made to help teachers to record what they know about children in terms which give information to other professions and carry weight with them. It is becoming more common for long-term assessment centres to employ teachers on their staff not only to occupy and teach the children but to observe the child's behaviour in response to group activity and academic tasks.

Successful teaching of handicapped children requires, in addition to certain desirable qualities of personality, a higher level of specialised knowledge and teaching skill than is needed with the ordinary child.

Because of handicapped children's varied difficulties, much less can be left to chance and to the child's curiosity, resilience and drive towards maturity. For example, the teacher of an educationally subnormal child needs a very clear understanding of the learning process and the maturation of abilities. Teachers of physically handicapped children will have to devise methods of overcoming specific learning disabilities which are rarely encountered in ordinary schools. They may have to teach reading to children who cannot speak. Teachers of maladjusted children – and indeed all teachers of handicapped children – need to understand how emotional problems affect learning and the growth of personality. While it is desirable that all teachers should know something of these problems, it is important that those who teach handicapped children should have specialised training, preferably in addition to their basic training. At the present time, additional training is not compulsory except for teachers of blind and deaf children where specialised teaching techniques are essential.

Teachers who wish to work with handicapped children are usually encouraged to start their teaching career in ordinary schools, on the grounds that familiarity with the standards of non-handicapped children and confidence in their ability as teachers will form the best foundation for work with the handicapped later. There is considerable force in this argument which also derives from the recognition of the common needs of all children. When teachers with a minimum of two years' experience transfer from ordinary to special schools, they usually do so without further training, but in their new school they have the guidance of an experienced head who usually has some additional qualification. Teachers are then eligible after five years' total experience to apply for secondment to one-year courses leading to the diploma or certificate in the education of handicapped children. Much theory which had little impact during their basic training is now more easily assimilated and seen to be related to classroom practice.

It is desirable that all teachers should receive this additional training within three years of taking up work with handicapped children, as they do already for blind and deaf children. Unfortunately, it has not been possible to achieve this standard because of the general teacher shortage which makes it difficult for local education authorities to second an adequate number of teachers for further training. Moreover, the arrangements may have the result of discouraging some enthusiastic young teachers who wish to work with handicapped children from the start. There would, therefore, be obvious advantages in increasing the understanding of handicapped children among young teachers during their initial training.

It is inevitable that many teachers find themselves having to teach handicapped children in ordinary schools, work for which they have not been prepared and that they have to do without the guidance of a head trained in special education. Some of these teachers later take one-year courses at institutes of education and usually the staffs of the institutes are glad to have teachers from ordinary and special schools intermingling in these courses. There are strong grounds for giving extended opportunities for training to those teachers in ordinary schools who actually have handicapped children in their classes. The proposed inclusion of severely subnormal children in the education system inevitably raises more forcibly the question of relevant training to teach children with severe learning difficulties. We therefore advocate a range of courses for teachers to equip them for work with handicapped children.

The basic training of teachers
Many organisations stated in evidence that the basic three-year course in colleges of education gives students inadequate preparation to help even the handicapped children they are almost certain to meet in ordinary schools. All teachers inevitably encounter children with slight physical or sensory defects and must be helped to understand the educational effects of these. The most serious problem confronting the teacher in the ordinary school is providing for slow learners and emotionally disturbed children. We think that all students in training should be given some understanding of serious learning problems. In introducing students during their basic training to ways of helping handicapped children, stress should not be placed on the rarer and more sensational disabilities, such as autism, blindness or aphasia but more time should be devoted to child development, the psychology of learning and the techniques of teaching the basic skills to children who have not acquired them at the usual age.

We think it should be possible for students during their basic training to opt for special education as an advanced subject. This course might be called "an optional study of children with learning difficulties". There is a danger that this course might be considered a soft option for less academically gifted students. This would be unfortunate and quite unjustifiable, since the study of learning difficulties is complicated and difficult, and students in this course would have access to a large body of research which at present makes far too little impact on classroom practice. Students who have taken such an option during their basic training would be able to teach more effectively in primary schools with a large proportion of disadvantaged children, in the remedial streams of secondary schools, and in special schools.

Advanced courses

These will probably contine to be the main means of qualifying teachers in special education, especially those who are aiming at promotion. We welcome the recent tendency to establish courses covering a wider range of handicaps, while recognising the value of separate courses which concentrate in depth on the needs of one particular group of handicapped children.

Degrees in education

It is important that the prestige of those engaged in special education should be high. Unfortunately, this is not always so and it would obviously add to the prestige of special education as a whole if a greater number of its teachers were university graduates. At the present time, only York University has accepted special education as a subject in the bachelor of education degree. If special education is included in courses for the B.Ed. degree, it is essential that practical experience of handicapped children should be part of these. We would like to see three-year trained teachers after suitable experience in ordinary or special education returning to complete a B.Ed. in special education. Some of the present diploma courses might be converted into completion courses for the B.Ed. degree. It has, as part of its syllabus, a thesis or dissertation which may be on some aspect of special education. This is an appropriate qualification for lecturing and advisory posts.

Training of teachers of severely subnormal children

The first training courses for teachers of severely subnormal children were established by the National Association for Mental Health in 1945. At first they were one-year courses for experienced staff, but later a two-year course was established for new recruits aged 18 and over. Then in 1963 a Training Council for Teachers of the Mentally Handicapped was established by the then Ministry of Health to promote and approve courses and award a diploma. The number of trained people in this work has been growing gradually during the last ten years and is now about one third of the total employed.

When training centres and hospital schools are transferred to local education authorities, it will be necessary for all teachers of the severely subnormal to have recognised training and professional status equal to that of teachers in other schools. The Secretary of State for Education and Science announced in November, 1969 that all staff holding the above diploma and with not less than five years experience in teaching severely subnormal children will be recognised as qualified teachers. A new category of qualified teachers has been agreed to in principle.

The Department of Education and Science has asked institutes of education to consider the best way of developing three-year courses with special reference to mentally handicapped children within the general framework of teacher training. They will take place in colleges of education which already have diploma or certificate courses in the education of handicapped children. This would result in the creation of a new type of course offering a basic training in special education, which should have equal status with general teacher training. There would then be two main ways by which a teacher could become qualified in special education. It will be important to ensure that there is an interchange of teachers between training centres and special schools, particularly for educationally subnormal children, especially if these institutions remain separate. It would help to avoid educational backwaters if teachers who had begun their professional career in ordinary schools worked alongside teachers with an initial specialist training. This situation already exists in schools for deaf children.

Re-orientation courses
A number of teachers who are interested in handicapped children are nevertheless reluctant to make a change from ordinary to special schools or classes unless they can have additional training. Reorientation courses would enable such teachers to undertake this work with more confidence, particularly in special classes in ordinary schools. One-term courses of this kind have been established by some institutes of education and more could be provided by local education authorities in conjunction with teachers' centres.

Refresher courses

Conditions are so constantly changing that teachers and other professional workers need to keep themselves up to date. Short courses provide an opportunity for such refreshment and also for experienced professional workers to exchange experiences and views. Refresher courses for teachers are run by most local education authorities, by the Inspectorate of the Department of Education and Science, and by many voluntary organisations, such as the National Association for Mental Health, the Spastics Society, the Association for Special Education, the College of Special Education and other professional associations with teachers among their members.

One disadvantage of this way of providing courses is a general lack of co-ordination. There is nothing, for example, to prevent two organisations in the same area having a conference at roughly the same time on a similar theme which might then be neglected for several years. Therefore we welcome the setting up of the Joint Council for the Education of Handicapped Children, established by eight organisations, which has among its aims co-ordinating conferences and courses.

When courses are run by government departments or different departments of a local authority they are seldom multi-disciplinary. We hope that local health, education and social services departments will provide local refresher courses jointly for health, educational and social workers concerned with handicapped children.

Ancillary staff in schools

Because handicapped children need more personal care than ordinary children, special schools should have a high staff-child ratio. All members of staff, including caretakers, cooks and domestics, have a part to play in the community. In addition, most special schools employ non-teaching staff who work directly with the children. Some of these are nursery assistants who work with younger children. They may attend to the child's toilet needs, but also work in class alongside the teacher, making apparatus or joining in free educational activities.

Special schools also employ untrained helpers, often married women, who are selected on grounds of personality. They may work as bus attendants or guides accompanying children to school. They also work in schools for physically handicapped children, helping them to dress and to move about the school. In schools for maladjusted children attendants, even without training, have proved valuable in giving individual attention to a child who might be in a difficult mood and unable to tolerate the group. This often is difficult work and it is not wise that it should be left in the hands of completely untrained staff (Dinnage and Pringle, 1967).

There is need for a scheme of training for such helpers which would give a qualification equivalent in status to the National Nursery Examination Board. Until this can be achieved it would be valuable if local education authorities and social services departments were to run short courses for people working as helpers in special schools. So far as we know, this has not been done, though satisfactory results can be obtained when the staff of a special school takes steps to involve ancillary staff in the care of the children and in the understanding of the children's needs. In schools for maladjusted children, there is a good case for employing young men as general helpers. Some community service volunteers have done valuable work in this way.

Nursery nurses are trained to work with children up to the age of 7. A two year in-service training recognised by the National Nursery Examination Board is provided in 96 training establishments in England and Wales. The planning of tuition is left to those in charge of the training establishments, who often work in conjunction with colleges of further education, but the N.N.E.B. organises an external written examination leading to a nationally recognised certificate. During training, students directly observe the development of children in the particular establishments where they work. The emphasis is on normality but inevitably students will be expected to note deviations, especially in social and emotional development.

School counsellors

In every special school the teacher's role includes concern for the social and emotional well-being of pupils. We hope that teachers will receive more training and guidance in this and help from school medical officers, educational psychologists and social workers.

The Seebohm Report comments as follows on school counsellors:

"Recently, training courses for school counsellors have started at some universities and colleges of education. These aim to equip teachers for educational and personal counselling. There are problems when one person tries to perform all these functions. To give only one example, educational counselling obviously needs extensive development to meet the expanding opportunities in higher education and many schools are not yet able to advise over the full range. The person prepared to undertake this work may well be different from the one whom a boy or girl will choose to question or confide in about personal relationships. While we welcome the development of educational counselling, we should like to emphasise that we see the primary need as the provision of opportunities for *all* teachers to gain further knowledge of the social factors affecting their pupils. As a further development within the school, we suggest the establishment on an experimental basis of a recognised post of special responsibility in some schools for liaison with outside social agencies, particularly with the social service department. Such a post might be combined with counselling or with remedial teaching."

If counsellors were thus employed, they would have an important function in safeguarding the interests of handicapped children who are being educated in ordinary schools. One year courses in counselling for experienced teachers now exist in three universities. The development of school counsellors is still in a fluid state and there are differing views as to whether counsellors should be primarily teachers or primarily social workers.

Careers officers

At present careers officers are the only local education authority officers whose task continues with young people after they have left school for employment. In consultation with schools' staff, the child and his parents, they see all school leavers, assess the child's employment prospects and from their knowledge of local opportunities are responsible for suggesting openings and for placing some young people in employment. Careers officers have usually had previous experience in either education or industry and need to be knowledgeable about both. Some education authorities employ careers officers with a particular interest in handicapped children but there is no special training for this. They also have an important function in advising young people about further education as well as placing them in work. The Institute of Careers Officers commented to the Working Party that many social agencies seem to be unaware of this. Because of a break in continuity when children leave school, a careers officer often finds himself concerned with the social as well as the employment problem of handicapped school leavers. When the continuity of care which we advocate becomes a reality, it will be important, as we have said in chapter 10, for careers officers and social workers to have contact well before the child leaves school. The government is at present reviewing the whole future of the youth employment service.

There is a one year course for the diploma of the Youth Employment Service Training Board which can be taken at two universities (one in Scotland) and two colleges. The qualifications for entry to training include: a university degree, or diploma in social science or equivalent qualifications from local government, industry or elsewhere. Some time is spent during the course on the needs of handicapped workers.

Residential child care staff

Before the 1939 war, training of residential child care staff was being provided by two voluntary organisations. Much progress has been made in such training since the Central Training Council in Child Care was set up by the Home Office in 1947. Education authorities as well as children's departments now recognise the importance of trained staff and are working to improve the status of this relatively new career. Even if children's homes and boarding schools do not attempt to take the place of a child's family, we believe it is the function of child care staff to create a home-like atmosphere (see also chapter 8). In considering the appropriate training of those who care for handicapped children, it is important to remember that among children received into care by local authorities there is a large proportion with special difficulties, particularly emotional disturbance and educational retardation, and also children with severe physical handicaps. Even if such children receive their education in a boarding special school, they often return to a children's home during the holidays. As we have argued from another angle in Chapter 8, some understanding of handicapped children is therefore important for all child care staff but especially vital for those who work in schools or homes which provide for children with severe disabilities (Dinnage and Pringle, 1967).

Although residential child care work is basically the same, whether in homes or schools, there are some differences. The chief of these is that in the school setting teaching and child care staff are members of the same community, working closely together. If this co-operation is to be successful both branches of the staff must share a common philosophy. The Plowden Report (1967) emphasised the importance of co-operation even where home and school are separate. Where the two are – even temporarily – united under one roof, differences of attitude can have harmful effects.

Harmony is not, however, inconsistent with a differentiation of role and we believe it to be important for all boarding schools to recognise the need for staff whose main purpose is to compensate for the lack of a normal home life. Though some teachers, especially in boarding schools for maladjusted children, have successfully combined the functions of teaching and child care, such a combination is not easy. We therefore stress the importance of the child care function in boarding special schools. Recognition of this function is shown by the fact that there were in 1969 about 1,000 child care staff in boarding special schools, though unfortunately the great majority of these were not trained either in basic child care or in the special needs of handicapped children.

The common employment of teaching and residential child care staff in boarding schools emphasises differences in status, because teachers have a longer training, higher salaries, longer holidays and frequently better accommodation. Yet residential child care staff feel quite rightly that their work is equally important and that they should have equivalent salary, status and privileges. Their prospects of promotion in boarding schools are more limited than in children's homes since the head of the school is usually a teacher. Nevertheless, it has been possible in some boarding schools to establish a staffing structure which gives residential child care staff full responsibility, under the head, for the physical care, social training and emotional well being of the children, and to create a ladder of promotion with senior and principal residential child care staff providing guidance for the less experienced. In these schools, teaching and child care staff share the same common room, attend case conferences and are consulted by visiting specialists and parents. The situation will not, however, be remedied until ultimately residential child care staff have training and status equal to that of teachers. The survey conducted by the Williams Committee (1967) showed that in various types of boarding special schools the number of untrained staff varied from 56%–66%. The highest percentage (15%) of staff with the certificate in residential child care was in schools for the maladjusted. Returns to the Department of Education in January 1968 suggest that even these figures over-estimate the percentage of trained staff.

Residential training in child care, sponsored by the Central Training

Council in Child Care, is based on one-year courses, open to both men and women, usually in colleges of further education. The 12 courses now in existence train about 300 students a year. Candidates are normally expected to have had at least one year's residential experience before taking the course, which leads to the Central Training Council certificate in the residential care of children.

In recent years 42 further education courses on this subject have been established. These are open to school leavers of 16 years and over and lead to a preliminary certificate in residential child care. The Central Training Council also provides a syllabus and guidance to local authorities and voluntary organisations who run their own in-service training schemes, respectively for new entrants and for previously untrained but experienced staff. A detailed guide syllabus has been issued which includes compulsory and optional subjects. One of the options – 15 seminars on "special problems in caring for handicapped children" – is compulsory for staffs of boarding special schools. Such in-service courses have the advantage of direct relevance to the students' actual field of work. They do not lead to a qualification but students who complete the course are eligible to receive the Central Training Council's certificate of attendance at an approved in-service study course.

At present the Central Training Council is considering ways of expanding not only the numbers of students on training courses, but also the provision of a range of training facilities which will widen the area of recruitment into the service, so that people with different educational backgrounds and experience can obtain training at an appropriate level.

Clearly, one year's training is too little time in which to gain understanding of child development, the skills of home-making and the organisation of leisure activities. It is not to be expected that much time would be available for attention to specific handicaps. Nevertheless a number of the one-year training courses offer their students an option in a particular handicap. The Williams Committee envisaged that a similar development might take place in some of the basic two year courses in residential care which they recommended, recognising that the care of children who are handicapped, and some other groups, would need further study. They say: "It may be that certain centres would include a detailed study of one of these groups as the recognised emphasis of the course, but this should not militate against the concept of children's development as a continuing and integrated process. We agree with the view that – as in the teaching profession – specialised training in the needs of handicapped children should normally follow basic training in the care of all children."

The next stage should be progress in specialised advanced training. For several years the Central Training Council has sponsored two advanced courses in university departments of education, primarily for students with relevant basic training followed by not less than three years' further experience. These courses include a special study by each student in greater depth of some aspect of child care. Further developments of this kind could form the basis of specialised training in the residential care of handicapped children.

The Williams Committee stressed the unity of the residential "caring" profession and advocated a combined two-year course covering the residential care of adults and children. The Committee thought that interchange between different types of residential care work would result in a better career structure. Although we sympathise with this view, we think that in practice comparatively few people would wish to change from working with children to working with adults or vice versa, or to make residential care a life long career. The residential child care staff's need for a better career structure might be more effectively met by common training for field and residential child care staff. This different point of view is well argued in the Report of the Castle Priory Study Conference (1969). Courses for child care officers and residential child care are sometimes provided in the same college of further education and share some facilities. Plans for the development of a residential option in a few child care officer training courses are under discussion. Such an option already exists in one university applied social studies course.

Even when it becomes possible for all child care staff to obtain suitable qualifications, there will still be a need for refresher courses on handicapped children such as those which the Central Training Council has run for some years past. We hope that some of these courses will be run jointly for residential child care staff and members of other professions working with such handicapped children. Some courses should emphasise the needs of particular groups of handicapped children. For example, in a school for the blind, child care workers well versed in the needs of sighted children may be aware that – unlike teachers of the blind – they have no specific training to help them to understand the effects of sensory loss. In a school for the deaf, the development of communication is as important out of school hours as in the classroom. Similarly, while we recognise that all courses in child care stress emotional development, those who work with maladjusted children need further expertise and insight. Even though the first need is to extend basic training in residential child care to as many staff as possible, there must eventually be more advanced courses offering specialised training for work with handicapped children, some of which may be general, covering a wider range of handicaps, others concentrating in depth on the special needs of particular groups.

Boarding special schools also benefit from having a matron or domestic bursar who combines skilled housekeeping with understanding of children. To meet this need, a two year course of training for matron-housekeepers has been established by the Institutional Management Association. The aim is to train people to take charge of the domestic side of small communities of children (50–60) in which the organisation approximates as nearly as possible to that of a "home". On completion of this course students in their early 20's are not usually able to take full charge of homes and schools of this size but after some years of child care work would be well fitted to do so. A greater emphasis on the child care aspect would strengthen its appeal in the case of children's homes and boarding special schools.

Social work with the families of handicapped children

As we have said in chapter 7, a continuing and comprehensive casework service for the families of handicapped children does not exist at present. Mental welfare officers are concerned with families when there is a severely subnormal or mentally disturbed child; social welfare officers with physically handicapped school leavers; psychiatric social workers and caseworkers in voluntary organisations with a limited number of particular groups. Deficiencies were noted by our witnesses in three main situations: *1.* in the pre-school years, *2.* when a child is separated from his home to go to a boarding school and *3.* after he leaves school and responsibility passes from the education to the welfare services. We agree with the Seebohm Report that:

"a family or individual in need of social care should, as far as possible, be served by a single social worker. In support of this proposition it can be argued that the basic aim of a social service department is an attempt to meet all the social needs of the family or individual together and as a whole. The new department, by escaping from the rigid classifications implied in the present symptom-centred approach will provide a more effective family service. But for this advantage to be realised it is essential that the family or individual should be the concern of one social worker with a comprehensive approach to the social problems of his clients. It follows that a single worker, and through him the social service department as a whole, can be held accountable for the standard of care the family or individual receives (or fails to receive) much more easily than if responsibility is fragmented between several workers."

This is now made practicable by the Local Authority Social Services Act with the possible exception of education welfare. We ourselves hope that in most cases this social worker would become the "trusted friend" referred to in the Association of Education Committee's evidence to us. The Seebohm Report goes on to say:

"there would sometimes be good reasons for involving other social workers with a family or even with an individual – for example in some problems involving adolescence or in some marital problems. But this should happen as a decision taken by the social worker primarily responsible, in consultation with his supervisor and with the client, and not simply because the administrative structure requires more than one social worker to be involved."

The Report also envisages that the social services departments will provide consultation for field workers and others, that advanced training will be necessary in particular areas of knowledge and practice, for example, handicapping conditions; and in specific settings such as residential homes or schools. Even with better generic training there will also be a need for social workers with special knowledge of particular handicaps. It is significant that of the four sections in the newly constituted British Association of Social Workers one is concerned with physical illness and handicap, and another with mental health. These are interest sections not specialisations.

We think it particularly important that social workers attached to special schools should fully understand the work of the school as well as the needs of the families so that co-operation in the interests of the child may be encouraged. We are glad to note the Seebohm Report's recommendation that social workers based on an area office of the social services department should be seconded to a school or group of schools. Where, as often happens, children in special schools come from a wide catchment area, this will mean that the social worker will not always be the same person as the family social worker. As we have said in chapter 8, we are not convinced by the argument of the Seebohm Report that, so far as residential schools are concerned, the responsibility for maintaining contact between the home and the school should rest with the social services department of the area in which the school is situated. In our view the authority placing the child should take responsibility for ensuring regular visiting as part of the review of progress.

Social workers attached to day or boarding special schools will gain understanding of the needs of particular groups of handicapped children and should therefore be in a better position to advise parents on the special management problems of handicapped children. It is important, however, to recognise that an adequate family casework service based on a unified social services department would not eliminate the need for some other forms of counselling inside the school system to which we have referred above. This is both an educational and social work function as an integral part of the school's operation. The Local Authority Social Services Act does not include education welfare: it is thus left open to any given local authority to transfer this (of course excluding school attendance) if it so wishes. The current emphasis is on generic casework training and on developments in group and community work and that specialization in training should follow, not be a part of basic training. Responsibility for sponsoring the training of social workers is at present spread among three councils: the Advisory Council for Probation and After-Care, the Central Training Council in Child Care, and the Council for Training in Social Work, and two professional associations, the Association of Psychiatric Social Workers and the Institute of Medical Social Workers. Under the Local Government Social Services Act there will be one comprehensive Central Council for Education and Training in Social Work covering the United Kingdom and the whole range of social work. This and the institution of one professional association should improve planning, raise standards and make more economic use of social work teachers in universities and colleges of further education, and of field work supervisors.

L

Conclusion

We have said much about the need to improve interdisciplinary co-operation in services for handicapped children. It is only too easy to say that people must work together, less easy to say how this can be made possible. We comment elsewhere on organisational means for improving co-operation. We would like to re-emphasise the part that training can play. We conclude:

a. That the training of all professional people likely to have contact with handicapped children should include understanding of the functions of other related professions.

b. That there should be more interdisciplinary in-service training.

c. That common courses are desirable at the basic training stage for different professionals working with children.

d. In some instances further specialised or "hybrid" courses are also desirable.

References

CENTRAL ADVISORY COUNCIL FOR EDUCATION (ENGLAND) (1967) *Children and their Primary Schools* (Plowden report) HMSO London.

COMMITTEE ON LOCAL AUTHORITY AND ALLIED PERSONAL SOCIAL SERVICES (1968) *Report of the Committee* (Seebohm Report). HMSO London.

DEPARTMENT OF EDUCATION AND SCIENCE (1968) *Psychologists in Education Services.* (Summerfield Report). HMSO London.

DEPARTMENT OF HEALTH AND SOCIAL SECURITY (1970) *National Health Service.* HMSO London.

DINNAGE, R. AND PRINGLE, M. L. KELLMER (1967) *Residential Child Care – Facts and Fallacies* Longmans, London.

FROOD, L. 1969. Unpublished paper.

MINISTRY OF HEALTH STANDING ADVISORY COMMITTEE (1967) *Child Welfare Centres* – Report of a sub-committee (Chairman, Sir Wilfrid Sheldon). HMSO London.

NATIONAL COUNCIL OF SOCIAL SERVICE (1967) *Caring for People:* report of the committee of enquiry. (Williams Report) Allen and Unwin, London.

RESIDENTIAL CHILD CARE ASSOCIATION (1969) *Residential Task in Child Care.* R.C.C.A., Beechholme, Banstead, Surrey.

Acts

Health Visiting and Social Work (Training) Act, 1962.

Local Authority Social Services Act, 1970.

12. National, regional and local planning and co-ordination of services

"It has become painfully apparent that there is a desperate need for the care of these handicapped children to be transferred to a central department which can cover the health, education and social welfare aspects throughout the country. The present arrangements result in local government servants of mediocre ability attempting to administer inadequate facilities with insufficient funds. This leads to lack of co-ordination, 'buck-passing' and intolerable delays."

Letter from the father of a handicapped child

Extension of services

The need for an extension of services for handicapped children and their families is apparent in two contexts. First, the very considerable variation in provision between local authorities indicates that some authorities are not making the required effort to ascertain the needs in their areas and then to meet them. What is required here is that the services in all local authorities should be lifted to the level of the best. Secondly, there are certain specific shortcomings which affect most if not all authorities. For example, it has been estimated that there are over 3,000 autistic children in England and Wales between the ages of 5 and 14 but at the most only 250 of these children are receiving the specialised education and treatment that they require. Over and above the specific, unmet needs, there are more general deficiencies which must be rectified. The pages of this report abound with examples of these. There is a shortage of hospital beds, whilst some children retained in hospital could with adequate support for the family be at home or in hostels or other special accommodation. Assessment procedures are too often determined by the nature of the presenting symptoms and fail to take account of the total needs of the child. Assessment is too often seen as an event rather than a continuous process. Long-term comprehensive planning for handicapped children is infrequent, so that at best valuable time is lost and at worst an opportunity is gone for ever.

We suggest (in chapter 6) that it should be the duty of the social services department to ensure that every handicapped child's case is reviewed annually by the assessment team and for this purpose to gather all necessary reports, as well as being responsible for seeing that agreed follow-up action is taken by the services primarily concerned. Furthermore, we envisage that responsibility for ensuring continuity of care from detection, whether at birth or later, onwards should rest with the social services department.

It is important to be quite clear here that it is not suggested that the social services department should be playing the major role throughout the life of a handicapped child. Its actual involvement may be minimal at certain times and substantial at others, just as with other departments. What is proposed is that it should additionally assume a continuity role. In the past, no one local authority department has been accountable for this continuity and co-ordination aspect. Since it is so vital, it seems sensible to charge one department with this task; and the social services department appears to be the most likely candidate.

Just because so much needs to be done, the establishment of priorities is extremely difficult where everything is interdependent. More emphasis on prevention would result in fewer handicapped children. Better detection would lead to earlier assessment and more appropriate provision which in turn would minimise the handicapping effect of disabilities. More effective support for the families of handicapped children would reduce rejection, stress and anxiety and also enable parents to cope better with their problems. Better planning for work placement would make it possible for more handicapped young people and adults to realise their full employment potential and make less demands upon social care and other services. Where should we make a start?

Since it is, unfortunately, inconceivable that all handicaps could be prevented, a disproportionate allocation of resources to this would be unwise. Again, the most highly sophisticated assessment services are of little avail if treatment provision is inadequate. It is arguable whether special educational treatment should attempt to raise the vocational aspirations of handicapped children in the absence of reasonable employment opportunities. It is clear that no area of potential advance can be neglected. Progress must be made along a broad front.

If there is one dictum which will ensure that this broadly based progress is in the right direction, it is that the total needs of the handicapped child and his family should be carefully considered and kept under constant review. At any point in time, the child's most urgent needs may be relatively specific: orthopaedic treatment, auditory training, further education, psychotherapy. But, first and foremost, the handicapped child is a child: a delicately balanced organism with a complex of abilities, disabilities, aspirations, fears and temperamental idiosyncrasies. It is not possible to "treat" one aspect in isolation and our approach should be comprehensive and sensitive enough to detect adverse reactions or new needs as they arise. Above all, the emotional and social adjustment of the child should be closely watched.

Our ability to discern, understand and meet the needs of the individual child is to some extent limited by our lack of knowledge of the needs of handicapped children in general. This is particularly true of the handicapped adolescent. Time and money devoted to research and evaluation would be well spent.

Research and evaluation

Some research in this field is undertaken at government level and a good example of this is a survey carried out by the Government Social Survey of the adult chronic sick and handicapped living at home. A report on this is expected in 1970. In addition, most government departments have research sections which undertake some research of their own.

However, the principal role of central government here is to stimulate and finance independent research. The Medical Research Council, which is financed from government funds, has its own research programme and also supports University and other independent research. The more recently established Social Science Re-

search Council at present has only a limited research programme of
its own and most of its research funds are allocated to Universities and
other bodies. The most useful form of sponsorship, whether direct from
a government department or from one of these councils, is often a
programme grant, which permits a degree of continuity normally
lacking in the isolated piece of research. It is well known – and
inevitable – that most research poses as many questions as it answers
and unless there is some follow through, research effort can be dissipated
and disjointed. One of the most urgent needs is for some evaluation of
existing practice.

New legislation is introduced, too, with no machinery for rapid
feedback or objective assessment of its strengths and weaknesses. With
resources which are inevitably limited, it is short-sighted in economic
terms, quite apart from other considerations, to neglect the possibility
of some evaluation which could guide future action or legislation.

Many of the larger local authorities are now forming research and
intelligence departments and their contributions could be invaluable.
However, the problems of the large authority may well be different in
kind from those of the smaller one. A great deal of useful information
can be assembled in an authority of any size with some attention to the
standardisation of records. This suggestion almost invariably meets with
some initial opposition from individual fieldworkers or administrators.
However, the maintenance of basic records in some standard form need
not restrict the individual who wishes to add supplementary information and it can go a long way towards providing a ready means of
monitoring existing procedures and pointing the way towards useful
modifications.

The need for co-ordination

It has been suggested that existing facilities need to be developed and
extended on a broad front. It is also recognised that much of this
demands additional resources. The Joint Under-Secretary of State of
the Department of Health and Social Security said in a debate in the
House of Commons on the private member's Chronically Sick and
Disabled Persons Bill (second reading, 5th December 1969), "inevitably
there are strict limits on the growth of public expenditure, both
centrally and locally. Though the local health and welfare authorities
are no less likely than the Government to continue saying that the

social services must command priority, the financial resources cannot be stretched indefinitely". He went on to add that there are also limits to the qualified manpower resources which the country can reasonably allocate to any particular service.

Fortunately, from this viewpoint one of the most urgent needs – if not *the* most urgent need – at the present time is also one of the least expensive in terms of finance or of manpower. It is for better and more efficient co-ordination of services for the handicapped. In the evidence which was submitted to the Working Party, this theme recurred again and again. From all sources there was widespread concern about the inadequacies of the present machinery for drawing together the best available knowledge and applying it to individual cases. From parents, professionals and voluntary societies came many comments on the problems which arise when responsibility is shared with, or passes on to, another discipline or agency. Perhaps, it would be more accurate to represent these views by saying that too often the handicapped child seemed to be everybody's responsibility yet nobody's.

For example, a young couple with an eighteen months old child handicapped by cerebral palsy and retarded mental development had been separately seen by the general practitioner, a child health clinic doctor, two hospital paediatricians, a medical social worker and a health visitor. Some had been more hopeful, some more helpful than others, but no attempt had been made to hold a case conference. After nearly a year, the parents were quite confused as to what was wrong, what the future implications of the handicaps might be and to whom to turn for continuing advice and support.

Such examples were neither rare nor confined to one locality or handicap. The volume of evidence left no reasonable doubt that, despite instances of good progressive care, the present health, education and personal social services do not, within and between them, have sufficient built-in channels of communication and systems of co-ordination.

The effect of proposed new legislation

The Local Authority Social Services Act, 1970 largely implements the recommendations of the Seebohm Report. All major local authorities (*ie* at present county and county borough councils) are to set up unified social services departments. These departments will take over all the functions of children's and welfare departments; and the personal social services at present provided by the health departments, including services for the sick and mentally disordered, (family case-work and other social work, day centres, clubs, residential care in the community, adult training centres and workshops). Other health department functions to be taken over include day nurseries, child minding and the provision of home helps. The care and aftercare of the sick and mentally disordered, so far as social work is concerned, will thus be a responsibility of the social services department.

The Green Paper, *National Health Service* (1970) says: "The Government has decided that the services should be organised according to the main skills required to provide them rather than by any categorization of primary user. Any alternative would involve the establishment of more than one local service deploying the same skill. Broadly speaking, the decision is that the health authorities will be responsible for services where the primary skill needed is that of health professions, while the local authorities will be responsible for services where the primary skill is social care or support". The Government is still considering where responsibility for the child guidance service should lie, though it is suggested that social workers in child guidance teams might be employed by the social services department. The Seebohm Report recommended that education welfare should be a function of the social services department because of the desirability to consider a child's whole environment both at home and at school as a unity. The Government agrees in principle that family casework should be concentrated in the social services department but leaves it open to local authorities to transfer this from education welfare to the social services department if they so wish. The general consequence of setting up these new social services departments will be a more comprehensive and co-ordinated service and the lessening of un-certainties about where responsibility lies for providing particular social care services. This should also mean that people will be more aware that these services exist. So far as can be judged at this early stage, the proposed re-organisation would make possible that continuity of care from the personal social services without respect to age or categorization for which we have argued throughout this report. In saying this, we also assume that some powers of welfare departments which are at present only permissive will become mandatory, under the Chronically Sick and Disabled Persons Act. These powers will of course be transferred to the social services department. A consequence of this legislation and of the proposed re-organisation of the National Health Service is that there will be unified and coherent health and social services alongside the education services. The problem of how to interrelate these services, and the different professions within them, in the interests of handicapped children still remains to be solved.

This Green Paper also embodies the Government's decision that the various parts of the National Health Service should be united under area health authorities directly responsible to the Secretary of State though closely associated with the local authorities. Thus it proposes to abolish the present division into hospital, general practitioner and local authority health services. This, says the Green Paper, means that: "all decisions on staffing, planning and the deployment of resources must be governed by the total health needs of each area". It is proposed to include the school health service. As the Green Paper says: " . . . the new arrangements will help to secure continuity in the medical . . . care of children from birth through their school days. This continuity will be beneficial whether the child is in good health or has a physical or mental handicap that calls for constant medical supervision and perhaps special educational arrangements". Our own findings suggest the extreme importance of adequate and acceptable health facilities for handicapped young people after they leave school. The Green Paper suggests that the routine medical examinations under the Factories Act "will be replaced by a more selective system concentrating on those young persons in need of medical advice and based on the area health authority's programme of medical supervision of school children."

It is also proposed to set up about 14 regional health councils for overall planning of the hospital and specialist services and certain other purposes. About 90 area health authorities are envisaged. Thus some 104 authorities would supersede the 168 now directly responsible to the Secretary of State and, in addition, the 158 local health authorities. The Green Paper emphasises the importance of close co-operation between the area health authorities and the local authority social services departments. These are proposals for discussion, apart from the decision to unify the National Health Service outside local government, to make the boundaries of area health authorities the same as those of unitary authorities, and to organise services according to the main skill required.

In the White Paper on *Reform of Local Government in England* (1970) the Government accepted most of the recommendations of the Redcliffe-Maud Report (1969) and the principles that the divisions between town and country should be abolished and the number of local authorities greatly reduced. It proposes to reduce the number of local authorities from 1,210 at present to 51 unitary authorities with considerably increased populations (a minimum of 250,000). They would be responsible for all local government services. There will also be five two-tier metropolitan authorities (in addition to Greater London). It is proposed that education should be a first tier and social services a second tier service. This could create difficulties from the point of view of an effectively co-ordinated and continuous social care service for handicapped children and their families unless there is close consultation between the two authorities and common agreement about the best form of service. No decision will be reached about the Redcliffe-Maud proposal for provinces with wider planning powers until the Royal Commission on the Constitution has reported.

The re-organisation of local government and of the National Health Service into much larger units, together with the abolition of a distinction between town and country, should do much to overcome some of the difficulties mentioned in this report: the problems created by the differences between regional hospital board and local authority areas; and the small size of many local authorities and thus their inability to provide a proper range of services for children with different handicaps. In particular, it is to be hoped that in future residential schools would not be so remote from some children's home areas.

The unification of the personal social services as well as of the National Health Service, together with common boundaries and a considerable increase in the size of authorities, should make it easier to identify gaps and inadequacies in the services, to deploy scarce professional staffs more effectively and to provide a more comprehensive range of specialist services.

Of course to change boundaries, whether physical or administrative, does not itself solve problems and may create some new ones. In particular, there is the real danger that larger units may make the personal social services less "personal", unless there is well planned decentralisation and deployment of staff. However, it is to be hoped that as a result of any amalgamation of services there will be a levelling up of standards rather than the reverse. Certainly the possibilities of more effective co-ordination are enhanced.

Regional co-ordination

Regional planning of services for handicapped children is essential. Much of the evidence submitted to the Working Party stressed that children placed in residential special schools often have to travel inordinately long distances. This means that effective contact between the school and the parents or local authority services is difficult if not impossible. Furthermore, a five-day week at the schools is impracticable for such children; they may, therefore, feel depressed or rejected at week-ends. Regional planning and co-ordination of provision would not solve this problem overnight but could have an immediate impact upon new placements.

The children's regional planning committees set up by the Children and Young Persons Act, 1969, will undoubtedly need to work in close consultation with hospitals and the education and health services and voluntary children's organisations. It would seem, then, a sensible and reasonable step to extend the responsibility and function of these committees to cover planning for most residential accommodation for handicapped children including hostels. Such an extension of function would mean that the education and health authorities would play a more central role in the children's regional planning committees than at present envisaged. Further developments in more general regional planning, particularly in health and education, may follow from the Government's proposal for regional health councils, and when it has been decided whether to set up provincial councils as part of the reform of local government.

National co-ordination

In the context of national planning, the reply of the Joint Under-Secretary in the debate on the second reading of the private member's Chronically Sick and Disabled Persons Bill, was particularly illuminating. Apologising for the fact that he could not personally answer the many points raised by members, he commented, "At the latest count, there are *nine* Departments involved in dealing with the Bill."

Overall national planning of services and provision for handicapped children – and adults – is at the present time conspicuous by its absence, largely for the reason that so many government departments are concerned. The four departments most directly concerned with the handicapped are the Department of Education and Science, the Department of Employment and Productivity, the Department of Health and Social Security and the Home Office. Each has shown over a long period close and continuing interest in its function in relation to handicapped children but there is no single authority responsible for looking at total needs and total resources. Moreover, there is no specific provision for integrated planning between them. This is not to say that no links exist but effective machinery for comprehensive and co-ordinated appraisal and policy determination in relation to the well-being of handicapped children is lacking, though urgently needed.

The case for a national advisory council on handicapped children

As we have said, the evidence to the Working Party from many voluntary organisations and from parents' letters stressed the confusion, gaps, overlapping and lack of co-ordination whether in statutory or in voluntary services for handicapped children. They emphasised the need for a comprehensive national council or other advisory body covering all forms of handicap and all relevant disciplines and services.

It was suggested that such a body should be able to:
1. collect, sift, summarise and assess published literature on all aspects of the care of children with handicaps;
2. study in the field and report on experiments and innovations;
3. act as an information centre for parents and central and local organisations, both statutory and voluntary;
4. show by collating available information, where there are gaps in present provision and to make proposals about new or improved services;
5. stimulate research on the care, treatment and education of handicapped children;

6. encourage collaboration between all the specialist services concerned with handicapped children;

7. assist voluntary and statutory services in planning extensions of their services;

8. advise government departments on the formulation of policy in relation to handicapped children.

Necessary as all these functions are, we consider that their range is too wide to be encompassed within one body; moreover, a council advisory to government departments is necessarily different in kind from one which would be free to arouse public opinion and to give advice to individual parents of handicapped children. We believe, therefore, that there is a strong case for setting up two councils, one an independent voluntary body, and the other within the ministries concerned.

The case for an independent voluntary council

The independent voluntary council suggested in evidence to us would aim to bring together the separate voluntary organisations and others with an interest in handicapped children; to provide a meeting ground for discussion of necessary action and for publicity to further the well-being of such children and their families; to undertake studies and enquiries; and to act as a comprehensive source of information for parents and others about facilities which already exist. This last function should be of much value in assisting local authorities to discharge their new information giving responsibilities under the Chronically Sick and Disabled Persons Act.

Much of the evidence submitted to the Working Party suggested that the functions envisaged for the proposed council would be appropriate for the National Bureau for Co-operation in Child Care to undertake. The Working Party considered all the possible alternatives, including the setting up of a new body specifically for this purpose. The issue was not an easy one, nor one that had been envisaged when the Working Party was set up. After careful discussion we came to the conclusion that no other organisation in the children's field is sufficiently comprehensive and that the Bureau has the added advantage of not being exclusively concerned with handicapped children; hence the basic concept that the handicapped child is first and foremost a child would be maintained.

Nonetheless, the Working Party was told that certain of the functions suggested for the new council might present some difficulties. The Bureau has always specifically avoided the role of a pressure group because of its wide membership, which includes the great majority of local authorities, as well as government departments in consultative membership. In so far as it is important for the new council to act as a pressure group and to provide an advice and guidance service for individuals, the Bureau itself might not envisage that such functions would be appropriate for it. If this proved to be a serious difficulty, there is also the possibility that the proposed council should have a separate existence under the Bureau's auspices, serviced by it and with access to its research expertise, library and information facilities. The information, documentation and library service envisaged for the council would in this case be an extension of an existing facility.

With these various considerations in view, we decided to commend to the Executive Committee and Council of the National Bureau for Co-operation in Child Care the proposal that the Bureau should take on the functions outlined for an independent voluntary council for handicapped children, recognising at the same time that considerable funds would be required to implement this proposal, particularly in relation to a central information service. Alternatively, we suggest that the Bureau should consider setting up a council under its auspices, appropriately constituted, to discharge the functions as envisaged.

The case for an inter-departmental advisory council

In central government the problem is primarily that several vertically organised departments have responsibility for different aspects of handicap, when the health, education, social and employment needs of handicapped children themselves are essentially horizontal and closely interrelated. We see no way to meet this problem except by some kind of inter-departmental machinery with a developmental, consultative role to achieve common policies.

The possibilities are either an advisory council set up by the initiative of the ministers concerned, probably within one ministry but with representation from the others and from outside interests; or an advisory council set up by legislation. In any event, the council should have a constitution and its chairman should have access to the ministers concerned.

There are existing advisory committees concerned with handicap in two of the ministries. The Secretary of State for Education and Science has an Advisory Committee on Handicapped Children whose terms of reference are: "To advise the Secretary of State on such matters relating to children requiring special educational treatment as he may submit to them or they may consider require investigation". The Secretary of State for Health and Social Security has an Advisory Committee on the Health and Welfare of Handicapped Persons. When the much more comprehensive Personal Social Services Council comes into existence this Committee's functions will be merged in the wider Council.

Both the Advisory Committee and the projected Personal Social Services Council are specialised in that one is primarily concerned with special education and the other with the personal social services. Thus neither can be said to cover the comprehensive needs of handicapped children. The council which we propose would have to fill a difficult but crucial developmental and consultative role. It should, however it is set up, bring together the particular interests in handicapped children of the Department of Education and Science, the Department of Employment and Productivity, the Department of Health and Social Security, the Home Office and other government departments including those responsible for housing and technological developments. It should also include other interests, notably the local authority associations, the health authorities, voluntary bodies, professional associations, universities and other research institutions. It should have access to any available information it needed; it should also have the necessary staff and other resources at its disposal to undertake independent enquiries and to commission research. It would clearly need to set up various sub-committees. It should present an annual report to Parliament, which should be published. In this report, amongst other matters, it would comment on the annual returns from local authorities about comprehensive assessment, the numbers and types of children on the registers of handicapped children, the services provided for them, variations in different parts of the country, and the changing pattern of incidence and provision (see chapter 6).

We envisage that the council would be based in one of the four departments primarily concerned. It should be the responsibility of the chosen department to ensure that the other departments had adequate representation. What chiefly matters is the will to make the council an effective body, constantly consulted and able to make its voice heard on the different but closely interrelated needs of handicapped children.

References

DEPARTMENT OF HEALTH AND SOCIAL SECURITY (1970) *National Health Service.* HMSO London.

MINISTRY OF HOUSING AND LOCAL GOVERNMENT (1970) *Reform of Local Government in England.* HMSO London.

Royal Commission on Local Government in England (1969) (Chairman: Lord Redcliffe-Maud). HMSO London.

Acts

Children and Young Persons Act, 1969.
Chronically Sick and Disabled Persons Act, 1970.
Local Authority Social Services Act, 1970.

Appendix A

Professional associations, voluntary organisations and individuals who responded to the Working Party's invitation to submit evidence

Association of Children's Officers.
Association of Education Committees.
Association of Educational Psychologists.
Association of Hospital Welfare Administrators.
Association of Psychiatric Social Workers.
Association for Special Education.
Association of Social Workers.
Association of Teachers of Maladjusted Children.
Association of Workers for Maladjusted Children.
British Diabetic Association.
British Epilepsy Association.
British Medical Association.
British Paediatric Association.
British Psychological Society.
British Red Cross Society.
British Society for Music Therapy.
Central Council for the Disabled.
College of Special Education.
College of Speech Therapists.
College of Teachers for the Blind.
Cystic Fibrosis Research Foundation.
Deaf, Blind and Rubella Children's Association.
Disabled Living Foundation formerly Disabled Living Activities Group
    of the Central Council for the Disabled.
Dr Barnardo's Homes.
Elfrida Rathbone Association.
Guild of Teachers of Backward Children.
Health Visitors Association.

Inner London Education Authority.
Institute of Medical Social Workers.
Institute for Research into Mental Retardation.
Institute of Careers Officers.
Invalid Children's Aid Association.
Lady Hoare Thalidomide Appeal Fund.
London Boroughs Association.
Muscular Dystrophy Group of Great Britain.
National Association for Education of the Partially Sighted.
National Association of Head Teachers.
National Association for Maternal and Child Care.
National Association for Mental Health.
National Association of Schoolmasters.
National Association of Youth Clubs.
National Children's Home.
National College of Teachers of the Deaf.
National Deaf Children's Society.
National Society for Autistic Children.
National Society for Mentally Handicapped Children.
Nursery School Association.
Pre-School Playgroups Association.
Residential Child Care Association.
Royal College of Nursing.
Royal National Institute for the Blind.
Royal National Institute for the Deaf.
Save the Children Fund.
Society of Medical Officers of Health.
Society of Teachers of the Deaf.
Spastics Society.
The Joint Four (The Joint Executive Committee of the Associations of Head Masters, Head Mistresses, Assistant Masters and Assistant Mistresses).
Women's Royal Voluntary Service.

Dr D. Dale, Institute of Education, University of London.
Dr R. M. Forrester, Consultant Paediatrician, Wigan and Leigh Hospitals.
Professor R. S. Illingworth, University of Sheffield.
Dr J. D. Kershaw, Medical Officer of Health, Colchester.

Dr R. C. MacKeith, Newcomen Centre, Guy's Hospital, London.

Miss M. Procter, Senior Educational Psychologist, Inner London Education Authority.

Dr C. E. Williams, Consultant Psychiatrist, Borocourt Hospital, Reading.

Mr. H. J. Wright, Senior Educational Psychologist, Portsmouth.

Mr M. Colborne Browne wished to be associated with the evidence submitted by the Royal National Institute for the Blind.

Dr K. S. Holt wished to be associated with the evidence submitted by the British Paediatric Association.

Mr. J. Loring wished to be associated with the evidence submitted by the Spastics Society.

Evidence also submitted to Working Party from:

Association for All Speech Impaired Children.

Mr W. Crudge ⎫
Mr A. Field ⎬ Headmasters of Shaftesbury Society Schools.

Devon and Cornwall Association for Spina Bifida and Hydrocephalus.

Mrs D. M. Dixon, teacher, Stoke-on-Trent.

Dr R. E. Faulkner, Stevenage, Herts.

Mr B. J. Fleming, Health and Welfare Department, Kent County Council.

Miss C. P. S. Griffiths, John Horniman School.

Dr R. H. Martin, Medical Officer, Northampton.

Medical Women's Federation.

Mrs H. Milner ⎫
Miss M. Roberts ⎬ Speech therapists, York Education Committee.

Orpington Mental Health Association.

Mr. J. L. Smith, Teacher-in-charge, Assessment Unit, Warwickshire Education Committee.

University of Bradford Undergraduate School of Studies of Applied Social Study.

Miss M. Voysey, Aberdeen.

Appendix B

Summary of the evidence submitted by voluntary organisations, professional associations and individuals

Approximately 116 voluntary organisations, professional associations and individuals concerned with handicapped children were invited to submit written evidence to the Working Party. A list of those who did so is given above. Suggested guidelines were provided (see below) to structure and make comparable the views expressed on present gaps and weaknesses, and on suggested changes. It was hoped that respondents would also comment on new trends in the treatment and care of handicapped children.

Several organisations set up special committees to consider and compile evidence; some organisations collected evidence from their branches in different parts of the country; and some asked individual members to prepare evidence on their behalf.

The whole Working Party made use of the evidence both in discussions and in the preparation of the report; in addition three sub-committees were set up to consider it from the educational, medical and social care point of view and to summarise the topics most frequently mentioned.

Although many of the organisations or professional associations had specialist interest, most of them expressed concern about certain general topics. These included the need for early detection of difficulties; for more support for the families of handicapped children; for the development of a greater variety of provision, particularly for children of pre-school age and for school leavers; and for improved and extended training of all professional workers dealing with handicapped children and their families. The most frequently mentioned need was for improved co-ordination of services and a closer liaison between all departments, organisations and professional workers involved with handicapped children and their families.

It is not possible to analyse and summarise systematically evidence of this kind. An attempt has been made to highlight the major points which emerged and to illustrate some of these with quotations. These are only a small selection but, in our findings and conclusions, we have, of course, taken all the evidence into account.

Guidelines suggested for submitting written evidence
Views on some or all of the following aspects listed below would be appreciated.

Identification of handicap
Medical treatment of handicapped children
Education, further education and training of handicapped children
Supportive services available to handicapped children
Needs of parents and families of handicapped children
Needs of professional workers
Pattern of organisation　　*a.*　statutory bodies
　　　　　　　　　　　　　　b.　voluntary bodies
Co-ordination of services and interdisciplinary co-operation
Geographical distribution of provision of services

Identification of handicap

Many organisations stressed the need for a team approach to diagnosis and assessment, free communication between all disciplines concerned with the full diagnosis and recommendations and for centres to be available at various levels and of different types.

Many organisations commented that assessment needed to be ongoing throughout life.

The need was frequently expressed for early detection of difficulties, which often only became obvious at the first stages of schooling; observation/diagnostic units for children who experienced difficulty in adjusting to school could discover early stages of maladjustment; records kept in school of all children who might need special help could lead to early identification and subsequent help. Some organisations also stressed a need for improved facilities for psychological testing; for continuous educational assessment; for continuous appraisal of children with certain handicaps, *eg* the visually handicapped; for careers assessment.

Quotations from the evidence

SOCIETY OF MEDICAL OFFICERS OF HEALTH:

"*Assessment centres.* We see these as involving various types of centres. Some of these will need to be highly specialised in the facilities and services they provide and can be established only in specialist paediatric hospitals and units, probably on a regional basis. Others, of a more general character, will serve areas corresponding to 'district general hospital' catchment areas. It may well be necessary, in some places, to have a further type of peripheral centre to carry out continuing 'field level' observation and assessment.

Observation centres. We consider it important to have centres or units in which handicapped children can be kept under skilled surveillance. Some of those will be residential and some day units. It may be convenient for those to be established in places primarily intended for care and education (*eg* nursery units in junior training centres and special schools for the educationally subnormal) but some of them may be within or attached to assessment units of the type mentioned above. We would stress again that the child's response to care is an important facet of assessment, so that all places where handicapped children are receiving care or education, whether special establishments or ordinary nurseries and schools accepting a small number of handicapped children, should be closely linked with assessment centres.

Assessment teams. We consider that each locality should have assessment teams, consisting of doctors in all branches of the National Health Service and appropriate para-medical and non-medical workers, who would be associated with assessment as such and with all places where handicapped children are receiving care or education.

Organisations. The responsibility for the establishment of assessment teams should be placed with the local health and education authority who, working in collaboration with the hospital services, would decide on the number and location of assessment and diagnostic units."

LONDON BOROUGHS ASSOCIATION:

"There are advantages in the attachment of assessment units where possible to large comprehensive special schools especially for children with multiple handicaps as compared with similar units placed, as suggested, at District and Regional hospitals.

The advantage for the handicapped child of locally based medical assessment units appear now to have been widely realised and the problems of how, where and when to set up such units are now actively exercising the minds of doctors and others at many levels in this country and in the committees of the World Health Organisation. In Hounslow two such local authority assessment units have flourished for over ten years and have attracted a stream of visitors from all parts of the world.

The team at the purpose-built medical assessment unit for all types of paediatric handicapping conditions at Martindale and at the purpose-built audiology unit at Heston are truly multi-disciplinary. Here are the great benefits which can accrue from the combination in one team of hospital consultants, local authority medical and para-medical staff and the teaching staff of the immediately adjacent special schools and satellite special classes.

A further advantage may be added. When professional staff from a wide range of disciplines constantly work together, they come to understand each other's distinctive approach. They soon appreciate what each one can contribute towards the total assessment and treatment, and equally important they get to know the limitations of the various skills available.

If they are accustomed to working in the situation where education and treatment are taking place they are less likely to make unrealistic or impracticable recommendations, and they are more likely to apply practicable ones with understanding and imagination than if they are working in a hospital remote from the community in which the children live."

British Paediatric Association:
"Assessment of the child is a continuous and collaborative process. There is now no place for the brief interview and the dogmatic outcome. Even if accurate, this procedure is rarely acceptable to parents . . . No doctor (or other professional worker) must be allowed to forget that he is trying to help the child and his family to an understanding of the handicap; to explain this at leisure and in a comprehensible manner; to make sure that his advice is matched to the available facilities; and if he is not satisfied that the facilities available are adequate, to move heaven and earth to make them adequate. This has implications in the education of the paediatrician and of the local authority doctor."

ASSOCIATION FOR SPECIAL EDUCATION:

"The main weakness at present in many areas is the lack of planned facilities for the early detection and assessment of handicap. Children with gross handicaps are usually identified, and many minor physical defects noted, but the less obvious handicaps which may have an important effect on the child's learning and behaviour are often not discovered until after a start at school. Examples of this are speech and language difficulties, perceptual difficulties, early emotional disturbance. Environmental conditions which lead to the child's being deprived of the experiences necessary for successful intellectual development can be extremely harmful at this stage.

We believe it should be compulsory for all local authorities to ensure the early detection of handicap and to provide appropriate special educational guidance and treatment."

Medical treatment

A number of organisations noted the wide variation of services for medical treatment in different parts of the country, both in quantity and quality.

Quotations from the evidence

DR. BARNARDO'S:

"*a*. Experience gained in caring for socially handicapped children deprived of maternal care is often not applied in the case of physically and mentally handicapped children *eg*, there can be a too easy acquiescience to prolonged or even permanent hospitalisation, particularly where mentally handicapped children are concerned; many babies have unnecessarily long hospitalisation before placements have been sought in homely residential settings.

b. Children's hospitals and subnormality units often do not provide a proper setting for the emotional and social development of the handicapped child.

c. The paediatric service has tended to be clinical in outlook and only comparatively recently has developmental paediatrics come to be recognised in its own right."

INVALID CHILDREN'S AID ASSOCIATION:

"*a*. There is a need for a more efficient hospital appointment service.

b. There is a need for improved transport facilities for those attending out-patient departments. At present, due to an inadequate service, a child and mother may spend many hours at hospitals waiting for transport.

c. There is a lack of liaison and information between hospital specialists and general practitioners.

Examples

i. A mother was told by a hospital always to take the child to hospital for his frequent rises in temperature, as the doctor was uncertain about the diagnosis. Mother found it an intolerable strain, and upsetting to the child who had long stays in hospital. She arranged herself with the general practitioner for him to be seen at home. Reports are periodically sent to the general practitioner from the hospital.

ii. A child suffering from severe asthma was referred to a hospital by the general practitioner. The paediatrician treated him and recommended a period at boarding open air school. Parents and child found this course hard to accept, but finally did so. Subsequently, the boy was transferred to the care of another doctor at the same hospital who did not believe in boarding school. He changed the treatment and cancelled the application for boarding school placement.

The point to be made here, is that of families under stress because of lack of continuity in treatment – the general practitioner hands the case over, sometimes completely, to the hospital consultant. The child may then be treated by various registrars at the hospital, and have a variety of specialists for different aspects of his handicap, without any one person to whom the parents can refer back."

ASSOCIATION OF SOCIAL WORKERS:

"We wish to point out the enormous variation in the standard of provision of medical services, physiotherapy, occupational and speech therapy. We recognise here that it is not only services which need expanding, *eg,* more hospital beds, special adolescent units, more adequate physiotherapy and speech therapy, and more transport facilities to take children for treatment, but there is also a great shortage of staff to carry out these services. Rural areas are particularly hard hit in the treatment available, and there is the problem of distance to get to treatment centres. A particular lack is noted in the provision of speech therapy before school age.

We would like parents to have more opportunity to consult the doctors in charge.

One person should have overall responsibility for the medical care of the handicapped child with the authority to co-ordinate the medical and surgical care, psychiatric services, and able to plan the whole treatment of the child."

Education, Further Education and Training

Most organisations stressed the need for more nursery type provision for all types of handicapped children; these could be in small units attached to existing nurseries; in pre-school play groups specially for the handicapped; or in groups and day nurseries and nursery schools for normal children – a flexible pattern is advocated. Fee support from local authorities to voluntary organisations to set up and operate nurseries was also suggested.

The need for the development of a variety of provisions for handicapped children was stressed by a large number of organisations. These included:

Regional comprehensive special schools, with hostel accommodation. The attachment of units, classes, etc to ordinary day schools for children with minimal cerebral dysfunction; who are educationally subnormal or physically handicapped, or those with communication disorders, or who are mildly disturbed, or borderline educationally subnormal.
Special care units for particular types of handicaps, *eg* maladjusted, autistic, severely disturbed children of low intelligence, children with spina bifida, those who are severely multi-handicapped.
More provision for maladjusted adolescents.
More provision for children with speech disorders.

Several professional associations commented that if special classes were provided in ordinary schools they should be planned as part of the special education service. Placement of classes would need to be constantly under review, choice of school and head-teacher would be an important factor in placement of classes, and careful study should be made of whether the school could cater for individual children's needs.

The view was frequently expressed that the siting of all special schools should be carefully planned, and should be community based, not isolated (especially residential schools) and as near the children's homes as possible. The need for study of the premises for all special schools was emphasised by a large number of organisations; also that existing buildings should be adapted to meet the children's needs.

Many organisations referred in their evidence to the need for residential schools to be planned to maintain contact with the home. Schools for the maladjusted especially should be planned as part of therapeutic provision for the whole family. Provision should be made for parents to visit the school before admission and during their child's stay, thus giving opportunity for observation, parent education, interchange of information, etc.

Weekly boarding was suggested by a large number of organisations. A system of staggered holidays would ensure continuous provision, particularly for the maladjusted.

The need for improved services of further training and education, placement in employment, follow-up and after care was emphasised.

Official responsibility for handicapped young people up to the age of 18 or 21 was frequently suggested. Some organisations thought this responsibility should rest with the health department, some with the education authority, and some with another different department. Closer liaison with all departments dealing with the young person was necessary.

Much of the evidence stressed the need for more "work experience" schemes, work training, simulated workshops, etc. These schemes could only be fully used if the laws relating to the employment of children and young persons were amended.

The need for hostels run in connection with further training facilities occurred again and again. These should include after-care hostels for educationally subnormal and maladjusted children who need further help or who cannot return to a satisfactory home environment; and for young people who have to move away from home because there is no suitable work for them locally.

A number or organisations pointed out the need for more specially trained careers officers. Contact with young people at an earlier age in schools was required so that more attention could be given to preparation for employment. The range of employment and activities could be widened; in many cases it was thought that the sights were set too low. More help and preparation was especially needed for the handicapped young person of above average ability. More use could be made of regular or special courses in colleges of further education.

Quotations from the evidence
a. pre-school provision
SOCIETY OF MEDICAL OFFICERS OF HEALTH:
"We consider that more provision should be made for pre-school handicapped children but would not advocate a uniform system; a special nursery for handicapped children may be best for some and a special nursery school or class for others (especially those who may require specialised remedial education) while a substantial number may benefit from admission to an ordinary nursery, nursery class or nursery school. In many cases transport will have to be provided."

ASSOCIATION FOR SPECIAL EDUCATION:
"Apart from the compensatory value of nursery education we feel that the nursery teacher is ideally placed to identify the child with special needs, so that he can be added to the 'at risk' register and given appropriate treatment. Parents too need help and advice at this early stage and this might be given via the nursery school if it were accepted that diagnostic and special educational facilities should exist as an integral part of an expanded system of nursery education.

We also believe in the need for flexible organisation which would permit children whose development is markedly retarded in any respect to be given the benefit of a longer stay in a nursery school before proceeding to an infant school, or subsequently in an infant school before proceeding to a junior school."

PRE-SCHOOL PLAYGROUPS ASSOCIATION:
"The improvement in a handicapped child can sometimes be quite dramatic, and the hope reflects back into the home. In cases where there is no hope, the mother is better able to accept it when she finds that the child and she are accepted as they are anyway. One such mother is running a lovely, lively playgroup while her 3-year old lies in a carry-cot unable to give even a smile of recognition, his face usually smeared with catarrh.

It was the playgroup that put her back in circulation again, and she is now leading it happily and confidently. She says with genuine surprise, 'It always strikes me as a bit odd that the other mothers come to *me*, of all people, to be cheered-up or smoothed down! But I know just how they feel. I've got just one person belonging to the playgroup that I can phone up when I'm feeling really desperate. You must have someone, mustn't you?'

b. special education

ASSOCIATION FOR SPECIAL EDUCATION:

"We would stress that special education in ordinary schools should be special in fact as well as in name. The curriculum, methods, staffing, equipment and facilities should be very similar to those in special schools. If handicapped children are to be integrated within the ordinary school instead of being merely attached to it, there must be co-operation, understanding, and acceptance by the whole staff. Special classes in ordinary schools should be planned and organised as part of the special education service, with a mutual interchange of information, methods and personnel."

LONDON BOROUGHS ASSOCIATION:

"There is or should be a greater emphasis on the treatment of the child in the locality and community although residential school will still be the best placement in certain cases. The advantages of day school provision are:

a. the children and their families are known to the medical and psychological services in the area;

b. the child is not separated from his family environment and there is therefore no problem of re-integration as there is when a child finally leaves a residential school;

c. the day school avoids for the local education authority the disadvantage of keeping contact with residential schools in all parts of the country, especially the independent residential schools in which the staffing and physical conditions can deteriorate very rapidly;

d. the provision of day special schools and local treatment is very much less costly than places at residential schools. Furthermore the residential schools have increasing difficulty in securing satisfactory staff and costs are very likely to rise still further. Even so, present costs are probably artificially low because the buildings were

acquired many years ago. If new residential special schools are
purpose built to modern standards, the cost per pupil is likely to be
nearer £1,500 per annum than £1,000;

e. the provision of day special schools and local treatment will be
in harmony with the closer integration of all the social service
agencies recommended by the Seebohm Report and indeed by
other reports and investigations, and the establishment where
necessary of community homes for children rather than specialized
residential provision at a school."

ASSOCIATION OF CHILDREN'S OFFICERS:
"There is a growing realisation of need for the involvement of the local
community for the enrichment of the lives of both the children and
their neighbours. What is practically more difficult is the positive
encouragement of parental visiting and parental participation in the
life of the school. Perhaps all schools could follow the example of the
Royal National Institute for the Blind in providing for parents to get
to know the school and to help parents in home care of the child before
admission, and to provide accommodation for parents and child on
initial visits to the school and thereafter.

Effective bonds between residential schools and families are difficult
to maintain due to schools being long distances away and difficult to
reach.

It is questioned whether schools should completely close down each
holiday without regard for children whose parents cannot cope with
them for the full holidays, or who have no family at all."

ASSOCIATION OF SOCIAL WORKERS:
"Although we favour the extension of day school facilities for handicapped
children wherever possible and advocate financial help being given to
parents to enable them to move into areas where their children can
attend day schools, at the same time, we see a need for the development
of regional comprehensive schools for all children with different
handicaps being educated together where possible, but being taught in
separate groups for specialised help. Many children could then return
home at weekends, which is not now possible if they are sometimes
placed two hundred miles from their homes. In general we see a place
for more residential facilities of both a long and short term nature,
making for a wider variety of provision. However, we also see a danger

in segregation, where society is not allowed to come to terms with its handicapped."

c. school leaving, further training and education, and employment

NATIONAL ASSOCIATION OF SCHOOLMASTERS:
"There are far too many children leaving the residential schools ill-equipped to deal with the demands of a modern society. Many have been isolated in what is largely an artificial environment for up to ten years, and it is ludicrous to expect them to deal adequately with the work situation without thorough preparation. In their last year or eighteen months at school every effort should be made through work experience, youth club movements, Duke of Edinburgh Award Scheme, youth hostelling, etc, to re-establish links with their contemporaries in ordinary schools and therefore to prepare them in part for the kind of people they can expect to meet when they go out to work at the end of their school days. The education of the child takes place outside as well as inside the classroom, and it must be remembered that, for many of these handicapped children, social training and adjustment is often as important as what may be called classroom work. Children must be made to feel adequate to deal with the unexpected and the new situation, and the schools must be prepared to embark on an intensive programme of such activities for their school leavers."

DISABLED LIVING FOUNDATION:
"In view of the practical difficulties which are likely to arise it is essential that the young people likely to need special arrangements should be identified in good time, ie at least 12 to 18 months before they are eligible to leave school. This will enable parents, often very anxious, to be re-assured; the individual needs of each child to be properly assessed; the priorities to be put into some sort of order; time for sufficient consideration of the programme by both parents and children, and their full approval secured in good time for appropriate arrangements to be made so that the young person does not fall into a void on leaving school."

BRITISH PAEDIATRIC ASSOCIATION:
"The co-ordination of the services for handicapped school leavers needs very close examination. They present a formidable problem. There is not much point in looking after the handicapped child in great detail if

we fail to realise that he becomes a handicapped adult with emotional, educational and employment problems."

ASSOCIATION FOR SPECIAL EDUCATION:
"Further educational facilities for the handicapped are insufficient. Many special schools have developed well thought out schemes for pupils in their final year to prepare them for the transition to employment and to life outside the school. Such schemes need extending to all special schools. There should be flexibility about the age of leaving so that some children might be allowed to leave before 16, while others are encouraged to remain after reaching that age. Decisions should be individual ones based upon the child's all round development. Some may be considered to need a period of vocational training after leaving school before entering employment, and the Department of Education and Science should have the responsibility for providing such opportunities up to the age of 18. Legal difficulties are preventing experiments with work experience schemes for children still at school and a working party set up by this Association in 1966 made the following recommendations: That consideration be given to the amendment of the appropriate laws and bye-laws to enable work experience schemes to be undertaken by those handicapped children 'at risk' from an employment point of view, as part of an integrated school leavers' programme, such work experience to be undertaken during the final year of compulsory education. Control of these schemes should be exercised by the schools (acting through the Local Education Authority) and the youth employment service, in co-operation with employers and trade unions."

NATIONAL ASSOCIATION FOR MENTAL HEALTH:
"The National Association for Mental Health has three hostels: one for boys and one for girls leaving schools for the educationally subnormal and the third for boys who were at schools for the maladjusted; all these young people need to live away from their own homes at this vital stage in their development.

The hostels have helped many boys and girls to gain confidence and self-assurance sufficient for them to move to lodgings and maintain themselves in employment. Without the hostels it may be supposed that at least some of the young people may have found the adjustment too difficult and would never have been able to realise their potential to be capable, independent young adults.

The applications for all three hostels confirm the fact that there is a great lack of 'places to put' difficult adolescents. This is particularly apparent where the hostels for the educationally sub-normal are concerned. We so often get applications for a disturbed adolescent who is barely in the educationally subnormal range, and where we feel that the children's department is so desperate for accommodation that the appropriateness of our hostels has barely been considered."

ASSOCIATION OF EDUCATION COMMITTEES:
"Voluntary institutions for the vocational training of the disabled, together with government training centres, are undoubtedly making the most of the limited means at their disposal. The major criticism of present facilities is that sights are inevitably set too low; the range of employment available to the handicapped is too restricted. This, in the past, has been the inevitable consequence of a limited knowledge of what the individual handicapped person is capable of doing. The suggestions already made – that ascertainment should be regarded as a continuous process, that there should be extended facilities for general education, coupled with opportunities for diagnostic testing, and the functional assessment of physical capability – should result not only in considerably higher standards of educational attainment, but also in a far more detailed and accurate assessment of individual potential. If this could be achieved, the natural and logical consequence would be a very considerable widening of the range of activities open to the handicapped, and the demand for an increased variety of training facilities would inevitably be created."

ASSOCIATION OF SOCIAL WORKERS:
"For the older child, we would like effective planning for work to start at 13–14 years and there should be good consultation between the youth employment officer, the welfare officer and the school from that time onwards. Youth employment officers should have special training to fit them for work with handicapped children."

LONDON BOROUGHS ASSOCIATION:
"The paramount necessity is for the development of pre-employment training of handicapped children either in their last year at school or between school and employment. The eight to five regime, and fairly long periods of unsupervised work (even at low level) is something to which each school leaver should be well accustomed before leaving school, if the handicapped children are to fulfil our aim of being ready

to face employment and life. At this stage more attention should be given to their social training and to the opportunities to engage in cultural pursuits.

Much local industry is interested and ready to help in this problem but is, of course, deterred by the present regulations from employing any child under the compulsory school leaving age, even when this is arranged by the local education authority. This should be remedied."

Supportive services and the needs of families of handicapped children

In their evidence many organisations stressed the need for supportive work with parents to help them to deal with emotional problems. The provision of information on the services available, on equipment, and on general care of children with particular handicaps was also stressed. Suggestions were made for the preparation of leaflets, etc, for information to be available in libraries and for some form of national clearing house for information on available services.

More practical help for families with handicapped children was suggested by several organisations. This included: home helps, baby-sitter services; home nursing; laundry services; issue of aids and appliances; play facilities for pre-school handicapped children; finanical help: tax allowances, or extra family allowances; opportunities for holidays and breaks for parents, siblings and the handicapped child.

Several organisations suggested some form of advisory and information service for all those involved with handicapped children, local authorities, parents, workers, voluntary groups, etc. This should offer advice and information on special schools, placements, service etc and be either nationally or regionally organised.

Quotations from the evidence
a. counselling
NATIONAL ASSOCIATION OF SCHOOLMASTERS.
"Where a handicapped child is a member of a normal family group, that group, both adults and children, should receive advice, and if necessary instruction, on how to treat the 'odd' man out. This is particularly important for the child away from home in a residential school. There should be as little rupture of the normal family way of life, when he

or she returns home either for holidays or at the end of their school days."

DISABLED LIVING FOUNDATION:
"Suggestions and advice to parents are needed so that they have a better realisation of their child's capabilities. Parents are very often completely unaware of how much the child can do, given encouragement and opportunity. The need for suggestions is particularly necessary for children below school age, and for those at home during the school holidays where in many cases no programme has been arranged because of lack of relevant information."

DR BARNARDO'S:
"There is not enough appreciation of how frequently time is needed for parents to grow into an acceptance of their child's handicap, and slowly to absorb the problems involved. Often at first they cannot consciously accept the news, and need to be told the facts clearly and compassionately over and over again."

ASSOCIATION OF EDUCATION COMMITTEES:
"Guidance is needed as to the nature and limiting effects of the handicap and the precise requirements where medical treatment or the taking of drugs is involved. Families are in urgent need of a 'sheet anchor', a trusted friend who may be relied upon to advise on a wide range of minor and major problems, and who can relieve anxiety and create confidence by the very knowledge that he is available if the need arises. Such a person may be the health visitor, or the psychiatric social worker of the child guidance service, or some other welfare worker – what is important is he should be the most suitable person for the case in question. It is equally important that the identity of the responsible person should be known to all other bodies having a legitimate interest in the family concerned. Such an arrangement should help to eliminate the complaints of overlapping of effort that sometimes arise."

SPASTICS SOCIETY:
"There is a growing awareness of the need to see the family as a whole and of the importance of looking at the problems and feelings of parents and siblings as well as those of the handicapped child. There is, however, still a great deal more to be done in this field. Communication is a very real problem and parents frequently say that they are not given adequate practical information and details about a whole range of services, from

types of wheelchairs and where to obtain them to the facilities available
through statutory and voluntary bodies. The role of the health visitor
in this field needs to be clarified and more emphasis laid on the need
for skilled social work help to families, particularly at the time when
they first learn that their child is handicapped."

ASSOCIATION FOR SPECIAL EDUCATION:
"The needs of the handicapped child must be viewed within the context
of his family. No provision aimed at meeting such needs can be
regarded as complete in the absence of an adequate continuing system
of parent counselling and help.

When a child is first identified as handicapped in any way or in any
degree, the parents should be immediately consulted and advised and
their co-operation sought. Lack of consultation at this stage may lead
to antagonism later. When administrative decisions are taken, on the
advice of specialist officers, by a local education authority, every
attempt should be made to explain such decisions to the parents, and
their rights as parents should also be clearly explained. Pamphlets on
handicaps meant for parents, and letters addressed to them, should not
be written as is too often the case in an impersonal style or in language
comprehensible only to the expert.

Much advisory work and counselling of parents has always been
done by teachers, and this should continue, but trained social work help
is essential. We welcomed the suggestions made in para 255 of the
'Plowden Report' that some education welfare officers might be
trained to carry out wider social work functions. A new type of training
for health visitors might qualify them to give the guidance required to
parents of very young handicapped children."

LONDON BOROUGHS ASSOCIATION:
"One should first consider the crisis which occurs at the moment of
discovery by the parents that their child is handicapped and is going
to need special educational and training facilities. This discovery is
always a distressing experience and if the parents are left to face it
alone they may be overwhelmed and find difficulty in making a healthy
adjustment to the situation. Parents are so often emotionally upset at
the disability from which their child suffers that they are unable to
give the young pre-school child the training which is required. Quite
serious irrational fears and ill-founded feelings of guilt are not

uncommon, the baby may be rejected, particularly if it is of an unattractive appearance, or it may be hidden; and thus as it grows older its development may be retarded through over-protection. It is perhaps at this stage that the parents need help from experienced social workers to enable them as parents to understand the nature of the handicap and all the facilities, medical, educational and social, from which the child will later benefit. Early and accurate assessment will help the parents to understand the problem that besets them. Subsequent discussion of the prospects and proposals for care may then go a long way to restore the parents confidence in their capacity to overcome the difficulties and lead their child to the greatest attainable measure of independence. A patient and sympathetic attitude by all members of the multi-disciplinary team is of crucial importance in this aspect."

b. practical help
ASSOCIATION OF SOCIAL WORKERS:
"There is a great need for a co-ordinated information service about material aids and nursing aids, eg, facilities for dealing with a permanently incontinent child. The health visitor normally provides such information, but when she stops visiting there is no obvious way in which parents can know of new facilities.

The service for handicapped children and their families would be greatly improved by more imagination in the design and allocation of houses. It is cheaper to build for the handicapped than adapt existing dwellings, and perhaps a percentage of houses might be built with this in mind. Local housing authorities should allow priority for re-housing of families with a handicapped child, particularly where specially adapted, or enlarged, and more spacious accommodation would help to alleviate at least some of their problems.

Equipment, such as wheelchairs and hoists, should be improved, as much that is already in existence is heavy and awkward to handle.

We suggest in considering these domiciliary services that more attention should be given to the family's social needs and the status it holds in society, for example, a car and a telephone, would be essential for many of these families if they are to remain socially active.

More attention should be given to design for buildings for the whole age range of handicapped people, taking into consideration their whole environment, homes, schools, places of work, public buildings, thus helping to facilitate their easy movement to and from these buildings."

DISABLED LIVING FOUNDATION:
"In many cases the living environment of handicapped children appears to be lacking in standards of good practice; as for example, suitable accommodation and accessible buildings for such children. In one of the most important standard works for architects, namely 'Designing for the Disabled' by Selwyn Goldsmith, the word 'children' or 'child' does not appear in the index. So far as we know, no documented study is available on space requirements of disabled children in schools or elsewhere. It is, therefore, only by chance that purpose-built buildings for disabled children can be appropriate to their needs."

ASSOCIATION OF EDUCATION COMMITTEES:
"There are a number of supportive services which do much, and could do more, to give handicapped children a greater sense of independence and a better opportunity of participating in normal society. Amongst them are the provision of suitable domiciliary services designed to extend the range of personal mobility and activity; the provision of specially adapted transport; diversionary occupations and recreational services. It is suggested that the present provision of these services, both by local authorities and voluntary bodies, be kept under review in order that the goal of maximum fulfilment and participation by the individual handicapped person may be kept constantly in mind."

SOCIETY OF MEDICAL OFFICERS OF HEALTH:
"There are many ways in which the child's family may be involved in extra expense in giving him proper care or in which stress and strain could be reduced if more money were available. At present, monetary help can be provided only through limited 'unofficial' funds or by Social Security if the family's income is very low. We consider that some financial help should be more generously available. One way would be by allowing necessary extra expense to rank for income tax relief but this would assist only the families whose income is already fairly adequate. We would, therefore, favour the payment of a substantial extra family allowance in respect of a handicapped child."

LONDON BOROUGHS ASSOCIATION:
"There should be better facilities for holiday care for handicapped

children. Sometimes it is highly desirable for the whole family, including the handicapped child, to participate in a joint holiday, and in other circumstances it may be necessary for the parents themselves to take holidays with the remainder of their children in the family knowing that their handicapped child is being safely cared for either on a separate holiday or in a hostel during their absence."

Needs of Professional workers

Several professional organisations expressed the need for some part of the teacher training basic curriculum to be concerned with the education of handicapped children and more information about the various handicaps to be given, so that teachers in ordinary schools would have a greater awareness of handicap and be able to recognise divergencies from normal patterns of development.

The evidence referred to the need for more extensive training of all doctors at undergraduate and postgraduate level in the care of handicapped children and the physical, emotional and social problems this involves.

The need for better training for doctors working in child health centres in the assessment of handicapped children was suggested by a number of professional organisations. Refresher courses in methods of assessment for health visitors and district nurses were recommended.

The desirability of more short-term training facilities, courses, conferences, etc was mentioned by a number of organisations, who all stressed the need for professional workers to have wide contacts, and opportunities to discuss common problems.

Shortages of certain professional staff were noted frequently, particularly educational psychologists, child and family psychiatrists and speech therapists.

A number of organisations emphasised that social workers should have further knowledge about handicap and its implications, and about the wide variety of services available in a particular locality.

Quotations from the evidence
ASSOCIATION OF EDUCATION COMMITTEES:
"The present trends towards the integration of the handicapped in society make it extremely desirable that all teachers should have a

knowledge of handicapped children. Those teachers whose work is
mainly with handicapped children require a far more intensive training.
There should be a wider range of facilities for this purpose, particularly
since many teachers at present working in special schools have no
appropriate training. This is especially true in the case of teachers in
schools for educationally sub-normal pupils."

BRITISH PAEDIATRIC ASSOCIATION:
"We draw attention to the relatively poor training of most paediatricians
and local authority doctors in the problems of the handicapped child."

SOCIETY OF MEDICAL OFFICERS OF HEALTH:
"Present shortcomings are due to three main factors – shortage of staff,
inadequate professional training in some fields and the failure of some
workers to appreciate the problems of the handicapped child and the
family as a whole.

It is clear that for some time to come too many professional disciplines
will be competing for too few potential recruits. We consider that
better use might be made of existing staff, partly by the more generous
provision of transport and partly by giving wider training to such
general field workers as health visitors and child care officers.

To promote better understanding between different workers, we would
recommend various kinds of multi-disciplinary training. Thus, some
post-graduate courses for doctors should be open to general
practitioners, child health service doctors and paediatricians. Part of
the basic training of health visitors and social workers might be taken
in common. We believe that much could be done by local authorities
in the way of inter-disciplinary in-service training through short
courses, seminars and conferences and that there is also scope for
professionaly organisations and voluntary bodes to provide these."

HEALTH VISITORS' ASSOCIATION:
"Doctors and health visitors need regular refresher courses to keep their
knowledge of methods of assessment up-to-date. Health visitors feel
that they would also benefit from refresher courses devoted to the needs
of handicapped children and their parents."

ASSOCIATION OF CHILDREN'S OFFICERS:
"There should be flexibility in the service and sufficient training

schemes to enable staff movement between services for the handicapped and those for more normal children. Constant refresher courses are required and should include inter-disciplinary joint courses. The emotional deprivation of handicapped children needs a caring staff who should be in equal partnership with the educational and medical staff. This presupposes equality in training and salaries with better working conditions, as outlined in the Williams Report."

COLLEGE OF SPEECH THERAPISTS:

"Frequent resignations and staff shortages promote an unstable speech therapy service thereby providing only sporadic treatment for many speech handicapped children. There are still too few senior speech therapists to set up effective services and provide continuity of guidance and treatment for speech handicapped children and their parents. There is also a lack of senior therapists to whom their less experienced colleagues can turn for discussion and advice."

DR BARNARDO'S:

"Social workers in general are not trained to deal with the special problems of the families of the handicapped: those who would like more knowledge find that training facilities are almost non-existent.

If residential child care training courses could include some training in the care of physically and mentally handicapped children, this could mean that many more handicapped children who cannot live in their own homes could be cared for in residential homes rather than hospitals."

LONDON BOROUGHS ASSOCIATION:

"The professional social workers engaged at any stage and in any environment in dealing with handicapped children must be particularly knowledgeable of all the supportive services available in the locality. One would expect them to have the normal professional social work skills but beyond this they would need a liking for and an understanding of children, particularly the type and grouping of children with whom they will be undertaking social work."

ASSOCIATION OF SOCIAL WORKERS:

"It was felt that professional social workers in particular need more knowledge about handicap and its implications. All workers need to keep up to date in a field which is subject to change because of medical developments, and all need to have a full knowledge of special facilities

available. A central clearing house of information or a National Bureau
for Co-operation in the Care of the Handicapped Child would be of
considerable value here."

Patterns of organisation, co-ordination of services and inter-disciplinary co-operation

There were many pleas for one co-ordinated service to be responsible
for all handicapped children. Suggestions included the appointment
of one person to act as a co-ordinator, or a co-ordinating body, or a
new separate service. One organisation suggested this could be linked
with the child guidance service.

There was need for much closer liaison between all departments and
people involved with a handicapped child, especially at times when
transfer of responsibility is involved, *eg* pre-school, at school leaving,
when change of placement has to take place. Closer liaison between
residential schools and local education authorities in the home area is
advocated. Several organisations mentioned closer communication
between medical and non-medical staff.

The importance of the role played by voluntary organisations was
emphasised by many organisations, particularly in the pioneering of
certain services and in augmenting statutory provision. Closer
co-operation between voluntary and statutory bodies was suggested in
order to pool resources and prevent overlap.

Quotations from the evidence
ASSOCIATION FOR SPECIAL EDUCATION:
"The statutory bodies are often too small to provide the full range of
services necessary, and there is often inter-departmental jealousy and
inter-authority jealousy. We would urge that all services for handicapped
children be co-ordinated under one local authority department. Until
there is a change in local government boundaries, local authorities
should make greater efforts to co-operate in the provision of services
for handicapped children on an area basis. This does not merely mean
allowing a neighbouring authority to take a few places in a special
school but a real fusing of efforts in forward planning for a comprehensive range of services.

Voluntary bodies have played a most important part in the development of services for handicapped children and we believe that they

will still have a unique function in the future. As patterns of handicap change there will inevitably be gaps in the statutory provisions and it is here that the voluntary bodies can play a useful part by pioneering new methods and techniques and by acting as pressure groups on government departments. We would like to see closer co-operation between the many voluntary bodies so that resources can at times be pooled and overlapping and duplication of effort avoided."

LONDON BOROUGHS ASSOCIATION:
"Co-ordination of services is difficult on occasions because so many services may be involved and the same applies to inter-disciplinary co-operation. A local and single source of service would be more efficient and inter-disciplinary co-operation would be easier."

DISABLED LIVING FOUNDATION:
"It seems that there is a very great need for much better co-ordination of services, together with inter-disciplinary co-operation. The group has found that in all its studies concerning the disabled one of the points which is continually made is the great lack of communication between all those concerned with the same subject.

If the National Bureau could achieve better co-ordination and communication between all those organisations concerned with the physically handicapped child, greater economies related to finance and personnel might be achieved, much time could be saved, and inevitably the disabled child would benefit."

SPASTICS SOCIETY:
"There is generally a great need for better communication, co-operation and co-ordination, especially between different disciplines. The team approach has been talked about often enough, but except in isolated areas it is still theory rather than common practice."

NATIONAL ASSOCIATION FOR MENTAL HEALTH:
"While handicapped children are the responsibility of a number of departments and need the services of members of several professions, there would seem to be a need for some agency to provide opportunities for these workers to meet together to look at their common problems in helping handicapped children. The point of transfer from school to employment and from boarding school to home or hostel or lodgings, are clearly potential crisis times when the maximum number of helping agencies may be involved. For this reason this Association

has provided a forum for inter-disciplinary discussion for all those
concerned with the educationally subnormal school leaver and
subsequently for those working with children leaving schools for the
maladjusted."

SOCIETY OF MEDICAL OFFICERS OF HEALTH:
"We deplore the way in which some voluntary organisations have
difficulty in growing out of the pressure group stage and continue to
look on local authorities with suspicion or even hostility. We have no
magic recipe to suggest for breaking down this attitude but would feel
that the increasing tendency of local authorities to make use of the
services of voluntary bodies and to guide them in the provision of the
services, combined with representation of the authorities on the local
committees of the voluntary bodies, would encourage moves in the
right direction."

ASSOCIATION OF SOCIAL WORKERS:
"Although the voluntary bodies are in the main parent-promoted, there
seems little shortage of money once established. Many of these societies
have admirable facilities and resources, and it seems to us that the
co-operation which has existed between the statutory and voluntary
societies needs to be reinforced and strengthened. We are aware of
tensions which arise between voluntary and statutory bodies but feel
this arises from an under-estimation of their dependence upon each
other, a dependence which we do not see being lessened in the future.

There is a danger of the proliferation of these voluntary societies
tending to lead to a greater overall cost whilst providing a less effective
service. We would welcome a social work department which would
incorporate all the field work provisions for the handicapped."

WOMEN'S ROYAL VOLUNTARY SERVICE:
"All work by volunteers for handicapped children can only succeed if
both the professional workers and the parents have complete
confidence in the volunteer. There are, therefore, advantages, when
non-professional help is required, in inviting a voluntary service such
as WRVS to provide volunteers. It is not every willing helper who is
able or suitable to 'sit in' with a helpless child or to take a blind or
deaf child on a long journey. WRVS is able to select from among its
members those of proved reliability who are used to children and
also to ensure that a substitute is found if there is any last minute crisis.

No mother of a handicapped child should be 'at her wits end' or suffering a breakdown because she is denied help through lack of communications. This does happen today and equally there are many capable people, including young ones, to whom the idea of helping handicapped children makes the strongest possible appeal, but who are unable to find the opportunity."

NATIONAL ASSOCIATION OF SCHOOLMASTERS
"Voluntary organisations provide a valuable service and their existence should be encouraged and fostered. The service of many would be improved if they were to receive financial assistance from official sources. It would then be more reasonable to expect such organisations to adjust their functional role to meet particular needs and to accept some direction/advice from a co-ordinating body. The existence of many bodies is a good example of the healthy social attitude of the public to the less fortunate of this world. It is the right of the individual to contribute to a 'good cause' and this should be encouraged as often as the voluntary body comes into being to meet the needs of those whose needs are not being met by existing society. It would be of great value, however, if the various voluntary and statutory bodies could agree to the 'direction' of a co-ordinating body who could look objectively at the needs of the handicapped and could ascertain the most economical and effective means of meeting such needs. Ideally national standards of provision and facilities should be agreed and provided."

Geographical distribution of provision of services

The uneven geographical distribution of services was one of the concerns expressed by almost all organisations who submitted evidence.

Quotations from the evidence
NATIONAL ASSOCIATION OF SCHOOLMASTERS:
"It is most obvious to anyone concerned that the needs and incidence of handicapped children vary from area to area. Some local authorities make token provision which is little more than a gesture whilst others have elaborate, comprehensive services. Finance is often the reason for restricted provision, especially in some of the rural or depressed areas. It is, therefore, necessary to ensure that all areas make sufficient provision to meet needs and the money is not the sole reason for limited provision. Obviously for this to be so it is necessary to have available

additional funds, possibly on the lines of educational priority areas, for the handicapped."

PRE-SCHOOL PLAYGROUPS ASSOCIATION:
"In high density areas playgroups tend to be over-loaded with handicapped children. In deprived areas the need for playgroups is so urgent that large halls are passed for 40 or even 50 children, from 2–5 years, and with a ratio of handicapped children far higher than 1 : 10."

ASSOCIATION OF EDUCATION COMMITTEES:
"There are obvious difficulties of making adequate provision in rural areas. Many handicapped children are in the position of having no facilities within reasonable distance of their homes; transport is either non-existent or too time-consuming. The magnitude of the economic and financial problems involved have to be recognised, but this does not alter the fact that many young people in rural areas are being denied the opportunities which are available in urban centres."

Appendix C

Analysis of replies from selected local authorities

Introduction

Regrettably a national survey of the provision for handicapped children was not possible for financial reasons. Instead the Working Party invited ten local authorities to supply information and opinions in order to give some concrete illustration of how different authorities contend with the problems peculiar to their area, population, etc. Each of the authorities approached showed keen interest in the project and responded generously to initial discussions and meetings, the completion of questionnaires and the further follow-up of certain questions.

The selected authorities consisted of two large county boroughs, one in the north and one in the south of England; three large county councils, one mainly industrial, one rural and one mixed; an isolated rural county; two small county boroughs, and two of the new London boroughs created in 1965.

Separate questionnaires were designed for the clerk to the council, the medical officer of health, the chief education officer and the children's officer. It was intended that replies should indicate the practice and policy of each authority in relation to such topics as the early detection of handicap, assessment procedures, provision for pre-school children, special educational treatment, school leaving and employment, supportive services to families, the role of voluntary organisations, the training of staff and co-ordination of services.

Detection, assessment and screening

At risk register:

All ten local authorities keep some form of register of babies "at risk". This register relates to "those who are 'at risk' by reason of unfavourable heredity or adverse experiences in the pre-natal, perinatal, or immediate post-natal period" (Annual Report of the Ministry of Health 1957).

There is considerable variation between the different authorities in the way in which the registers are compiled and maintained. The percentage of live births placed on the register varies from 6 % to 28 %. The decision whether a child should be placed on the register is made in a number of ways. In some authorities registration is automatic after referral without any further investigation, but in the majority the decision is made after a senior medical officer has received all the available information. There is an annual review of the register in a few authorities and more frequent reviews in others.

The criteria for removal of names from the register vary considerably. One authority has no specific criteria; one has not, so far, removed any names, but is proposing to assess children at eighteen months and then either remove them or place them on the handicapped register. Several authorities remove the names when the child appears to be developing normally; in one authority this takes place at nine months, and in another the child remains on the register until he begins to attend an ordinary day school.

One large county borough maintains a register of all children with an abnormality, irrespective of whether it results in a handicap. The maternal and child welfare service is responsible for keeping a check on these children and for forwarding information to the mental health department and to the school health service, thus ensuring a continuous record. In addition, this county borough maintains a register of all children who have been in special care hospital units. These children are followed up by health visitors and are called for full medical developmental assessment at two years of age.

Routine follow-up examinations by the local health department of all the children on the "at risk" register take place regularly in eight out of the ten authorities. High risk children in one county authority are followed up by the paediatric service, and in a large county borough with a well equipped hospital service the majority of the children on the register remain under hospital supervision.

Screening and assessment
There are some schemes for the screening of all pre-school children,

who are seen by local authority clinic doctors, health visitors and general practitioners who hold child welfare clinics. These schemes vary considerably but only two of the ten authorities state that they have no screening procedures. In the majority of authorities plans are in hand for full developmental examinations of all infants but there is some variation in the application of these comparatively new skills. Screening for hearing defects, and for phenelketenuria, is usually carried out by health visitors.

In one large county borough, routine developmental examinations are carried out at local authority clinics, the clinic doctor assuming overall responsibility for the examination and for tests given by domiciliary midwives and health visitors. In this authority there is also a special clinic for pre-school children with a handicap, or whose development needs follow-up. Here the extent of the problem is assessed and supportive counselling is given to the parents.

Medical screening of the school population
In addition to regular school medical examinations, special screening of vision and hearing is carried out in most of the ten authorities. Audiometric sweep testing and surveys are usually given in the first year at school, and in two of the ten authorities a further check is made when the child is 7–8 years old. In eight of the authorities, vision testing is carried out at regular intervals during the child's school life; one authority used to screen all children when they were eight years old, but this has had to be discontinued for lack of staff (see Table B). Assessment of suspected handicaps detected through screening is usually instigated by maternity and child welfare and school medical officers who may refer certain cases to consultant paediatricians, orthopaedic surgeons, opthalmologists, ear nose and throat specialists and psychiatrists. Two authorities have established specialist clinics for the deaf. One education authority arranges for the educational psychologist to take part in the assessment of all children of school age with handicaps; in another authority, head teachers take part.

Educational screening
This is limited. Four of the ten authorities give details of some form of educational screening. In one, group tests are given to all children in the first year at the junior school; children needing further investigation have follow-up individual testing. In another authority, all children of 8 years are given a group test, and those scoring below a certain score

have individual tests. The main purpose of this is to plan the year's work for the remedial teachers but it has also proved to be a means of tracing some hitherto undetected educationally subnormal children. In one authority all 7 year olds are screened to detect "slow learners"; this is carried out with help of the school psychological service; as a result some children are then referred for a full medical examination and their needs are considered by panels based on the special schools in the county borough.

One authority has an educational test service which gives advice on group tests of ability and attainment; agreed testing procedures are established for each of the junior school years and infant schools use an intelligence test suitable for non-readers. The latter serves to screen children likely to need education at a special school, who can then be admitted at the end of their infant school period. One local education authority's system of continuous assessment includes verbal reasoning and intelligence tests which provide pointers to educational subnormality. Two education authorities state that in the past they have used some group screening tests, but no longer do so. In one large metropolitan authority each school keeps a special book in which teachers enter the particulars of any pupils who appear for any reason to need some special help; this book is inspected by the school doctor on his regular visits and any necessary action is taken.

There appears to be some participation by parents in assessment and in decisions regarding placement and treatment of their children in all ten authorities, but this ranges from the authority which states that parents' feelings are considered when decisions about placement are being made, to the authority in which parents are always involved in the process of decision making. Most medical officers have an opportunity to discuss problems with the parent when the child is examined but few authorities give any indication of how much follow-up takes place and by whom it is carried out. In one large urban authority, the health department runs a pre-school assessment clinic where parents receive considerable support and guidance. In another authority, the person who first detects a handicap discusses with the parents the need for further consultations with other professionals; an interdisciplinary group then meets and decides on the most suitable person to help the parents.

Opportunities for parents to help in observation and assessment units depends largely on the facilities available. In three county boroughs where there are a number of services for handicapped children, parents are encouraged to observe and help in assessment at such centres as audiology clinics and units, speech clinics, or the school for cerebral palsied children, while in one area parents work one day a week in a cerebral palsy unit. In one county council where the nursery special school caters for different handicaps, parents may stay as long as they like to observe and help in assessment.

Special educational treatment

Pre-school provision

The provision for pre-school handicapped children is still limited, and varies considerably in the ten authorities. All make some provision for deaf children, either by peripatetic teachers or in audiology units or schools for the deaf, but in some cases only a very small number of children receive help. In two authorities, deaf children are the only ones for whom provision is made. Pre-school children with other handicaps are admitted to day nurseries, playgroups and nursery schools in some authorities, although the numbers are small.

Special mention should be made of one county and one county borough. In the comparatively sparsely populated county, a nursery special school has been purpose built for children of two and upwards with any handicap. This school also serves as an assessment and treatment centre. The fairly small county borough provides a wide variety of services for pre-school children. There is a nursery class and a special playgroup for mentally handicapped, emotionally disturbed and socially deprived children; the day training centre admits severely subnormal children from the age of 3 years; a playgroup for maladjusted children operates at a psychiatric unit at the local hospital; there is a unit for children with cerebral palsy run jointly by the hospital and local education authority; there is a nursery class for deaf and partially hearing children and in addition domiciliary auditory training is carried out by specially trained health visitors; the day nurseries admit a small number of physically or mentally handicapped children. A small purpose built unit for six to eight physically handicapped children has just been added to an existing day nursery.

Provision for school age children

The education of handicapped children is provided in a number of ways, the variety and extent of provision depending both on the handicap and the policy of each local authority. The usual provision is in day special schools, or in residential special schools either maintained by the local authority or another authority, or by a voluntary organisation or an independent body. Provision is also made in hospital schools, in the child's own home and in some special groups for children with cerebral palsy. Special classes in ordinary schools are also provided by most of the ten authorities. These primarily cater for partially hearing, physically handicapped, maladjusted and delicate children. A number of authorities have classes for educationally subnormal children in the ordinary schools, but it is not possible to obtain precise particulars about these as they are not required in Department of Education and Science statistics.

The total number of handicapped children and the number per 10,000 school population receiving, or recommended for, special education in January 1969 in the ten authorities is shown in Table A.

The waiting list policies of the ten authorities differ considerably. The numbers of children waiting for special education range from 12 to 290; numbers in county boroughs are much lower than in county council areas. It is not clear whether this is the result of a policy of not keeping long waiting lists or whether county boroughs make more adequate provision.

Changing patterns of provision
Some interesting features of the changing patterns of provision emerge when a comparison is made with the statistics for 1967/68 and 1968/69. One noticeable change is the decrease in the numbers of physically handicapped and delicate children in some areas, but an increase in others. Three of the ten authorities report fewer delicate children receiving special educational treatment and one reports fewer physically handicapped children but in one large county authority there are twice as many physically handicapped children receiving special educational treatment in residential schools as in the preceding year, though fewer are in day schools. The number of ascertained delicate children in this authority has dropped dramatically. In another large industrial county borough, the number of ascertained delicate children has increased considerably. There has been a significant increase in the provision for maladjusted children in two authorities, and in two other authorities there are now more places for

maladjusted children in residential schools. In one large county borough, however, the provision for maladjusted children appears to have decreased and numbers are less than half those of the previous year. The number of deaf children receiving special educational treatment has diminished in two authorities, but in one authority they have substantially increased.

The overall number of children receiving special educational treatment in the ten local authorities has not substantially changed during the past year, with the exception of one county council in the south of England where there has been an increase in numbers, particularly of educationally subnormal and maladjusted children, and one large county in the north of England where the provision appears to have decreased. It is not possible to discover whether this is as a result of children moving to other areas, or to a real reduction in the number of children with particular handicaps, or whether the children have been absorbed into ordinary schools and so are not shown in the statistics of those receiving special educational treatment.

Day and residential special schools
The nature and severity of the handicap is one of the main determining factors in whether day or residential provision is made. Small numbers result in nearly all blind children being sent to residential schools. The population distribution is another factor contributing to the provision of day and/or residential schooling. In the county boroughs, the percentage of all handicapped children attending day schools ranges from 68% to 91%. In the county councils it ranges from 9% to 69%. Two authorities have unusually low percentages of children at day special schools; in one the policy has been to keep the children in ordinary schools if possible and so there is very little special school provision; the other is a sparsely populated county where it is considered more practicable to provide residential schools.

There are wide differences, therefore, in the numbers of children in the different authorities who attend residential special schools. These range from 9% of all children receiving special educational treatment in one large county borough, to 90% in two county council areas. Similarly, arrangements for the placement of children away from home differ from one authority to another. Two authorities appear to make no provision for parents to visit the schools before the child is placed, and education welfare officers escorting children to and from school seem to be the only liaison between home and school. Two authorities specify standard procedures prior to placement; arrangements are made for parents and children to visit the residential special schools before parents are asked to give their final consent to the child being admitted. This, then, makes them feel that they have had some choice in the matter.

While the child is attending a residential special school, parents are encouraged to visit the school and some authorities give financial assistance for this in case of need. One county borough finances a termly visit for each family and, if special circumstances arise, further help is given. There appears to be little evidence of supportive help to parents while the child is in a residential special school; in some cases this was said to be due to shortage of staff.

The extent of the contact between a given local authority and other local authorities or voluntary schools where children are placed varies. A few send information and receive regular school reports, but two state that no arrangements are made. One county borough education authority keeps close contact with the schools outside the area; they are all visited regularly by a school medical officer and/or a senior educational psychologist or a social worker, and a child's progress is reported directly back to the home authority. One large county council, the majority of whose handicapped children are in residential special schools, states that while a child is at school they consider he is the responsibility of the local authority administering the school but some liaison takes place with the professional staff.

Special educational treatment in ordinary schools
The policy about keeping handicapped children in ordinary schools varies only slightly in the ten different authorities. In the main, this is done wherever possible. One large county borough believes they should be kept there provided they do not fail, while another smaller one maintains that the decision to keep a child in an ordinary school has to be based on the needs of the child and the ability of the school to meet those needs. One authority with newly developing services has included in its building programme a new school for physically handicapped children near an existing secondary school, so that there can be as much integration of senior pupils as possible.

Where there are special classes and units for certain types of handicapped children in ordinary schools these are included in the Department of Education and Science statistics. All the ten authorities, except one small county borough, have special classes for partially hearing children, two have classes for the partially sighted, two authorities make provision for a very small number of physically handicapped children in a special unit, and five authorities have some provision in special classes for maladjusted children. Facilities for educationally subnormal children in special classes are not recorded on Department of Education and Science Form 21M so no details can be given of the total numbers of these children receiving special educational treatment. Because of this, the official number of educationally subnormal children presents an underestimate of known incidence. One large county borough has 94 special classes for these children, catering for approximately 2,000 children. One large county council, whose policy has been to keep educationally subnormal pupils in the ordinary schools if at all possible, has set up a number of classes for such children in purpose built classroom units attached to infant and junior schools. There appear to be over 200 pupils in these classes and plans are in hand to increase their number.

In addition, most of the ten authorities make some provision for children needing extra help, including peripatetic remedial teachers and teachers of the deaf, and remedial classes and units. The extent of this provision cannot be gauged. The criteria for and the process of selection for such help are not specified; for instance it is not known whether the children who are on the waiting list for special educational treatment are receiving this help.

Provision for multi-handicapped children
The placement of multi-handicapped children in each of the ten authorities appears usually to be made according to the major handicap. Several base the decision where to place these children on their educational needs, but two authorities think it is preferable to aim at the most sympathetic placement, taking into account social and environmental factors, rather than simply considering the major handicap. In one authority, where the majority of multi-handicapped children initially attend a nursery special school, there is a prolonged process of assessment to determine the most suitable ultimate placement.

Provision for severely subnormal children

The provision available for severely subnormal children in the ten authorities varies considerably. It is difficult to assess whether it is adequate as actual numbers are not readily obtainable. Numbers are given of places in junior training centres, and also some details of other types of provision, but it is not known how many children remain at home (see Table D). In addition to training centres, some authorities provide special care units which are usually attached to the centres. Hostel accommodation is provided by three authorities, where children stay and attend the local centre; it is also used for temporary or short term care during holidays. In two authorities there is provision for severely subnormal young children in special day nurseries and play groups.

For those severely subnormal children who have to remain at home, the main source of help appears to come from mental welfare officers. However, one county authority gives details of special classes held twice weekly in three small towns.

The procedures for reaching decisions about the placement of children who are borderline subnormal/severely subnormal are similar in most of the authorities. One county borough appears to have no set procedure, though there are three special classes which cater for 5 to 7 year olds of doubtful "educability"; these classes also fulfil a diagnostic function. In another small county borough, borderline children are put in special classes in ordinary schools pending a permanent decision, but it is not stated when, how and by whom this decision is made. In one large county borough, reports on such children are considered each term by a committee consisting of an educational psychologist, school medical officer and head teacher while a diagnostic unit at one of the schools for the educationally subnormal is equipped to assist in the assessment. A similar attempt in another large county borough is limited by lack of places. Remedial/diagnostic units have been set up in one county borough for 16 children aged 5 to 7 years whose progress is observed and reviewed before decisions are made. If it is considered necessary, a further period of observation can take place in the observation unit of the primary school for educationally subnormal children. Trial periods, either in a special (educationally subnormal) or an ordinary school are given in all the county authorities.

Handicapped school leavers, employment and after care

In some areas the youth employment service is provided by the local education authority, but in others it is part of the Employment Exchange Service run by the Department of Employment and Productivity. Eight of the ten authorities provide a youth employment service. Five of the authorities state that specialist careers advisory officers have been appointed to work exclusively with handicapped school leavers.

The procedures adopted for guidance and assistance in finding employment differ considerably in the ten authorities. Seven of them make special arrangements. One holds annual case conferences to discuss handicapped school leavers. Separate meetings, which include interviews with parents and children, are held to discuss the placement and employment of those attending schools for the educationally subnormal and other special schools, as well as ordinary schools. All departments and agencies involved attend these school leaving conferences.

In one highly populated county borough, a specialist careers advisory officer visits special schools each week and is included on the timetable for careers lessons. Counselling, guidance and practical information is thus given in a continuous and more informal way. In another county borough, there are two vocational specialists who deal exclusively with handicapped children; working in conjunction with a special school education welfare officer, they have particular responsibility for placement in employment and follow-up after a child has left school.

The amount of guidance given to children in residential special schools varies. All authorities arrange for reports to be sent from the careers officer in whose authority the school is situated; discussion and consultation then usually takes place with the home based careers officer. One authority has a regular arrangement whereby the child is interviewed while at home during the school holiday, and then placement can be discussed at the school leavers' conference in the home authority. In another large county borough, continued training and placement becomes the responsibility of a specialist careers officer after the young person returns home.

When it is recommended that school leavers should receive further training, seven of the local education authorities use local provision such as colleges of further education, training centres; all make use also of independent establishments, assessment centres, and vocational training centres run by voluntary bodies for specialist training. The extent to which this is done is difficult to determine, for many authorities list a large number of centres but do not state how frequently they are used and by how many of the school leavers. Two authorities arrange for some children to attend classes at colleges of further education or technical colleges and one of these runs special evening classes for slow readers. One authority makes provision for "work experience" for educationally subnormal children, and another has set up an industrial unit in which a number of educationally subnormal boys (and recently girls also) in their final year at school can spend most of their time.

One large county borough welfare department makes it possible for all ambulant handicapped adolescents to attend work centres until they find employment.

Supportive services to parents

Information about the amount of practical help provided by local authorities to parents of handicapped children was difficult to obtain. This is partly because health and welfare departments are not able to break down their figures of home help and home nursing services so as to show how many families with handicapped children receive such help. However, four authorities were able to state how many families had received some home nursing help for their handicapped child. These ranged from one family receiving help in one small county borough to twenty-six in one county council area. Very few families received a home help service in the four areas where figures were given. Six authorities were able to give some information about short-term day or residential centres, usually for mentally handicapped children. In one county council authority, children spend short periods in a residential centre in order that parents may have a break, and a summer holiday scheme also operates under which mothers can leave their children during the holiday at the nursery special school. In one highly populated area provision is made for both day and residential centres and places are available in units in day nurseries; temporary admission is arranged during periods of special difficulty.

In another area, a number of delicate children are sent by the local authority to a holiday home for two weeks.

The role of voluntary organisations
The role of voluntary organisations in most of the selected authorities appears to be mainly supportive. Parents' groups are run in most areas; in six areas there are youth clubs which are run by voluntary organisations.

Financial help is often given by the local authority to voluntary groups for a variety of activities. These include grants to youth clubs; financial help for provision of equipment to some centres; assistance to enable some children to go on holiday or to convalescent homes run by voluntary organisations; and rent free accommodation for centres, meetings, etc. In one area the Women's Royal Voluntary Service are responsible for transporting all the children who attend the special school and partially hearing units. A mileage allowance is paid by the local education authority. Active participation by members of the local authority staff on committees and boards of management is specified by three of the authorities. Meetings between local authority officials and members of voluntary organisations take place in nine of the areas but usually only one department is involved; whether or not these contacts are regular is not specified.

The extent to which schools and training centres run by voluntary organisations are used by the local authority depends to some degree on the authority's own provision; one county borough which has a considerable number of day special schools does not need to use any schools run by voluntary bodies. One large county council makes use of a number of voluntary schools, centres, etc which the local authority does not itself provide for children with specific handicaps. This situation also occurs in authorities where limited numbers suffering from a specific handicap make it impracticable to build a special school for such children.

Handicapped children in care

(NB One children's department did not complete the questionnaire) The proportion of children in the selected local authorities who are in care, either in foster or children's homes, shows a fairly wide range. In county authorities the percentages range from ·3% to ·5% of the total population under 18 years; in the county boroughs this percentage is slightly higher, ranging from ·6% to 1·7%. The proportion of children in care who are also handicapped varies considerably. The range is from 6% of all children in care in one small county borough to 27% in another county borough.

It is difficult to gather information about handicapped children in care because official child care statistics do not include this specific information. It is thought that the number of handicapped children in care is increasing. This makes it even more important that accurate information should be made available.

The commonest handicaps among children in care are clearly educational subnormality and maladjustment. The proportion who were ascertained as educationally subnormal ranged from 23% to 32% and those who were maladjusted from 9% to 37% (see Table C).

The placement of handicapped children in children's homes, residential special schools or foster homes presents problems in all authorities. Approximately 30% of handicapped children in care are in residential special schools. Only half the authorities are able to provide regular placements in their home area during the holidays. One of these authorities in a rural area states that regular placement is difficult for children who have behaviour and personality problems or who come from homes with such problems. In the remaining authorities, it appears impossible to provide regular holiday homes for about half the handicapped children because of their handicap. One authority finds it difficult to fit their severely handicapped children into small family group homes, even for holiday periods. The child's handicap also makes placement in foster homes difficult. One large county borough has only one handicapped child in a foster home because it is almost impossible to find foster parents who will accept handicapped children. In another county authority, however, with a sparse rural population, more handicapped children are in foster homes than in other placements. The disproportionate amount of time and energy demanded by these children clearly warrants the higher payment to foster parents which is made by seven of the nine authorities.

Consultant help to staff dealing with handicapped children in care, whether foster parents, residential staff or field staff is limited in all nine authorities; some provision is made for consultative help to

residential staff, and in one large county council there are group
discussions for field staff arranged by a training officer. The staff of
child guidance clinics and consultant psychiatrists give what help they
can when the child has an appointment at the clinic or hospital, but
this is limited.

Probably the most serious deficiency is the lack of adequate provision
for maladjusted children in care, particularly adolescents. There are
long delays in appointments with psychiatrists and these are usually
for diagnosis rather than treatment. Five of the nine children's
departments stressed the need for special accommodation and supportive help for these children, and for the staff who deal with them.
Severely disturbed children in care appear to present the greatest
single problem to children's departments.

Staff training in the education and health departments
Regular in-service training courses related to some aspect of handicap
are run by five of the ten local health authorities for some of their staff.
One provides training for health visitors in audiometric and vision
testing, for general practitioners and school nurses on disturbed
children and for school medical officers on educationally subnormal
children; every second year a week's refresher course is held for mental
welfare officers. Another authority in a rural area runs an annual
course for medical officers and health visitors on audiology and
screening for hearing loss; also courses are held occasionally for the
lay staff of the department in vision and hearing screening. Two other
authorities provide courses for teachers of mentally handicapped
children and for trainee assistants in training centres. One authority
runs regular courses for nursery nurses, for health visitors and school
nurses on the problems of handicapped children. This same authority
has special courses for interested teachers in both special and ordinary
schools arranged by the school psychological service.

Few in-service courses for teachers are organised by any of the ten
authorities. One large county borough holds such courses regularly for
teachers of educationally subnormal children and one large county
council has annual courses for staff in ordinary schools. One county
council has started a pilot course to help teachers to become more
aware of the problems of partially hearing children in ordinary

schools. The Inner London Education Authority, however, provides many day time and evening courses.

Some in-service training for workers in residential schools is either provided or being planned by four of the ten authorities. One large authority in an area where there are many facilities arranges for its staff to attend lectures and courses, including some in hospitals or run by professional organisations.

The number of teachers who have attended full time courses on the education of handicapped children during the last three years varies considerably. It is not always clear whether the attendance was at one year, one term or even shorter courses. The numbers range from one teacher in the last three years in a small county borough to 30 teachers in the same period in a large county borough. One of the large county councils was unable to give exact numbers of the teachers who had been seconded but believed this was substantial.

Co-ordination of Services

Within the local authority
Regular meetings of members of the education and health departments to discuss treatment and placement of handicapped children appear to take place in seven of the ten authorities. One authority's departments gave conflicting replies and another authority only occasionally holds such meetings. Six of the departments base their meetings on admissions and discharges of children to or from special schools, but only two authorities specify that the heads of these schools also take part. In one authority, case conferences are held to discuss referral and placement of children showing signs of emotional disturbance; workers directly involved with each child are invited.

One county borough has a well developed system of regular interdepartmental meetings covering a wide range of topics; these include a pre-school study group meeting once a month to consider all pre-school children with emotional, physical or mental handicaps; a clearing house conference, similar to the pre-school study group which meets once a fortnight and includes a review of school age children; a panel concerned with handicapped school leavers meets regularly to discuss placement and employment policy for all school leavers. The fact that the school health service operates within the education service rather than as an outside agency is felt to facilitate co-ordination. A similar arrangement operates in another large county borough so that the senior medical officer has almost daily contact with the adviser for special schools and the assistant education officer.

The availability of information and reports on handicapped children, together with contacts between the local health and education departments and the schools, varies a great deal from authority to authority. When a handicapped child is in an ordinary school, the amount of communication ranges from one authority where relevant information and records are available, to another authority where head teachers are invited to examinations and assessments, are informed of results and specific recommendations by hospital consultants and by school medical officers, who make follow-up visits to discuss any problems which may arise. In all ten authorities there is usually some form of inter-departmental contact about handicapped children.

The co-operation between local authorities when children are placed in residential special schools outside their home authority, appears to depend on the concern and interest of the home authority. Two authorities apparently have no co-ordinating arrangements with the authority in which the residential school is located. The latter is asked to make arrangements for medical supervision, etc. Another large authority with a high proportion of children in residential special schools consider that they are the responsibility of the other authorities. Progress reports are received in some areas, but with varying degrees of regularity. One education authority asks the receiving schools to keep them informed of progress, and regular visits are made by officers. Two authorities stated that they obtain prior information about any independent schools that they plan to use. In general, contacts appear to vary both in quantity and quality.

Co-ordination with general practitioners, hospitals and consultants

The local authority health departments have some contact with general practitioners and hospital consultants. Very few referrals and reports on handicapped children are received from general practitioners and in only a few of the ten authorities do they take part in discussion and decisions about placement or specific problems. The health department of one county council consider this may be due to lack of knowledge by general practitioners about the local authority powers, facilities and responsibilities. This same authority states that a minority of doctors regularly seek co-operation but as a group tend to resent any intervention on the part of the local authority.

The practice of attaching health visitors to general practices is increasing and most of the ten local health departments thought that this was working well. Only two authorities gave specific details of how the health visitors work with handicapped children. In one large county borough, the health visitors pay regular visits to all pre-school handicapped children at the request of the health department and maintain the necessary contact with general practitioners. In one rural county a health visitor works full time with handicapped children and their families, and keeps a close liaison with their general practitioners; other health visitors then keep in touch with her.

The contact between local health departments and hospital consultants appears to be adequate although there is variation in the way in which reports are sent. Only two authorities state that they automatically receive reports on handicapped children who have been seen by hospital consultants. In one large county borough, with a number of hospitals in the area, the consultants have expressed some difficulty in deciding which reports will be most useful, particularly in relation to educational problems. This same authority states that it is not always possible to follow the consultant's advice because of social and environmental factors but liaison in this field is good and often the consultants will modify their comments to make them more realistic.

Joint circular no 7/66 and 9/66

In 1966 a joint circular was issued by the Department of Education and Science and the then Ministry of Health asking local authorities to review arrangements for the co-ordination of education, health and welfare services for handicapped children and young people (see Appendix 4). The Working Party questionnaire asked the ten local authorities to give details of the ways in which this joint circular had been implemented.

Nine out of the ten local authorities responded by giving some account of the original discussions and subsequent action; while the original replies were not quoted in their entirety, it was evident that each authority placed emphasis on different aspects of the services for handicapped children.

Details and recommendations submitted by the local authorities follow:

In one large county council, staff discussions took place and it was felt that the arrangements for co-operation and co-ordination are complete, flexible and under continuous review; these include frequent discussion and liaison between the staff of the local authority departments and professional staff in other fields. All welfare arrangements are administered through the health department and it is felt there is never any doubt which department is responsible for a handicapped person.

Another authority listed the procedures adopted as well as those in process of formulation. The local health authority, together with the regional hospital board, has devised a system of case records for infants which will be computerized and the analyses circulated to all relevant departments. Co-operation between the hospital and the local authority has been strengthened by the establishment of a special out-patient clinic for children with chronic handicaps at which general practitioners and a medical officer are invited to attend to discuss particular cases. All the medical officers are on the staff of the local hospital and act as medical liaison officers in the paediatric department of the hospital.

One county council had instigated certain changes in order to improve co-operation prior to the publication of the joint circular. These included the establishment of joint files on handicapped children compiled by the health and education departments. Subsequent discussions on the whole disclosed close co-operation between the various services, and there are continuous efforts to improve co-ordination. Two examples of the ways in which this closer liaison has been achieved is the development of the school psychological service and the strengthening of the link between the school health service and the employment service, which in this area is run by the Department of Employment and Productivity.

The county medical officer of health of one large county council gave a comprehensive review of all the services available to handicapped children. It was emphasized that because many of the services are currently being developed, some duplication of functions is still occurring. It was suggested that within the local authority there might be one supervising department which could deal with all handicapped children. A specialist officer might be responsible for maintaining a central index of handicapped children and allocating cases to the most appropriate worker. The health department's reply suggested that the most appropriate person to assume this responsibility would be the county medical officer of health, who could, in addition, co-operate closely with the education and children's departments as well as with the youth employment service. The liaison with hospitals in a large county obviously varies and this local health authority would welcome more information from consultants and medical social workers, particularly on a child's discharge from hospital, so that a continuing service could be given. It was felt that many general practitioners are not aware of the extent of the health authority's services for handicapped children. In the county there are local co-ordinating committees, composed of representatives from the main voluntary organisations, co-opted general practitioners and medical officers and these meet with other local authority officers to form a central co-ordinating committee. These meetings provide an opportunity to disseminate new ideas and receive reports on any new project.

The officers of a rural county council discussed the circular and met with the local medical committees and representatives from the then Ministry of Labour. It was considered that while adequate liaison existed between these bodies there was still some scope for improvement within the council's organisation and in its relationship with other bodies. The council's main concern was that services should not break down when handicapped children moved from one school to another or at the school leaving stage. As a result a number of procedural changes were introduced. The welfare department is now notified of all seriously handicapped children aged 14 years in order to establish contact before they leave school; and of all other young handicapped people who experience difficulty in training, placement or work. Procedures were also reviewed for transfer of information from one school to another. A problem in this authority was whether to divulge relevant social and medical information to the staff of various departments within the authority; caseworkers would like this to be available, though used with discretion, but the official view is that this might constitute a breach of confidence. The authority hoped for some comments on this contentious point from the Ministries concerned.

In one large county borough details were not given, but as a result of the discussions there was felt to be better understanding by the local authority of the difficulties of the hospital services and of general practitioners. Quarterly meetings of senior officers of the health and education departments were established to have a systematic review of handicapped children in order to ensure continuity of supervision and to maintain family contact through the most appropriate worker. The regional hospital board have appointed a consultant physician for handicapped children and there are arrangements for him to be called in by the local authority for appropriate cases.

The procedures for co-ordination between departments concerned with handicapped children were listed fully by one county borough. This authority has a number of interdisciplinary committees and conferences which have been set up to ensure close collaboration between all those dealing with handicapped children at various stages. This ensures that all staff involved know what contribution each is making and who is assuming responsibility. A pre-school committee discusses assessment of the children with general practitioners, receives reports from consultants and keeps close contact with health visitors; thus much information is available when the child reaches school age, and adequate provision can then be made as soon as possible. Two handicapped school leavers, committees help boys and girls with placement and employment. There is close liaison with hospital consultants and medical social workers, consultants regularly attend local authority vision and audiology clinics and health visitors attend premature baby clinics. This authority feels that exchange of information between hospitals, general practitioners and medical staff of the local authorities could be improved by the introduction of a master card for information but it is recognised that the confidential nature of medical records could prove a complication.

One large county borough after discussions with other professions and organisations listed eight aspects in which they felt improvements could be made. These aspects included:

a. inadequate information from consultants to the health department;

    b. general practitioners requested that they should be brought into the picture more fully than at present and thus help the authority more by supplying further information about handicapped children and notifying the existence of subnormal children. There is now co-operation about this;

    c. it was thought that the scope and completeness of the handicap register could be re-examined to see whether improvements could be made to facilitate interchange of information;

    d. consistent advice and continuing support to families was considered necessary but not always achieved; the lack of social workers is curtailing support to the families of school age children;

    e. voluntary organisations felt that information about statutory and voluntary services should be readily available; a handbook produced by the local council of social service has now been brought up to date;

    f. the welfare department felt there should be closer consultation with other departments concerning severely handicapped school leavers to ensure contact with the child and his family; the amalgamation of the health and welfare departments is proposed.

The Inner London boroughs set up a working party to consider the joint circular. This group was composed of representatives of health, welfare and children's departments, the Inner London Education Authority, and regional hospital boards. It was agreed that in view of the complexity of London government co-ordination of services was adequate. However, several recommendations were made:

    a a register of all handicapped children should be kept in each London borough; this could be an extension of the "at risk" register but the names of children could be put on at any age and kept on until the age of 21;

    b. there should be a regular review of the register to ensure that up-to-date information was included;

    c. all statutory and voluntary organisations should supply relevant information to the medical officer of health;

    d. if possible, a standard format should be devised to facilitate ease of transfer to other authorities;

  e. when a child has been placed on the register, one chief officer
      should be made primarily responsible for co-ordinating all the
      services at all levels, this nominated officer could be changed at
      subsequent times as the situation changed;

  f. welfare and mental welfare officers should be brought into the
      consideration of the child's future at a much earlier age than
      at present;

  g. a simple pamphlet should be produced giving information on
      all available services for all handicapped children in each
      London borough;

  h. the medical officers of health should be asked to give reasonable
      forecasts of the demands for provision in each category of
      handicap in order that different departments might be able to
      plan accordingly;

  i. a survey should be made of handicapped school leavers to assess
      the value of the services given;

  j. co-ordination and adequate exchange of information between
      local authorities and hospitals appeared more satisfactory when
      local authority social workers were able to attend hospital
      clinics, and it was hoped that this practice would be extended.

Table A. Provision for handicapped children
1. Number of handicapped children receiving education in special
   schools, independent schools, boarded in homes, receiving education
   in special classes and units and in accordance with Section 56 of the
   Education Act 1944 in hospitals and at home awaiting admission
   to special schools, in January 1969.
2. Incidence of above per 10,000 school population.

Local Education Authority	School Population (approximate)	Blind		Partially Sighted		Deaf		Partially Hearing		Physically Handicapped	
		1	2	1	2	1	2	1	2	1	2
A	65,000	8	1·2	13	2·0	48	7·4	55	8·4	76	11·6
B	43,000	4	0·9	13	3·0	18	4·1	30	6·9	90	20·9
C	10,000	4	4·0	1	1·0	4	4·0	3	3·0	20	20·0
D	29,000	5	1·7	2	0·7	5	1·7	35	12·0	69	23·7
E	71,000	16	2·2	20	2·8	68	9·5	34	4·7	126	17·7
G	167,000	26	1·5	44	2·6	22	1·3	125	7·4	213	12·7
H	170,000	34	2·0	25	1·4	50	2·9	68	4·0	187	11·0
I	88,000	13	1·4	20	2·2	12	1·3	43	4·8	90	10·2
J	51,000	13	2·5	13	2·5	5	0·9	41	8·0	99	19·4

Area F is omitted as it was not possible to give a breakdown of figures.

Delicate		Maladjusted		Educationally Subnormal		Epileptic		Speech Defect		All Handicaps		Local Education Authority
1	2	1	2	1	2	1	2	1	2	1	2	
97	14·9	163	25·0	389	59·0	10	1·5	4	0·6	863	132·7	A
27	6·2	93	21·6	324	75·3	5	1·1	–	–	604	140·4	B
4	4·0	48	48·0	40	40·0	3	3·0	1	1·0	128	128·0	C
26	8·9	155	53·4	338	116·5	3	1·0	2	0·7	640	220·6	D
227	31·9	40	5·6	641	90·2	7	0·9	3	0·4	1182	166·4	E
44	2·6	154	9·0	226	13·5	21	1·2	3	0·1	878	52·5	G
111	6·5	70	4·1	1141	67·0	8	0·5	1	0·05	1695	99·7	H
34	3·8	147	16·7	991	112·0	4	0·4	1	0·1	1355	153·9	I
28	5·4	52	10·1	297	58·2	7	1·3	1	0·1	556	109·0	J

Table B. Vision and hearing testing of school age children

Local Authority	Vision	Hearing
A	Primary school children seen yearly by health visitor/school nurse Secondary school children seen biennially Boys given colour test at 11+	Survey of all children in 1st year of primary school
B	No screening procedures	No screening procedures
C	Testing at 8 years	No screening procedures
D	Annual test except at 6 years Colour test at 12 years	Sweep test in 1st year of infant school
E	Tests at 7, 9, 11, and 13 years	Sweep test at 6 years
F	Test on admission to school and subsequently 3 or 4 tests during school life	Sweep test at 5 years and at secondary school
G	Tests at 5, 7, 11 and 14 years	Survey of children at 5 years
H	No screening procedures	Sweep test at 5–7 years and at 7+
I	Tests at 8 years	Screening test at 6 years
J	Tests by school nurse at 5, 7, 11 and 14 years	Sweep test at 5 and 8 years

Table C. Handicapped children in the care of the children's department.

Local Authority	Percentage who are assessed as handicapped	Percentage of handicapped children who are educationally subnormal	Percentage of handicapped children who are maladjusted
A	10%	26%	35%
B	27%	23%	30%
C	6%		50%
D	No returns		
E	17%	39%	9%
F	19%	29%	37%
G	21%	32%	35%
H	14%	52%	20%
I	16%	52%	12%
J	12%	46%	14%

Table D. Provision for severely subnormal children

Local Authority	Approx. School Population	No. of Training Centres	No. of Children Attending	Other Provision
A	65,000	2	234	30 place special care unit; 19 places at short term residential hostel
B	43,000	1	50	6 children attend day training centre run by another local authority; 2 children attend residential training class; 4 children in residential care (voluntary organisation); 35 children in 2 subsidised play-groups; Spastic centre; No provision for those at home
C	10,000	1	50	No facilities; Visiting by mental welfare officers for those at home
D	29,000	1 (including special care unit)	93 + (25 in special care unit)	Social work support for those who remain at home
E	71,000	2	215	Special care unit – 40 places for severely subnormal children under 16 who have a physical handicap; Support by mental welfare officers to those at home. Short term care at hostel can be given

	Population	Use made of places in adjacent boroughs		Provision
F			35	30 children in 2 day nurseries; 12 children in special care unit; Home tuition and community care for those at home
G	167,000	6	408	Parent counselling by mental welfare officers – 465 children; Short term care facilities available
H	170,000	7	273	2 special care units – 13 severely subnormal and physically handicapped; Hostel accommodation for 20 children who attend local training centre; Health visitor visits those at home – 38 children
I	88,000	7	238	Support by mental welfare officers and other welfare officers for 300 families; Assessment clinics at local hospitals
J	51,000	2 (part-time) 3	130 15 (part-time)	Hostel accommodation for 40 children; 3 special classes held twice weekly; Visits by mental welfare officers, health visitors, medical officers; Short term residential care available

Appendix D

Department of Education and Science and Ministry of Health Joint Circular 9/66 and 7/66 March, 1966.

Co-ordination of education, health and welfare services for handicapped children and young people

1. The Secretary of State for Education and Science and the Minister of Health have recently reviewed, in consultation with the Minister of Labour and with their respective Advisory Committees, aspects of the care of physically and mentally handicapped children and young people, following joint study of the Report of a Working Party, commissioned by the British Council for the Rehabilitation of the Disabled, on the Handicapped School Leaver. They have also taken into account a Report to the Carnegie United Kingdom Trust on Handicapped Children and their Families. It is a recurrent theme in these reports that while individual services for handicapped children and young people may be good they are often not adequately co-ordinated. This frequently results in the handicapped, and particularly those who have more than one handicap, being deprived of beneficial services and continuous care, and in their families receiving inadequate support.

Review of Services
2. The Ministers are aware of arrangements which have already been made by various authorities to co-ordinate services, but nevertheless consider that there is still considerable scope for improvement. After consultation with the appropriate association of local authorities, they invite all education, health and welfare authorities to review their own practices and to join with hospital authorities and Executive Councils in a review of aspects of common concern. The Youth Employment Service should be brought into discussion of questions of vocational guidance and placing in employment. Voluntary organisations providing services in the area need also to be brought into consultation. Local authorities are asked to take the lead in initiating discussions. Copies of this memorandum have been sent to hospital authorities, Executive Councils and Local Medical Committees.

362

3. The matters to which the reviews should be directed are:

    i. The earliest detection and complete diagnosis of handicap, whether physical or mental, taking account of all evident or suspected disabilities of the child's general health, and assessment of practicable measures to deal with the handicap.

    ii. Regular review of medical, educational and social factors to enable an optimum service to be given in the interest both of the child and of the family; and in due course, consideration of employment prospects and the need for welfare services in adult life.

    iii. Consistent advice and continuing support to the family and, as appropriate, to the child or young person.

4. The objective of the review should be to establish arrangements which will ensure that there is co-ordination in the care of every handicapped child and that essential information about the existence of a handicap, its nature and degree, and the family situation, is available to all departments and services which may have a contribution to make. It will be of particular importance to examine the arrangements made for children with more than one handicap, and for all children at stages in their life where a change of responsibility occurs. Such changes occur when a family moves from one area to another, when a child is admitted to or discharged from hospital, or when the child goes to school and leaves school. Children who go away to residential schools need to be kept well in mind, especially during school holidays.

5. Whilst ascertainment will often be made by the local authority health services, clinical responsibility will remain throughout with the general practitioner and the hospital specialist. Within the local authority, the health department will have primary responsibility for children in the pre-school period, will retain it for those who are found to be unsuitable for education at school and will resume it in the case of many educationally subnormal or maladjusted children who find difficulty in adjusting to adult life after school. The education department, including the education authority's school health service, will be primarily responsible during the school years, in certain cases from the age of two years, and perhaps after leaving school if a substantial amount of further education is provided. Welfare services may well be needed at any age and welfare officers should in any case be actively concerned towards the end of the time at school. At this stage and afterwards the Youth Employment Service has responsibility for the employment of handicapped young people, covering their vocational guidance, placing and review of progress at work. The responsibilities of each of these services in relation to children with various single handicaps or with multiple handicaps need jointly to be examined and agreement reached about the services to be made available. This implies flexible arrangements for co-operation between the departments and a clear understanding by field workers, and others, as to the role they are to play.

6. The arrangements made will, of course, vary to meet local circumstances and the requirements of different handicaps. Factors of importance will be the

extent to which various kinds of staff are severally available to the education, health and welfare services and the extent to which each service has developed. To get the best results, it may be necessary to pool staffing resources and enable a nominated worker of the staff to work continuously with a child and his family even though his department may cease, from time to time, to be primarily responsible. For example, arrangements might be made for joint employment by the education and health departments of staff who are in touch with maladjusted or educationally subnormal children at school so that the same workers, in collaboration with the Youth Employment Officer, can continue to help children they know (and who know them) in the period of adjustment to employment and adult life.

In many cases, more then one department and more than one worker may need to be in touch with the child and his family. Clear arrangements must be made to ensure that all the staff involved know each other and the contribution each is making. The aim should be to reach agreement between them that one of them has responsibility for keeping in touch with the child and family. Case conferences are useful in keeping all concerned informed and reaching consistent decisions. Such conferences are particularly important when the handicap is first found and when the time comes to give vocational guidance and seek suitable employment. In all this, it is essential to consider the child and family together, for their problems interact and the services and advice offered must be adapted to the situation of the family, who may require a wider range of services and advice than is needed by the handicapped child alone. Even when a child is away from home continuing support and re-assurance to the family may be needed.

7. Timely communication of information is essential. All those in the education, health, welfare and employment services who are to work with a handicapped child or his family must have all the relevant medical and social facts about their needs if they are to give effective help. There might be advantage in reviewing the form of records kept by all departments to ensure that relevant information is readily available to those concerned with the family. A free exchange of information between hospitals, general practitioners and the medical staff of the local authority is specially necessary and consideration should be given to arranging for this as a matter of routine.

8. The consequences of failure of co-ordination for individual children or their families may be serious. It is advisable, therefore, to consider what overall form of supervision can be adopted in the area to secure that no child is lost to sight (this is particularly necessary if a handicapped child attends an ordinary or independent school far from his home) and that evident needs are not being neglected. It may be right that either the health or the welfare department should be allocated a responsibility for general oversight of nominated families where there is a clear prospect that their services will be needed in later life. In some cases one member of the staff would be in touch with the child from an early stage and could help to exercise oversight, eg the mental health worker in the case of the severely subnormal child, or the social

worker with the blind where blindness is the major handicap. In many cases special schools are the main point of contact with the family and act as focal points for the co-ordination of services for their pupils.

Report on Reviews

9. The Ministers would be glad to know by 30th September 1966 what steps have been taken to undertake reviews, what changes have in consequence been made, and of any problems encountered or new methods or developments deserving wider publicity. In order to assist in the collation of information it would be helpful if authorities would set out their replies so that they refer to arrangements for co-ordination in the order in which they occur in the life of the child.

It would be appreciated if authorities would send this information both to the Secretary of State for Education and Science and to the Minister of Health.

Appendix E

Copy of article by Anne Allen
published in the Sunday Mirror on August 11th, 1968

The people who need people

I imagine that the greatest cross the parent of a handicapped child has to bear is exhaustion. But it may be something quite different – anger, sadness, embarrassment, an illogical feeling of guilt. And what of the handicapped child himself? What are his greatest needs? Education? Friends? Parents who are unharassed in crises? An opportunity to get out and about? I am only guessing, but parents who have a mentally or physically handicapped child know his needs. Their views and experiences can help the National Bureau for Co-operation in Child Care to carry out an inquiry, backed by the Carnegie U.K. Trust.

The Bureau know the services for disabled or retarded children are patchy. They suspect that some people get virtually no help while others are well looked after. They are sure there are some splendid and imaginative experiments going on in the world of education, medicine, welfare or private charity. What they need, however, are details from the people most concerned – parents of handicapped children, young disabled adults, or disabled children. They are finding out from Medical Officers of Health, Chief Education Officers and Children's Officers in some areas how many handicapped children they know about, and what facilities there are for them locally. They are trying to discover how many are "in care," how many need special education, what training is available for school leavers, whether there are any youth clubs for handicapped young people, whether parents

366

are helped by day centres, home nursing or home helps. From the answers they will build up the official picture. From the parents they want the individual pictures.

If you have a child who is blind or partially sighted, deaf or hard of hearing, epileptic, delicate, physically handicapped, the Bureau would like to hear from you. Or if your child suffers a speech defect, needs special education for emotional reasons, is educationally sub-normal or too backward to be educated at all, they would also like you to write. Send your letters to me, Anne Allen, Sunday Mirror, 33 Holborn, London, EC1 and I will forward them to the Bureau. No names or localities will be mentioned when the research is published.

The Bureau are not in a position to help people who write. Their job is to find out what is lacking, and where, so that life can be made a little easier in the future. But they will be grateful for all letters. Have you, for instance, a local group where mothers with similar problems get together and help each other? Are there voluntary societies at work? If your child is in a residential school are you happy about the amount of contact you have with the school? Do people realise that your child needs what every other child needs, secure affection and the satisfaction of a day well spent? Does he have the chance to live life to his fullest capacity? With music, with hobbies, with friends, with the worship of God, according to his needs? Or is life for him, or her, a matter of not moving from one spot in the corner of the living room? Are there special money worries caused by wear on clothes or shoes, violence at home, long journeys to clinics? I know many of your letters will be desperate. I hope some, at least, will be contented.

There are magnificent schools and places for over-eighteens, such as the villages run by the Camphill Village Trust, which are imaginative and safe refuges for life. It would be nice to hear that some of the children who must go through life with a permanent disadvantage, whether mental or physical, had met with kindness, fun, excitement and the awareness that they were people-with-a-handicap rather than handicapped people. It would be nice to know that some of us care, not just in a woolly, sentimental way, but practically.

Bibliography

All references from chapters are included in this bibliography, the arrangement of which is in alphabetical order.

BLACKSTONE, T. (1969) "Where Nursery Schools Are". *New Society*. Vol 14, No 367, pages 560–561.

BLAND, G. A. (1968) *Education in Hospital Schools for the Mentally Handicapped* College of Special Education, London.

BLOOM, B. S. (1964) *Stability and Change in Human Characteristics*. Wiley & Sons, New York.

BRENNAN, W. K. AND HERBERT, D. M. (1969) "A survey of assessment/ diagnostic units in Britain". *Educational Research*, 12, No 1, 13–21.

BRITISH COUNCIL FOR REHABILITATION OF THE DISABLED (1964) *The Handicapped School Leaver*. Report of a Working Party. British Council for the Rehabilitation of the Disabled, London.

BRITISH PSYCHOLOGICAL SOCIETY (1966) *Children in Hospitals for the Subnormal –* A survey of admissions and educational facilities. The British Psychological Society, London.

BUTLER, N. R. AND BONHAM, D. G. (1963) *Perinatal Mortality*. E. & S. Livingstone Ltd, Edinburgh.

BUTLER, N. R. AND ALBERMAN, E. D. (ed.) (1969) *Perinatal Problems*. E. & S. Livingstone Ltd, Edinburgh.

CARLSON, E. R. (1952) *Born that Way*. Arthur James, The Drift, Evesham, England.

CARNEGIE UNITED KINGDOM TRUST (1964) *Handicapped Children and their Families*. Dunfermline, Scotland.

CENTRAL ADVISORY COUNCIL FOR EDUCATION (ENGLAND) (1967) *Children and their Primary Schools* (Plowden Report). HMSO London.

CHAZAN, M. (1965) "Factors associated with maladjustment in educationally subnormal children". *British Journal of Educational Psychology*. Vol 35, pp 277–85.

CLARKE, A. D. B. (1966) *Recent advances in the Study of Subnormality*. National Association of Mental Health, London.

COMMITTEE ON LOCAL AUTHORITY AND ALLIED PERSONAL SOCIAL SERVICES (1968) *Report of the Committee* (Seebohm Report). HMSO London.

DAVIE, R.; BUTLER, N. R. AND GOLDSTEIN, H. *From Birth to Seven*. In the press.

DEPARTMENT OF EDUCATION AND SCIENCE AND MINISTRY OF HEALTH. 9/66 and 7/66. *Co-ordination of Education, Health and Welfare Services for Handicapped Children and Young people*. HMSO London.

DEPARTMENT OF EDUCATION AND SCIENCE (1966) *The Health of the School Child*. HMSO London.

DEPARTMENT OF EDUCATION AND SCIENCE (1969) *The Health of the School Child*. HMSO London.

DEPARTMENT OF EDUCATION AND SCIENCE (1967) Education Survey No 1. *Units for Partially Hearing Children*. HMSO London.

DEPARTMENT OF EDUCATION AND SCIENCE (1969) Education Survey No 6. *Peripatetic Teachers of the Deaf*. HMSO London.

DEPARTMENT OF EDUCATION AND SCIENCE (1968) *Psychologists in the Education Services* (Summerfield Report). HMSO London.

DEPARTMENT OF EDUCATION AND SCIENCE (1968) List of Independent Schools in England and Wales Recognised as Efficient under Rule 16 (List 70). HMSO London.

DEPARTMENT OF EDUCATION AND SCIENCE (1969) List of Special Schools for Handicapped Pupils in England and Wales (List 42). HMSO London.

DEPARTMENT OF HEALTH AND SOCIAL SECURITY (1968) *Annual Report of Chief Medical Officer*. HMSO London.

DEPARTMENT OF HEALTH AND SOCIAL SECURITY (1970) *National Health Service*. HMSO London.

DINNAGE, R. AND PRINGLE, M. L. KELLMER (1967) *Residential Child Care – Facts and Fallacies*. Longmans in association with the National Bureau for Co-operation in Child Care.

DINNAGE, R. (1970) *The Handicapped Child*. A research review, Vol 1. Longmans in association with the National Bureau for Co-operation in Child Care.

DIXON, P. J. (1968) "The Tenant". Paper read before the Health Congress of the Royal Society of Health.

DOUGLAS, J. W. B. (1964) *The Home and the School*. University of London Press.

FROOD, L. (1969). Unpublished paper.

GARDNER, L. (1969) "Planning for planned dependence". *Special Education*, Vol 58, No 1.

GOLDIE, L. (1966) "Psychiatry of the handicapped family". *Developmental Medicine and Child Neurology*. Vol 8, No 4, pp 456–462.

GOLDSMITH, S. (1967 revised) *Designing for the Disabled*. Royal Institute of British Architects, London.

GOULD, B. (1968) "Working with handicapped families". *Case Conference.* Vol 15, No 5.

GRAHAM, P. AND RUTTER, M. (1968) "Organic brain dysfunction and child psychiatric disorder". *British Medical Journal.* Vol 3, No 5620, pp 689–700.

GULLIFORD, R. (1969) *Backwardness and Educational Failure.* National Foundation for Educational Research, Slough, Bucks.

GUNZBURG, H. C. (1963) Progress assessment charts. National Association for Mental Health, London.

HALL, T. *et al* (1969) "Preparation of immature and educationally sub-normal school leavers for a life in industry". *The Lancet,* Vol 1, Part 7599, pp 830–832.

HANCOCK, L. E. *et al* (1969) "Areas of Concern". *Concern No 2.* National Bureau for Co-operation in Child Care, London.

HEWETT, S. (1967) *Handicapped Children and their Families.* University of Nottingham Press, Nottingham.

HEWETT, S., WITH NEWSOM, J. AND E. (1970) *The Family and the Handicapped Child.* Allen and Unwin, London.

KERSHAW, J. D. (1961) *Handicapped Children.* Heinemann, London.

KIRK, S. A. (1958) *Early Education of the Mentally Retarded.* University of Illinois Press, Urbana, Illinois.

KUSHLICK, A. (1967) "Comprehensive services for the mentally subnormal" Chapter 38 in: *New aspects of the Mental Health Services* Freeman and Farndale ed. Pergamon Press, London.

MALLINSON, VERNON (1956) *None can be Called Deformed.* Heinemann, London.

MAPSTONE, E. (1969) "Children in Care". *Concern No 3.* National Bureau for Co-operation in Child Care, London.

MARSHALL, A. (1967) *The Abilities and Attainments of Children Leaving Junior Training Centres.* National Association for Mental Health, London.

MINISTRY OF EDUCATION (1955) *Report of the Committee on Maladjusted Children* (Underwood Report). HMSO London.

MINISTRY OF HEALTH (1957) *Annual Report of the Chief Medical Officer.* HMSO London.

MINISTRY OF HEALTH (1968) Memorandum to Medical Officers of Health, 28th June, 1968. Reference F/H1/2.

MINISTRY OF HEALTH STANDING MEDICAL ADVISORY COMMITTEE (1967) – *Child Welfare Centres* – Report of a sub-committee (Chairman, Sir Wilfrid Sheldon) HMSO London.

MINISTRY OF HOUSING AND LOCAL GOVERNMENT (1969) *Council Housing Purposes, Procedures and Priorities.* HMSO London.

MINISTRY OF HOUSING AND LOCAL GOVERNMENT (1970) *Reform of Local Government in England.* HMSO London.

MINISTRY OF LABOUR (1962) *Report of the Working Party on Workshops for the Blind.* HMSO London.

MITCHELL, R. (1969) Personal communication.

MONCRIEFF, JEAN (1966) *Mental Subnormality in London*. A survey of community care. Political and Economic Planning Report, London.

MORRIS, P. (1969) *Put away*. Routledge and Kegan Paul, London.

NATIONAL COUNCIL OF SOCIAL SERVICE (1967) *Caring for People*: report of the committee of enquiry. (Williams Report) Allen and Unwin, London.

NATIONAL SOCIETY FOR MENTALLY HANDICAPPED CHILDREN (1967). *Stress in Families with a Mentally Handicapped Child*. National Society for Mentally Handicapped Children, London.

NORRIS, D. (1961) "Education in the training centre". *Journal of Mental Subnormality*. 7, 62–66.

NORRIS, D. (1968) Some observations on the school life of severely retarded children. *Journal of Mental Subnormality*. Monograph.

O'CONNOR, N. AND HERMELIN, B. (1963) *Speech and Thought in Severe Subnormality*. Pergamon Press, London.

PACKMAN, J. AND POWER, M. (1968) "Children in need and the help they receive". Appendix Q in the *Report of the Committee on Local Authority and Allied Personal Social Services* (Seebohm Report) HMSO London.

PETERSON, O. L. *et al* (1967) "What is value for money in medical care? Experiences in England, Wales, Sweden and the USA". *Lancet*, Vol 1 No 74/93, pp 771–776.

PRINGLE, M. L. KELLMER (1964a reprinted 1967) *The Emotional and Social Adjustment of Blind Children*. Occ. Public. No 10, National Foundation for Educational Research, Slough, Bucks.

PRINGLE, M. L. KELLMER (1964b reprinted 1969) *The Emotional and Social Adjustment of Physically Handicapped Children*. Occ. Public. No 11, National Foundation for Educational Research, Slough, Bucks.

PRINGLE, M. L. KELLMER, ed. (1965) *Investment in Children*. Longmans, London.

PRINGLE, M. L. KELLMER (1965) "Emotional adjustment among children in care: a firm friend outside". Chapter 11 in: *Deprivation and Education*. Longmans, Green & Co., London.

PRINGLE, M. L. KELLMER, (1966) *Social Learning and its Measurement*. Longmans, London.

PRINGLE, M. L. KELLMER, ed (1969) *Caring for Children*. Longmans in association with the National Bureau for Co-operation in Child Care.

PRINGLE, M. L. KELLMER, BUTLER, N. R. AND DAVIE, R. (1966) *11.000 Seven Year Olds*. Longmans in association with the National Bureau for Co-operation in Child Care, London.

PRINGLE, M. L. KELLMER, DAVIE, R. AND HANCOCK, L. E. (1969) *Directory of Voluntary Organisations Concerned with Children*. Longmans in association with the National Bureau for Co-operation in Child Care.

PRINGLE, M. L. KELLMER AND FIDDES, D. O. (1970) *The Challenge of Thalidomide*. Longman, London.

RESIDENTIAL CHILD CARE ASSOCIATION (1969) *Residential Task in Child Care.* R.C.C.A., Beechholme, Banstead, Surrey.

Royal Commission on Local Government in England (1969) (Chairman: Lord Redcliffe-Maud). HMSO London.

RUTTER, M. (1968) "Concepts of autism" Chapter 6 in: *Aspects of autism* (ed. Mettler, P. J.). The British Psychological Society, London.

SAMPSON, O. C. (1965) "The wide mesh of welfare". *The Times Educational Supplement*, 4th June.

SHERIDAN, MARY (1965) *The Handicapped Child and his Home.* National Children's Home, London.

SKINNER, A. AND CASTLE, R. (1969) *78 Battered Children: a Retrospective Study.* The National Society for Prevention of Cruelty to Children, London.

SMITH, R. (1970) Further education, training and employment of handicapped school leavers. Personal communication on on-going research of National Bureau for Co-operation in Child Care.

TANSLEY, A. E. AND GULLIFORD, R. (1960) *The Education of Slow Learning Children.* Routledge and Kegan Paul, London.

TIZARD, J. (1960) "Residential care of mentally handicapped children". *British Medical Journal*, 1960, 1, pp 1041–6.

TIZARD, J. AND GRAD, J. C. (1961) *The Mentally Handicapped and their Families.* Oxford University Press, London.

TIZARD, J. (1964) *Community Services for the Mentally Handicapped.* Oxford University Press, London.

WHITMORE, K. (1969) "An assessment service for handicapped children". *The Medical Officer.* Vol 22, No 3199, pp 263–267.

WIGGLESWORTH, R. (1967) "The Handicapped Child – towards helping the family in the community". Paper given to the Paediatric Group, Institute of Medical Social Workers.

WIGGLESWORTH, R. (1969) Personal communication.

WILLIAMS, C. E. (1968) "Behaviour disorders in handicapped children". *Developmental Medicine and Child Neurology.* Vol 10, No 6.

WILLIAMS, C. E. (1968) "Psychiatric problems of Blind Children". Chapter 6 in: *Mental Health and Subnormality.* (ed. O'Gorman, G.). Butterworth, London.

WILLMOTT, P. (1967) *Consumers' Guide to the British Social Services.* Penguin Press, Harmondsworth, Middlesex.

WOLFF, S. (1969). *Children under Stress.* Penguin Press, Harmondsworth, Middlesex.

WOODWARD, M. (1963) "The application of Piaget's theories to research in mental deficiency". Chapter 8 in: *Handbook of Mental Deficiency.* (ed. Ellis, N. R.). McGraw-Hill, New York.

WORLD HEALTH ORGANISATION (1967) *Report of a Working Group on the early detection and treatment of handicapping defects in young children.* Regional Office for Europe, WHO, Copenhagen.

YOUNIS, M. (1966) "The Way I See Things". Chapter 10 in: *Stigma,* ed. Paul Hunt. Geoffrey Chapman, London.